Dale Van Gelder

THE CONQUEST OF THE OCEAN

THE
CONQUEST
OF THE
OCEAN

THE ILLUSTRATED
HISTORY OF SEAFARING

BRIAN LAVERY

LONDON, NEW YORK, MUNICH, MELBOURNE, DELHI

Senior Editor Angela Wilkes
Senior Art Editor Michael Duffy
Editors Hugo Wilkinson,
Andy Szudek,
R.G. Grant,
Hannah Bowen,
Debra Wolter,
Anna Streiffert,
Georgina Palffy,
Jane Perlmutter
Designers Katie Cavanagh,
Jane Ewart,
Steve Woosnam-Savage
Picture research Sarah Smithies,
Surya Sankash Sarangi
Jacket Designer Laura Brim
Jacket Editor Manisha Majithia
Jacket Design Manager Sophia M.T.T.
Producer, Pre-production Adam Stoneham
Production Controller Mandy Inness
Managing Editor Stephanie Farrow
Senior Managing Art Editor Lee Griffiths
Publisher Andrew Macintyre
Art Director Phil Ormerod
Associate Publishing Director Liz Wheeler
Publishing Director Jonathan Metcalf

First American Edition, 2013

Published in the United States by
DK Publishing, 345 Hudson Street
New York, New York 10014

13 14 15 16 10 9 8 7 6 5 4 3 2 1
001–186985–Sept/13

Copyright © 2013 Dorling Kindersley Limited.
All rights reserved.

A catalog record for this book is available
from the Library of Congress.

ISBN 978-1-4654-0841-9

Printed and bound by
South China Printing Company, China.

Discover more at **www.dk.com**

DK books are available at special discounts when purchased in bulk
for sales promotions, premiums, fund-raising, or educational use.
For details contact: DK Publishing Special Markets, 345 Hudson Street,
New York, 10014 or SpecialSales@dk.com

THE MARINERS MIRROVR

Wherin may playnly be seen the courses, heights, distances, depths, soundings, flouds and ebs, risings of lands, rocks, sands and shoalds, with the marks for thentrings of the Harbouroughs, Havens and Ports of the greatest part of Europe: their seueral trafickes and commodities: Together wᵗʰ the Rules and instrumēts of NAVIGATION.

First made & set fourth in diuers exact Sea-Chartes, by that famous Nauigator Lvke Wagenar of Enchuisen. And now fitted with necessarie additions for the use of Englishmen by ANTHONY ASHLEY.

Herein also may be understood the Exploytes lately atchieued by the right Honorable the L. Admirall of England and his Mᵗⁱᵉ Navie with sōe former seruice don by that worthy Knight Sᵗ FRANC DRAKE,

Contents

Introduction

W hat is the ocean? Today we refer to five individual oceans—the Atlantic, Pacific, Indian, Arctic, and Southern. But in ancient and medieval times, "the ocean" was the whole mysterious and frightening mass of water surrounding the only known lands—Europe, Asia, and Africa. In fact, nothing separates the oceans from each other. There is no moment when one passes from the Atlantic to the Indian Ocean, or from the Indian Ocean to the Pacific. The ocean is a great unity. As the *Encyclopaedia Britannica* said in 1911, it is "the great connected sheet of water which covers the greater part of the surface of the earth."

Ocean voyages were made as long ago as 1000 BCE, when Polynesians began migrating across the Pacific. From Europe, Viking sailors originating in Scandinavia crossed the North Atlantic to Iceland in the 9th century CE and had reached North America by 1000 CE. In the Middle Ages, sea trade routes linked China to Egypt and Venice to London. Most seafarers kept close to coastlines whenever possible, however, and for the learned scholars of the Muslim Middle East and Christian Europe, the ocean remained the subject of fear or denial. According to the Arab geographer Al-Masudi in 957 CE, the Pillars of Hercules at the exit from the Mediterranean Sea into the Atlantic had statues indicating that there was "no way beyond me." The German chronicler Adam of Bremen wrote in 1076: "Beyond Norway, which is the farthermost northern country, you will find no human habitation, nothing but ocean, terrible to look at and limitless, encircling the whole world." Around 1290, an Englishman, Richard of Haldingham, presented a map to Hereford Cathedral. In medieval fashion, it showed the world as consisting of three continents—Europe, Africa, and Asia. Even the Mediterranean was not accurately drawn, with a triangular

Italy and the eastern end of the sea curving to the north. The band of oceans surrounding the great landmass was not much wider than the rivers and seas—the oceans were simply not considered important.

This narrow view of the world was soon to change, however. Venetian Marco Polo's 1298 account of his travels in the east, including a sea journey from China to the Persian Gulf, broadened the scope of knowledge. By 1400, Europe had rediscovered the works of the ancient Greek geographer Ptolemy, written in the 2nd century CE. Ptolemy had plotted the Indian Ocean, though he showed most of India as an island and enclosed the ocean with land. In the 15th century, sailors began to explore the world more systematically. Between 1405 and 1433, the Chinese admiral Zheng He led a series of voyages into the Indian Ocean, traveling as far as the east coast of Africa. Portuguese caravels, meanwhile, began probing tentatively down Africa's west coast and into the unknown mass of the Atlantic, reaching the Azores in 1427. The expanding view of the world is summarized in a great map made by the monk Fra Mauro in Venice around 1450. Fra Mauro writes that he does not believe "the Sea of India is enclosed like a pond," since a junk—perhaps part of Zheng He's expedition—

had crossed the Indian Ocean in 1420 and "sailed for 40 days in a south-westerly direction without ever finding anything, except wind and water." Fra Mauro's map also recognized the Atlantic as an

THE HEREFORD MAPPA MUNDI
Created around 1300, this medieval map of the world is the largest surviving example of its kind.

ocean. The European experience soon spread to the rest of the world. Adventurous mariners backed by aggressive and acquisitive monarchs set out in search of trade, land, and plunder. Christopher Columbus established the first sustained maritime link between Europe and the Americas with his famous voyage to the West Indies in 1492. Setting out in 1498, Vasco da Gama led a Portuguese fleet around the southern tip of Africa to India. In 1519, Ferdinand Magellan, a Portuguese in the service of Spain, set off on a voyage around South America, his crew completing a circumnavigation of the globe after his death in the Philippines. By 1527, a world map produced by Diogo Ribeiro gave a reasonably accurate representation of the Atlantic and Indian Oceans, plus a sketchier Pacific. The age of ocean denial was over.

Once humans could travel over vast areas of sea, it was perhaps justifiable to use the term "conquering the ocean." Yet for centuries, ocean voyagers confronted discomfort and danger. Land travel was not without dangers, but those of the sea were of a different order. Without prior knowledge or charts, sailors could never be sure what was under the surface of the sea. If bad weather came, it was often not possible to find shelter. Diseases, such as scurvy, killed thousands of people at sea, and accidents were commonplace in the dangerous environment of a sailing ship. Sea travelers might run out of food or water, and it was not possible for a sailor in trouble to call for help beyond the horizon. Waves often made traveling by sea intolerably uncomfortable— seasickness was perhaps the greatest deterrent to ocean travel, apart from the danger.

In the golden age of sail from the 16th to the 19th century, ocean-going sailing ships were central to world trade, empire building, and warfare, yet they remained entirely at the mercy of the currents and above all the winds, which are often unpredictable even to a modern weather forecaster. A sudden gale could scatter or sink a fleet. A dead calm or adverse winds might slow or halt a voyage, adding weeks to a journey. The constancy of predictable winds was highly prized. The American seaman Richard Henry Dana, writing in 1840, described "the blessed trade-winds… that have blown in one direction, perhaps from the Creation, never falling away to a calm & never rising to a furious gale…" The other bugbear of ocean travel was the lack of navigational techniques. Observing heavenly bodies, continually measuring the ship's speed, and using the magnetic compass could at best achieve a fair degree of precision in calculating a ship's position. Sailors out of sight of land often had only a vague notion of where they were and the lack of accurate charts added to their difficulties, but years of technological progress and maritime experience gradually improved ocean travel. By the 19th century, scurvy was almost eliminated and navigation was greatly improved. As ocean-going steamships replaced sail in the second half of the century, sailors no longer had to rely on fickle winds and the time spent at sea was reduced. By the 20th century, ocean travel had become reasonably safe, at least in time of peace.

In a sense, the ocean has not been "conquered," and never will be. Nothing we do can intentionally control the currents, waves, and weather, and human impact has mostly been negative and unwanted. But humans have at least developed the means to travel over vast areas of sea, and this achievement has been the product of many centuries of adventures. Seafarers from ancient times down to the present day have faced a hard struggle against the elements, demanding endurance, skill, and ingenuity, whether engaged in trade, exploration, warfare, or the colonization of distant shores. The record of their lives includes barely credible stories of voyages into uncharted waters and survival at sea against awesome odds. Their experience deserves to be celebrated, as does the essential contribution of sailors and their ships to the evolving history of the human world.

The First Ocean Sailors

TO 1450

In many different parts of the world, the first simple boats were built for local travel in sheltered, inland waters such as lakes, rivers, and estuaries. Voyaging on seas and oceans, however, was a far riskier venture. The Polynesians were the first ocean sailors, crossing wide expanses of the Pacific in outrigger canoes propelled by paddles and sails, while in the Mediterranean, the Phoenicians, based in what is now Lebanon led the development of maritime trade from around 900 BCE, and the ancient Greeks and Romans practiced large-scale naval warfare from oared galleys. The Mediterranean peoples also operated far beyond the confines of their native sea—the Phoenicians, for instance, sailed to the Canary Islands, and the Romans maintained a fleet in Britain. After the decline of the Roman Empire in the 5th century CE, new societies emerged in northwestern Europe, some of which developed impressive seafaring skills—the Vikings of Scandinavia were probably the first European sailors to reach North America, for example, although they left no permanent settlements. While oared galleys remained the elite ships of the Mediterranean, medieval northern Europeans built seagoing sailing ships descended from the Viking longships, and used them for trade and war.

Meanwhile, after the rise of Islam in the 7th century CE, Arabs developed a flourishing and extensive seaborne trade in the Indian Ocean. Maritime routes linked the Red Sea to India, the islands of Indonesia, and China. The Chinese had their own sophisticated tradition of boatbuilding and sailing, focused on navigation along major rivers and in coastal waters. The establishment of the Ming dynasty in the 14th century was followed by a program of naval construction and the dispatch of fleets into the Indian Ocean. By the mid-15th century however, China had abandoned its interest in oceanic voyages, just as Europe stood on the verge of a new age of extraordinary maritime exploration and expansion.

Exploring the Pacific

IN JANUARY 1778, on his third voyage across the Pacific, Captain Cook wrote in his journal, "How shall we account for this Nation spreading itself so far over this Vast ocean?" He was speaking of the Polynesians, a people he found scattered across thousands of Pacific islands in a great triangle between New Zealand, Hawaii, and Easter Island, and who had apparently colonized the region in simple boats without the aid of charts, compasses, or even written instructions.

One possible answer had already presented itself to Cook on his second voyage, when he visited the Southern Cook Islands and discovered three Tahitians who had foundered there while exploring other islands. This had led him to wonder if the Polynesian settlers had spread by chance, but such an event was unlikely. Founding a new society by accident would have required that a large group of men and women with a suitable range of skills—and fully provisioned with tools, plants, seeds, and animals—had all been at sea and came aground on an uninhabited island. Not only was this improbable, the pattern of colonization in Polynesia deviates from the prevailing winds and currents of the Pacific, suggesting that the natives did not simply drift from island to island, but that they deliberately set out to explore—and if the winds and currents were as predictable then as they are today, then they did so with at least some hope of returning if a voyage proved fruitless. Another factor that favored exploration was that the islands lie in the tropics, where the sun and stars are rarely obscured, and where storms tend to be seasonal. And there was no need to worry about capsizing, as Joseph Banks, Captain Cook's naturalist, observed; "They [the boats] are frequently upset but the people are almost amphibious and care little for such accidents." They were "such good swimmers that only seals can be compared with them."

One thing that is certain is that the Polynesians learned ocean navigation gradually. Archaeological evidence shows that their ancestors probably came from Southeast Asia around 40,000 years ago, and that they moved from one island to another along the coast without ever losing sight of land. By 30,000 years ago, they had reached the Solomon Islands in the South Pacific, where they settled for some

POLYNESIAN SEAFARING

25,000 years, giving them plenty of time to improve their boat-building and navigational skills. Then, for 2,500 years or so, they again spread from island to island, making voyages of hundreds of miles at a time. Between 1000 BCE and 500 BCE, they discovered routes from Fiji and Tonga to Samoa, and then to the Cook Islands. By 750 CE, they had reached Easter Island and Hawaii, and by 1500 they had settled in New Zealand and the Chatham Islands. In a separate movement, people from the Philippines and Indonesia settled on the Northern Mariana Islands and Caroline Islands to the northeast from 1000 BCE, and moved farther east until around 500 CE.

As for why the Polynesians went to sea, they may have simply done so for adventure, in spite of the obvious dangers. This sense of restlessness is poignantly expressed in the Tikopian lament:

> The voyaging mind has been made up
> Your being borne off there into the ocean
> When it's done you are wailed over by your people. The foot floats off...
> The mind of a young man who jumped aboard to go

Another possibility is that new islands were discovered on extended fishing expeditions, and that these were then returned to by skilled navigators to confirm their positions. Once the position of an island had been established, boats could then carry families, goods, and animals to it in reasonable safety. In Tahiti in 1847, Henry Byam Martin of the British Royal Navy encountered one such vessel—an ocean-going double canoe fit to transport an entire community: "Thirty eight persons crossed in her from Pomotoo—about 250 miles... They seem to be families who have come to see what is to be seen and picked up."

Some islands may have been inhabited gradually, perhaps being used by fisherman or hunters for part of the year, while huts were built and small settlements gradually appeared. Others may have been settled quickly, perhaps by large groups that intentionally set out to found a new colony. The group might have included a chief or his son, carpenters, and people adept at fishing, hunting, and farming. Three or four large canoes would probably have traveled together, sharing an experienced navigator. If sailing west, they would probably have chosen a season when the winds were from the east, and perhaps during winter when the trade winds were less forceful.

There is little archaeological evidence of ancient Polynesian boats, and no written descriptions exist before those of the first Europeans who visited the region centuries later, so we have to imagine what the

LONGEST OCEAN CROSSING BY
POLYNESIAN EXPLORERS:

2,000 MILES
(3,200 KM)

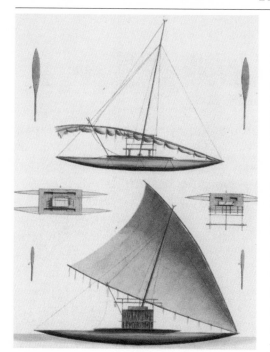

POLYNESIAN BOAT
Characterized by twin hulls, raised bows, and simple deck shelters, Polynesian boats could carry entire tribes from island to island, sometimes to found new settlements.

ancient Pacific boats looked like. Joseph Banks described the traditional boats of Tahiti and Tonga in 1769. Crafted with excellent workmanship from stone tools, there were simple log rafts, dug-out log boats, and boats made from planks bound together—all open to the elements, though some had a small hut on deck. There were also large, double-hulled fighting canoes with bows 17–18 ft (5.2–5.5 m) high, and small fishing vessels. The boats that were used to travel between islands were 30–60 ft (9–18 m) long, each with "a small neat house 5 or 6 feet broad and 7 or 8 long fastned upon the fore part of them, in which the principal people...sit when they are carried from place to place." They were very narrow, but were stabilized by having two hulls, which were lashed together, or by having an outrigger—a smaller, second hull, which acts as a float. The islanders steered these boats using large paddles with long handles and flat blades. Each boat had either one or two masts and the sails were "narrow, of a triangular shape, pointed at the top and the outside curvd." This type of sail was "borderd all round with a frame of wood and has no contrivance either for reefing or furling, so that in case of bad weather it must be intirely cut away." In foul weather, the sailors would shelter on islands, hauling the boats onto the beaches rather than leaving them afloat.

When islanders set out to sea, they lived crowded together on relatively small boats for up to three weeks. The larger groups included women, children, and babies. According to Banks, everyone on board paddled when needed—except "those who set under the houses"—and they could "push themselves on pretty

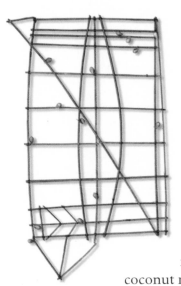

MODEL POLYNESIAN CHART
This wood-and-shells map of the Marshall Islands shows the islands, currents, and routes between them.

fast through the water." The boats could sail close to the wind, "probably on account of their sail being borderd with wood which makes them stand better than any bowlines could possibly do." They were often very leaky and "one person at least is employd almost constantly in throwing out the water." The men and women were segregated as much as possible, the women staying mostly in the shelter. Everyone slept on coconut matting beds in any space they could find.

The navigator was the most important person on board, with a status equal to that of a chief or a priest. His skills were vital, since any mistakes could mean death for the entire group, and his authority was supreme. He navigated without any instruments, using the stars and the high volcanic islands as reference points. According to Banks: "In their longer Voyages they steer in the day by the sun and in the night by the Stars. Of these they know a very large part by their Names and the clever ones among them will tell in what part of the heavens they are to be seen in any month when they are above their horizon; they also know the time of their annual appearing and disappearing to a great nicety, far greater than would easily be believed by a European astronomer."

This method of navigation was demonstrated more recently in a voyage from Tikopia to Anuta in 1983, in which waves were also used to navigate:

> Suppose the sky becomes bad; the sky is covered by clouds and the stars are not clear. Only the expert navigator sits at the helm. He sees the waves; the crests of the groundswell resulting from the wind, and the island's summit... Thus he will go... but the island has not yet appeared... At that point, he looks for the group of waves—of the land waves—which have begun to beat upon the bow... He will place the canoe; will align directly with the land waves so that they strike precisely on the bow.

MATAVAI BAY, TAHITI
Captain Cook encountered traditional Polynesian
craft in Tahiti on his voyage in the 1770s. In this
1776 painting, the British ships HMS *Resolution* and
HMS *Adventure* anchor near them.

The flight paths of birds were even used as a last resort: "[Mount]
Anuta does not yet stand. It is close. He sits in his canoe and finally
sees the bird of Anuta's summit... Thus, the navigator will align the
canoe to follow the tropic-bird's path as it descends towards the bow."

Landing in pounding surf was eased by the great length and high
sterns of the boats, which were then hauled as far up the beach as
possible. Then the men unloaded the animals, tools, and supplies,
and went about setting up home and searching for food.

Despite their epic feats of seafaring, the Polynesians had no reason
to build bigger ships, since their populations were comparatively small
and they conducted very little trade. The skills of their navigators,
however, were immense, and their legacy endures to this day. Two of
their inventions—the outrigger and the catamaran—became
common features of yachts and ferries in the late 20th century.

Seafaring in the Mediterranean

MINOAN TRADERS from the island of Crete are known to have been active in the eastern Mediterranean by the 2nd millennium BCE, but it was the Phoenicians—a civilization based to the north of present-day Israel—who first spread across the entire sea, doing so between 1200 BCE and 900 BCE. Before this, the Egyptians had developed the sail by around 3500 BCE, and on the strength of it they became the world's dominant naval power, but the Egyptian Empire had collapsed in 1085 BCE, giving the Phoenicians a chance to flourish. Their civilization was based on trade, which they conducted by sea, traveling in oar-powered sailing vessels that the Greeks called *gauloi* (meaning "tubs"), from which the word "galley" derives. Their trade routes spanned the Mediterranean, the west coast of Africa, and the Canary Islands, and their colonies included Carthage (in present-day Tunisia), and towns in Ibiza, Sicily, and southern Spain. By far their greatest invention was the bireme, which was a galley with two rows of oarsmen on each side of the ship. The design was adopted by the Greeks, another great culture that was thriving on islands and city-states by the sea, and who in turn developed the trireme—a galley with three rows of oarsmen on each side. Homer's *Odyssey*, written in around 700 BCE, gives a description of seamen at work aboard a typical Greek galley—probably a single-decked, 50-oared ship known as a penteconter:

> Telemachus shouted out commands to his shipmates: "All lay hands to tackle!" They sprang to orders, hoisting the pinewood mast, they stepped it firm in its blocks amidships, lashed it fast with stays and with braided rawhide halyards hauled the white sail high. Suddenly wind hit full and the canvas bellied out and a dark blue wave, foaming up at the bow, sang out loud and strong as the ship made way, skimming the whitecaps, cutting towards her goal.

Military triremes and penteconters gave the Greeks their greatest naval victory at Salamis, in 480 BCE, when they defeated an invading force of much larger Persian vessels. Such victories proved that naval strength was the key to political power in the region—a fact that convinced the Romans, who were not natural seafarers, to build a navy of their own. The majority of the Greeks' ships, however, were trading vessels that followed the routes established by the Phoenicians. Few accounts of life on board such vessels survive, but those that do show how difficult even the simplest of voyages could be. The best of these comes from Synesius, a 27-year-old man from a wealthy Greek family who boarded a ship in Alexandria, Egypt, in 397 CE. Synesius was well-educated—in later life he became a military commander and a Christian bishop—and he recounted his near-disastrous voyage to Libya in a letter to his brother.

The ship that Synesius boarded was not an elegant galley, but a squat and ill-equipped merchant vessel, whose captain was on the verge of bankruptcy. She had a single mast and was probably very old—ships of the period sometimes served for 80 years or more with a great deal of repair. Synesius was uneasy when the ship scraped the bottom more than once before it was out of the harbor—this was a bad omen: "... it might have been wiser to desert a vessel which had been unlucky from the very start. But we were ashamed to lay ourselves open to an imputation of cowardice..."

EARLY MINOAN SEAFARING
Dating from around the 16th century BCE, this fresco depicts Bronze Age Minoan ships voyaging in the Mediterranean.

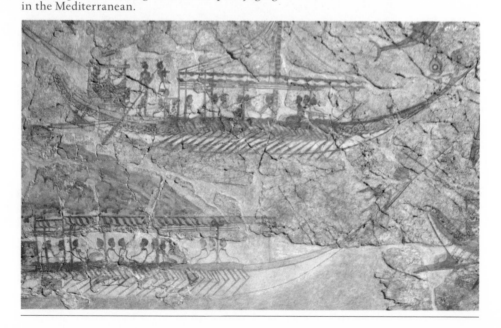

The First Sailing Vessels

The first boats and ships were probably built in Egypt between 3500 BCE and 2500 BCE. After that, the Mediterranean became a crucible of naval invention, with the rise of the Greek trireme and the multi-sailed Byzantine dromon.

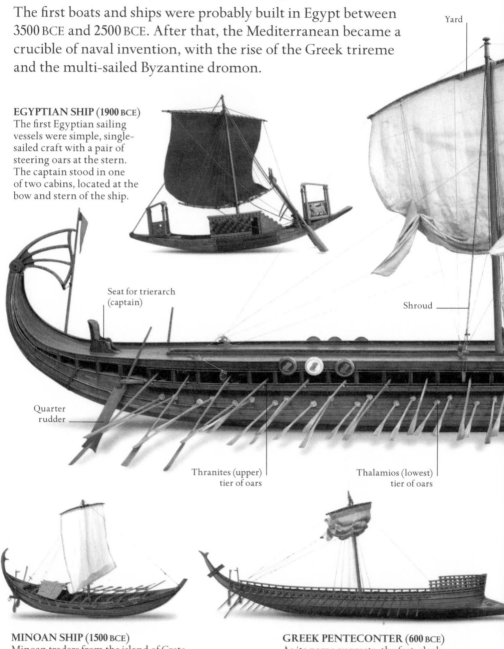

Yard

EGYPTIAN SHIP (1900 BCE)
The first Egyptian sailing vessels were simple, single-sailed craft with a pair of steering oars at the stern. The captain stood in one of two cabins, located at the bow and stern of the ship.

Seat for trierarch (captain)

Shroud

Quarter rudder

Thranites (upper) tier of oars

Thalamios (lowest) tier of oars

MINOAN SHIP (1500 BCE)
Minoan traders from the island of Crete flourished in the eastern Mediterranean in the 2nd millennium BCE. Their ships were usually small, with a single bank of oars.

GREEK PENTECONTER (600 BCE)
As its name suggests, the fast, sleek penteconter was powered by 50 oarsmen. It was probably the first Greek ship to be designed with a ram in its bow.

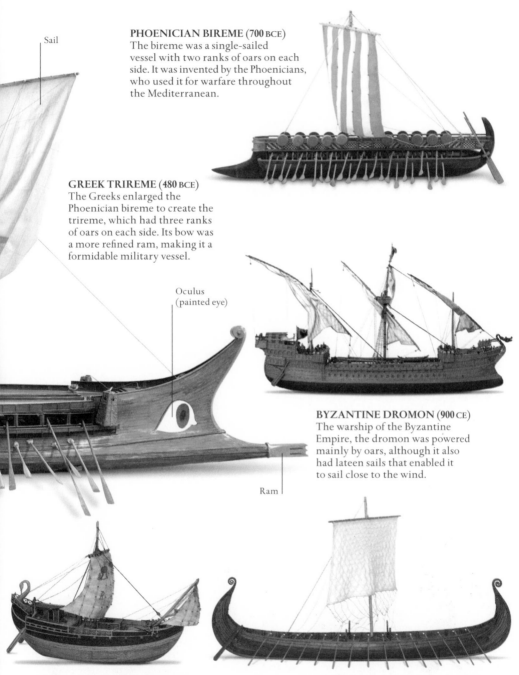

Sail

PHOENICIAN BIREME (700 BCE)
The bireme was a single-sailed vessel with two ranks of oars on each side. It was invented by the Phoenicians, who used it for warfare throughout the Mediterranean.

GREEK TRIREME (480 BCE)
The Greeks enlarged the Phoenician bireme to create the trireme, which had three ranks of oars on each side. Its bow was a more refined ram, making it a formidable military vessel.

Oculus (painted eye)

BYZANTINE DROMON (900 CE)
The warship of the Byzantine Empire, the dromon was powered mainly by oars, although it also had lateen sails that enabled it to sail close to the wind.

Ram

ROMAN MERCHANTMAN (200 CE)
Roman merchant ships were used mainly for transporting grain from Egypt to Rome. They were broad and had no oarsmen to maximize space for cargo.

VIKING LONGSHIP (800 CE)
With its shallow-draft hull designed for speed, the longship carried the Vikings across the Atlantic and through the Mediterranean to the Black Sea.

Off Alexandria, the state of the ship's crew began to worry Synesius. The surly captain, Amaranthus, did not inspire confidence and there were thirteen seamen aboard, which was deemed unlucky. Half of them were experienced sailors, but the rest, according to Synesius, were "a collection of peasants who even as late as last year had never gripped an oar"—and each had "some personal defect." While working they called each other by their nicknames, such as "the 'Lame,' the 'Lefthanded,' and the 'Goggle-eyed.'" Finally, most of them (including the skipper) were Jews who, according to Synesius, were "fully convinced of the piety of sending to Hades as many Greeks as possible."

There were fifty passengers aboard, including a unit of Arab cavalrymen. Synesius could not help noticing that about a third of his companions were women, mostly "young and comely." But, as he wrote to his brother with a hint of disappointment, "Do not, however, be quick to envy us, for a screen separated us from them and a stout one at that, the suspended fragment of a recently torn sail..." Once clear of the harbor, the ship headed out to sea, and Synesius was put in mind of the poet Homer. The captain made straight for a rocky island "with all sails spread, to all seeming bent upon confronting Scylla, over whom we were all wont to shudder in our boyhood." This was a reference to the famous story of Odysseus passing between the rock of Scylla and the whirlpool Charybdis, at what is now the Straits of Messina. Back in the real world, Synesius and his fellow passengers were alarmed at the

A MERCHANT SHIP UNLOADS
Depicted on a fresco, a mechant ship from the ancient Roman port of Ostia unloads its cargo of grain around the third century BCE.

jagged rocks passing close to the ship, and "all raised so mighty a cry that perforce he gave up his attempt to battle with the rocks." They believed that they alone had persuaded the captain to turn away in time, but reading between the lines it seems that he simply enjoyed teasing his ignorant passengers: "All at once he veered about as though some new idea had possessed him, and turned his vessel's head to the open, struggling as best he might against a contrary sea."

A fresh southerly wind got up and carried the ship out of sight of land. Soon Synesius was looking longingly at the larger merchant ships they passed, "the double-sailed cargo vessels, whose business does not lie with our Libya." These larger merchant ships were carrying grain from Egypt to feed the city of Rome. In his tiny, run-down coaster and with no land in sight, Synesius could see no reason for going so far north out to sea on a voyage along the coast. The volatile Amaranthus was getting tired of hearing complaints, and stood on the stern "hurling awful imprecations" at his passengers and proclaiming, "We shall obviously never be able to fly... How can I help people like you who distrust both the land and the sea?" To which Synesius replied, "What do we want of the open sea? Let us rather make for the Pentapolis, hugging the shore."

It was a typical conflict between the landsman who wanted the reassuring sight of land, and the seaman who knew that coastal sailing was full of hidden dangers. Amaranthus felt justified when the wind suddenly turned northerly and became much stronger, forcing the sail back against the mast and—Synesius thought—almost capsizing the ship. The triumphant captain thundered, "See what it is to be master of the art of navigation. I had long foreseen this storm, and that is why I sought the open... But such a course as the one I have taken would not have been possible had we hugged the shore, for in that case the ship would have dashed on the coast."

The storm abated and the rest of the day passed peacefully, but the wind picked up after nightfall. The passengers became alarmed again during the Jewish Sabbath, when the captain dramatically ceased to carry out his duties at "a time during which it is not lawful to work with one's hands... Our skipper accordingly let go the rudder from his hands the moment he guessed that the sun's rays had left the earth, and throwing himself prostrate..." At first the passengers assumed he had succumbed to a fit of despair. The wind subsided shortly afterward, but the waves began to swell in size and the captain was still prone on the deck and the rudder unattended. Synesius noticed that the sea was often even more unpleasant when the wind died down: "when the wind has suddenly relaxed its violence… the oncoming waves fight against those subsiding."

With the ship tossing violently on the waves, one of the soldiers tried to threaten Amaranthus into action with his sword, but the captain "proved at such a moment to be an orthodox observer of the Mosaic law" and stayed put. One might suspect that he knew there was nothing he could do with no wind, and was again deliberately mocking his passengers. In any case, Amaranthus finally went back to the helm in the middle of the night, with a characteristically unreassuring explanation: "We are clearly in danger of death, and the law commands."

The storm worsened, with "groaning of men and shrieking of women." People prayed to their various gods, and Synesius's thoughts returned to Homer. "Achilles, the most high-spirited and the most daring of all, shrinks from death by drowning and refers to it as a pitiable ending." The other passengers began to don their finest gold and jewelry, which they believed might pay for the ferry over the River Styx in the underworld. Synesius was more pragmatic: "It is a matter of necessity that the corpse from a shipwreck should carry with it a fee for burial, inasmuch as whosoever comes across the dead body and profits by it… will scarcely grudge sprinkling a little sand on the one who has given him so much more in value."

The wind abated at daybreak and they were able to furl the sail "like the swelling folds of a garment." It would normally have been replaced by a smaller sail, but Synesius noted dryly that Amaranthus's was, "already in the hands of the pawnbroker." They finally set anchor along a remote desert coastline, where the relieved passengers "touched the dearly beloved land, we embraced the earth as a real living mother." They waited for two days for better weather, then set off at dawn with a stern wind that lasted for two more days. Another fierce storm blew up from the north, in which "the winds raged without measure, and

PHOENICIAN PENDANT
Dating from the 4th-century BCE, this piece of jewelry depicts a Phoenician ship. The Phoenicians were the first civilization to expand their shipping routes all the way across the Mediterranean.

"It is a matter of necessity that the corpse from a shipwreck should carry with it a fee for burial"

the sea became deeply churned up." As the ship was battered by the elements, the yard holding up the sail broke under the strain and fell, nearly killing some of the passengers. In this state, "we carried along during a day and a night... before we knew it, behold we were on a sharp reef which ran out from the land like a short peninsula." Faced with this perilous passage, "The sailors were terrified, whereas we through inexperience clapped our hands and embraced each other."

They were in severe danger of running onto the rocks, but suddenly, a man "in rustic garb" appeared on the shore and signaled to the crew, directing them to a place of relative safety. He then went out to the ship in a boat and took the helm from the captain, who "gladly relinquished to him the conduct of the ship." Guided by their mysterious benefactor, they anchored in "a delightful little harbour" called Azarium on the Libyan coast. They had sailed a distance of some 640 km (400 miles).

Although now safe from the raging seas, the passengers were short of provisions and began to forage for food, fishing and gathering limpets. The whole time, however, Synesius and his stranded companions were "lamenting in concert on desert shores, gazing out towards Alexandria to our heart's content, and towards our motherland Cyrene." Synesius's letters do not reveal how they resolved their predicament, but, like Odysseus, he eventually returned safely home. He later wrote to his brother, "never trust yourself to the sea."

Homer's *Odyssey* was set at the beginning of the classical age; he describes a place of unknown seas and islands, which is perhaps how the Mediterranean appeared to seafarers more than 3,000 years ago. Synesius, on the other hand, lived at the end of that age, when the power of Rome was being challenged by the Huns. New civilizations were rising to power, and before long, the Mediterranean would cease to be under the control of classical cultures.

The Mediterranean Sea

The Mediterranean Sea is almost enclosed by southern Europe,
North Africa, and the Middle East. It loses three times more water by
evaporation than it gains from rainfall and rivers, leading to high salinity.
The loss is balanced by an inflow from the Atlantic Ocean through the
Strait of Gibraltar, which causes a slight counterclockwise circulation of
current. A strong current passes through the Strait of Messina between
Sicily and mainland Italy, which inspired the Greek myth of Scylla and
Charybdis. The climate is mild; winds are mostly local, and are known
by names such as the sirocco, a hot southerly wind that blows off the
Sahara, the northwesterly mistral, and the gregale from the northeast.

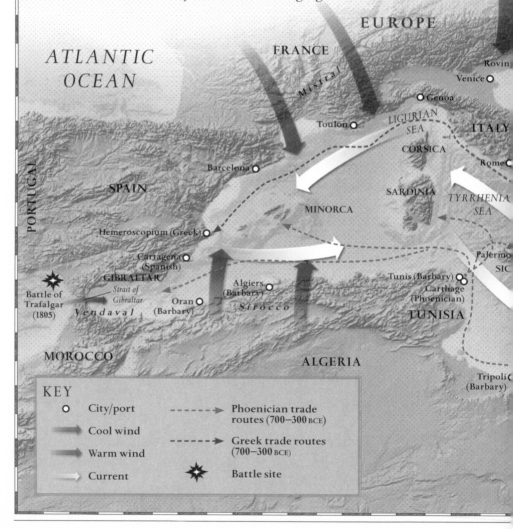

EUROPE

ATLANTIC
OCEAN

FRANCE

Rovin

Venice ○

○ Genoa

LIGURIAN
SEA

ITALY

Mistral

Toulon ○

CORSICA

Rome ○

Barcelona ○

SPAIN

SARDINIA

TYRRHENIA
SEA

PORTUGAL

MINORCA

Hemeroscopium (Greek) ○

Palermo

Cartagena ○
(Spanish)

SIC

GIBRALTAR

Algiers ○
(Barbary)

Tunis (Barbary) ○

Carthage
(Phoenician)

Battle of
Trafalgar
(1805)

*Strait of
Gibraltar*

Oran ○
(Barbary)

Sirocco

Vendaval

TUNISIA

MOROCCO

ALGERIA

Tripoli
(Barbary)

KEY

○	City/port	– – –▸	Phoenician trade routes (700–300 BCE)
➡	Cool wind		
➡	Warm wind	- - -▸	Greek trade routes (700–300 BCE)
➡	Current	✷	Battle site

MEDITERRANEAN CULTURES

Until exploration of the world's oceans began in earnest in the
15th century, the Mediterranean was the center of the known
world for many different peoples (see pp.20–27). These included
great civilizations and island cultures such as the Egyptians,
Phoenicians, Minoans, and Greeks—all of whom migrated,
fought, and traded on the sea. The whole region was under the
control of the Roman Empire by 30 BCE, but the Empire's fall in
476 CE led to an era of political and religious strife. Later, conflict
between Christian north and Muslim south dominated.

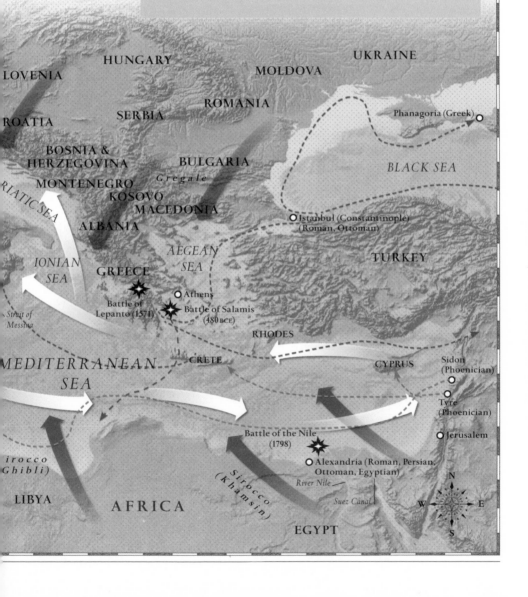

HUNGARY

UKRAINE

LOVENIA

MOLDOVA

ROATIA

SERBIA

ROMANIA

Phanagoria (Greek)

BOSNIA &
HERZEGOVINA

BULGARIA

BLACK SEA

MONTENEGRO

Gregale

RIATIC SEA

KOSOVO

MACEDONIA

ALBANIA

Istanbul (Constantinople)
(Roman, Ottoman)

IONIAN
SEA

AEGEAN
SEA

TURKEY

GREECE

Battle of
Lepanto (1571)

Athens

Battle of Salamis
(480 BCE)

*Strait of
Messina*

RHODES

MEDITERRANEAN
SEA

CRETE

CYPRUS

Sidon
(Phoenician)

Tyre
(Phoenician)

Battle of the Nile
(1798)

Jerusalem

*irocco
Ghibli)*

Alexandria (Roman, Persian,
Ottoman, Egyptian)

*Sirocco
(Khamsin)*

River Nile

Suez Canal

N

LIBYA

AFRICA

W   E

EGYPT

S

The Voyages of the Vikings

"ON THE [7TH] OF JUNE [793 CE], they reached the church of Lindisfarne, and there they miserably ravaged and pillaged everything; they trod the holy things under their polluted feet, they dug down the altars, and plundered." Thus chronicler Simeon of Durham describes the sack of the monastery at Lindisfarne, off the northeast English coast, by Viking raiders. He continues: "Some of the brethren they slew, some they carried off with them in chains, the greater number they stripped naked, insulted, and cast out of doors, and some they drowned in the sea." The famous island monastery, which had produced one of the most beautiful manuscript books of gospels, had been destroyed by the Vikings, a savage and heathen people who came by sea. The monks were humiliated, enslaved, or dead. It was not long before Alcuin, the advisor to the Frankish Emperor Charlemagne, was speculating, "Either this is the beginning of greater tribulation, or else the sins of the inhabitants have called it upon them." It was indeed the beginning of a long nightmare for the Celts and Anglo-Saxons of the islands, as it was for many in Europe.

The term "Viking" may originate from the Norse word "vik," meaning "creek" or "bay," suggesting a pirate who hid there looking for prey. In Spain, however, the raiders, who mostly came from Denmark and Norway, were known as "heathen wizards"—a tribute to their sailing abilities, for they roamed the seas with more daring than anyone else of that age. There was a militaristic intent to much of their voyaging, and they exploited the weaknesses of surrounding nations, such as the

LINDISFARNE CARVING
The Vikings' brutal attack on the monastery at Lindisfarne is commemorated in this 9th-century carving. They were hardy sailors as well as fierce warriors, and their expeditions were often a mixture of discovery and violence.

THE VOYAGES OF THE VIKINGS

division between the English and the Irish, and the disarray on continental Europe after the death of Charlemagne in 814 CE. They had no charts or compasses and, like earlier sailors, navigated by the stars; the only aid they had was a sun shadow board, which provided a primitive but effective way of sailing east or west along a line of latitude. Their longships, however, were masterpieces of shipbuilding, and it was in these that they sailed to and settled in Orkney and Shetland, founded Dublin, conquered much of England, colonized Normandy, and traded and settled along the great rivers of Eastern Europe.

In addition to colonizing much of Europe, the Vikings discovered new lands long before other western civilizations, most notably North America. They also reached Iceland via the Faroe Isles in 873 CE, and Greenland in 895 CE—the latter name disguising the true climate of the island, it is said, because the Viking explorer Eric the Red wanted to encourage migration to the land he had discovered. A Viking merchant named Biarni is believed to have been the first European to discover North America in 985 CE. One summer, he sailed to Iceland to visit his father and learned that he had moved to Greenland. Biarni decided to follow him, although his crew objected—and he himself conceded that the voyage was foolhardy, since none of them had been there before. Nevertheless, they set off and sailed for three days, "until the land was hidden by the water, and then the fair wind died out, and north winds arose, and fogs, and they knew not whither they were drifting."

After many days they saw land—now thought to be Newfoundland, off the American coast. Biarni knew that this was not Greenland, for it did not have ice-covered mountains but was "level, and covered with woods." They found a flat, wooded place on the coast and Biarni's crew urged him to go ashore in search of food and water. He replied, "Ye have no lack of either of these," so his expedition never set foot on the new land. They sailed northward, eventually sighting more land, whereupon Biarni remarked, "This is likest Greenland, according to that which has been reported to me." By chance, they found Biarni's father at his settlement in Greenland and found that he knew nothing about the vast lands they had narrowly skirted.

It was generally agreed among the Norsemen that Biarni had lacked enterprise in his expedition. Wanting to explore the land properly, Leif Ericsson, son of exiled Viking explorer Eric the Red, bought Biarni's ship and recruited a crew of 35 men. After a long voyage, the company went ashore on the new land—also believed to have been Newfoundland—and built huts. On one occasion, a crewman went inland and returned with vines and grapes, so Leif named the country Vinland. The ship's keel was damaged, so they replaced it with local wood and erected the old timber on a headland, which they named Keelness. They then returned home with a rich harvest of grapes.

LEIF ERIKSSON
The famous Viking explorer is thought to have started his voyage to Newfoundland from Brattahild, South Greenland, where this statue of him stands today.

TOP SPEED OF A VIKING LONGSHIP:

12 KNOTS

Leif's brother, Thorvald, was the next Viking to make the long voyage to Vinland, though his landing was less successful. His party stumbled across three canoes manned by nine natives, eight of whom they slaughtered. The surviving native escaped, and the next day Thorvald was awoken with a frantic cry: "Awake, Thorvald, thou and all thy company, if thou wouldst save thy life; and board thy ship with all thy men, and sail with all speed from the land!" They were surrounded by hundreds of "Skrellings," or Inuit in canoes, who attacked them. As the Vikings hurried to their ships, Thorvald was killed by an arrow. His last words were reputedly, "This is a rich country... there is plenty of fat around my belly. We've found a land of fine resources, though we'll hardly enjoy most of them."

The next voyage to Vinland came in 1009, when Thorfinn Karlsefni, a wealthy Norwegian, put together an expedition of three ships and 160 men with the intention of settling in the new land. The company included Thorhall the Sportsman, who had plenty of experience of wild and uninhabited lands, but who was also, according to the *Saga of Eric the Red*, "overbearing in temper, of melancholy mood, silent at all times, underhand in his dealings, and withal given to abuse." There were also five women with the party, including Thorfinn's wife Gudrid, and Eric the Red's fearsome daughter Freydis, who was accompanied by her henpecked husband.

After sailing in northerly winds, they rediscovered Keelness, then continued and found some creeks. They sent ashore two Scottish slaves—a man and woman, called Kaki and Haekja—who returned two days later with a bunch of grapes and an ear of wild wheat. Thorfinn concluded that they had found "good and choice land," so they proceeded up a firth where they found an island so heavily populated with birds that "scarcely was it possible to put one's feet down for the eggs." Farther up the firth, they unloaded their stores and cattle to settle for the winter. However, the winter was hard and the fishing was poor, and the Norsemen (most of whom had been converted to Christianity) prayed to God to relieve their hunger. One day, Thorhall disappeared and was found sitting on a rock in a trance, reciting something. He was calling upon his old god, Thor—an appeal that seemed to be answered when a whale was washed ashore. The men cut it up and feasted on the meat, but they soon fell sick. There were more "supplications to God's mercy," and the fishing later improved. The expedition also went hunting and gathered birds' eggs.

When summer came, Thorfinn decided to explore the south, where he thought the land would be better, and Thorhall was sent to explore the north. Lacking wine, and forced to carry water to his ship, Thorhall lamented, "The clashers of weapons did say when I came here that I should have the best of drink… Eager God of the war-helmet! I am made to raise the bucket; wine has not moistened my beard, rather do I kneel at the fountain." His party set off north, but a gale drove them out to sea and over to Ireland, in what was possibly the first direct crossing of the North Atlantic. The voyage ended in disaster, as they were defeated and enslaved by the Irish.

Meanwhile, Thorfinn's party proceeded south, and eventually reached a land that they called Hop, which seemed like paradise. It boasted "fields of wild wheat wherever there were low grounds; and the vine in all places where there was rough rising ground. Every rivulet there was full of fish." Two weeks later, the group saw canoes heading toward them, their occupants whirling staves. Thorfinn was doubtful, but his son Snorri said, "It may be that it is a token of peace; let us take a white shield and go to meet them." The Norsemen were indeed left in peace. They built settlements there and spent a winter free of snow. In the spring, more Skrellings arrived. The Vikings raised their shields as a sign of peace and the two cultures began to trade. The Skrellings bartered red cloth in exchange for furs and gray skins. They also wanted to buy swords and spears, but Thorfinn and his son forbade it, fearing danger.

All was quiet for another few weeks, then a great fleet of canoes appeared. The natives catapulted large stones, which "struck the ground with a hideous noise." The Norsemen retreated to some rocks, despite Freydis's taunts: "Why run you away… Let me but have a weapon, I think I could fight better than any of you." She seized a sword, bared her breasts, and struck her chest with the flat of it. This was enough to frighten the attackers away.

WARRIOR TRADITION
This pre-Christian runestone from Gotland Island, Sweden, shows the Viking god Odin's ship carrying the souls of heroic slain warriors off to the afterlife.

Another account suggests that Thorfinn deliberately retreated, to take up a good position among the rocks. The Inuit were armed with stone axes and knew very little about iron. One of them picked up a Viking axe and tested it by swinging it at one of his companions, who fell dead. A man of "large size and fine bearing," possibly the chief of the Inuit, picked up the axe, examined it suspiciously, and threw it into the sea. Then, "they fled helter skelter into the woods." Over the winter, Thorfinn's followers became fractious and in the spring, Thorfinn decided to leave, as the threat of war with the Skrellings was looming constantly over them.

A few years later, Freydis mounted another expedition to Vinland with her own ship and another commanded by the brothers Helgi and Finnbogi. There was dissension as winter set in, and Freydis's men captured the brothers' party while they slept. They killed the men but refused to execute the women, until Freydis took up an axe and carried out the deed herself. The party was sworn to secrecy, but when they returned to Greenland, word of their actions spread. Freydis's brother Leif declined to punish his sister, but "no one from that time forward thought them worthy of aught but evil."

Freydis's was the last recorded expedition to Vinland, the Vikings' outpost in what is now North America. If the Vikings had retained the fighting spirit with which they conquered so much of Europe, they might have made short work of the Inuit, but they seem to have lost the urge to expand, and were growing increasingly less warlike as they began to adopt the values of Christianity. Their power gradually declined, but they had left an indelible mark on much of Europe and the north. Indeed, their influence on shipbuilding contributed to the rediscovery of the Americas nearly five hundred years later (see pp.64–71).

The North Sea and Baltic

Connected to the Atlantic Ocean via the English Channel
and the Norwegian Sea, the North Sea has long been an
important European shipping lane. It has a surface area of
around 466,028sq miles (750,000sq km). The North Sea meets
the Baltic, a brackish inland sea, at the Kattegat Strait between
Sweden and Denmark. The low salinity of the Baltic waters
creates a phenomenon whereby the two seas meet but do
not mingle, resulting in a visible division between the dark,
choppy waters of the North Sea and the calmer Baltic.

NORTH ATLANTIC DRIFT

SHETLAND
ISLANDS

ORKNEY
ISLANDS

Scapa Flow

SCOTLAND

North
fishing gr

ATLANTIC
OCEAN

Edinburgh ○ Rosyth

Batt
Dog
Bank

Newcastle ○

Spanish Armada
(1588)

Battle
Flambor
Head (1

IRELAND

IRISH SEA

Royal Charter
(1859)

ENGLAND

WALES

Felixstov
○

London ○

B

ENGLISH CHANNEL Battle of Winche
(1350)

FRANCE

KEY

○   City/port

→   Cool wind

→   Warm wind

→   Current

⚓   Naval base (WWI)

✦   Battle site

⚙   Shipwreck site

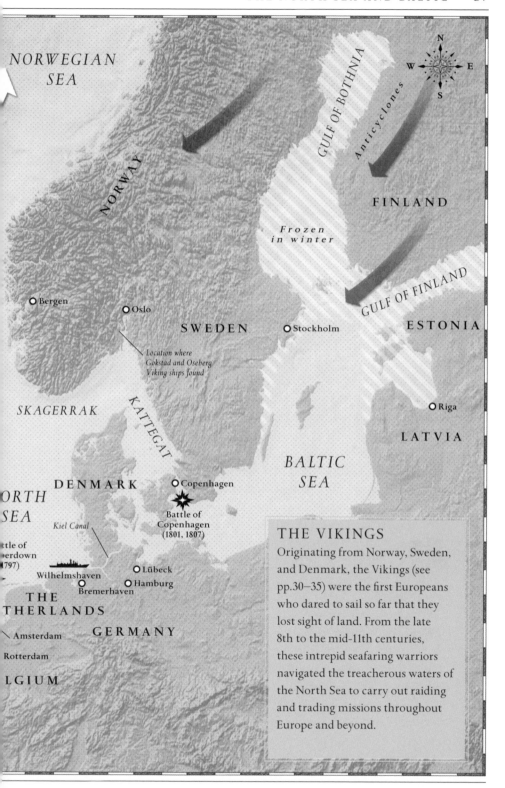

NORWEGIAN
SEA

GULF OF BOTHNIA

Anticyclones

FINLAND

NORWAY

*Frozen
in winter*

O Bergen

O Oslo

SWEDEN   O Stockholm

GULF OF FINLAND

ESTONIA

*Location where
Gokstad and Oseberg
Viking ships found*

SKAGERRAK

KATTEGAT

O Riga

LATVIA

BALTIC
SEA

DENMARK   O Copenhagen

ORTH
SEA   Battle of
                   Copenhagen
Kiel Canal   (1801, 1807)

tle of
erdown
797)

Wilhelmshaven   O Lübeck
           O   O Hamburg
THE   Bremerhaven
THERLANDS

GERMANY

Amsterdam

Rotterdam

LGIUM

THE VIKINGS

Originating from Norway, Sweden,
and Denmark, the Vikings (see
pp.30–35) were the first Europeans
who dared to sail so far that they
lost sight of land. From the late
8th to the mid-11th centuries,
these intrepid seafaring warriors
navigated the treacherous waters of
the North Sea to carry out raiding
and trading missions throughout
Europe and beyond.

Arab Seafaring

IN THE MIDDLE OF A GREAT STORM in the South China Sea, in the year of the prophet 338 (950 CE), the Muslim captain of a Persian merchant ship was harangued by his terrified passengers. Over the crashing of the waves, he calmly told them of his philosophy: "All of us captains are bound by oaths. We are sworn not to expose a ship to loss when it is still sound and its hour is not yet come. All us captains, when we board a ship, stake our lives and destiny on it. If the ship is saved, we remain alive. If it is lost, we die with it."

Such steadfast seamanship played a vital role in the spread of Islam, taking it as far afield as Bengal and Indonesia. Indeed, the Koran lists the ship among the miracles of God, so being a captain was considered a great honor for a Muslim seaman. After the death of the prophet in 632 CE, it was Muslim sea power that upheld the Abassid Caliphate, which ruled over northern Egypt, Israel, Iraq, Iran, and North Africa until the 13th century. In the Mediterranean, a conflict flared with the Christian Byzantine empire, and it was Arab light galleys (or Dromons)—built in Alexandria with wood from Lebanon—that won a great victory at Dhat-al-Sawari in 655 CE.

The Red Sea, the Persian Gulf, and the Indian Ocean, however, were more peaceful, serving more as theaters of trade than of war. The Arabs had established two routes from the Mediterranean to the east—via Suez and the Red Sea, and via Baghdad and the Persian Gulf. But such voyages were not without hazards. According to the 9th-century merchant Sulaiman, there were "... frequent outbreak of fires at Kanfu (Canton)... ships are sometimes wrecked on the way out or on the way back, or plundered..." The traders who traveled in these ships were mostly opportunists who would sell their goods wherever they could. They might be "forced to make long stops and sell their goods in non-Arab countries. Sometimes, too, the wind throws them on to Al-Yaman or other places and they sell their goods there." Such traders sought knowledge of the prices goods might fetch in every port. In 1065, for example, one merchant wrote to a colleague, "The price in Ramle of Cyprus silk, which I carry with me, is 2 dinars per little pound. Please inform me of its price and advise me whether I should sell it here or carry it with me to Fustat, in case it is fetching a good price there."

The ship that was caught in the storm in 950 CE was a typical Arab merchant vessel; a symmetrical (or double-ended) "dhow," which had a sharply angled bow and stern. This particular vessel was owned by Abu al-Zahr al-Batkhati, a prominent Persian merchant from Siraf, a port on the northern side of the Persian Gulf. The ship had set sail for Canton, carrying "men from China, India, Persia and the islands," many having rented two cabins; one for living in and one for storage, although there was also a hold for cargo. The ship had two masts—a main mast set forward of the center of the ship, and a smaller mizzen mast aft. Each mast was supported by moveable stays, rather than the fixed shrouds of western ships, and each carried a lateen sail, whose peaks could be raised some way above the mast. The sails were not quite triangular, each having a vertical forward edge carrying it down below the yard. In a storm, these sails were taken down and replaced by smaller sails—a procedure that was strange to western sailors, who shortened their sails by "reefing." Another difference from western ships was that Arab vessels rarely turned by "tacking" (with the bow facing the wind); instead they invariably turned by "wearing" (with the stern facing the wind), which was easier, but much more time-consuming.

By al-Batkhati's day, Arab dhows also used a stern-mounted rudder instead of a steering paddle. In 985 CE, the geographer Al-Muqaddasi described how such a rudder was used:

> The captain from the crow's nest carefully observes the sea. When a rock is espied, he shouts: 'Starboard!' or 'Port!' Two youths, posted there, repeat the cry. The helmsman, with two ropes in his hand, when he hears the calls tugs one or the other to the right or left. If great care is not taken, the ship strikes the rocks and is wrecked.

Another major difference between the dhow of this era and the boats of Europe is that many dhows were made of planks that were sewn rather than nailed together. According to ibn Jubayr in 1184, a sewn hull was vital

ARABIAN LATEEN-SAILED DHOW
The dhow's angled sails allowed it to tack sharply in the wind, so it did not have to rely on precise wind direction.

A MERCHANT'S DHOW
Taken from a 13th-century
Arab manuscript, this
illumination shows a
typical merchant vessel
of the time. The ship
has a single mast
supporting its sail,
and is steered with a
stern-mounted rudder.

because ships had to be kept "supple" due to "the many reefs that are met with in that sea." "They are sewn with cord made from *qinbar*, which is the fiber of the coconut and which makers thrash until it takes the form of thread, which then they twist into a cord with which they sew the ships."

The route to China taken by al-Batkhati's ship—from the Persian Gulf to Canton—had been in use from the 7th century, and by the 9th century it was "the longest in regular use by mankind before the European expansion in the sixteenth century." Ships left Gulf ports such as Siraf in September or October, before the seas became rough. They would usually stop over in Suhar, in Oman, where "one comes to the end of palms and other trees, people and ports and inhabited places." From there it was a ten-day voyage to Muscat, another great port in Oman, where the Persian Gulf opens onto the Arabian Sea: "It is a cape between two different routes, safe in every wind and possesses fresh water..." On leaving, the navigator would take account of a rock at the head, "which the traveler to and from any place sees, whether he aims for India and Sind or Hormuz or Mekran in the West."

Suitably equipped and stored, the ship was ready to cross the Indian Ocean. The captain might make landfall at Quilon, in India, beyond which "... every cape comes out to you so that you must swerve from it immediately you see it in the eastern monsoon." The ship would probably head south of Sri lanka, where there was "continuous lightning on the island to guide travelers." Passing south of the Nicobar Islands, it would head for the Kalah Bar on the Malay peninsula, to trade and replenish, before heading into the China Sea. According to another sailor of the time, "I was sailing... in the region of Sandal Fulah... when the wind dropped to a calm and the sea became still: we let out the anchors and rested where we were a couple of days." When there was a suitable wind, the ship then entered the South China Sea—a treacherous region notorious for its reefs and typhoons and where sailors bound for Canton had to avoid the Paracel Islands between China and Vietnam.

It was in this area that al-Batkhati's ship and its passengers were plunged into a storm. The gale was deafening, but the ship was "on the point of foundering, because of the crew's negligence and the state of the rigging, rather than because of the sea or the wind." After two days and nights of ferocious seas, there then appeared "a vast fire in front of them, that lit up the whole horizon." The captain's assurances failed to appease the passengers, who "burst into tears, every man bewailing his misfortune." But then an elderly stowaway came out of hiding:

> Be calm, the old man said. By the grace of God you will be saved. What you see is an island bordered and encircled by mountains, on which the ocean waves hurl themselves. During the night this produces the effect of an enormous fire, which frightens ignorant people. At sunrise the illusion disappears and melts into the water.

The passengers were relieved by the news and, as the gale died, they found that they were indeed close to an island—one of many volcanic islands that could well have caused the fiery haze they saw.

Despite the faith of her captain, however, al-Batkhati's ship had nearly been destroyed, and less by the elements than by the inadequacy of her crew, and it was to avoid such disasters in future that Muslim ships were given ever more complex crew structures. By the 15th century, a typical dhow had a captain, or Mu'allim, who was responsible for "...zealous observation on the high seas and near to land... of winds, storms, currents, movements of the moon and the stars, the stations of the year, seasons, bays and coastal shallows, capes, islands, coral shelves, entrances of straits, desert coasts, hills or mountains... At the same time he ought not to forget to pray to Allah and his prophet to remove all dangers." The captain's main function was navigation and seamanship, although he was warned, "Do not notice a disorder in your ship, and ignore it until a later date except when absolutely necessary for it will only get out of hand." Other crew members

9TH-CENTURY CHINESE GOLD CUP
This immaculately preserved gold cup, discovered in 1998, was one of a number of items salvaged from an Arab dhow that sank in the Java Sea on its way back from China over a thousand years ago.

"Beware of the negligence of the helmsman"

AHMAD IBN MAJID

included the Tandil, or the chief of the sailors; the Nakhoda-khashab, who supplied the passengers and assisted with the cargo; the Sarang, or mate, who superintended the loading and served as the captain's deputy; the Panjari, the lookout who sat astride the yard at the top of the main mast; the Gumati, who baled out bilge water; and various Khārweh, or common sailors. There were also several helmsmen, although as the navigator Ahmad ibn Majid warned, "One must especially beware of the negligence of the helmsman, for he is the greatest of your problems." The crew usually worked in three-hour watches, and since the tropical night was close to 12 hours long, that meant three changes in the hours of darkness.

In the 13th century, the Arabs had received the compass from the Chinese, so they were less dependent on the stars for navigation. Since then, according to Majid, the navigator also had to learn "all the more important properties of the lunar mansions, rhumbs, routes, bashis, stars and their seasons," as well as "the signs for landfalls." Majid himself was born in Oman in 1432, the same year that Zheng He's junks docked at Jeddah (see pp.46–51), and he lived to be one of the greatest navigators of his day. In 1490, he wrote an encyclopedia of navigational lore called the *Book of Useful Information on the Principles and Rules of Navigation*, which became a standard text for navigators for centuries to come.

Finding the Way

In order to navigate at sea with any accuracy, sailors needed to know exactly in which direction they were sailing. In ancient times, they had to stay in sight of land or rely on observation of the sun and stars. The invention of the magnetic compass was a major breakthrough, since it meant they could orient themselves and find their way even at night or when visibility was low. By around 900 CE, the Chinese had devised the first "wet" compass, in which a magnetized iron needle was floated on water until it pointed north. The true mariner's compass, using a pivoting needle in a dry box, was in common use in Europe by about 1300.

A cross marks the east point, indicating the direction of the Holy Land

The north point always stands out more than the others—this one takes the form of a *fleur-de-lys*

The pivoting, circular dial—the compass rose—is made of vellum and paper and displays the compass points

Before the compass

Early seafarers navigated the seas using their experience of the winds, tides, and currents, and the position of the heavenly bodies. The Vikings had no compasses so they had to rely on the sun and stars to help them steer a course when out of sight of land. They also used sun shadow boards—a simple form of sundial that enabled navigators to figure out the elevation of the sun at any time of day, in order to sail along a line of latitude (see pp.162–63).

REPLICA OF A WOODEN VIKING SUN SHADOW BOARD

The brass pivot cap in the center of the needle balances on a brass spike

MARINER'S COMPASS,
PROBABLY ITALIAN, c.1570

This compass has a diamond-shaped, iron needle that balances on a spike on the bottom of the bowl. The needle is attached to the underside of the compass rose, which turns as the magnetic needle pivots.

Most early compasses had wooden containers and lids. This one is made of ivory, so it probably belonged to someone wealthy

The compass is mounted in a brass gimbal ring, which reduces the effects of the ships's motion at sea

The outer ring of the hand-painted dial is divided into 32 points, to indicate the winds known to Mediterranean sailors

Compass development

The first European compasses were first described in Italy in about 1187, at the height of the Crusades. These compasses were similar in appearance to those from China dating back to the previous century, which may have been imported into Europe by Arab traders.

MING-DYNASTY COMPASS
Chinese seafarers at the time of the Ming dynasty (1368–1433) used an intricate 24-point box compass that featured a different Chinese character at each point.

MARINER'S COMPASS
This dry card compass, which dates from around 1776, has a steel needle, which retained its magnetism much longer than the iron needles used previously. The brass compass housing fits onto a spike in the bottom of the box that allows the compass to rotate, yet remain level at sea.

GYROCOMPASS
The gyrocompass was invented in Germany in 1906, and the German Imperial Navy adopted it for use in 1908. This entirely new type of compass finds the earth's true north, rather than its magnetic north, thanks to the gyroscope, a fast spinning wheel that orientates itself according to the earth's axis.

The Voyages of Zheng He

EVEN THE MOST CYNICAL MERCHANTS in the cities of Nanjing or Cheng-Chiang must have been moved in January 1431, as a huge fleet passed down the Yangtze River, heading away from China to voyage across the world. It was the seventh such naval expedition to be sponsored by the ruling Ming dynasty since 1405, and, like its predecessors, its aim was to assert imperial control over the major ports of South and Southeast Asia, Arabia, and East Africa, to collect tribute from them, and to foster trade.

There was a great fanfare as the fleet left Nanjing, but its 12-day passage along the 180 miles (290 km) of river was probably much quieter. The whole procession would have taken several hours to pass any single point, for it consisted of around 100 ships, including dozens of gigantic "treasure ships"—so-called because of the treasure they were expected to bring home—and numerous escort ships, message carriers, and shallow-hulled coastal vessels. Aboard this formidable flotilla were some 27,500 men, including soldiers, seamen, merchants, accountants, and doctors.

Supervising all of this was the imposing figure of commander-in-chief Zheng He, who, at more than 6 ft (1.8 m) tall, towered over his crewmen. Born to a Muslim Mongol family in Yunnan province around 1371, Zheng He was captured at the age of ten by the Ming army that had been sent to his homeland to fight against its leader, and, as was customary with young male prisoners, he was castrated and sent to serve the emperor at the imperial court in Beijing. As a eunuch, he was one of a powerful group who could be taken into royal confidence, and he distinguished himself as a soldier, gaining the title of Grand Eunuch and becoming a trusted

ZHENG HE
Explorer, diplomat, admiral, warrior, and favored adviser to the emperor, Zheng He commanded the largest fleet to sail the Indian Ocean until World War II.

CHINESE SEAFARING

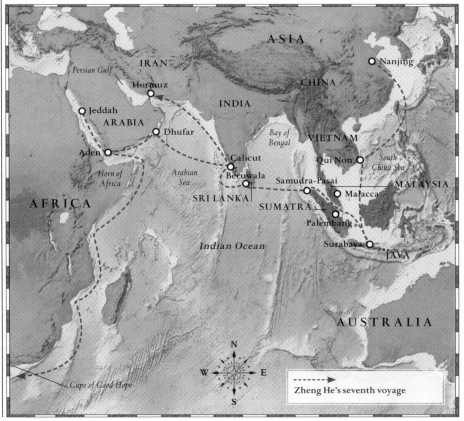

Zheng He's seventh voyage

advisor to the emperor. He was not learned in the traditional Chinese sense, but he had studied the art of war and had great wisdom and energy. He was given charge of the expeditions by Emperor Chengzu, whose aim it was to replace the overland trade routes that had been destroyed by Mongol invaders with shipping routes across the Indian Ocean. Exploration was only a secondary objective, since most of the places visited were already known to Chinese merchants, but the voyages do seem to have pushed the boundaries of the known world.

Much of what is known about the expeditions comes from the writings of Ma Huan, an Arabic-speaking court official who, as a boy, had read a book called *A Record of the Islands and their Barbarians*. "How can there be such dissimilarities in the world?" he had wondered—and, looking for an answer, he had joined Zheng He's fourth expedition in 1413 as a translator. He subsequently joined the fifth and seventh expeditions, in which he expanded his observations of the lands he had visited before. His accounts are strictly factual—no monsters or legendary characters make an appearance—and he is rarely judgmental, noting in detail the goods traded in each country, and the appearance and customs of the people at each port of call.

The treasure ships formed the core of each fleet, and they were designed to strike awe into the hearts of anyone who saw them. In 1420, Venetian merchant Niccoló da Conti noted that they were "like great houses and not fashioned at all like ours. They have ten or twelve sails and great cisterns of water within." They were divided into several compartments by watertight bulkheads, a technological innovation that did not reach the West until the 19th century. The largest ships had up to 12 masts, some of which were only raised in light winds, and had a crew of 1,000 men (600 sailors and 400 marines). One hundred years earlier, Marco Polo had observed that the largest vessels contained 50 or 60 cabins, but many of Zheng He's ships were even larger. In 1597, more than 160 years after Zheng He's voyages, Chinese writer Luo Maodeng described the largest as 450 ft (137 m) long and 180 ft (55 m) wide—as big as a 20th-century battleship—but it is more likely that they were about 250 ft (76 m) long, which is still enormous, and enough to overawe any Asian ruler. All of Zheng He's ships were propelled by mat-and-batten sails, the classic Chinese rig. Each sail was made up of numerous horizontal strips, with battens between them, and mounted with a small part of the sail forward of the mast. The battens could be lowered one by one to reduce sail in a strong wind. Each could be set at a slightly different angle than the one below, which was needed when the wind was stronger higher up. In good wind the ships could travel 346 miles (557 km) in two and a half days: an average of 138 miles (222 km) per day, or around 6 knots.

CHINESE TREASURE SHIP
The design of junks such as this one changed very little over 500 years or so, and showed minimal influence from Europe. Zheng He's fleet contained some of the largest junks of its era, recorded as being over 330 ft (100 m) long.

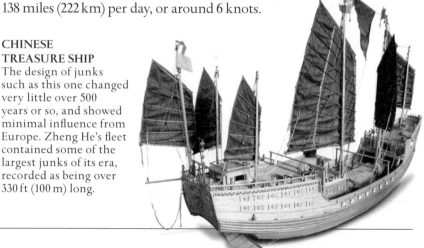

TOTAL DISTANCE TRAVELED BY ZHENG HE:

29,800 MILES
(48,000 KM)

Having left the Yangtze River, the fleet of the seventh expedition slowly made its way across the Gulf of Tonkin between south China and Vietnam, taking 15 days instead of the usual ten. After leaving Qui Non, in modern-day Vietnam, it sailed nearly 1,400 miles (2,250 km) south and arrived at Surabaya on the island of Java on March 7. Huan noticed the art form known as the Wayang Beber, in which the performer exposed sections of a picture one by one and explained it to the crowd who were "sometimes laughing, sometimes crying, exactly as if the narrator were reciting one of our popular romances." Eleven weeks later, the expedition reached Palembang on Sumatra, then the capital of a maritime empire. The ships had to tie up to brick towers on land before the men were rowed ashore in boats. The place was far better governed since Zheng He had suppressed a gang of pirates on his second voyage. The ships then left for Malacca in Malaysia, where a stockade "like a city wall" was built, including four watchtowers with gates, and patrolled by police. Inside that was another stockade with warehouses and granaries, where money and provisions were stored. Ships traveled to different parts of the region, and when they returned their valuables were stored until a southerly wind arrived to take them back to China.

Next came the 375-mile (603-km), ten-day trip to the small Muslim trading kingdom of Samudra-Pasai on the northeast coast of Sumatra. This was the slowest part of the whole voyage, the ships averaging a speed of 37 miles (60 km) per day. It was not a comfortable anchorage, either, as the waves were large and dangerous. The kingdom was an emporium for Eastern trade, but to Chinese eyes it was a primitive place, without walled cities, albeit with people who were "pure and honest." On November 2, the fleet then sailed on its first real ocean voyage, heading toward Sri Lanka to catch the monsoon winds from the northeast. They stayed south of the Nicobar Islands, where it was noted that "the people dwell in caves; men and women have naked bodies, all without a stitch of clothing" before rounding the southern tip of Sri Lanka and arriving at Beruwala on November 28. Ma Huan was impressed by the religious relics in the town, which included a single footprint in a rock face that was said to be that of the Buddha.

On December 10, they arrived at Calicut in southern India, dubbed the "City of Spices" and "the great country of the Western Ocean." Zheng He already knew the city, having visited it in 1407 to confer a title of honor and a grant of silver on the king and to give the chiefs hats and girdles. There, he erected a stone that declared, with some exaggeration: "Though the journey from this country to the Central Country [China] is more than a hundred thousand *li* [nearly 35,000 miles (65,000 km)] yet the people are very similar, happy and prosperous, with identical customs." There was a great deal of bureaucracy involved in trading with Calicut. The king sent a chief and an accountant to deal with one of the leading Chinese eunuchs, and between them they fixed prices for every article for sale, starting with the valuable silk embroideries. Such complex negotiations took at least a month or often three to settle. Presumably, the ships of the seventh expedition left some of their number behind while this was completed, or unloaded the goods, as the fleet only stayed for four days at Calicut.

On December 14, the main body of the fleet sailed for the next ocean passage, more than 1,400 miles (2,250 km) across the Arabian Sea. After a slow voyage, averaging 45 miles (72 km) per day, it reached the great

trading port of Hormuz at the entrance to the Persian Gulf, where artisans strung together exquisite pearls, and merchants dealt in precious stones and metals. Hormuz was linked by overland routes to the major cities of Iran, Central Asia, and Iraq, and Ma Huan noted that "Foreign ships from every place and foreign merchants traveling by land all

TRIBUTE GIRAFFE
Painted by Shen Du in 1414, this picture shows one of several giraffes that were gifted to the Chinese by foreign rulers (in this case an Indian prince) during Zheng He's voyages.

come to this country to attend the market and trade; hence the people of the country are all rich." They were also devout Muslims. The sailors found entertainment in the city and although he considered the juggling and acrobatics no more than average, Huan was impressed with the tricks of a goat on the top of a 10-ft (3-m) pole.

Some of the ships took a different route across the Arabian Sea, heading straight for Dhufar on the southeast coast of Arabia. On the way across they kept clear of the Laccadive Islands, where, according to Ma Huang, "If unfavourable winds and waters are met with, when the ship's master loses his bearings and the rudder is destroyed, ships passing these liu [islands]... become uncontrollable and sink." Moving on to Aden, they found a people of "overbearing disposition" with 7,000–8,000 well-drilled cavalry and foot soldiers, which made them valuable as an ally. Next they headed up the Red Sea and put into Jeddah, the port for pilgrims to Mecca. Huan was impressed by the appearance of Mecca's inhabitants, their religious devotion, and the good order of their society: "There are no poverty-stricken families. They all observe the precepts of their religion, and law breakers are few. It is in truth a most happy country."

Part of the fleet traveled down the African coast, where the Chinese had established a presence centuries earlier. Zheng He's fleet may have traveled even farther. The Venetian cartographer Fra Mauro wrote: "Around 1420 a ship, or junk, from India crossed the Sea of India towards the Island of Men and the Island of Women, off Cape Diab [southern Africa]... It sailed for 40 days in a south-westerly direction without ever finding anything other than wind and water." The ship sailed for 2,000 miles (3,200 km), then turned back to reach Cape Diab 70 days later. If this account is true, then the seventh expedition may have rounded the Cape of Good Hope decades before the Europeans.

On March 9, 1433, the fleet began its return journey, accompanied by a ship carrying a giraffe, horses, lions, and precious stones gifted by the King of Hormuz. The fleet largely retraced its steps, and from Calicut to Samudra-Pasai it made the fastest passage of all, covering nearly 1,500 miles (2,400 km) in 14 days. By June, they were back in Chinese waters. Toward the end of the trip, the 62-year-old Zheng He died and was buried at sea. Although he had extended the Middle Kingdom's wealth and power across a vast realm, its colonial period was drawing to a close, and no longer needed the offerings of foreign nations.

Pilgrims and Galleys

IN APRIL 1483, a group of twelve German Dominican monks arrived in Venice to find a ship to take them to the Holy Land. Among them was Felix Fabri, who had made the journey before, and who wrote a lively and informative account of his travels. He describes how at the port they were given a choice between two galleys; one commanded by Augustine Contarini (whom Fabri had sailed with before), but which was "small and cramped" and had only two rows of oars; and one that was new, had three banks of oars, and was captained by Contarini's arch enemy, Peter de Lando. The latter fixed the price at 45 ducats per person, and guaranteed that "The captain shall be bound to protect the pilgrims, both in the galley and out of it, from being attacked or ill-used by the galley-slaves"—and so they signed up with de Lando.

After a month of waiting, during which they bought bedding and other provisions, the pilgrims loaded their belongings into a large boat and sailed a mile out to sea to join their galley. The wind was foul and the water choppy, and it took nearly two hours to get all the passengers on board. The men met their fellow passengers, who included noblemen, knights, priests, and monks from many different nations, including "Sclavonians, Italians, Lombards, Gauls, Franks, Germans, Englishmen, Irishmen, Hungarians, Scots, Dacians, Bohemians, and Spaniards." There was only one woman among them, an "old beldame" from Flanders who was disliked because of her "silly talk and her inquisitive prying into unprofitable matters."

As the galley prepared to sail, the crew hoisted seven large silk flags, including the banner of St. Mark, with its red lion. They then raised the anchors and hoisted the yards "with exceeding hard toil and loud shouts." After that, Fabri writes, "the sails spread and filled with wind, and with great rejoicing we sailed away from the land." Trumpets were blown, "as though we were about to join battle," the galley-slaves shouted, the pilgrims sang Martin Luther's hymn "Here Is the Tenfold Sure Command," and the galley ploughed powerfully through the sea, leaving Venice far astern.

The ship was a typical Venetian galley, "built of the stoutest timbers, and fastened together with many bolts, chains, and irons." The prow was "sharp where it meets the sea, and has a strong beak,

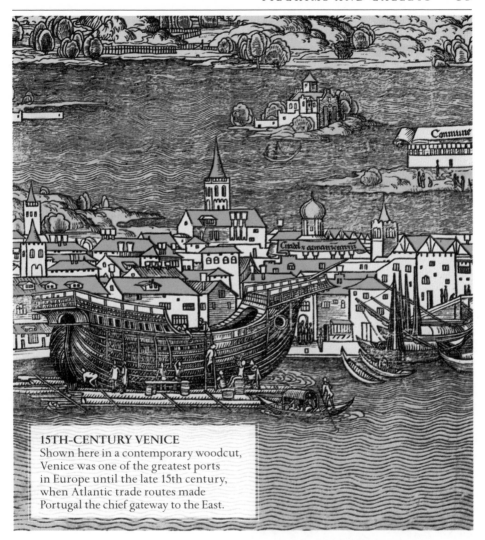

15TH-CENTURY VENICE
Shown here in a contemporary woodcut,
Venice was one of the greatest ports
in Europe until the late 15th century,
when Atlantic trade routes made
Portugal the chief gateway to the East.

made somewhat like a dragon's head, with open mouth, all of which
is made of iron, wherewith to strike any ship which it may meet." The
stern was considerably higher than the prow:

> The castle has three stories: the first, wherein is the steersman and the
> compass, and he who tells the steersman how the compass points, and
> those who watch the stars and winds, and point out the way across the
> sea; the middle one, wherein is the chamber of the Lord and captain of
> the ship, and of his noble comrades and messmates; and the lowest one,
> which is the place wherein noble ladies are housed at night, and where
> the captain's treasure is stored.

The space between the prow and the stern was filled with benches, on each of which three oarsman worked, ate, and slept. Various light swivel guns were mounted between the benches and two heavier *bombardanas*, which fired stone balls, were housed in the bow. There was a mast with a triangular (or "lateen") sail in the prow, and the mainmast stood amidships. Beside the mainmast lay an open space "wherein men assemble to talk…" and which the passengers called "the market-place of the galley."

Fabri described the cabin, where the pilgrims slept and spent much of their time, as "a great and spacious chamber" in which "… one berth joins the next one without any space left between them, and one pilgrim lies by the side of another… having their heads towards the sides of the ship, and their feet stretching out towards one another." The cabin was located just above bilge water, which produced "a worse smell than that from any closet of human ordure [excrement]." It was difficult to get to sleep in this cramped and unpleasant space, especially for monks who were used to single cells:

15TH-CENTURY RELIEF OF A GALLEY
This galley is a quinquereme—a medieval development of the Greek trireme— which has five banks of oars, as well as a single square sail.

… there is a tremendous disturbance while they are making their beds… great quarrels arise between those who are to lie side by side… for one blames his neighbour for overlapping a part of his berth with his bed, the other denies it. Some, after all lights are put out, begin to settle the affairs of the world with their neighbours… During many nights I never closed my eyes.

De Lando was indisputably the head of the ship, though "he does not interfere with the art of navigation, nor does he understand it, but merely orders the ship to be sailed hither or thither." His crew included "a brave and warlike man" who cared for the armament, a steward who was responsible for food, and a Caliph, or carpenter, who maintained the upkeep of the galley. The pilot had a chart, "whereon the whole sea is drawn with thousands and thousands of lines, and countries are marked with dots and miles by figures." The pilot also employed the services of "certain cunning men"— astrologers and soothsayers, who watched the stars and the sky and tried to predict the weather. The mate, or Cometa, had a silver whistle to convey orders. "All his subordinates fear him as they would fear the Devil," Fabri marveled, "because he strikes with staves, and punishes whomsoever he will with his fists and with ropes' ends..."

There were also nine skilled seamen, "who know how to run about the ropes like cats, who ascend the shrouds very swiftly up to the cap, [and] run along the yard standing upright even in the fiercest storms." Under them were the less skilled mariners. At the very bottom of the pecking order were the oarsmen, or galley-slaves, who were "for the most part the bought slaves of the captain, or else they are men of low station, or prisoners, or men who have run away, or been driven out of their own countries, or exiles, or such as are so unhappy that they cannot live or gain a livelihood ashore." They came from various Mediterranean nations, but Fabri remarked that he never saw a German galley-slave, because "no German could survive such misery." His journal paints a vivid picture of galley-slaves' lot: "they all are big men; but their labours are only fit for asses... these wretches, when they are pulling with their utmost strength, are still beaten to make them pull harder... They... work with bare backs, arms and shoulders, that they may be reached by whips and scourges." Their main function was rowing the ship in and out of harbor, which was often slow; it took two hours to row 1 mile (1.6 km) into one harbor when the winds were contrary.

The passengers found various ways to pass the time on the voyage. Many competed at chess, or played cards or dice games, sometimes for money. Others sang songs or struck up a tune on a musical instrument—Fabri mentions zithers, lutes, bagpipes, and clavichords being played. The more agile men ran up the rigging, or showed their strength by lifting heavy weights. The lazier ones lingered over flasks of wine, or snoozed in their berths. There was also the loathsome but necessary task of catching lice and rats. Four trumpeters announced dinner, and on the signal everyone dashed to the poop deck, since those who missed a place on the three tables there had to sit on the galley-slaves' benches. They were served wine, followed by "a salad of lettuce with oil, if green herbs can be come by; and at dinner mutton, and a pudding, or a mess of meal, or of bruised wheat or barley, or panada [bread soup] and thin cheese." Extra food could be bribed from the cooks, though this was not easy because the kitchen staff were bad-tempered, their workspace being "narrow, with many pots, many different things to be cooked, a small fire, and a great shouting going on..."

Not long into the voyage, they found themselves in a race with Captain de Lando's rival, Augustine Contarini, who had left Venice shortly after them. They feared that if Contarini arrived at the Holy land first, no more passengers would be allowed ashore until they had left—according to Fabri, "this would have been the death of us, and past our bearing." On June 4, de Lando took refuge in Rovigno (in what is now Croatia) in unfavorable winds, but sailed that evening when Contarini was seen passing. The next day Fabri witnessed one of the more difficult tasks with lateen sails, as the yard had to be brought from one side of the mast to the other:

> As the storm waxed fiercer the sailors wanted to gybe the mainsail, and the yard was already raised up above the 'top' of the mast, with the accaton furled round it, but when they let the yard fly round on the other side, the sail came loose, and fell upon the oars on that side. As the wind now suddenly filled the sail, and was raising it up with great force, it stuck among the oars, and the ship leaned over so much to that side that the yard itself touched the water, and the mast, and, indeed, the galley herself, threatened to go over on that side.

They stopped on June 9 to replenish their water but, "... lo! Master Augustine also came with his galley and passed us by... for a long way we could see his galley out at sea, sailing before a fair wind." They found Contarini again at Metona on the 14th, but, much to the annoyance of the captains, the passengers had grown tired of the race and did not share in the rivalry—making instead "a happy and merry fellowship." On June 21, they arrived in

VENETIAN MERCHANT GALLEYS ACTIVE IN 1450:

3,000

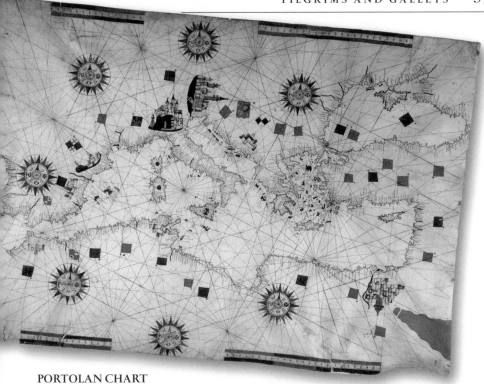

PORTOLAN CHART
Comprising "rhumb lines" originating from compass
points, portolan charts prefigured modern cartography. They
were used to plot courses between ports in the 13th and 14th
centuries; this 15th-century example was made in Italy.

Rhodes, only to find their rival there again, but he departed after
dinner. De Lando blew the trumpets to recall his passengers and
make chase and several were left behind, including the irritating
Flemish woman.

On July 1, the lookout in the maintop called out: "My lords
pilgrims, rise up and come on deck; behold, the land which you long
to see is in sight!" No one was sure if it was the Holy Land until the
captain, "with the voice of a herald," confirmed it. There was much
jubilation on board: "... it was a joyous thing to hear so many priests
singing the same song together out of the gladness of their hearts."
Both galleys had arrived almost simultaneously. When the pilgrims
landed, Fabri writes, "[we] cast ourselves down upon our faces and
kissed the sacred earth with great devotion. By merely touching the
holy land we received plenary indulgences for the remission of sins."

The Battle
of Winchelsea

IN 1350, KING EDWARD III OF ENGLAND was at peace—with Scotland, after capturing King David II at the Battle of Neville's Cross in 1346, and with France, after a decisive victory at the Battle of Crécy in the same year. For many years, however, trouble had been brewing with Castille—a Spanish kingdom whose navy had taken to raiding English ships in the Channel. A chance for restitution came when news reached Edward that a Spanish fleet had sailed to Flanders to trade wool. "We have for a long time spared these people," he announced, "for which they have done us much harm; without amending their conduct; for on the contrary, they grow more arrogant; for which reason they must be chastised." He resolved to intercept the fleet as it returned to Castille—a feasible operation in the narrow waters of the English Channel.

Edward assembled a fleet of 50 ships by the usual means of conscripting merchantmen and outfitting them for war, and issued a summons to his lords and knights. At least 17 lords and more than 400 knights responded, creating a top-heavy command structure on board ship; at the time, the title of "captain" was essentially a military one, and it was held by the lord or knight who commanded the troops on board. The fleet gathered off Winchelsea, then a significant harbor on the south coast and one of the Cinque Ports, which were obliged to maintain ships for the Crown in case of need. Edward's warrior son, the Black Prince, and the 10-year-old John of Gaunt were among the troops, as was Robert of Namur, Edward's favorite knight, who took charge of the *Salle de Roi*, which carried the King's household.

Meanwhile, the Spanish fleet of 47 ships had loaded up with linen at Sluys, in Flanders, where the English had sunk most of the French fleet 10 years earlier. Don Carlos de la Cerda, the Spanish commander, had heard of Edward's plans and armed his ships accordingly; as many cannons as he could find were lifted aboard, and the wooden "castles" atop the ships' masts were stocked with stones and iron bars to drop on the English vessels. When they raised anchor, the ships, according to the Flemish chronicler Jean Froissart, were "so beautiful, it was a fine sight to see them under sail."

SEAL OF WINCHELSEA
This 14th-century town's seal shows an English two-castle ship in detail, depicting its rudder, the tiller in the helmsman's hand, and two men hauling anchor.

Edward sailed in the *Cog Thomas*, commanded by Robert Passelow, and the fleet cruised between Dover and Calais. He enjoyed himself as he waited for the Spanish, encouraging Sir John Chandos, his tactician at the battle of Crécy, to sing with the royal minstrels. Eventually, late in the afternoon of August 29, the lookout caught sight of the Spanish. "I see two, three, four, and so many that, God help me, I cannot count them," he cried. The minstrels were silenced and the king offered wine to his knights, who drank and put on their helmets. Always conscious of his image, Edward stood at the prow of the ship, dressed, according to Froissart, in a black velvet jacket and a beaver hat, "which became him very much."

The Spanish had the wind behind them and could have declined battle (they had more to lose with valuable cargoes on board) but "their pride and presumption made them act otherwise." The king shouted to Passelow, "Steer for that ship for I want to joust with her," since he loved tournaments and had recently revived the Arthurian ideal of chivalry. Normally the master of the ship had the right to advise on such matters, but in this instance he remained silent:

> The sailor did not want to disobey his orders because it was the King who desired it, even though the Spaniard came on at speed sailing on the wind. The King's ship was strong and manoeuvrable, otherwise she would have split; for she and the great Spanish vessel struck with such force that it sounded like thunder and as they rebounded the castle of the King of England's ship caught the [top]castle of the Spanish ship in such a way that the mast levered it from the mast on which it was fixed and it fell in the sea. All those in the castle were drowned and lost.

But the Spanish ship was not the only vessel damaged in the collision. The seams between the planks of the *Cog Thomas* opened and she began to take on water. The knights pumped and baled, but did not dare to tell the King, who looked at the ship alongside the one he had "jousted" with and called out, "Grapple my ship to that one; I must have her!" One of the knights exclaimed, "Let her go, you'll get a better!" and soon another vessel drew near and the knights snared it with grappling hooks and chains:

> The English royal knights made strenuous efforts to take the ship they had grappled with because their own... was in danger of foundering as she had taken in so much water. At last the King and his crew fought so well that the Spanish ship was taken and everyone on board her was thrown over the side. Then they told the King of his peril from the sinking ship and that he should go on board the prize vessel. The King took this advice and went on board the Spanish ship with all his men leaving the other empty.

The battle raged around the English as they drew close to the Spanish, who shot arrows and pelted them with iron bars. Night was falling and the English were anxious to reach a conclusion, but the Spanish were "people well used to the sea and with large well-equipped ships." The Black Prince soon became embroiled in a fight of his own as his ship grappled a large Spanish vessel. His ship was holed in several places, perhaps by the iron bars, and was beginning to sink when the Duke of Lancaster came alongside in his own ship. The old crusader called out "Derby to the rescue!"—since he was also the Earl of Derby—and boarded the Spanish vessel. He was victorious, and again the captured enemy prisoners were thrown overboard.

The *Salle de Roi* was grappled by a large Spanish ship, which hoisted its sails and tried to drag her off. As the two ships passed the *Cog Thomas*, members of the royal household aboard the *Salle de Roi* cried for help, but there was no response. One of Robert's followers, called Hanekin, then leapt into action:

"If the English were thirsting for a fight, [the Spanish] appeared to be even more so, and this proved to be the case"

JEAN FROISSART

COMBAT AT SEA
This illustration from
Froissart's *Chronicles*
shows the hand-to-hand
nature of naval warfare
in medieval times.
It depicts the battle
between French and
English squadrons at
Sluys, Flanders, in 1340.

With his naked sword in his hand, he leapt on board the Spanish ship,
reached the mast, and cut the halyard and the sail collapsed and didn't
draw any more. And then with great effort he cut the four mighty
shrouds which supported the mast and sails so that they fell on the ship
and the ship stopped and couldn't go any more.

Robert's men boarded the ship with swords drawn, and, according to
Froissart, "fought so well that all on board were killed and thrown
overboard, and the ship taken." It was the end of the battle—an
indisputable victory for the English, who captured 20 Spanish ships at
the cost of only two of their own.

In spite of Edward's success, however, Winchelsea was only a flash
in a conflict that raged between the English and the Spanish for over
200 years, coming to a head with the defeat of the Spanish Armada in
1588 (see p.115). It was a typical naval battle of the late-medieval
period, both harking back to the ram-and-board tactics of classical
times and straining toward the early modern period, in which vessels
with designated gun decks were developed. It proved yet again that
merchant ships were ill-suited to housing cannons, and effectively
became hand-to-hand battlegrounds when they met each other in
combat. Little would change until the 16th century, when the first
true warships in the modern sense were built (see pp.72–73), heralding
an age in which ships could fire at each other from a distance, and
battles could be won or lost without boarding.

The Age of
Exploration
1450–1600

The ocean voyages of European mariners in the 15th and 16th centuries had a profound impact on world history. When Christopher Columbus, an Italian in the service of Spanish monarchs, crossed the Atlantic to the West Indies in 1492, he established the first permanent link between Europe and the Americas, and within 30 years European sailors had also blazed a trail to India around the Cape of Good Hope and circumnavigated the globe. The secret of their success was partly technological—the evolution of three- and four-masted sailing ships, combining the best of Mediterranean and northern European boat-building traditions, and the adoption of navigational devices, such as the astrolabe, the sextant, and the magnetic compass. But maritime expansion also depended upon the extraordinary ambition and drive that inspired seafarers to endure great hardship and risk their lives venturing beyond the known limits of their world.

The voyages of exploration allowed European states—particularly Portugal and Spain at first—to found overseas empires and fill their coffers with wealth from plunder, exploitation, and trade. However, while staking a claim to new territories, conquering indigenous peoples, and opening up advantageous trade routes, Europeans also found the energy to fight one another. During the 16th century, numerous cannons were mounted onto ships such as carracks or galleons, arranged to fire over the bows and stern, as well as through ports in the side of the ships. Naval power became a vital element in a continuous round of European conflicts. Privateers such as Sir Francis Drake conducted campaigns of licensed piracy and plunder against Spain's shipping and colonies in the Americas, and in 1588, the English fought off a powerful Spanish Armada in an attempted invasion of the realm of Elizabeth I. Mariners were learning to sail the oceans with confidence, but they remained exposed to countless hazards and uncertainties.

The New World

ON JANUARY 2, 1492, the long Moorish occupation of Spain was over. Forty-year-old Genoese seaman and adventurer Christopher Columbus watched as the Spanish royal flags were hoisted above the great fortress of the Alhambra in Granada. The Moorish king came out to kiss the hands of King Ferdinand II of Aragon and Queen Isabella I of Castile, and the country was now united under a strong Catholic monarchy. The same year, setting out under the patronage of the newly confident Spanish monarchy, Columbus became the first European to set foot on American soil—at least since the haphazard transatlantic journeys of the Vikings (see pp.30–35). In doing so, he began a golden age of exploration and expansion for his Spanish masters.

Columbus was a visionary with a keen interest in the geography of the world. Widely read, he may already have sailed as far north as Iceland and as far south as Guinea, and was convinced that it was possible to reach the great riches of China and India by sailing west. He had already tried to get support in France, England, and Portugal for such a voyage, before seeking patronage in Spain. His arrival was timely. Eager to establish colonies overseas, Ferdinand and Isabella financed three ships—the 58-ft (18-m) *Santa Maria* and the smaller *Niña* and *Pinta*—all of which were three-masted, in the style of the day. The *Santa Maria* was captained by Columbus, while the Pinzón brothers took command of the other two. The ships carried 40, 24, and 26 men respectively, all of whom slept on the deck (they later discovered hammocks in the West Indies—perhaps one of the greatest unsung discoveries of Columbus's voyage).

The expedition set sail from the Spanish port of Palos on August 3, 1492. It made its first stop at Gomera in the Canary Islands, which had been under Spanish control

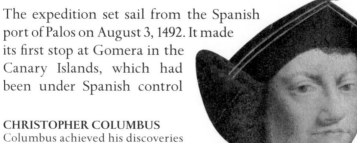

CHRISTOPHER COLUMBUS
Columbus achieved his discoveries through a mixture of accident and design. Nevertheless, he was the pioneer of European settlement in the New World.

VOYAGES OF COLUMBUS 1492–1506

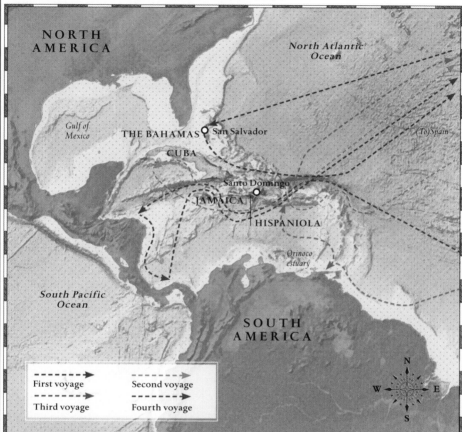

NORTH
AMERICA

*North Atlantic
Ocean*

*Gulf of
Mexico*

THE BAHAMAS ○ San Salvador

(To) Spain

CUBA

Santo Domingo ○

JAMAICA

HISPANIOLA

*Orinoco
estuary*

*South Pacific
Ocean*

SOUTH
AMERICA

------▶ First voyage	------▶ Second voyage
------▶ Third voyage	------▶ Fourth voyage

N
W   E
S

since 1402 and provided a good base for Atlantic exploration. Here they re-rigged the *Niña* and fixed the rudder of the *Pinta* before setting off west into uncharted waters.

Columbus's calculations tended to underestimate the earth's diameter, and he also understated the distance they were traveling, so that the crew, he wrote, "might not become disheartened." With no idea how far they had traveled, the sailors veered off course. The captain reprimanded his sailors for their sloppy steering. However, he knew that birds might indicate the presence of land, and began to record bird sightings with obsessive regularity after the crew of the *Niña* reported seeing a tern and a tropicbird— according to Columbus, these never flew more than around 100 miles (160 km) from land.

THE *SANTA MARIA*
At slightly over 100 tons, Columbus's largest
ship, the *Santa Maria*, was only a modestly
sized merchant vessel, even for her day.

The navigators could measure
latitude by taking a sight on the sun
daily at noon, but there was no accurate
way to measure longitude (see pp.162–63)
except by tracking the distance and direction of
the ships and both speed and the effect of currents
were impossible to gauge. When the ships' pilots were consulted on
September 19, the captain of the *Niña* reckoned she had traveled 440
leagues, or 1,760 miles, from the Canaries, the *Pinta* made it
420 leagues, and the *Santa Maria* made it 400 leagues. It rained later
that day, which Columbus interpreted as a sign that there were islands
north and south of the ships, but he pressed on west, determined to
find mainland Asia. The next day, they caught a bird that they
thought was a river bird, proof to them that land was nearby.

Legend has it that the crew were afraid of falling off the edge of
the world, but they were actually far more concerned about the
wind, which blew forever westward. How could it return them to
Spain? Columbus records that the crew became "very much excited"
when they encountered a headwind from the west, but this turned
to disappointment when there was a flat sea, suggesting that the
westerly wind was not enough to whip up great waves. On the 23rd,
however, the sea "without wind, rose greatly" and Columbus
compared it to the opening of the Red Sea in the biblical story of
Moses. When the storm had died down, Pinzón called out from the
poop of the *Niña* that he had sighted land to the southwest. Men
climbed into the rigging to look, then sank to their knees in prayer.
Columbus estimated that the land was 25 leagues away, and steered
toward it—but at noon the next day he conceded that all they had
seen were clouds. Columbus tried to sustain hope with more bird
spotting: "They saw a bird called the frigate-bird, which makes the
boobies vomit what they have eaten in order to eat it itself... nor
does it go more than twenty leagues from land," he wrote in the
ship's journal. But by October 1, the captain's secret log showed that
they had now gone 707 leagues without finding land. Even

Columbus's optimism waned. After more than a month at open sea, the crew could "bear no more" and began to complain about the long voyage. Sailing southwest again, the fleet spotted a stick with an iron tip, a small board, and land vegetation floating on the water. According to Columbus, they "breathed again and rejoiced." The captain called his men together and promised a silk doublet and 10,000 *maravedís* a year (almost a seaman's annual wages) to the first to sight land.

On the night of October 12, a sailor called out: "Land ahoy!" This time, it was no illusion: the ships reached a small island where they could see naked people on shore, and anchored. Columbus took possession of the land in the name of his king and queen, naming it San Salvador. More than 500 years later, there is still no consensus as to where Columbus first landed, but it may have been Watling Island in the Bahamas. He described the natives as a simple, trusting people, "well built, with very handsome bodies and very good faces." They could easily be converted to Christianity by "love rather than force," he wrote, and would also make very good servants.

The flotilla sailed on in search of the Asia described by Marco Polo. They were convinced it was near, and began to find new peoples, new animals, and new vegetation. Anchoring off the northwest point of Crooked Island in the Bahamas, they found that the people had fled in terror. They sailed on to the large island now known as Cuba, where they learned more about the natives' fears: the peaceful Arawak people were terrified of the fierce Caribs from the east, who raided them for slaves. The Spanish assumed that the Caribs were cannibals. Two of the crew ventured into the interior, where they discovered natives "on their way to their villages, men and women, with a brand in their hands, the herbs for smoking which they are in a habit of using." This was the first European encounter with tobacco-smoking—a habit that was taken back to Spain. On

"Gold is a treasure, and he who possesses it does all he wishes to in this world"

CHRISTOPHER COLUMBUS

The North Atlantic Ocean

The North Atlantic Ocean is dominated by a circular wind pattern that travels in a clockwise direction around its periphery. Trade winds blow southwest from Europe to the Caribbean and then up the east coast of North America. The Gulf Stream and North Atlantic Drift carry warm water to Europe, giving the continent a mild climate despite its northerly latitude. Depressions originating off Newfoundland bring strong winds and rain too. Drifting icebergs are common in the shallow waters around Greenland.

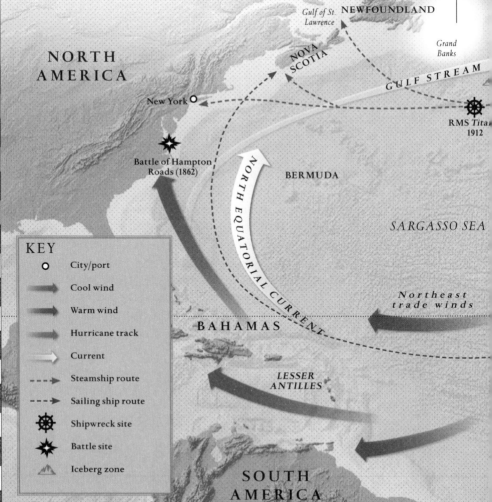

Semi-permanent area of fog

Gulf of St. Lawrence   NEWFOUNDLAND

Grand Banks

NOVA SCOTIA

GULF STREAM

NORTH AMERICA

New York O

RMS *Titanic* 1912

✶ Battle of Hampton Roads (1862)

BERMUDA

NORTH EQUATORIAL CURRENT

SARGASSO SEA

Northeast trade winds

BAHAMAS

LESSER ANTILLES

SOUTH AMERICA

KEY

O	City/port
→	Cool wind
→	Warm wind
→	Hurricane track
→	Current
---→	Steamship route
---→	Sailing ship route
⛭	Shipwreck site
✶	Battle site
⛰	Iceberg zone

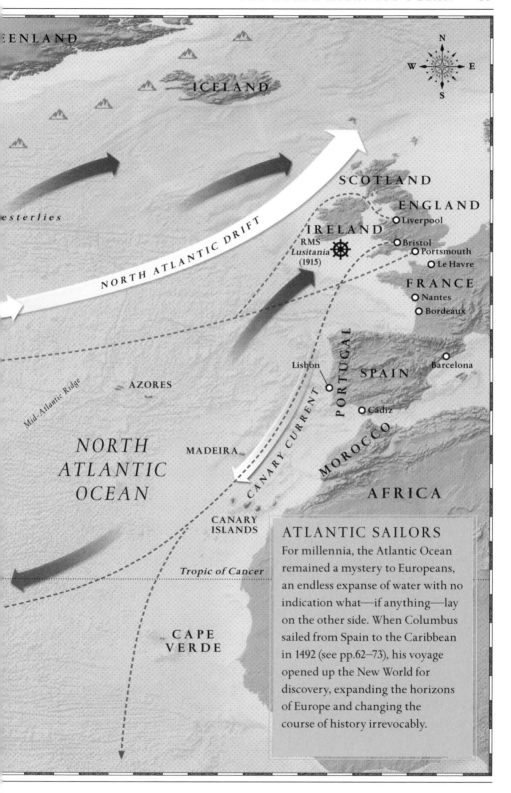

ENLAND

ICELAND

N
W   E
S

SCOTLAND

ENGLAND

O Liverpool

IRELAND

RMS
Lusitania
(1915)

O Bristol
O Portsmouth
O Le Havre

FRANCE

O Nantes
O Bordeaux

esterlies

NORTH ATLANTIC DRIFT

Mid-Atlantic Ridge

AZORES

Lisbon

PORTUGAL

SPAIN

O Barcelona

O Cádiz

CANARY CURRENT

NORTH
ATLANTIC
OCEAN

MADEIRA

MOROCCO

AFRICA

CANARY
ISLANDS

Tropic of Cancer

CAPE
VERDE

ATLANTIC SAILORS

For millennia, the Atlantic Ocean remained a mystery to Europeans, an endless expanse of water with no indication what—if anything—lay on the other side. When Columbus sailed from Spain to the Caribbean in 1492 (see pp.62–73), his voyage opened up the New World for discovery, expanding the horizons of Europe and changing the course of history irrevocably.

November 5, Columbus sailed southeast "to seek for gold and spices and to discover land." The *Pinta* sailed separately, which Columbus saw as desertion. The *Santa Maria* and the *Niña* came to a large island, which Columbus called Española (later known as Hispaniola), with excellent harbors and "some plains, the loveliest in the world, and as fit for sowing as the lands of Castile." Its soft-voiced people, "of good height, not black," exhibited "the most extraordinarily gentle behavior and appeared to live in fear of a people called the Caniba"—another name for the dreaded Carib.

The *Santa Maria* and *Niña* sailed around Hispaniola on Christmas Eve. That night, Columbus, feeling "secure from banks and rocks," went down for a rest, but the *Santa Maria* drifted onto a bank and heeled over; her seams opened, and Columbus and his crew had to abandon her. Since the *Niña* was too small to carry two crews, Columbus decided to leave 39 men on Hispaniola to found a town— the first European settlement in the New World—which he called Villa de Navidad (Christmas Town). The men were well armed and built fortifications from the ship's timbers, and Columbus was confident that they would enjoy the support of the local chief and the unarmed natives. He wrote, "the men whom I have left there alone would suffice to destroy all that land." The *Pinta* rejoined the *Niña* as she was setting sail.

On January 13, the expedition encountered the fearsome Caribs when a party of seven went ashore and was attacked by over 50 men with bows and arrows. After re-embarking, they sailed in search of the Carib homeland (and a legendary island inhabited by women), but found themselves caught in a westerly wind that sent them east across the ocean, back toward Africa. Columbus and the crew of the *Niña* lost sight of the *Pinta* amid "frightful waves" in a treacherous storm, and the crew drew lots to make a pilgrimage to Santa Maria di Loreto if they survived. Columbus drew the chickpea marked with a cross, but still, he wrote, "each one made his own individual vow, because no one expected to escape, owing to the terrible storm." He sealed the ship's log in a barrel for posterity. Finally, the winds abated and they anchored briefly in the Portuguese Azores.

When they encountered another storm, they experienced seas "which came upon them from two sides," and "winds, which seemed to lift the caravel into the air." They spotted land, and at daybreak

LANDING AT HISPANIOLA
Columbus was impressed both with the richness of the land and the friendliness of the native people.

headed for a harbor that they saw. Unfortunately, it turned out to be Lisbon. The Portuguese soon discovered that they had been to the Indies, and harrassed Columbus to reveal the route. Eventually, he was allowed to sail, and on March 15, 1493, after more than six months at sea, he crossed the bar into the Spanish port of Palos.

Columbus reported to the King and Queen in Barcelona, and was awarded the title "Admiral of the Ocean Seas." He was given 17 ships and 1,200 men for a much larger expedition, and set sail again on his second voyage in September 1493. He returned to Hispaniola, where he found that Villa de Navidad had been burned to the ground and his men had been slaughtered by natives.

After returning to Spain again, he embarked on a third voyage in 1498. This time he reached the mainland of South America, where he thought that the Orinoco estuary was Eden itself. In 1500, however, he was sent home in chains by Francisco de Bobadilla, the newly appointed royal governor of the Spanish colonies, accused of governing with excessive violence. He was restored to favor in Spain, and explored the Gulf of Mexico on a fourth voyage in 1502.

Columbus died in 1506, still believing that he had sailed close to Asia. However, an Italian navigator by the name of Amerigo Vespucci soon demonstrated that the lands Columbus had discovered were not the eastern shores of Asia, but an entirely different continent—one that would soon be named after Vespucci himself. This New World, as it was called, soon became a battleground in which rival imperial powers fought for territory, most notably in the Spanish conquests of the gold-laden countries of South America (see pp.94–95). Confined, inward-looking, overcrowded Europe had begun to break its bounds—a process that stimulated travel, navigation, and commerce, but brought with it the evils of slavery and genocide.

Medieval Ships

The medieval period saw a flowering of innovation in ship design, particularly in Europe, where a cross-fertilization between the Scandinavian and Mediterranean traditions produced a new generation of powerful, multi-masted vessels.

VIKING KNORR (c.1000)
The knorr was the type of cargo ship that the Vikings used to colonize Iceland, Greenland, and eventually Vinland. It was typically 56 ft (17 m) long and 15 ft (4.5 m) wide.

Mainstay

Foresail

Forecastle

Spritsail

BREMEN COG (1380)
The cog was the standard northern European ship during the Middle Ages. It had a single mast, a square sail, and a spar projecting from the bow to anchor the sail.

SPANISH COCCA (1450)
The Mediterranean equivalent of the cog was the cocca. It had a broad, rounded hull to maximize space for cargo and a crow's nest on its main mast.

FLEMISH CARRACK (1450)
The carrack became the standard vessel of Atlantic trade in the 16th century. This Flemish version had three crow's nests for lookouts.

ENGLISH COG (1485)
By the mid 15th century, the ships had "castles" fore and aft, which served as excellent platforms for bowmen in times of war.

SPANISH CARRACK (1490)

The carrack was a three- or four-masted ship developed by the Portuguese for sailing the Atlantic Ocean. This Spanish version was the largest European sailing ship of the 15th century.

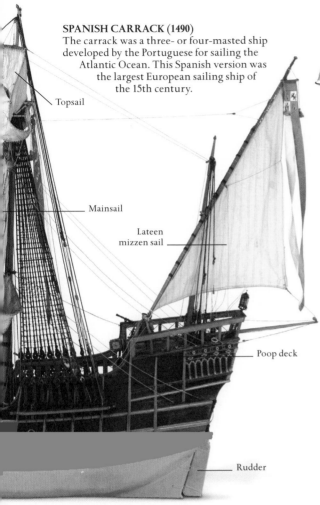

Topsail

Mainsail

Lateen mizzen sail

Poop deck

Rudder

PORTUGUESE CARAVEL (1490)

Another Portuguese invention, the caravel was a highly maneuverable sailing vessel. This version is a *caravela rodonda*, which had square sails on its main mast.

ENGLISH CARAVEL (1497)

This caravel is the *Matthew*, in which Italian explorer John Cabot sailed from Bristol to Newfoundland in 1497. Like Columbus, he had expected to find the eastern seaboard of Asia.

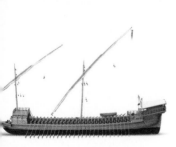

VENETIAN GALLEY (1500)

Oared galleys remained the chief fighting ships of the Mediterrean well into the 16th century. Each oar of this Venetian example was rowed by up to five oarsmen.

TREASURE SHIP (1400)

In the early 15th century, the Chinese sailed gigantic "treasure ships" across the world. Some are said to have been 450 ft (137 m) long and 180 ft (55 m) wide.

VENETIAN COCCA (1525)

This small cocca, with its high prow and stern, was typical of the merchant ships that sailed from Venice to the East in the early 16th century.

To India by Sea

IN 1497, SPURRED BY RIVALRY WITH SPAIN in the wake of Christopher Columbus's crossing of the Atlantic (see pp.64–71), King John II of Portugal commissioned Vasco da Gama to sail east on a voyage of discovery. Da Gama's expedition differed from Columbus's in many ways: he sailed east rather than west, traveled along coasts for much of the journey, and visited lands that had already been discovered by Europeans. However, he became the first European to reach India by sea, and opened a route to Asia that avoided both the Mediterranean and the dangerous waters of Arabia.

By the late 15th century, Portugal already had a long history of nautical exploration. With a long Atlantic seafront, good harbors, and skilled seamen, the nation had explored the west African coast under the leadership of Prince Henry the Navigator from 1415 until his death in 1460. Portuguese sailors discovered the Azores, to the west, in 1432, and the Cape Verde Islands, farther south, in 1456. Both of these were good bases for Atlantic exploration. In 1488, Bartholomew Dias sailed around the southern tip of Africa, discovering what he called the Cape of Storms—which was later renamed the Cape of Good Hope to make it sound less daunting.

King John II of Portugal had rejected Columbus's plan for a westward voyage, but when Columbus arrived at Lisbon in 1493 at the end of his first voyage, the king wanted to know all about the Spanish discoveries. Tensions developed between Spain and Portugal over the lands that were being discovered, until Spanish-born Pope Alexander VI intervened to settle the conflict. In 1494, at Tordesillas in Spain, the two nations signed a treaty to divide newly discovered lands along a meridian

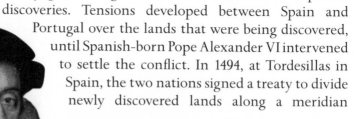

VASCO DA GAMA
The Portuguese nobleman's voyage was the first time a European had sailed to India. It opened up important trade routes, and was an extraordinary feat of seafaring.

DA GAMA'S FIRST VOYAGE 1497–99

EUROPE

ASIA

PORTUGAL
O Lisbon

INDIA

AFRICA

CAPE VERDE
ISLANDS

O Calicut

Malindi O
Mombasa O

Indian
Ocean

Mozambique O

NATAL

South
Atlantic Ocean

N
W   E
S

Cape of Good Hope

- - - - ▶
Outward journey
- - - - ▶
Return journey

halfway between the Portuguese Cape Verde Islands and Columbus's discoveries in the Caribbean. Spain was given all the lands to the west of the meridian, and Portugal received all the lands to the east (see p.86).

The Treaty of Tordesillas thus gave Portugal an incentive to explore to the south and east. It was felt that if Columbus had found a westward sea passage to the Indies, then the Portuguese could find one to the east. After King John's death in 1495, his successor, King Manuel I, continued to back exploration and invited one of his courtiers, Vasco da Gama, to lead an expedition.

·S· graviel

Vasquo da gama,

The Portuguese tended to build very large ships, but such deep-hulled vessels were not suitable for exploration, so da Gama assembled three smaller ships, of around 120 tons each, and an even smaller supply ship. He commanded the flagship, *São Gabriel*, his brother Paolo commanded the *São Raphael*, and Nicolau Coelho commanded the *Berrio*. Da Gama employed Diogo Dias, brother of explorer Bartholomew Dias, as his pilot, along with a total crew of 170.

The king's instructions were simply to "discover," to find the riches of the east, and to link up with Christian kingdoms that were believed to exist in the region, and which could be allies in controlling the ocean. On July 8, 1497, da Gama and his officers joined a procession of priests in Lisbon. The bishop gave them absolution for their sins and they boarded the ships, watched by a large crowd. Winds were favorable and they made a fast passage to the Cape Verde Islands, covering 1,590 miles (2,560 km) in 14 days. From there, the ships headed southeast, then looped out into the South Atlantic. They hoped to avoid the doldrums around the equator, but it took the flotilla 80 days to get far enough south to pick up westerly winds. After that they made a fast passage east.

On November 4, after a voyage of four months, da Gama and his men sighted land on the southwest coast of Africa. "Having put on our gala clothes, we saluted the captain-major by firing our bombards, and dressed the ships with flags and standards," an anonymous journal of the voyage records. But the pilot, Dias, who had sailed to the Cape of Good Hope with his brother, could not identify the place, so they did not land. The ships proceeded cautiously down the coast, anchoring in a sheltered bay they named St. Helena. Here they met "tawny-coloured" natives, who were dressed in skins with "sheaths over their virile members." An attempt to trade led to a mêlée—the first of many—that ended with da Gama and his men being attacked with spears.

The expedition sailed on, tacking to the east and at last sighted the Cape of Good Hope. They rounded the cape with the wind behind them, and three days later landed in another bay. Here they found much braver natives. Both sides kept their weapons handy, but a large party came to the shore bearing gifts and playing flutes, "some producing high

**16TH-CENTURY ILLUSTRATION OF
VASCO DA GAMA'S CARAVEL**
Caravels were small enough to navigate shallow water,
and could be rigged with either lateen or square-rigged
sails, making them very versatile.

notes and others low ones." Da Gama ordered his trumpeters to respond, and the sailors danced to the music. The Portuguese exchanged a trinket for an ox, which they roasted on the beach, finding "his meat as toothsome as the beef of Portugal." The crew erected a cross on a headland, but saw the natives dismantle it as they left.

A week later, the expedition entered unknown territory beyond the pillar erected a few years earlier by Dias at the farthest point of his exploration. Da Gama named the coastline Natal (after the birth of Christ) since they passed it on Christmas Day, 1497. Sailing warily on, the ships hove to at night in case of unseen dangers. At the Rio dos Bons Signaes (River of Good Tokens) they found "black and well-made" people, whose chieftains were "very haughty and valued nothing which we gave them." The natives had seen "big ships like ours" before, which was a sign that they were approaching the Arabs' trading area. "These tokens gladdened our hearts, for it appeared as if we were approaching the bourne of our desires," the anonymous chronicler notes. Nevertheless, the sailors stayed a month here because many of the men were now showing signs of scurvy.

On March 2, the flotilla arrived off the coast of Mozambique. Here they anchored and found a Mohammedan people akin to the Moors of North Africa, and four Arab ships in port laden with gold, silver, jewels, and spices. The sultan came on board, but "he treated all that we gave him with contempt, and asked for scarlet cloth, of which we had none," da Gama recounts. At "a repast when there was an abundance of figs and comfits" the sultan did, however, agree to provide the expedition with two pilots, and gave "a jar of bruised dates made into a preserve with cloves and cumin" to Coelho as a gift.

The Portuguese set sail again, but the Mozambique current forced them back into the port. Disembarking at dusk to get water, they were then confronted by about 20 men with spears, and in response fired

"The meats have become rotten, the butter has gone bad, and beer has run out"

VASCO DA GAMA
IN HIS DIARY, SEPTEMBER 17, 1497

their bombards (muzzle-loading cannons). The Mozambicans fled, and relations remained strained until the ships finally sailed on March 29. The pilot later told them that the sultan had taken them for Moors. "But when they learnt that we were Christians they arranged to seize and kill us by treachery."

The local pilots turned out to be unreliable—da Gama had one flogged for mistakenly claiming an island was the mainland—but soon the flotilla reached Mombasa, the finest port in the region. Small boats dressed in flags came out to meet the Portuguese, who put on a show too. Led to believe that there were Christians living there alongside Moors, the men were excited by the prospect of a welcome.

Instead, there was a tense standoff at midnight as a hundred men armed with cutlasses tried to board the ships. Four or five "of the most distinguished" were allowed on board, where they remained for a couple of hours. Da Gama suspected them of wanting to capture the ships. Despite the visitors' distrust, the next day the ruler sent gifts of oranges, sugarcane, and sheep, with a ring as a pledge of safety, conveyed by "two men, almost white, who said they were Christians." Two sailors then went ashore to meet the ruler and encountered supposedly Christian merchants; one was selling a picture that was said to be of the Holy Ghost, but which may have been of a Hindu deity. In any case, da Gama concluded that any Christians in the city were "only temporary residents, and... held in much subjection."

Increasingly nervous, da Gama suspected a plot against him and tortured two locals for information. That night, lookouts heard what sounded like fish below, and found several local people trying to cut the cables and board the ship. "Our Lord did not allow them to succeed, because they were unbelievers," the chronicler writes. The crew were glad to set sail again, and when two boats pursued them they captured one and took its 18 passengers prisoner, including an "old Moor of distinction" and his young wife.

Three days later, the flotilla arrived at Malindi, where the Portuguese handed over the hostages and were welcomed as potential allies against Mombasa. For nine days the sailors were entertained by "fêtes, sham fights, and musical performances."

On April 24, da Gama and his men set off across the Indian Ocean to their final destination of Calicut on the Malabar Coast of India, with the southwest monsoon behind them. An Indian pilot from Malindi helped

DA GAMA ARRIVES
This contemporary Portuguese tapestry
depicts Vasco da Gama's fleet landing at
Calicut, India, in 1498. His pioneering
route around the Cape of Good Hope
is still in use today.

them to avoid "a thousand or more islands"—the Laccadives—and after just 23 days they saw "lofty mountains." Thunderstorms and rain prevented them from landing at first, and they mistakenly anchored 8 miles (13 km) from Calicut, but eventually one of the crew was sent ashore and found Castilian-speaking Arabs, who told him, "You owe great thanks to God for having brought you to a country holding such riches!" Da Gama was invited to pay court to the local Hindu ruler, the Zamorin. He and 13 men "put on our best attire, placed bombards in our boats, and took with us trumpets and many flags," according to the journal of the voyage. The captain was carried in a palanquin by relays of six men to the palace, where they found the Zamorin reclining on a green velvet-covered couch. The latter asked da Gama to hand over the "golden virgin"—a statue of the Madonna—that had been seen on his ship, but da Gama refused, claiming it was not made of gold, and that it was essential for worship. The Portuguese had prepared gifts of cloth, coats, hats, coral, sugar, and a barrel of butter to impress their hosts, but the Zamorin's inspectors showed little interest, telling them "the poorest merchant who came from Mecca or the Imdios gave him more than that." The Zamorin declined to see samples.

On the way back to the ship, the palanquin traveled so fast that the rest of the party was left behind. Feeling agitated, the Portuguese suspected a trap and refused to signal for the ships to come closer. The tension ended when they were allowed to bring part of the cargo ashore to sell, but the sophisticated Arab traders despised their goods. The sailors were reduced to bartering what they could on the waterfront in exchange for essentials for the journey home.

The Portuguese stayed in Calicut for three months, but again relations soured. Da Gama proposed leaving two of his men, including Dias, to discuss trade, and taking emissaries from the Zamorin to Portugal. Instead, he was asked to pay duties. Believing that Dias was being held hostage, the Portuguese seized a group sent out to parley and raised their anchors to depart. Luckily for Dias, however, there was no wind, he was assured that he was not a prisoner, and the hostages were released.

All the same, da Gama decided it was time to sail for home: "inasmuch that we had discovered the country we had come in search of... and it appeared impossible to establish cordial relations with the people, it would be as well to take our departure. We therefore set sail and left for Portugal, greatly rejoicing at our good fortune in having made so great a discovery." This time, the fleet set off across the Indian Ocean against the monsoon winds, and the 2,300-mile (3,700-km) passage took 132 days—as opposed to the 27 days taken on the outward trip. Scurvy made a reappearance: "All our people again suffered from their gums, which grew over their teeth, so that they could not eat. Their legs also swelled, and other parts of the body," the anonymous journal records. Thirty men died, and it was only the oranges of Malindi, where the ships' crews rested and replenished for five days, that saved the rest.

Farther down the East African coast, they burned the *São Raphael*, since they no longer had enough crew for three ships. Once the two remaining ships rounded the Cape of Good Hope, where winds and currents would carry them to the Cape Verde Islands, they were delayed in calms. The *São Gabriel* and the *Berrio* parted company, Vasco da Gama making his way to the islands with his dying brother, while Coelho sailed back to Lisbon. Paolo da Gama died in the Azores. The *Berrio* arrived in Lisbon on July 10, after an absence of two years, and the *São Gabriel* followed on September 18.

Despite the loss of life and the trade failures, da Gama became a national hero and was heaped with honors on his return. He had shown that the eastern route to the Indies was viable, that there was no navy in the Indian Ocean to contest Portuguese power, and that lucrative trade was practicable if the right goods could be found. In subsequent voyages, his countrymen reduced the sailing times and established the first major sea route for trade between Europe and the Indies.

PORTUGUESE FORT AT CALICUT
The Portuguese were eager to capitalize on the newly discovered trade route, and set up a trading outpost in Calicut, where they constructed a fort in 1530.

Circumnavigating the Earth

IN A THREE-YEAR VOYAGE that lasted from 1519 to 1522, an expedition led by Ferdinand Magellan became the first to circumnavigate the earth. Magellan himself did not live to see his ship's triumphant return to Spain, but he claimed several other firsts en route: he was the first European to sail from the Atlantic into the Pacific, and the first to cross the Pacific Ocean—proving the existence of the long-dreamed-of western route to the Indies.

Since Columbus's first voyage in 1492, Spanish power had extended over the islands of Cuba, Hispaniola, and Jamaica, as well as Panama and Florida on the mainland. Only the Portuguese were serious rivals on the oceans, with a presence in Brazil and in the Indian Ocean. A Portuguese nobleman and veteran of expeditions to the Indies, Magellan had fallen out with King Manuel I of Portugal when the king refused to back a westward voyage to the famously rich Spice Islands, or Moluccas. In 1517, the disgruntled explorer left for Spain.

Spaniard Vasco Núñez de Balboa had glimpsed the Pacific Ocean from Panama in 1513, and in 1518, Magellan persuaded King Charles I of Spain to outfit out a small expedition to find a route into the Pacific. This venture was of particular interest to Spain since the Treaty of Tordesillas (see pp.74–75) had granted Spain all the lands west of the Papal Line of Demarcation—a political boundary halfway between the Portuguese Cape Verde Islands off West Africa and the Spanish Caribbean. Portugal had been given all the lands to its east.

Magellan assembled a fleet of five ships at Seville: his flagship, the 120-ton *San Antonio*, the 110-ton *Trinidad*, the

FERDINAND MAGELLAN
Magellan was born in 1480, into a noble Portuguese family. He enlisted on his first voyage, to the Indies, in 1505.

CIRCUMNAVIGATION OF THE EARTH 1519–22

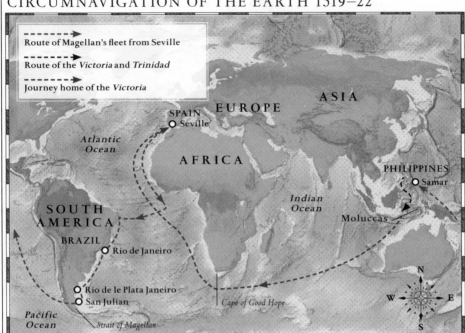

Route of Magellan's fleet from Seville

Route of the *Victoria* and *Trinidad*

Journey home of the *Victoria*

90-ton *Concepción*, and the *Santiago* and *Victoria*, both 75 tons. There were 15 Portuguese noblemen on the ships, plus their servants, four pilots, and Juan de Silva of Madeira, who was said to be a spy for Portugal and complained that the ships were "very old and patched up."

Rivalry between Spain and Portugal would dog the whole voyage. From the outset, Magellan believed "the masters and captains of the other ships of his company did not love him" because of antagonism between the nations, wrote Italian adventurer Antonio Pigafetta in his account of the journey. Of his own involvement, Pigafetta wrote: "I was in Spain in the year 1519, and from books and conversations I learnt that there were wonderful things to be seen in travelling the ocean, so I determined to discover with my own eyes the truth of all that I had been told."

Magellan had 237 men in his crews. The sailors were not told the full extent of the voyage, Pigafetta wrote, in case they were deterred by "amazement and fear." The captain organized them carefully, in three watches overnight that changed at midnight and "towards break of day." The watches alternated to allow continuous sleep for one night out of three. He also divided the crew into "companies," a system that

DIVIDING THE WORLD
This 1502 map shows the Papal Line of
Demarcation (vertical, in blue), which
divided the world between the Spanish
and Portuguese empires.

anticipated modern naval organization. Intent on keeping his fleet together, Magellan ordered that his own ship, the *Trinidad*, should be in the lead, and organized light signals for setting and reducing sail.

On August 10, 1519, the five ships sailed down the Guadalquivir river to the coastal port of Sanlúcar de Barrameda. There they took on supplies and went to Mass daily, and before setting off Magellan commanded all the men to confess their sins. They set sail on the 20th, stopping off at Spanish Gran Canaria before sailing south, bypassing the Portuguese Cape Verde Islands and continuing along the familiar West African coast. They kept the mountains of Sierra Leone in sight for several days.

In the equatorial region progress was slowed, Pigafetta wrote, by "a variety of weather and bad winds, as much on account of squalls as for head winds and currents which came in such a manner that we could no longer advance." During the storms they were comforted to see the bright violet glow of St. Elmo's fire, since sailors' lore dictated that no ship was lost when it appeared. The sailors also caught sharks, "which have teeth of a terrible kind," and were not good to eat.

The expedition crossed the equator and lost sight of the pole star. On November 29, the pilot, Francisco Albo, began to take sights of the sun and found that they had crossed the 7th parallel south. Soon after, they arrived at Verzin, or Rio de Janeiro, which had been discovered by the Portuguese in 1502. Here they enjoyed "refreshments of victuals, like fowls and meat of calves, also a variety of fruits, called batate, pineapples, sweet, of singular goodness and many other things," Pigafetta recorded.

Sailing on south to the Rio de la Plata, they arrived at the river's wide estuary and found a race that they believed were the cannibals that had eaten 60 men of a Spanish crew. They were approached by a man who was "great as a giant," and had "a voice like a bull." A hundred men chased after him, but "this kind of people did more with one step than we could do at a bound." Realizing that the river did not provide a passage through the continent, they sailed south to a new anchorage at Puerto San Julian, but by that time they had missed the southern summer and had to stay for five months.

With provisions much reduced, the winter was going to be hard. As they prepared to wait it out, the enormity of the task before them was dawning on some of the officers. They had no way of knowing how far south the continent stretched, and there were only speculative calculations on the distance to the Moluccas in Indonesia. Moreover, they distrusted their Portuguese captain, who had reasons to hate the Spanish. Magellan, however, had resolved "either to die or to complete his enterprise," and told his officers that they could get through the winter by hunting and fishing, and that summer would offer them "one perpetual day." So far, they had sailed only four degrees south of the Cape of Good Hope, which had regularly been passed by Portuguese sailors. To return without going further would be ignominious. If they pressed on, however, they might well find "a new unknown world, rich in spices and gold."

Magellan's conviction was not enough for three of his captains— Juan de Cartagena, Luis de Mendoza, and Gaspar Quesada. On April 1, the ringleader, Cartagena, boarded the *San Antonio* and locked its captain, the loyal Alvaro de Mezquita, in his cabin. Magellan counterattacked, boarding the *Victoria* and killing its mutinous captain, Mendoza. Outnumbered, the other ships surrendered. Magellan dealt harshly with the rebels: Quesada, captain of the *Concepción,* was executed, and Cartagena, too high-ranking to execute, was cast ashore and marooned along with the mutinous chaplain.

The bay in which they had anchored proved to be another land of "giants," whom Magellan called "Patagóns," possibly after the wild men encountered by the hero of *Primaleon,* a romance by Francisco Vázquez that was popular at the time. Pigafetta observed of the men, "Certainly these giants run faster than a horse, and they are very jealous of their wives." Relations with the Patagóns were friendly until Magellan made a clumsy attempt at capturing some of them by subterfuge. He fitted them with shackles, which the natives took to be body decorations until the sailors tried to fasten them. One man was killed in the ensuing mêlée.

On August 24, the expedition set sail again in search of a passage through the continent. The *Santiago* was wrecked in a storm, but its crew survived. After a stop at Santa Cruz, the remaining four ships arrived in another bay. The *Trinidad* and *Victoria* anchored while the *San Antonio* and *Concepción* went ahead to reconnoiter. Driven into a bay by a storm, they feared the worst, but instead of being dashed against the rocks, they found the entrance to a strait. Returning to report this to the others, they fired their guns and flew their flags. The men aboard the *Trinidad* and the *Victoria* were delighted, and all the crews thanked God and the Virgin Mary.

MAGELLAN IN THE PACIFIC
This illustration shows flying fish hitting Ferdinand
Magellan's ship in the Pacific. His expedition was one
of the greatest successes of Spanish exploration.

The ships still had to navigate the strait, which proved to be a
succession of bays with high mountains on each side, and a channel
"which at some places has a width of three leagues, and two, and one,
and in some places half a league." The strait was perilously narrow
and too deep to anchor, the sailors having to lash the ships to rocks
on shore when they stopped for the night.

The *San Antonio* and the *Concepción* were again sent ahead to check
the lie of the land. This time the pilot of the *San Antonio* rebelled,
putting the captain in irons and heading home. Magellan polled his
officers on whether to continue, but he had already made up his mind,

consulting them only "to please and content his people." He concluded that going on was "for the good of the fleet," and they sailed the next day. After more than five weeks they saw "a great sea on the other side," and Magellan ordered that guns be fired in celebration.

Magellan named the ocean he found the "Pacific" (meaning "peaceful"), and indeed they were lucky enough not to encounter any storms as they were "driven almost continuously by a very strong wind" over a sea "more vast than the mind of man can conceive." They headed west-northwest, reckoning that if they sailed due west they would miss the Cape of Good Hope and find nothing of value. They had no real idea of how far they had to go, however, and they encountered only two small, barren, and uninhabited islands. Food began to run short, Pigafetta recorded: "... we only ate old biscuit reduced to powder, and full of grubs, and stinking from the dirt which the rats had made on it when eating the good biscuit, and we drank water that was yellow and stinking." They ate the ox hides that protected the yards from chafing after steeping them in water for four or five days, and dead rats changed hands at half a crown each. Scurvy then broke out, killing 20 men.

On March 6, after more than three months at sea, they reached an island—probably Guam—where they could anchor and replenish their supplies. As they began to strike their sails, dozens of natives appeared and the Europeans had their first encounter with Polynesian seafarers: "there is no difference between poop and prow in these boats, and they are like dolphins bouncing from wave to wave." However, the natives stole one of the boats that was being towed astern, and Magellan ordered a raid on their villages in reprisal—40 or 50 houses were destroyed, and seven men were killed. The Europeans deemed the people, "poor, but ingenious, and great thieves," and sailed on with some regret, having seen women who looked "beautiful and delicate." After 10 days, they reached the island of Samar on the edge of the Philippines, where the people were far friendlier and offered them exotic fruits. Then they sailed to an island called Mazaua, where Magellan sent his Malay slave and interpreter Enrique ashore to negotiate. They traded gifts with the ruler and may have said Mass there on March 31,

DISTANCE OF MAGELLAN'S VOYAGE:

37,560 MILES
(60,440 KM)

THE *VICTORIA*
This was the only ship out of five to return home to Seville from the expedition. Of around 265 crew who set out, only 18 returned.

which was Easter Sunday. A week later they arrived at Cebu, where Magellan persuaded the ruler to convert to Christianity with a promise to "leave them the arms which the Christians use." The conversion was performed on an elaborate scaffold, followed by the baptism of the king, queen, and 800 others.

Magellan then made the fatal error of getting involved in tribal politics, taking sides in a war with a tribe that refused to convert to Christianity. He sailed to the island of Mactan with a small force to "prove how their lances wounded." Forty-nine men waded ashore and were met by some 1,500 islanders. The Spaniards fired muskets and crossbows, but the natives approached undaunted, shooting arrows and throwing spears at their enemies' unprotected legs and arms. Recognizing Magellan as the captain, the natives attacked him, and he, "like a good knight, remained at his post without choosing to retreat further," even after his helmet was knocked off. Wounded in the face, he struck an opponent with his sword, but, unable to withdraw it, he was surrounded, and "the Indians threw themselves upon him, and ran him through with lances and scimitars."

Magellan's men retreated, but the heart had gone out of the expedition. There were not enough men left to crew the remaining ships, so the *Concepción* was abandoned. The last two ships made it to the Spice Islands, where they loaded up with precious cloves and cinnamon, which eventually raised enough money to pay for the whole voyage. The *Trinidad* attempted to return eastward across the Pacific and the *Victoria*, under Sebastian del Cano, sailed westward around the Cape of Good Hope. The *Trinidad* never made it home, but the *Victoria* returned to Sanlúcar on September 1, 1522, three years after setting off.

The surviving crew of the *Victoria* were the first men to sail around the world, and Magellan became a posthumous hero for this great navigational achievement. However, around 232 men had died of starvation or disease on the voyage, and successive Spanish voyages across the Pacific were a failure. In 1529, Spain sold all the rights to the Spice Islands to Portugal for a generous sum of money.

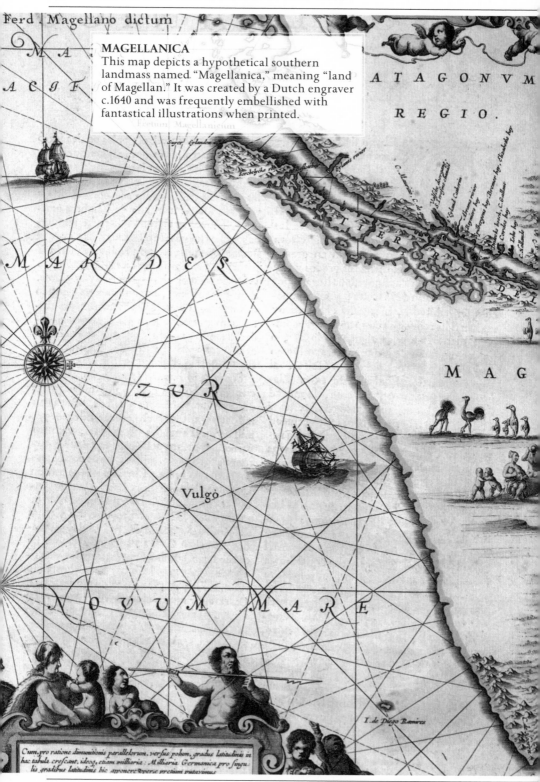

MAGELLANICA
This map depicts a hypothetical southern landmass named "Magellanica," meaning "land of Magellan." It was created by a Dutch engraver c.1640 and was frequently embellished with fantastical illustrations when printed.

B. Gallego

Ferfte Engelfe

Fretum Magellanicum

DES NORT

Nobilissimo,
Amplissimoque Viro,
D. GVALTHERO de RAET,
IVD. Curiæ Hollandiæ, Zee-
landiæ, West-frisiæque
Senatori eminentissimo.
D.D.D. Ioannes Ianssonius.

C. de Pennas

C. de St Ines

ANICA.

Verschoors Ree

Mauritius Landt

Valeyns Bay

Staert van Lemair

Staten
Eylandt

Schapenham by

Goet Rede

Nassausche Voerd

Terhalten eylandt

Lheremitens
eylandt

Sweeaks eylandt

F. de Gonçalo

AUSTRAE.

Barnevelts Eylanden

TABULA
MAGELLANICA.

The Conquest of Mexico

TWENTY-FIVE YEARS after Columbus's first voyage to the New
World in 1492 (see pp.66–73), the Spanish were well established in
the West Indies, and in 1517, Governor Diego Velásquez de Cuéllar of
Cuba sent three ships under the command of Francisco Hernández de
Córdova to explore the mainland to the west. The voyagers landed at
a cape they called Catoche (from the native Maya word for "homeland"),
on the Yucatán Peninsula, but they were ambushed immediately and
had to fight their way back to their ships. They were considerably more
cautious when they landed at Champotón, on the west side of the
peninsula, but again they were attacked, and the expedition returned
to Cuba in defeat. Of the whole sorry affair, a young soldier called
Bernal Díaz del Castillo lamented, "Oh! what a troublesome thing it is
to go and discover new lands..." Nevertheless, when Velásquez sent
Juan de Grijalva on a second expedition with three ships and 240 men
the following year, Díaz went with them as a junior officer. Again, they
encountered hostile natives, but this time they brought back gold
worth 4,000 dollars, and 600 axes. They assumed that the axes were
also made of gold, but in fact they were made of copper, Díaz recording,
"there was a good laugh at us, and they made fun of our trading." Still
convinced that the new lands were rich in gold, Velásquez ordered a
third expedition, this time commanded by Hernando Cortés, a minor
nobleman and veteran of several expeditions, with 10 ships at his
disposal. This flamboyant leader, according to Díaz, who chronicled
the expedition, "wore a plume of feathers with a medal, and a gold
chain, and a velvet cloak trimmed with knots of gold, in fact he looked
like a gallant and courageous captain."

The new expedition was beset by difficulties from the start. Shortly
before it set sail, Velásquez revoked Cortés's commission, afraid that
he would establish his own settlement on the mainland to rival
Velásquez's on Cuba, but Cortés left regardless. Soon after they set
sail, however, the flagship ran aground and had to be unloaded and
refloated. The leaders were eager to take horses, but only 16 could be
found. Cortés took "a vicious dark chestnut horse," which died early
on the voyage, while Juan Sedeño "passed for the richest soldier in the
fleet" when he arrived in his own ship with a chestnut mare and a
negro slave. Captain Pedro de Alvarado was sent ahead in "a good ship

"We came to serve God and to get rich, as all men wish to do"

BERNAL DÍAZ DEL CASTILLO

named the *San Sebastian*" with 70 soldiers, and the rest followed. On the way, Cortés's ship again had trouble when she lost her rudder and had to be fitted with a spare. When Cortés caught up with the *San Sebastian* off the Yucatán Peninsula, he found that her pilot had disobeyed orders and gone ashore, so Cortés had him put in irons.

Disembarking on the island of Cozumel, Cortés found a priest who had spent eight years as a slave to the local Maya people after a shipwreck. Jerónimo de Aguilar proved to be "a useful and faithful interpreter," though he knew nothing of the local geography, wrote Díaz: "having been a slave, he knew only about hewing wood and drawing water and digging in the fields." Setting sail once more, the expedition continued westward along the coast, and on March 12 arrived at Tabasco, where they found "twelve thousand warriors" lined up on shore. Undeterred, Cortés landed his men—100 sailors and 508 soldiers, including 32 crossbowmen and 13 musketeers—some brass cannons, and four light guns known as falconets. Fighting in the river and marshland, the natives were soon overwhelmed—so much

CORTÉS MEETS DOÑA MARINA
On landing in Tabasco, Cortés was given the chief's daughter, Doña Marina. She converted to Christianity, learned Spanish, and became an excellent interpreter.

so that they believed Cortés to be the feathered serpent god Quetzalcoatl, whose return from the west had been predicted. After capitulating, the natives presented Cortés with gold and 20 women, including the chief's daughter, Doña Marina, who converted to Christianity and became an excellent negotiator and interpreter. For the first time, the Spaniards heard the name "Mexico," and learned that the natives called themselves "Aztecs."

Cortés sailed on to San Juan de Ulúa, where he was treated with respect by the governor, a representative of the Aztec emperor Moctezuma II, who lived in the city of Tenochtitlán, some 50 miles (80 km) inland. Each side was eager to impress the other. The natives painted realistic pictures of people, ships, and horses, and the Spaniards gave displays of horsemanship and loaded their guns with "a great charge of powder so that they should make a great noise when fired off." The emperor's messengers were astounded, not least by the horsemen, whom they saw as beasts with two heads and six legs.

As several expeditions went inland, however, there were stirrings of unrest among those who were left behind; life was uncomfortable in the mosquito-infested dunes, and 35 soldiers had died of their wounds already. Particularly unhappy, Díaz recorded, were "some of the soldiers who possessed Indians in the island of Cuba." Determined to press on, Cortés reassured them:

> ... it was not good advice to recommend going back without reason; that hitherto we could not complain of our fortune, and should give thanks to God who was helping us in everything, and as for those who had died, that always happened in war and under hardships.

Nevertheless, a faction attempted to seize one of the ships and sail it back to Cuba. When Cortés heard of the plot he had the sails and rudder removed from the ship, and sentenced conspirators Pedro Escudero and Juan Cermeño to be hanged, pilot Gonzalo de Umbria to have his feet cut off, and the sailors who had supported them to

THE ROUTE TO TENOCHTITLÁN
It took Cortés and his men three months to march from the east coast to the Aztec capital of Tenochtitlán. On the way they made an alliance with numerous native tribes that were unhappy with the rule of Moctezuma II.

MAYAN CODEX
This bark paper painting from the Mayan civilization encountered by Cortés on his journey to the heart of the Aztec Empire shows the god of death beating the celestial snake with his axe to produce rain.

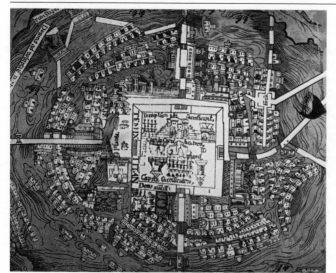

CORTÉS'S MAP OF TENOCHTITLÁN
Attributed to Cortés, this drawing shows the fortified Aztec capital in the middle of Lake Texcoco. The city was connected to the land by a number of causeways.

receive 200 lashes each. Cortés then took the advice of his officers "not to leave a single ship in the port, but to destroy them all at once, so as to leave no source of trouble behind"—a consultation that was probably a sham, serving only to spread responsibility for the action among his officers. Everything of value was taken from the ships, which were then destroyed, and Cortés and his men, joined by the ships' sailors, set off inland toward Tenochtitlán, the capital of the Aztecs.

Tenochtitlán was an island city in the mountains, and the capital of Moctezuma II. Its construction was a remarkable achievement for a people who did not have iron, horses, the wheel, or even a written language. It was the largest city in the world at the time, and, being completely surrounded by water, it was believed by the natives to be impregnable. Díaz was impressed:

> Gazing on such wonderful sights, we did not know what to say, or whether what appeared before us was real, for on one side, on the land, there were great cities, and in the lake ever so many more, and the lake itself was crowded with canoes, and in the Causeway there were many bridges at intervals, and in front of us stood the great City of Mexico, and we—we did not even number four hundred soldiers!

Cortés noted the large, fine houses, many two stories tall, which, Díaz wrote, "in addition to having fine and large dwelling rooms, have very exquisite flower gardens." His soldiers thought the great marketplace larger and better regulated than that of Rome, and the city's numerous waterways reminded the sailors of Venice. One member of the party described it as having, "many wide and handsome streets; of these two or three are the principal streets, and the others are formed half of hard earth like a brick pavement, and the other half of water, so that they can go along on land or by water by the boats which are made of hollowed wood..." However, as Cortés climbed the 114 steps of the city's great temple—declining help, to show that he and his companions never tired—he saw that they led to a platform on which human sacrifices were being made. Díaz noted, "they were burning the hearts of the three Indians whom they had sacrificed that day. All the walls of the oratory were so splashed and encrusted with blood that they were black, the floor was the same and the whole place stank."

Cortés was then welcomed into the city by Moctezuma, who by all accounts treated him as a god. According to Bernardino de Sahagún, Cortez was greeted with the words:

> My lord... You have come to your city: Mexico, here you have come to sit on your place, on your throne... This is what has been told by our rulers, those of whom governed this city, ruled this city. That you would come to ask for your throne, your place, that you would come here.

Moctezuma then pledged his allegiance to the King of Spain, giving Cortés the right to treat any subsequent rebellion as treason.

Thus ended the first stage of the Spanish conquest of Mexico. Cortés moved into the Palace of Axayácatl, where he effectively held Moctezuma hostage. Within weeks, however, Governor Velásquez of Cuba sent an expedition to bring Cortés back to Spain to try him for mutiny, so Cortés had to leave the city to fight these Spanish troops, whom he defeated. While he was away, however, the men he left behind massacred some natives at a religious gathering, and Cortés returned to find that the Aztecs were in open rebellion, having chosen a new leader, Cuitláhuac, to replace the hapless Moctezuma. In an attempt to quell the rebels, Cortés ordered Moctezuma to speak to his people, but on doing so Moctezuma was stoned to death and the Spanish were driven out of the city. It was July 1520, just seven months after Cortés had entered Tenochtitlán.

DOUBLE-HEADED AZTEC SERPENT
This Aztec mosaic statue is thought to symbolize rebirth and renewal. The serpent is associated with several Aztec gods.

Cortés returned to the city the following spring. He was supported by many of the local tribes, who for years had paid tribute to the emperor—both in goods and in human sacrifice—and mistakenly believed Cortés to be their liberator. Díaz records that Cortés no longer had his ships, but he did have sailors and carpenters, and since the only way to penetrate the city in force was by water, he ordered Martin López, "a good sailor in all the wars," to design 13 small gunboats known as brigantines. Each boat would have a sail and be rowed by 12 men, and would have enough space to carry a dozen musketeers or crossbowmen, a gunner, and a captain, and have a single light gun or falconet mounted in the bows. Cortés sent for all the rigging, anchors, and ironwork that had been saved from his ships, and López "worked like a strong man" hewing lumber, assisted by many of the natives. Four sailors were sent into the forest to extract resin from pine trees to caulk up the seams between the planks. The pieces were then carried to Texcoco where the vessels were assembled.

According to Aztec drawings, these were larger than ship's boats, and were fitted with forecastles and poops. They were too big to carry, so 8,000 natives dug a canal between Texcoco and the lake. Cortés had difficulty manning the boats because he did not have enough sailors for the task. The captains of the launches included Zamora, a ship's mate, and Colmenero, "a seaman and a good soldier." Cortés maintained that the boats were "the key of the whole war." The Aztecs, meanwhile, relied on dug-out canoes, adding "bulwarks of wood" to the sides to protect themselves from Spanish weaponry.

Battle orders were given. According to Díaz, each Spanish captain was carefully instructed in "what he was to do, and to what part of the causeway he was to go, and with which one of the captains who were on land he was to cooperate," and on May 31 they set off. Gonzalo de Sandoval led the land troops to Itzapalapan to the south of the lake, while Cortés joined the boats to cross by water, using both sails and oars. As they crossed the lake, they took a hill known as Tepepolco with 150 men. The Aztecs then set out from the city with a great fleet of canoes. The men on the hill quickly re-embarked, and Cortés ordered them to hold their positions and wait for the enemy. The Aztecs approached, stopping "two crossbow shots" away. As soon as a strong wind sprang up behind them, Cortés and his men attacked: "… although they fled as fast as they were able, we dashed into the midst of them and broke up numberless canoes and killed and drowned many of our enemies. It was the most wonderful sight in the world to behold!"

Cortés took advantage of his victory by landing 30 men with three large cannons on the causeway. Their fire was devastating, but it ended when a gunner accidentally ignited the powder supply. Sandoval's land reinforcements arrived, but were attacked from both the land and the lake. Cortés ordered that causeway be breached so that boats could pass to the other side and attack the Aztec's canoes, but the Aztecs retreated into waters too shallow for the Spanish vessels. Sandoval and his men attacked along the western causeway, but the Aztecs destroyed parts of it to impede them. Two of Cortés's launches were sent to bridge the gaps. After six days of fighting, Cortés heard of a third causeway to the north, where "the people of Mexico came and went as they pleased." He set out to capture it with a large land force and 250 men in the launches. They fought their way into the city but could not hold it.

Fighting continued around the city, but by June 15, Cortés was confident enough to divide his launches, using six to protect his camp and giving three each to his lieutenants, Sandoval and Alvarado. On June 30, the defenders launched a devastating counterattack, trying hard to capture one of the boats as Díaz and six others were pushing it out of shallow water. Sandoval came to the rescue, calling out, "Oh! Brothers put your strength into it and prevent them carrying off the launch." The men made a final push and the boat was saved.

The Spanish suffered heavy losses in the battle, and had to watch while their companions were sacrificed at the top of the temple tower. However, after a grueling siege that lasted for 85 days, Tenochtitlán was finally captured on August 13, and the Aztec empire was destroyed. Mexico City was established on its ruins, and Cortés was appointed governor of New Spain, a crucial stage in the establishment of the Spanish Empire in the Pacific.

Exploring Canada

FRENCH SEAMEN WERE ALREADY FAMILIAR with the shores of the "new world" when François I came to the French throne in 1515, for Bretons had been fishing on the Grand Banks off Newfoundland for years. A 1524 expedition claimed Newfoundland for the king, and in its wake the skilled Breton seafarer Jacques Cartier set out to discover more of the western lands and to find a northwest passage to China. In 1534, he reached and reconnoitered the Gulf of St. Lawrence, in the land he came to call Canada, returning with two sons of a native chief and a vow to go back and trade. He set off again in 1535, in the name of François I, to further explore these lands of "fertility and richness" and the "great river" that he had glimpsed.

Cartier started out from St.-Malo, France, in May, at the head of a flotilla of three ships: the *Grande Hermine*, the *Petite Hermine*, and the *Emerillon*. The crossing was "bad and stormy," and the ships were separated from each other, but all eventually reached Newfoundland about two months later. Cartier sailed along the north coast of the Gulf of St. Lawrence looking for a possible passage, before venturing up the St. Lawrence river. The sons of the Iroquoian chief Donnacona, Taignoagny and Domagaya, who had traveled to France with Cartier, piloted the boats.

Cartier records that the ships anchored at Stadacona (present-day Quebec) where the "lord of Canada," Donnacona, came out to meet them with 12 canoes "moving his body and his limbs in a marvelous manner, as is their custom on showing joy and contentment," when he saw his sons. The two larger boats anchored upriver at "a forking of the waters… where there is a small river and a harbour with a bar," which they named Ste-Croix. The *Emerillon* stayed on the main river, ready for exploration.

Soon after their cordial welcome by the Iroquoian chief, cultural differences began to cause friction. Donnacona complained that the French had too many weapons and was told that it was the French custom, while the visitors found the natives' habit of presenting them with children embarrassing. Cartier realized this was a bribe to stop him from exploring upriver and declined the gift, but Domagaya assured him the children were a sign of alliance.

The Iroquoians, however, were determined to prevent the French from traveling upriver and tried to scare them off. "They dressed up three men as devils, arraying them in black and white dog-skins, with horns as long as one's arm and their faces coloured black as coal," Cartier wrote. Floating downriver in a canoe, the devil-men were said to be messengers from the god Cudouagny, warning the visitors not to continue or they would perish in ice and snow. The Frenchmen laughed it off, but the natives refused to offer them a guide unless they left a hostage behind. Undeterred, Cartier and his men equipped two longboats and the *Emerillon* for the voyage upriver, leaving the *Grande* and *Petite Hermine* behind.

Cartier and his men set off on the tide. Cartier's respectful attitude toward the natives contributed to continuous good relations along the way. After a journey of 135 miles (217 km), they reached Hochelaga (present-day Montreal), where he recalls a rapturous welcome from "more than a thousand persons, both men, women and children, who gave us as good a welcome as ever father gave to his son, making great signs of joy; for the men danced in one ring, the women in another and the children also apart by themselves."

Cartier donned his armor and went ashore. "The village is circular and is completely enclosed by a wooden palisade in three tiers like a pyramid…" he wrote. The chief, Agouhanna, came out to meet them, carried on a deerskin by 10 men because he was paralyzed. Gesticulating toward his limbs, he asked the French to touch them, hoping to be cured. Cartier rubbed the chief's legs and "many sick persons, some blind, others with one eye, others lame and impotent, and others again so extremely old that their eyelids hung down to their cheeks" came out to be cured. Cartier tried to oblige. He also read from St. John's Gospel and made the sign of the Cross.

THE *GRANDE HERMINE*
Cartier sailed in the *Grande Hermine*, a 120-ton carrack, with several gentlemen from the royal household.

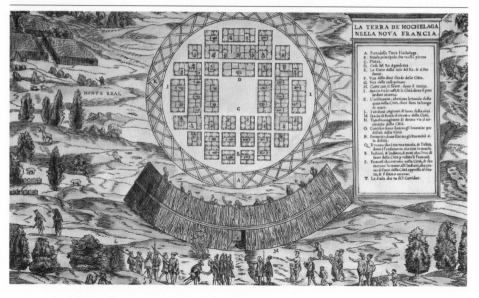

THE INDIAN VILLAGE OF HOCHELAGA
The symmetrical layout of the village impressed
Cartier, who also took note of the numerous houses
and the communal central space.

To find out what lay ahead of them, the French climbed a nearby
mountain, which they named Mont-Réal. The view stretched over
100 miles (150 km), described by Cartier:

> Towards the north there is a range of mountains, running east and west,
> and another range to the south. Between these ranges lies the finest land
> it is possible to see, being arable, level and flat. And in the midst of this
> flat region one saw the river extending beyond the spot where we had left
> our long boats. At that point there is the most violent rapid...

The rapids were clearly an obstacle to onward travel and dashed their
hope of this being the northwest passage. The natives told them about
silver and other riches upriver, but also warned them about a warlike
tribe. The disappointed party returned to Ste-Croix, and Cartier
discovered that the sailors had built a fort there, "enclosed on all sides
with large wooden logs... with artillery pointing every way, and in a
good state to defend us." Despite this obvious sign of mistrust, Chief
Donnacona arrived the next day to greet Cartier, "feigning to be
pleased at his return." It was too late in the season to sail home, so the
French dug in for the winter. Relations with the natives deteriorated
and the men became jumpy. They saw five scalps, proof of the warlike

nature of Donnacona's tribe. Cartier ordered that the fort be "strengthened on every side with large, wide, deep ditches, and a gate and drawbridge." Fifty men were to guard it at night.

In November, the river froze. The ice was "more than two fathoms in thickness," and the snow on shore "higher than the bulwarks of our ships." In December, 50 natives died of a strange illness. Inside the fort, the French also began to fall ill. It was scurvy and, soon, "of the 110 men forming our company, there were not 10 in good health." Eight men died. In the end, it was a native remedy that saved the French. Cartier noticed that Domagaya had recovered and found out that it was by drinking the bark of the white spruce tree boiled in water. A whole tree was stripped of its bark to cure the Frenchmen.

Chief Donnacona had set off on a long winter hunting trip but the French were dubious about its real purpose. When the chief returned in April, Cartier's servant Charles Guyot was sent into the village and found "wigwams so full of Indians, who he had not been in the habit of seeing, that one could not turn around inside them." Suspecting a plot, the French took the chief captive. That night the natives howled "like wolves" and called Donnacona's name, but Cartier persuaded him to travel back with them to France to meet the king, vowing he could return home in a year. They set sail, and arrived in St.-Malo 13 months later. Donnacona never did return to Stadacona and is believed to have died in France in 1539.

Cartier made a third voyage to Canada in 1541, as chief navigator under the command of Jean-François de La Rocque de Roberval. Their aim was to find gold in the legendary kingdom of Saguenay, beyond a river that Cartier had seen but not explored. The French set up a colony upriver from Stadacona, but the local tribes were now more hostile and about 35 settlers were killed. It was 1605 before the French made a permanent settlement in the area, but it was Cartier who had alerted them to the possibilities of the new territory, more cheaply in terms of ships and lives than many other explorers.

"I am rather inclined to believe that this is the land God gave to Cain"

JACQUES CARTIER

The South Atlantic Ocean

The South Atlantic Ocean has just a few, small islands that served as stepping stones for exploration, and two southern exits known to sailors since the 16th century—the Cape of Good Hope and Cape Horn. By the early 20th century, these had been superseded by the Suez and Panama canals. The trade winds are circular, as in the North Atlantic, but counterclockwise. In the middle lie the doldrums, a belt of light winds or calms that shift north and south with the seasons.

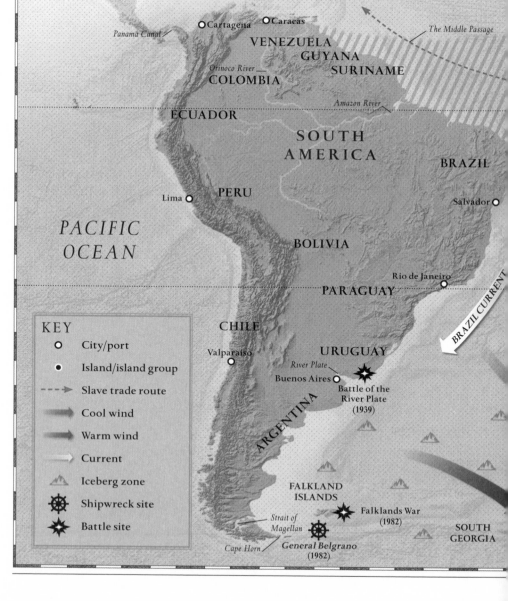

Panama Canal

Cartagena   Caracas

VENEZUELA

GUYANA

Orinoco River   SURINAME

COLOMBIA

The Middle Passage

ECUADOR

Amazon River

SOUTH
AMERICA

BRAZIL

Lima   PERU

Salvador

PACIFIC
OCEAN

BOLIVIA

Rio de Janeiro

PARAGUAY

BRAZIL CURRENT

CHILE

URUGUAY

Valparaíso

River Plate

Buenos Aires

Battle of the
River Plate
(1939)

ARGENTINA

FALKLAND
ISLANDS

Falklands War
(1982)

SOUTH
GEORGIA

Strait of
Magellan

Cape Horn   General Belgrano
(1982)

KEY

- ○ City/port
- ● Island/island group
- - - → Slave trade route
- ➡ Cool wind
- ➡ Warm wind
- → Current
- 🔺 Iceberg zone
- ☸ Shipwreck site
- ✦ Battle site

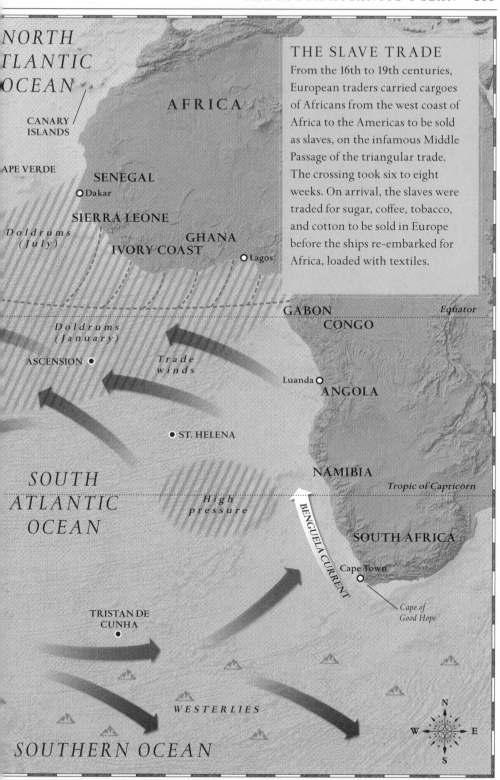

NORTH
ATLANTIC
OCEAN

CANARY
ISLANDS

CAPE VERDE

AFRICA

SENEGAL
○ Dakar

SIERRA LEONE

*Doldrums
(July)*

IVORY COAST

GHANA

○ Lagos

THE SLAVE TRADE

From the 16th to 19th centuries,
European traders carried cargoes
of Africans from the west coast of
Africa to the Americas to be sold
as slaves, on the infamous Middle
Passage of the triangular trade.
The crossing took six to eight
weeks. On arrival, the slaves were
traded for sugar, coffee, tobacco,
and cotton to be sold in Europe
before the ships re-embarked for
Africa, loaded with textiles.

GABON   *Equator*

CONGO

*Doldrums
(January)*

ASCENSION ●

*Trade
winds*

Luanda ○

ANGOLA

● ST. HELENA

NAMIBIA

Tropic of Capricorn

SOUTH
ATLANTIC
OCEAN

*High
pressure*

BENGUELA CURRENT

SOUTH AFRICA

Cape Town
○

*Cape of
Good Hope*

TRISTAN DE
CUNHA
●

WESTERLIES

N
W   E
S

SOUTHERN OCEAN

Drake's Plunder

Privateer, sea captain, slave trader, and explorer Sir Francis Drake was born in 1540, in Devon in the southwest of England. His father, a staunch Protestant, was chaplain to the naval ships in the Chatham dockyard in Kent, and the young Francis learned much of his seamanship among the nearby islands and banks. He joined his cousin John Hawkins on an expedition to raid merchant shipping, also becoming involved in the African slave trade. In 1568, their small fleet was surprised by the Spanish at San Juan de Ulúa, Mexico, and Drake only just escaped with his life. He was now an implacable enemy of Spain. The combination of his deep-seated hatred of Catholicism, his greed for gold, his determination, and his seamanship made him a very dangerous foe. In the following years, he made several expeditions plundering and pillaging in the Spanish Caribbean and Panama, and in 1573, he returned to England an experienced buccaneer with a bounty of gold.

The idea for a Pacific voyage may have originated with Drake, but it was backed by Sir Francis Walsingham, Queen Elizabeth I of England's foreign policy adviser. The plan was to go through the Strait of Magellan (see p.85), the only known way to reach the Pacific by sea. Spain had established power in the Pacific by traversing the South American continent to build ships on its west coast, and felt so secure in its domination of those waters that most of its ships were barely armed.

Drake's mission was purportedly to seek out commodities in areas that were not subject to "the obedience of princes"—but he knew that Spain had claimed the whole territory, and he was really looking for Spanish gold and silver. He recalled conversations in which it was agreed that, "… her Majesty had received diverse injuries of the Kings of Spain, for the which she deserved to have some revenge." Unofficially she was in full support of the voyage. Since the two countries were not at war, however, there was no question of Drake having a "letter of marque," which would have protected him from charges of piracy.

In view of its warlike intentions, Drake's fleet traveled well armed. His flagship, the 100-ton *Pelican*, carried seven broadside guns per side below decks, with two more firing forward. There were also six light guns above decks. The 80-ton *Elizabeth* was captained by John Winter, the

SIR FRANCIS DRAKE
Short and plump, with his fashionably trimmed red beard, Drake cut a distinctive figure. He enjoyed tacit royal support from Queen Elizabeth I for his privateering against the Spanish in the Pacific Ocean.

30-ton *Marigold* by John Thomas, the 50-ton *Swan* by John Sarcold, and the tiny 15-ton *Benedict* by Thomas Moore. The ships carried a number of gentlemen with court connections, some of them partners in the voyage, but who had no fixed role on board. These included Thomas Doughty and his brother John. The crews of the ships totalled about 150. For security reasons, they were told that they were going to trade with Alexandria in Egypt, where they would have faced raids by Barbary corsairs and possible obstruction by Spain. The true scale of the expedition was only revealed later.

Soon after setting off from Plymouth in December 1577, Drake's fleet captured six small Spanish and Portuguese ships, one of which, renamed the *Christopher*, was exchanged for the *Benedict*. Sailing south, Drake and his men raided Maio in the Cape Verde Islands, taking a Portuguese ship called the *Santa Maria*. Her captain, Nuno da Silva, was kidnapped, "because they knew him to be a pilot for the coast of Brasilia, and he might bring them to such places in those countries as had fresh water." The prize was renamed *Mary* and Thomas Doughty was put in charge of her. However, his leadership proved ineffective and Drake, growing suspicious of his behavior, had him brought on board the *Pelican* and lashed to the mast.

In June 1578, they arrived at San Julian on the coast of Patagonia, the same bay where Magellan had faced his mutiny more than half a century before (see p.88). Drake was now convinced that Doughty was "… a conjuror, a seditious fellow and a very bad and lewd fellow," and that his brother was "a witch, a poisoner…" He put them on trial, despite not being able to prove his right to do so when challenged. Doughty was found guilty. He met his death with dignity, as the ship's chaplain, the Reverend Francis Fletcher, recounted in his journals:

After dinner, all things being brought in a readiness… without any dallying, or delaying the time, he came forth and kneeled down, preparing at once his neck for the axe, and his spirit for heaven; which having done without long ceremony… he desired all the rest pray for him, and willed the executioner to do his office, not to fear nor spare.

As the severed head was held up, Drake announced, "Lo, this is the end of traitors." This was a turning point for Drake and his apprehensive men. Ahead of them was a voyage traveled by only one expedition before them, into little-known, perilous waters. If ever a crew needed an inspirational speech, it was now.

Drake chose this moment to use a phrase that became a motto for British naval power: "I must have the gentleman to haul and draw with the mariner, and the mariner with the gentleman." Class differences and personal rivalries were to be forgotten: "Let us show ourselves to be all of a company," he went on, appealing to his men's patriotism and pride:

> … if this voyage should not have good success, we should not only be a scorning or a reproachful scoffing stock unto our enemies, but also a great blot to our whole country for ever, and what triumph it would be to Spain and Portugal.

To signify a new start and assert his total authority, he dismissed the ships' officers and reappointed them in his own name. He renamed his flagship the *Golden Hind*, reflecting the coat of arms of the expedition's patron, Christopher Hatton.

DRAKE'S DRUM
Marked with Drake's coat of arms, this drum was carried on his voyage. It became the subject of songs and poems.

Navigating the Strait of Magellan was easier than expected, but the climate was cruel and several men died from cold and hunger. The *Marigold* was lost and when Captain Winter was separated from the others in a storm, he used the opportunity to take the *Elizabeth* home.

On September 6, the *Golden Hind* sailed out of the Strait, now on her own, and was caught by a strong wind that blew her west-southwest. By accident, Drake and his crew explored the land south of the Strait but it is not known if they reached Cape Horn. When the wind changed, Drake headed north, capturing several unarmed Spanish ships on the way. Off Valparaiso he seized a vessel carrying 200,000 pesos in gold

—making the voyage profitable— and a set of charts for the coast. By early 1579, the crew had dwindled to 70 men, many of them sick, but the *Golden Hind* still caused panic in Lima, capital of the Spanish Viceroyalty of Peru, when she raided the port of Callao.

GOLD AND SILVER CAPTURED BY DRAKE IN A SINGLE RAID IN 1573:

20 tons

Drake heard of another Spanish treasure ship at sea and offered a reward to the first man to sight it. This turned out to be his cousin John Drake, at midday on March 1. Drake did not want to attack in daylight, so he hung some empty wine jars astern to slow the *Golden Hind* down. Around 8 pm, the captain of the Spanish galleon, *Nuestra Señora de la Concepcion*, hailed the approaching ship. Drake cut away the wine jars to pass under the galleon's stern, calling out, "We are a ship of Chile."

The *Nuestra Señora* came alongside but a cry went up of "English! Strike sail!" Captain San Juan de Anton defiantly invited them to attack. A whistle was blown on board the *Golden Hind*, followed by a trumpet and a hail of shot and arrows. A chain shot knocked down the Spanish ship's mizzenmast, and the arrows drove the Spanish crew below, leaving Anton alone on deck. Forty men from Drake's pinnace boarded from the opposite side and the ship surrendered. Anton was taken captive on the *Golden Hind*. The English found an impressive haul of riches: there were 360,000 pesos of silver on board, or, according to one account, 80 lb (36 kg) of gold, 13 chests of pieces of eight, and 26 tons of silver and jewels.

The captured Spanish ship was nicknamed the *Cacafuego*, or "Shitfire." One of the ship's boys joked that she ought to be called "*Cacaplata*" or "Shitsilver," which amused the sailors "both then and long after." Every seaman and ship's boy, if he survived the voyage, would be comfortable for the rest of his life, and Drake could set himself up as a country gentleman.

With all this plundered wealth on board, it was now time to find the way home. Drake considered several possibilities. If they went back the same way they had come, the Spanish would be looking out for them. Other options were Magellan's route across the Pacific

THE DEFEAT OF THE SPANISH ARMADA
The Spanish commander sailed "in the confident
hope of a miracle," but fortune seemed to favor the
English fleet, whose ships were also more agile than
the larger, heavily armed Spanish vessels.

(see p.85), or an attempt to discover either the fabled northeast passage around Russia, or the equally legendary northwest passage around the top of North America.

In the end, Drake headed northwest, landing on the coast of California. Here he abandoned his pilot da Silva, fed with misinformation to trick the Spanish, then crossed the Pacific along the route used by Spanish treasure galleons to and from the Philippines. He passed through the Molucca Passage in Indonesia, stocking up with provisions and spices. When the *Golden Hind* ran aground on a reef, tensions on board surfaced again. Chaplain Fletcher claimed the stranding was punishment for executing Doughty, for which he was forced to live in cramped quarters below deck with the crew. Drake felt vindicated when the ship refloated. He stocked up on supplies in Java, then set off for the long voyage around the Cape of Good Hope, arriving back in England in September 1580, after three years at sea, with only 57 of the original 164 men on board.

Elizabeth I was delighted with Drake's success, and knighted him in 1581, but the voyage contributed to mounting tension between England and Spain, exacerbated by English support for the Protestants in the Dutch Revolt against Spanish rule (1572–85). From 1585 to 1604, England and Spain waged war with one another. Drake led raids against Spanish ports in the West Indies, while Sir John Hawkins built up a modern navy. In 1587, Drake led a preemptive strike against Spanish naval forces assembling at Cádiz—known to the English as "singeing the King of Spain's beard"—which destroyed 37 ships.

Felipe II sent his great Armada against England in 1588. Drake was second-in-command of the English fleet set against it, and harassed the Spanish ships as they proceeded up the English Channel. After a number of skirmishes, the Armada was dispersed off Gravelines and retreated north, around Scotland and Ireland, where it was devastated by storms. The English were happy to attribute this to divine intervention. The war dragged on for another 15 years, but England had won a decisive victory.

Drake died of dysentery on an expedition to the West Indies in 1596. His reputation remains ambiguous. On the one hand, he was a brutal pirate. On the other, he was an important founder of British sea power and empire.

The Age
of Empire

1600–1815

By the mid-17th century, the earlier dominance of Spain and Portugal over the world's oceans had been superseded through the skill and enterprise of Dutch and British seafarers, who established colonies and trading posts around the globe from the Americas to Africa, India, the East Indies (Indonesia), and even Japan. From the 1660s, under Louis XIV, France also expanded its navy to enter the competition for worldwide trade and empire. Naval warfare reached a new level of intensity as the British fought first the Dutch and then the French for global supremacy at sea. The victory of Admiral Nelson at Trafalgar in 1805 confirmed a British dominance of the oceans that would last for a century.

Life for seafarers remained hard, but advances in navigation and nautical charts, ship design, and medical knowledge increased the speed of travel and reduced death rates on long voyages. The rising power of regular navies was accompanied by a decline in lawlessness at sea. Pirates and buccaneers, highly active in the 1600s, became considerably less of a threat during the following century. In war, privateers were replaced as commerce raiders by fast-moving naval frigates.

Along with the expansion of overseas empires, a large-scale trade in slaves developed. Millions of Africans were transported across the Atlantic to provide forced labor in colonies in the Americas. During the 18th century, British sailors became the leading participants in this shameful commerce. Whaling was another growth area, with the slaughter of marine mammals increasing as ships penetrated ever deeper into the Arctic and the South Oceans. Official missions of scientific discovery led men such as French Admiral Louis Antoine de Bougainville and British Captain James Cook to the islands of the Pacific, Australia, and New Zealand. Such oceanic adventurers were heroes of this age of expanding European empire.

Colonies
in America

THE ENGLISH SHOWED an early interest in North America. In 1496, King Henry VII commissioned the Italian explorer John Cabot for a voyage that led to the discovery of Newfoundland. It was not until 1584, however, that the first attempt was made to found an English colony in the Americas. In defiance of Spanish claims to control most of the American continent, the English courtier and seaman Sir Walter Raleigh sent an expedition to colonize the central part of the eastern seaboard of North America, which he later called Virginia in honor of the "virgin queen," Elizabeth I. Raleigh's colony, on Roanoke Island, off present-day North Carolina, was short-lived. Raleigh promoted a second colony in the same region in 1587, with around 100 settlers. Shortly after this, the expedition's leader, John White, sailed back to England for supplies, and by the time he returned in 1590, the colonists had mysteriously vanished.

At the time, England and Spain were at war, and English navigators mostly concentrated on pillaging Spanish colonial territories. After making peace with Spain in 1604, the English began to look again at the possibility of colonization, rather than plunder. Cambridge-educated lawyer Bartolomew Gosnold was the driving force behind the first permanent English settlement in North America. He had been inspired to pursue this mission after reading the epic volume *Principal Navigations, Voyages, Traffiques and Discoveries of the English* by the influential geographer Richard Hakluyt, a fervent advocate of Elizabethan overseas expansion. Gosnold began by leading privateering voyages westward, and, in 1602, he settled on an island off the southeast coast of Massachusetts, naming it Martha's Vineyard after his mother-in-law. However, he soon discovered that living there was unsustainable. Undeterred, Gosnold approached the nobility for financial support for his colonization project. In 1606, the Virginia Company was formed, with a royal charter from King James I, with the goal of settling on the eastern coast of North America between latitudes 34° and 41° N.

JOHN SMITH
A former mercenary, soldier, trader, and privateer, Smith's tenacity and leadership were vital in successfully establishing the colony at Jamestown.

The directors of the Virginia Company recruited Christopher Newport to command the maritime aspects of the expedition. A vastly experienced captain who had given up privateering in favor of trade, Newport had an unrivaled knowledge of the West Indies. Gosnold was also appointed as a captain, along with John Ratcliffe. They were joined by Edward Maria Wingfield, one of the project's main investors, and by John Smith, an Englishman who had already enjoyed a remarkable career, having served as a soldier in campaigns against the Turks in southeast Europe and Asia, and escaped from slavery after being taken prisoner. The site chosen for the colony was the vast estuary of Chesapeake Bay, with its good harbors and fertile land. As Smith puts it: "It might well be thought, a country so fair (as Virginia is) and a people so tractable, would long ere this have been quietly possessed, to the satisfaction of the adventurers, and the eternising of the memory of those that effected it."

There were a lot of "gentlemen" on the expedition—29 of the 105 colonists—who, rather than "haul and draw with the mariner" as Francis Drake recommended (see p.112), instead sported an attitude of lazy entitlement. The fleet also carried four carpenters, a blacksmith, two bricklayers, and a mason, along with numerous laborers, a surgeon, and at least four boys. The lead ship was the 120-ton *Susan Constant*, a typical merchant vessel; she carried 71 colonists on her crowded decks. The *Godspeed*, commanded by Gosnold, was of 40 tons and carried 52 passengers, while the 20-ton *Discovery* carried 21 men and was captained by Ratcliffe.

The passengers embarked on London's River Thames on December 19, 1606, but unfavorable winds forced the ships to anchor off the east coast of Kent for six weeks of the winter. This was a severe trial for those on board, including the expedition's chaplain, who is recorded as badly affected by disease and seasickness, "making wild vomits into the black night." The fleet finally sailed from English waters in January 1607. Taking the trade route south, it reached the Canary Islands in mid-February. Already, factions were appearing among the colonists. As they headed west across the Atlantic, Smith became the target of a conspiracy, probably led by Wingfield, who accused him of intending to "usurp the government, murder the council, and make himself king." They placed Smith under restraint for the rest of the voyage.

Once in the Caribbean Sea, the fleet landed on Dominica, where they traded with "cannibals," and then took six days of rest at Nevis. There, a gallows was apparently erected to hang Smith, but the execution was not carried out. The water on Nevis was sulphurous and so the expedition traveled on, finding "an excellent bay able to harbour a hundred ships" at Tortola in the Virgin Islands, according to the colonist George Percy. They resumed the voyage north, longing for a sight of Virginia. After battling a storm, the men started to believe they had bypassed their destination—even Newport did not know this area. Then, on April 26, they "fell in with Cape Henry, the very mouth of the Chesapeake Bay" and sailed in. The ships anchored offshore, but at first only a few men were allowed to land.

The Virginia Company directors had put the names of the men appointed to form the council of the new colony in a sealed box, to be opened on arrival. That night, with due solemnity, it was revealed that the councilors were to be Wingfield, captains Newport, Gosnold, and Ratcliffe, two of the "gentlemen," and the maligned John Smith. He was released from captivity, but Wingfield did his best to exclude him from the council. The expedition found a flat, rectangular peninsula on the James River, which Smith thought "a very fit place for the erecting of a great city." They landed their stores there and began to build a fort. They named the place Jamestown, after the English king.

Newport set off to explore upriver with 40 men in a pinnace (a ship's boat), in search of gold and a passage through to the Pacific. Although he found neither, he made contact with the Native American chief Powhatan, a powerful ruler of over 30 tribes. Jamestown had been founded within the territory of Powhatan's expanding empire. When Newport returned to the colony, he feared imminent attack by the local tribes, and hastened the construction of the fort, described by Percy as "triangle-wise; having three bulwarks, [one] at every corner, like a half-moon, and four or five pieces of artillery mounted in them; we had made ourselves sufficiently strong for these savages."

MAP OF VIRGINIA
This detailed 17th-century map shows Virginia and
Chesapeake Bay, as well as the figure of the Native
American leader Powhatan in the top left-hand corner.

Bartholomew Gosnold died four months after arrival in Virginia.
Captain Newport sailed off for England with the *Susan Constant* and
Godspeed to fetch supplies and reinforcements, leaving the *Discovery*
behind to service the colony. Smith and Wingfield, who was president
of the council, competed for control. The settlers were experiencing
difficulties, and decided to opt for Smith's practical skills. Wingfield
was deposed on a trumped up charge of "atheism" and "combining
with the Spaniards to the destruction of the colony." Smith took
control of the colony and instituted a policy of firm discipline: "There
are many in Virginia… [who were] devoted to pure idleness," he
wrote in his account of the early days of the colony. He ordered the
settlers to farm with the words: "He that will not work shall not eat."

In December 1607, Smith headed upriver and was captured by
natives. According to his own account, they were ready to beat out his
brains when "Pocahontas the King's dearest daughter, when no entreaty
could prevail, got his head in her arms, and laid her own to save him
from death; whereat the emperor was contented he should live." Smith's

tale of Powhatan's daughter saving his life is disputed, and it is possible that he misunderstood a tribal ritual. Nevertheless, relations between the parties improved. The Englishmen observed the customs of the Native Americans, out of self-preservation as well as curiosity. They watched as the native men hunted and fished and the women farmed: "They live upon sodden wheat beans and peas for the most part, also they kill deer, take fish in their weirs, and kill foul in abundance," one colonist wrote soon after landing. But the displaced English struggled for subsistence, as Percy recalled: "Our men were destroyed with cruel diseases as swellings, fluxes, burning fevers, and by wars, and some

VILLAGE OF SECOTON
Depicted by Theodor de Bry, this settlement
was part of the Powhatan territory. Though he
illustrated them, de Bry never visited the Americas.

"There were never Englishmen left in a foreign country in such misery as we were in this new discovered Virginia…"

GEORGE PERCY,
JAMESTOWN COLONIST

departed suddenly, but for the most part they died of mere famine." With help from the native population, and Smith's leadership, 38 out of the original 104 colonists survived the first winter.

In September 1608, Newport finally returned with supplies and new colonists, including the first two women settlers. In London, the Virginia Company sent out another supply fleet, led by the 240-ton *Sea Venture*, in June 1609, but she ran into a storm and was wrecked in Bermuda, then uninhabited. The stranded party showed great enterprise in building two pinnaces from the wreckage, aboard which they eventually completed the voyage to Jamestown in May 1610. By then, the colony had suffered disaster. Their leader Smith had gone back to England after being injured in a gunpowder accident. In the winter of 1609, severe drought had worsened the situation. The "starving time" had reduced the population from 500 to about 60 by the time the *Sea Venture*'s pinnaces arrived. They decided to abandon the settlement but, just as the ships were setting off for home, another three vessels arrived from England with fresh supplies, and colonists to continue the venture.

Elsewhere on the east coast, Dutch and Swedish settlers moved in, while the French claimed Canada (see pp.104–09). However, in the years that followed, the Virginia colony suffered many more tribulations. In 1613, Governor John Rolfe, who later married Pocahontas, introduced a new strain of tobacco which proved popular in Europe. The first 20 African slaves were imported in 1619, and turned out to be the best labor force on the tobacco plantations. Virginia became rich and cultured—the first permanent, successful, English-speaking settlement in America, the origin of what became the United States.

Early Modern Ships

The early modern period saw the transformation of the carrack into the galleon—which in turn became the ship of the line—and the domination of the oceans by European powers.

DUTCH WARSHIP (1670)
In the 17th century, Holland had one of the most powerful navies in the world. This Dutch warship had 80 guns on two gun decks.

Main topmast

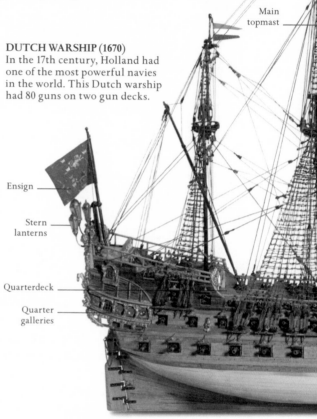

KOREAN TURTLE SHIP (1592)
In the 16th century, the Korean fleet included triple-sailed ironclad "turtle ships," each of which had 15 cannons.

Ensign

Stern lanterns

Quarterdeck

Quarter galleries

ENGLISH WARSHIP (1669)
The majestic, 90-gun *St. Michael* was an English ship of the line. She was rebuilt and renamed the *Marlborough* in 1706.

FRENCH SHIP OF THE LINE (1636)
The *Couronne* was a 68-gun warship. She was the finest ship in France's first regular navy, which was developed by Cardinal Richelieu.

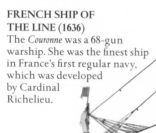

BRITISH TWO-DECKER (c.1717)
This ship carried 470 crew and 60 guns. Like many British vessels of the era, its priority was to provide heavy firepower.

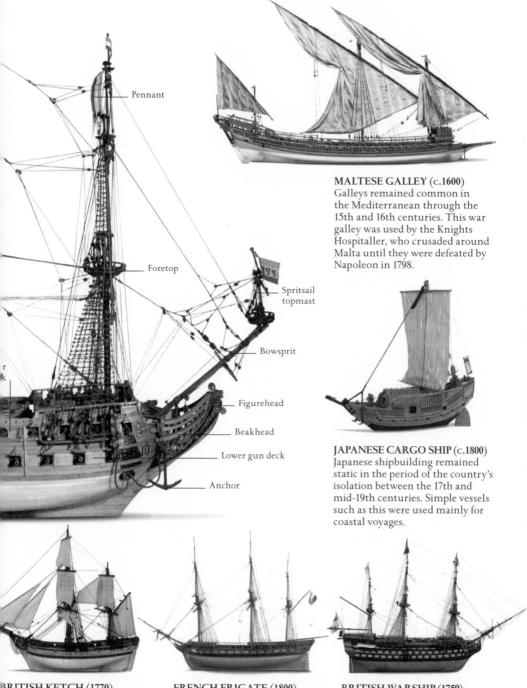

Pennant

Foretop

Spritsail topmast

Bowsprit

Figurehead

Beakhead

Lower gun deck

Anchor

MALTESE GALLEY (c.**1600**)
Galleys remained common in the Mediterranean through the 15th and 16th centuries. This war galley was used by the Knights Hospitaller, who crusaded around Malta until they were defeated by Napoleon in 1798.

JAPANESE CARGO SHIP (c.**1800**)
Japanese shipbuilding remained static in the period of the country's isolation between the 17th and mid-19th centuries. Simple vessels such as this were used mainly for coastal voyages.

BRITISH KETCH (1770)
This British merchant vessel was 73 ft (22 m) long and 27 ft (8 m) wide. Her wide beam left plenty of room for cargo.

FRENCH FRIGATE (1800)
Frigates were lighter and faster than ships of the line, and were used mainly for scouting. This French frigate had 46 guns.

BRITISH WARSHIP (1759)
The British HMS *Victory* was a 104-gun ship of the line. She served as Lord Nelson's flagship at Trafalgar (see pp.174–81).

The Wreck of the *Batavia*

THE NETHERLANDS became Europe's leading maritime nation, and a rapidly expanding colonial power, during a long struggle for independence from Spanish rule that began in 1568. Despite 80 years of almost constant warfare—interrupted by a 12-year truce from 1609—the Dutch flourished, enjoying a "golden age." They became the world's leading civil engineers, building dykes, dams, and canals, and there was a flowering of the arts that included the advent of the first real marine paintings, with realistic seas and ships.

The Dutch developed efficient and economical merchant ships called *fluyts*, which became the carriers of much of Europe's trade. Entering the Indian Ocean, they took hold of the highly valuable trade in spices between the East Indies (now Indonesia) and Europe, establishing the town of Batavia (now Jakarta) on Java to control the production and marketing of mace, nutmeg, pepper, and cloves. The Dutch also settled in Brazil and established a staging post at Cape Town in South Africa. The trade to the east was controlled by the Dutch East India Company. Embarking on a voyage to the East Indies was a demanding and hazardous enterprise. In 1621, a ship called the *Gouden Leeuw* made the 15,000 mile (24,000 km) journey in 127 days, but most could expect the passage to take much longer. None had a worse experience than the ill-fated ship the *Batavia*.

In October 1628, the *Batavia*, an East Indiaman (see pp.134–35), was among several large ships anchored at Texel at the mouth of the Zuyder Zee—where vessels from Dutch ports such as Amsterdam sailed into the North Sea—loading for a voyage to the East Indies. She was 160 ft (48 m) long and would carry 341 passengers and crew. Like

most Dutch ships of the age, she had a high, narrow stern, flat aft, and was probably decorated by a painting or carving representing her name. Her bottom was flat and her hull was not deep since she had to negotiate the

18TH-CENTURY BOTANICAL ILLUSTRATION
As spices like this nutmeg plant became more valuable, the Dutch pioneered an ocean route from the Cape of Good Hope to Indonesia.

BATAVIA, JAVA
On the northwest coast of Java, Batavia was
established as a trade and administration post by
the Dutch East India Company in the 17th century.

sandbanks of her native waters. Her cross section was square to get in
the maximum cargo and she had a long, elegant, and spindly
framework in the bows, supporting a modest figurehead. Although a
merchant vessel, she was armed with 32 guns for defense against
pirates and privateers. Batavia was a *retourschip* (return ship), which
meant she was to return to the Netherlands loaded with goods instead
of staying out to serve the Dutch East India Company in the east.

Just before sailing from Texel, the *Batavia* and the six ships that
accompanied her were placed under the command of an "upper-
merchant" for the Dutch East India Company, Francisco Pelsaert—the
company's chief representative in the fleet. He shared the great cabin at
Batavia's stern with her skipper, Ariaen Jacobsz, who was responsible for
navigation and the crew, under the upper-merchant's direction. Joining
them on the voyage was an apothecary and under-merchant for the
Dutch East India Company, Jeronimus Cornelisz. An unconventional
character, Cornelisz played a key role in the events that followed.

The Indian Ocean

The Indian Ocean is the third-largest ocean on Earth, lying between
Africa and Australia. High pressure over India from November to
April pushes surface water in the Arabian Sea toward Africa, generating
currents, while during the monsoons between June and September,
low pressure over India gives rise to southwesterly winds. Below the
Equator, regular trade winds blow from the southeast. South of the
Tropic of Capricorn, westerlies travel as far as Australia.

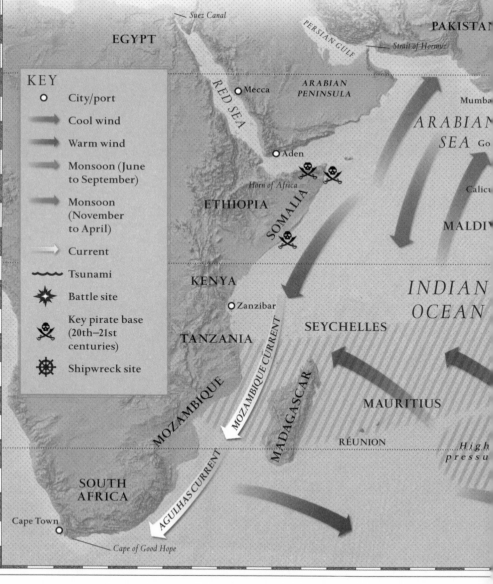

KEY

O	City/port
→	Cool wind
→	Warm wind
→	Monsoon (June to September)
→	Monsoon (November to April)
→	Current
〜	Tsunami
✸	Battle site
☠	Key pirate base (20th–21st centuries)
☸	Shipwreck site

Suez Canal

EGYPT

PERSIAN GULF

PAKISTAN

Strait of Hormuz

RED SEA

Mecca

ARABIAN PENINSULA

Mumbai

ARABIAN SEA   Goa

Aden

Horn of Africa

Calicut

ETHIOPIA

SOMALIA

MALDIVES

KENYA

INDIAN OCEAN

Zanzibar

SEYCHELLES

TANZANIA

MOZAMBIQUE CURRENT

MADAGASCAR

MAURITIUS

RÉUNION

MOZAMBIQUE

High pressure

SOUTH AFRICA

AGULHAS CURRENT

Cape Town

Cape of Good Hope

OCEAN TRADE

Historically, trade and travel across the Indian Ocean depended on the monsoons. Arab traders first set up a slave trade with East Africa in the 10th century, and in an epic series of voyages, Chinese admiral Zheng He (see pp.46–51) sailed from China around the Indian subcontinent and on to Arabia and Africa between 1405 and 1433. After Portuguese explorer Vasco da Gama's voyage of 1497–98 (see pp.74–83), the ocean and its shores came increasingly under European domination.

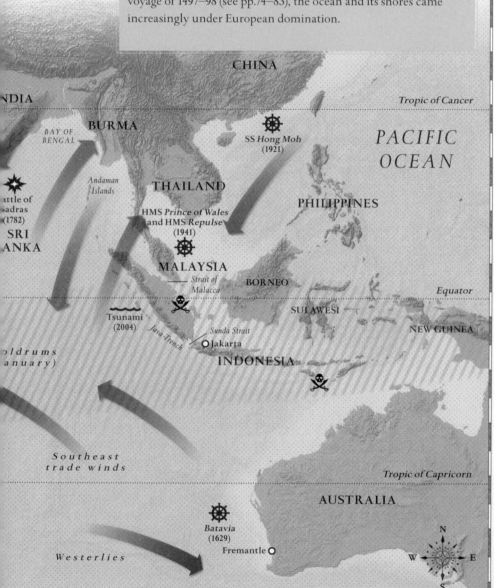

CHINA

NDIA

Tropic of Cancer

BAY OF BENGAL

BURMA

PACIFIC OCEAN

SS *Hong Moh* (1921)

Andaman Islands

THAILAND

PHILIPPINES

attle of adras (1782)

HMS *Prince of Wales* and HMS *Repulse* (1941)

SRI ANKA

MALAYSIA

Strait of Malacca

BORNEO

Equator

Tsunami (2004)

Java Trench

SULAWESI

NEW GUINEA

Sunda Strait

oldrums anuary)

Jakarta

INDONESIA

Southeast trade winds

Tropic of Capricorn

AUSTRALIA

Batavia (1629)

Fremantle

Westerlies

N
W E
S

The *Batavia* had 180 seamen, living on the upper deck forward of the mainmast. They were controlled by a strict code of discipline, which included the death penalty and keel-hauling (being tied to a rope and dragged under the hull of the ship)—one source claimed that a *retourschip* sailor was "like an untamed beast." A seaman slept in a hammock or on a straw mattress and his food was adequate, if unappetizing. Nicholas de Graef, a ship's surgeon, wrote that "… each mess gets every morning a full dish of hot groats, cooked with prunes and covered with butter or some other fat; at midday they get a dish of white peas and a dish of stockfish…" There were also 11 cadets on board and a company of soldiers. The soldiers did not get on with the seamen—who, it was said, would "show more concern for the death of a chicken than a whole regiment of soldiers"—and lived down below on the airless, lightless orlop, or cow-deck. There were also at least 22 women on board, including several soldiers' wives. Outstanding among this company was Lucretia ("Creesje") Jans, accompanied by her maid, Zwaanti Hendricx. Twenty-eight years old, beautiful, and wellborn, Jans was traveling to join her husband in the east.

During this period, the directors of the Dutch East India Company did not yet prescribe routes across the oceans—or "cart-tracks"—within which their ships should sail, but their orders were very detailed, and no stops were allowed before the Cape of Good Hope. Despite this, Pelsaert authorized a visit to Sierra Leone on the coast of West Africa, after which the ships spent some time becalmed in the windless doldrums of the equatorial zone. Scurvy set in, killing 10 seamen. Meanwhile, serious tensions were developing on board. The skipper, Jacobsz, had become infatuated with Creesje Jans. The apothecary Cornelisz, who had formed a friendship with Jacobsz, tackled him about it, but: "The skipper answered that because she was fair, he desired to tempt her to his will, and to make her willing with gold and other means." Jans resisted Jacobsz's advances, and the skipper then became infatuated with her maid, Hendricx, who was more willing.

The fleet anchored at the Cape of Good Hope, known as the "tavern of the ocean," on April 14, 1629. Jacobcz was rowed round the harbor with Hendricx, visiting ships and getting drunk. Pelsaert records that he "… behaved himself very pugnaciously, and at nighttime when he went to the ship *Buren*, he behaved even worse."

The upper-merchant called Jacobcz into their cabin and "chided him over his arrogance and the deeds committed by him." Later, on deck, the disgruntled skipper looked out at the other East Indiamen and confided to

TOTAL DEATHS FROM THE *BATAVIA*:

220

Cornelisz: "By God, if those ships were not lying there, I would treat that miserly dog so that he could not come out of his cabin for fourteen days. And I would quickly make myself master of the ship." The two began plotting to overthrow Pelsaert's command.

By the time the fleet sailed again on April 22, relations between Pelsaert and Jacobsz were at a very low ebb. During a storm, the *Batavia* was separated from the rest of the fleet. This may have been a deliberate ploy by Jacobsz to give him a chance to organize a mutiny, abetted by Cornelisz. Discipline was collapsing, and Jacobsz was becoming increasingly out of control. While Pelsaert was incapacitated by illness, at some stage Jans was molested by the ship's high boatswain, on the orders of Jacobsz.

The passage east from the Cape was along the "roaring forties," the zone of strong westerly winds that the Dutch explorer Hendrik Brouwer had discovered in 1611. Ships were ordered to steer east between 36° and 42° for nearly 3,000 miles (4,800 km) before turning north. However, navigation was approximate. The *Batavia* carried at least four astrolabes (see p.162) to measure the latitude accurately, but as with all sailors of the age, the ship's officers had no accurate way of finding longitude. Even dead reckoning was not done well by the Dutch (see pp.162–63). They did not use a log-line like most seafaring nations—instead, to calculate a ship's speed, according to one source they "took notice of any remarkable patch of froth, when it is abreast the foremost end of the measured distance, and count half-seconds till the mark of froth is abreast the after end." In the absence of certainty about a ship's position, keeping a careful lookout was essential to avoid disaster. Jacobsz was on deck on the night of June 3–4, when some spray was sighted, but he was told it was just the reflection of the moon. At around 5am, Pelsaert was jolted by a "rough terrible movement" that roused him from his bunk. The ship had strayed off course and grounded on the uninhabited Houtman Albrohos Islands, about

40 miles (65 km) off the west coast of Australia. With the ship breaking up in heavy surf, the crew and passengers were ferried to a nearby island with a few supplies. The island had no fresh water and scant food. Jacobsz and Pelsaert took a boat and set off with 46 others in search of a source of water. They landed at several points on the Australian coast but, finding it a "dry cursed earth," decided to head on to Java, some 1,800 miles (2,900 km) to the north. They reached Batavia on Java on July 7, more than a month after the wreck. Pelsaert reported in to the Dutch East India Company, and Jacobsz was put under arrest for negligence in causing the wreck. The high boatswain, meanwhile, was swiftly hanged for the assault on Creesje Jans.

Pelsaert was given the yacht *Sardam* to return to the island and rescue the stranded passengers and crew, but the voyage back was slowed by head winds. Back on the island, Cornelisz had revealed himself to be a truly dangerous and unstable man. Fearing the consequences if Pelsaert reported his complicity in mutiny to the governor in Batavia, the under-merchant devised a deranged plan to establish a new kingdom on the island, with himself as its ruler. Having commandeered weapons and food, he ferried a party of soldiers to another island nearby, supposedly to find water—in fact

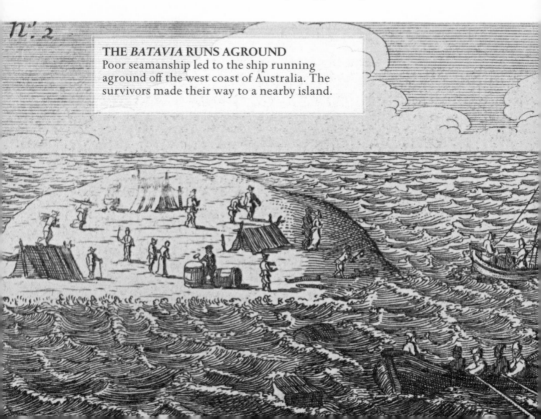

THE *BATAVIA* RUNS AGROUND
Poor seamanship led to the ship running aground off the west coast of Australia. The survivors made their way to a nearby island.

he intended to leave them there to die. He then gathered a makeshift militia comprising various men from the crew, and used them to terrorize the remaining survivors. Under Cornelisz's sadistic direction, his supporters set about massacring more than 100 of the passengers and crew, including 17 women and seven children, by stabbing, strangulation, drowning, or starvation.

Unknown to Cornelisz, however, the abandoned soldiers on the other island had succeeded in finding water, and survived. Having learned of the slaughter taking place on the main island from a handful of escaped survivors, they improvised some basic weapons and returned to the site of the wreck to attack Cornelisz and his murderous followers. When Pelsaert eventually returned with his ship on September 17, he interrupted a pitched battle between the soldiers and the mutineers, and heard the extraordinary tale of Cornelisz's descent into madness, which he described as "a horror in the ears of all good Christians." Pelsaert's men joined forces with the soldiers and they overpowered the mutineers. After a summary trial, Cornelisz and six other perpetrators were hanged. Pelsaert then carried just 68 men, five women, and one child back to Java—the sole survivors of the original 341 on board the *Batavia*.

East Indiamen

The largest merchant ships of the 17th and 18th centuries, the massive East Indiamen were built to carry goods to trade with Asia. Primarily cargo ships, they also carried soldiers and civilian passengers out to colonies, and were armed against attack on the long, hazardous journeys. They originated in the Netherlands and Britain, but other European countries soon began building them to compete in the Asian trade.

Ship characteristics

The East Indiamen's main purpose was to carry cargo, facilitated by their large, square holds. However, with ornate decor and guns for protection, they could easily be mistaken for warships.

DOUBLE GUN DECKS
East Indiamen were armed with cannons to deal with the threat of pirates, and were made to look even more heavily fortified than they were—not all the gun ports had working guns.

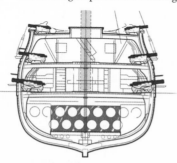

THE TUMBLEHOME PRINCIPLE
To counteract the instability created by the heavy cannons, East Indiamen were designed according to the "tumblehome principle": the hull becomes narrower above the waterline, making the ship more stable.

Mizzenmast

Officers' quarters, under the poop deck

Cargo of tea chests, cases of china, and bales of cloth

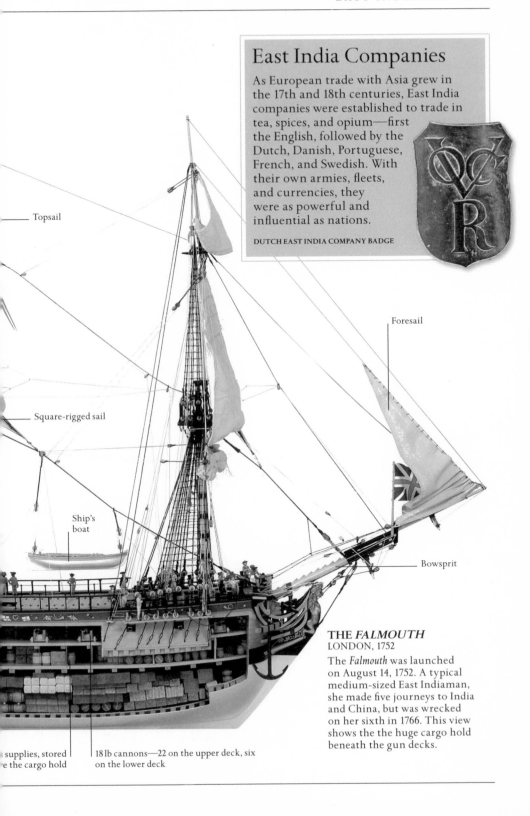

East India Companies

As European trade with Asia grew in the 17th and 18th centuries, East India companies were established to trade in tea, spices, and opium—first the English, followed by the Dutch, Danish, Portuguese, French, and Swedish. With their own armies, fleets, and currencies, they were as powerful and influential as nations.

DUTCH EAST INDIA COMPANY BADGE

Topsail

Square-rigged sail

Ship's boat

Foresail

Bowsprit

THE *FALMOUTH*
LONDON, 1752

The *Falmouth* was launched on August 14, 1752. A typical medium-sized East Indiaman, she made five journeys to India and China, but was wrecked on her sixth in 1766. This view shows the the huge cargo hold beneath the gun decks.

supplies, stored
e the cargo hold

18 lb cannons—22 on the upper deck, six on the lower deck

A Life of Piracy

B Y THE 17TH CENTURY, piracy had existed for millennia—it had been rife in the Mediterranean at the time of the Roman Empire. Also known as "buccaneers," "freebooters," or "corsairs," pirates were freelance maritime predators, but their activities were not always clearly defined as criminal. Piracy often shaded into privateering— state-sponsored attacks on the ships and ports of a hostile power. Some raiders, such as English sea captain Sir Francis Drake attacking the Spanish in the 1570s, were supported covertly by their governments in peacetime. In wartime, privateers had their raids on the enemy explicitly legalized through government-issued "letters of marque." Pirates flourished when state navies were weak. The Muslim Barbary corsairs of North Africa, who preyed on Christian shipping for many centuries, were strong enough in the 17th century to raid in the Atlantic, the British Isles—in 1631, they captured about 120 people in an attack on the village of Baltimore on the coast of Ireland—and as far north as Iceland. Later in the century, English and French buccaneers roamed the Caribbean at will, plundering the rich but sparsely populated territories of Spain's empire in the Americas.

One pirate, the well-educated French gentleman Raveneau de Lussan, published a book about his exploits. Born in 1663, Lussan had an overwhelming urge to wander, believing that: "For a person never to get out of his native country, and to be ignorant of how the rest of the earth stands, appeared to me a matter that would be appropriate to a woman only." He first joined the army, but siege warfare against the Dutch offered little excitement, so he went to sea. He loved the ocean: "That element, which to the generality of men, seems very frightful, appeared to me the most amiable and delightful of any in the world." After various vicissitudes, Lussan ended up on the West Indian colony of Saint-Domingue on Hispaniola, heavily in debt. Considering the quickest methods of making money that were open to a man of his skills, he decided to take to piracy. As he wrote with characteristic ingenuousness, he intended to pay his creditors off, he said, by "borrowing as much money as I could from the Spaniards, for these sort of borrowings have this advantage attending them, that there is no obligation of repayment."

SOUTH SEA PIRACY

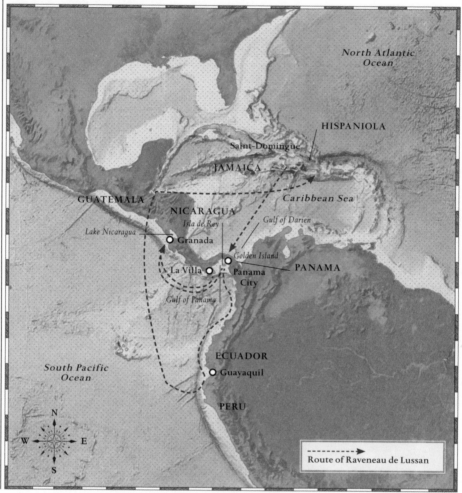

Lussan joined Dutch pirate Laurens de Graff in search of ships to seize in the Caribbean, but the pickings were slim in the winter of 1684–85. They anchored off the coast of the Spanish-controlled Isthmus of Darien (now Panama), a narrow strip of land that linked the Atlantic and Pacific oceans and was a hot spot for buccaneers. There they found a message from other pirate captains who had begun to operate in the Pacific and needed crews. Lussan decided to leave Graff and join a small party of men who were to be led on foot across the isthmus by Darien Indians to join a pirate fleet at Isla del Rey on the Pacific side of the isthmus. The party traveled for six days across the wild,

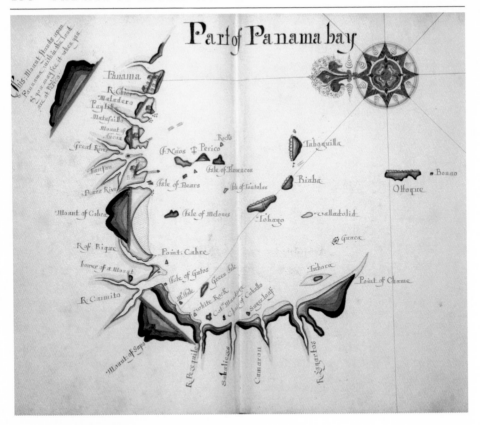

PANAMA BAY
This map showing Panama Bay was
an English version of a map captured
from a Spanish ship in 1680.

largely uninhabited terrain, via "mountains, precipices and impenetrable forests," according to Lussan, until they reached a river where they were put into canoes. For the next stage they had to travel under the cover of night, because they had heard that 1,000 Spanish troops were out searching for them. Finally, they reached the mouth of the river, where the well-organized pirates had left two small ships to take them out to join their fleet.

There were eight pirate ships at Isla del Rey waiting for crews. One, a 36-gun ship from Hamburg, was commanded by Captain David, an English buccaneer of Flemish origin. David had captured the ship off the coast of Africa; he and his crew had behaved so badly, even by pirate standards, that they had had to flee into the Pacific. Another was a small 16-gun frigate which, it was claimed, had originally been outfitted under Captain Sammes by the Duke of York, the king of

England's brother, for a peaceful expedition to the Pacific. The fearsome Captain David had confronted Sammes' ship at sea, and the Englishman had agreed to join him in piracy. The two men had gone on to capture six other ships. With the addition of Lussan's party, their fleet now had 1,100 men. Command was shared between English and French pirates, including captains Groignet, Townsley, and Henry.

Lussan professed to be religious, but he felt that pirate raids on the Spanish settlements on Darien were morally acceptable, because of "the unjust usurpation [the Spanish] have made... from the aborigines, over whom they have made themselves masters by such tyrannical and cruel methods as have been heard of throughout the world." Moreover, France was technically at war with Spain at the time, though it is not clear if any of the captains had a letter of marque legitimizing their activities.

On April 27 1685, Lussan went on his first operation when 500 crew manned 120 canoes for a raid on a town near Panama City. En route, they met two small Spanish ships, whose crews ran them aground and then retreated to a rocky island. The pirates proceeded up a river to the town, but their desire for plunder was frustrated as all the inhabitants had fled with their valuables. On May 8, the fleet sailed past Panama City and were reminded of perhaps the most audacious pirate raid of all. In 1671, the Welsh buccaneer Henry Morgan had attacked what he describes as "the famous and ancient city... the greatest mart for silver and gold in the whole world." Although his haul—to the modern value of about $45,000—was disappointing, Morgan had made good, and after a brief period of disgrace, he was knighted and made governor of Jamaica. Now Lussan and his fellow raiders could see the fortified new town of Panama City, "whose churches and houses seemed to us to be finely built," alongside the ruins of the old one.

The pirates then lay in wait off the coast of Panama City for a Spanish treasure fleet that was due to arrive from Peru. Capturing her, Lussan wrote, would bring "wealth enough to live at ease," and the men took an oath that they "would not wrong one another to the value of one piece of eight, in case God gave us victory over the Spaniards." A French captain, Groignet, was posted to keep watch for the treasure fleet, and at noon on June 7, he sighted the Spanish ships. The crews tossed their hats into the air, thinking they already had the better of the Spaniards.

"To succeed out here and amass a considerable fortune... all that is required is a good boat supplied with enough provisions to last for a long period"

RAVENEAU DE LUSSAN

The Spanish ships had much greater gun power, so it was vital for the buccaneers to have the "weather gage"—to have the wind behind them—since this would allow them to dictate the tactics of the battle, and in particular to board the ships, the favorite pirate tactic. They seemed to be successful in getting to windward, but night was falling and David ordered the ships to anchor until morning. The Spanish took advantage of their better knowledge of local currents, and as dawn broke, they were to windward of the raiders. The Spanish vice admiral rapidly sailed up to David's ship and fired into it. Sammes's ship was damaged early in the attack and could not go to David's assistance. Captain Henry's ship, with Lussan on board, received 120 hits. The raiders had to rely on their superior seamanship to get them out of trouble, breaking off contact and sailing to islands where they could repair the damage. David's ship had lost half her rudder and Sammes's poop deck had almost been shot off, but the captains were thankful they had lost only a few men.

Having had little success, differences began to appear among the pirate crews. Both the English and the French liked to believe that they were doing their work in the name of religion, but for the English this involved destroying the Roman Catholic symbols they found in Spanish churches. According to Lussan, "... they made no scruple when they got into a church, to cut down the arms of a crucifix with their sabers, or to shoot them down with their fusils and pistols." This came to a head the following spring, when David was away on the southern coast of Darien and Sammes had gone to the East Indies. The French found they were in a majority and boarded Captain Townsley's ship to confront him: "Then we let the captain know that we were honester men than he, and that though we had the upper hand, yet we would not take the advantage of revenging the injuries they had done us," Lussan wrote. The buccaneers reunited for a raid on Granada, a "large and spacious town" on the shores of Lake Nicaragua, "whose churches are very stately and houses well enough built." A party of 345 men captured the town. Some of them mused that they could easily take canoes eastward from Granada down the San Juan River to return to the Caribbean, but instead they went back to their ships. When it came to dividing the spoils of the raid, four men who had been permanently disabled in the fighting were each given 1,000 pieces of eight (the Spanish coin that became well known to pirates), while the rest received 600 "as it was our constant custom in those seas."

After Granada, there were further disagreements, and the ships divided into two fleets: Groignet went west, while Lussan sailed southeast toward Panama City with Captain Townsley. They captured the town of La Villa, taking 300 prisoners for ransom and acquiring a booty of 15,000 pieces of eight, but as they were leaving in canoes they were ambushed by the Spanish and the booty was retaken. The surviving pirates returned to the site of the ambush to find the burned or decapitated bodies of their colleagues. They were furious, and beheaded four prisoners in retaliation. The Spanish then began to negotiate the ransom for the remaining captives. Lussan wrote that the pirates "... cut off the heads of two prisoners and gave them to the messenger to carry to the Alcide [governor] telling him that if he sent us no other answer, we would cut the heads off the rest." The Spanish paid 10,000 pieces of eight.

On October 21, 1686, the raiders were anchored off the island of Taboga in Panama Bay when they spotted three Spanish ships very close. At first, the Spanish held the weather gage, but the pirates tacked five times to gain the advantage, and

PIECES OF EIGHT
The Spanish dollar—also known as the *peso de ocho*, or piece of eight, valued at eight *reales*—was a popular international currency, and as such was the type that often ended up in the hands of pirates preying on international shipping.

"THE SPANISH ARMADA DESTROYED BY CAPTAIN MORGAN"
Depicted in this 1681 engraving, Captain Henry Morgan's raids on Spanish vessels and settlements were made semi-legitimate by England's war with Spain at the time.

MYTH AND LEGEND
The pirates of the 17th and 18th centuries were
subject to mythologizing and fanciful portrayals.
Here, a gang of Arab pirates is pictured cutting
off the arm of a ship's captain.

the Spanish were too cautious to escape by passing between a rock and
the island of Taboguilla. The pirates threw grenades into the biggest
Spanish ship, starting a fire, and then boarded it. Eventually all three
ships were captured. Many of the raiders wounded in the fighting later
died—it was claimed that the Spanish had used poisoned bullets,
which Lussan self-righteously claimed was "so manifest a contravention
of the laws and maxims of a just war." Two more Spanish ships arrived
but were decoyed into surrender; the pirates were even more incensed
when they discovered ropes on board that were to have been used to
hang them. They began to negotiate with the governor of Panama for
a ransom. However, the negotiations did not go well, so the pirates
decapitated 20 of the captured sailors and sent their heads to him,
blaming the Spanish for making this necessary. If the governor had
used a conciliatory tone sooner, Lussan wrote, he "would have saved
the lives of those wretches, whose heads we have sent you, and whose
death you have been the occasion of." Lussan and his crew were
eventually paid a ransom of 20,000 pieces of eight.

The buccaneers then sailed to attack Puná Island off the coast of
Ecuador. They formed up in military order to attack the main fort.
Lussan was an ensign, carrying a banner, and was promised a
thousand pieces of eight if he was the first to plant his flag on the fort.

They canoed upriver to the town of Guayaquil, where they overcame 700 men in a pitched battle, but Captain Groignet was mortally wounded. Once they became masters of the town, the pirates soon discovered it was a rich prize: "[There were] several sorts of merchandise, a great many pearls and precious stones, a prodigious quantity of silver plate, and seventy thousand pieces of eight at least," Lussan marveled. They were soon captivated by the women, too, although the sentiment was not always returned, since the locals had been told that pirates were little better than monkeys and would eat them. The pirates used the island for their winter quarters, where they "lived mighty well."

After another summer of raids, the buccaneers had captured enough treasure to return home. Early in 1688, they began the long journey overland across Guatemala. After walking for 59 days, during which 84 out of 480 men were lost in the jungle or died of disease, they reached a river that took them to the Caribbean. Eventually they reached the colony of Sainte-Domingue on Hispaniola, where Lussan was welcomed by the governor, who described his adventures, with considerable exaggeration, as "the greatest and finest voyage of any in our age." Lussan returned to Paris, and published a highly successful account of his buccaneering exploits entitled *The Filibusters of the South Sea*.

A war over the disputed succession to the Spanish throne began in Europe in 1701, shortly after Lussan's return. Britain and France, who had been raiding Spain's New World empire, were at each other's throats, while the war itself allowed adventurous and avaricious young men to raid shipping legally as privateers. When the war ended in 1714, a so-called golden age of piracy began. It was different from earlier eras in that there was no longer even tacit state sponsorship. For six or seven years, men such as the notorious Edward Teach (Blackbeard) and Bartholomew Roberts (Black Bart) raided territories and captured ships carrying valuable cargoes in the Caribbean, along the eastern seaboard of North America, in the Indian Ocean, and off West Africa. These freebooters were eventually suppressed by regular navies. The North African Barbary corsairs, however, continued their predations until France occupied Algeria in 1830.

Slave Ships in the Atlantic

OLAUDAH EQUIANO was just 11 years old when he and his sister were kidnapped from their village in what is now Nigeria, tied up, and carried off on "a great many days journey." Separated from his sister, Equiano was sold to African slave owners. Under the relatively humane African domestic form of slavery, Equiano was well treated by his first masters, but in 1756, after six or seven months of captivity, he was sold again and transported to the coast. He had never seen the ocean before, but there was an even bigger shock in store for him, as he recalled in the autobiography he published 33 years later: "The first object which saluted my eyes when I arrived on the coast was the sea, and a slave-ship, which was then riding at anchor waiting for its cargo. These filled me with astonishment, which was soon converted into terror…" He was carried on board ship, where he was "immediately handled, and tossed up, to see if I were sound." His horror increased as he looked around him and saw: "A multitude of black people of every description chained together, every one of their countenances expressing dejection and sorrow." Equiano had been sold to British slave traders and was to be shipped across the Atlantic to Barbados.

Commerce in slaves was well established in Africa before European mariners entered the slave trade. Arab merchants had long been transporting slaves across the Sahara desert and through African ports. The Portuguese began to import African slaves for domestic

SLAVE SHIP
Kept in unsanitary, cramped, and overcrowded conditions, many slaves did not survive being transported. They were often shackled, and were sometimes subjected to abuse from the crew.

use in 1441. From the early 16th century, the development of European colonies in the New World led to a dramatic increase in the demand for agricultural labor to work in the plantations. The Portuguese started to supply Africans to the Spanish American colonies, as well as shipping their own slaves across the Atlantic to Brazil, and in the 1600s, the Dutch set up slave trading forts on Africa's west coast. The first British attempt to break into the Atlantic slave trade, by Sir John Hawkins and Francis Drake in 1562 (see p.110), was suppressed by the Spanish, but in 1672, the Royal African Company was founded to promote slaving voyages from West Africa. When the company's charter expired in 1698, the trade in human beings was thrown open to all British ships. In the 18th century, Britain became the leading nation in the Atlantic slave trade, which reached an industrial scale, with tens of thousands of Africans forcibly transported across the ocean every year.

The classic pattern for British slaving voyages was the "triangular trade." A ship would leave a British port carrying manufactured goods such as cloth and guns. It would sail along the West African coast, exchanging those goods for captive men, women, and children such as Equiano. When the hold was full of human cargo, the slave ship would embark on the long voyage across the Atlantic to the Caribbean, a journey known as the "Middle Passage." The slaves who survived the cramped, inhumane, and unsanitary conditions were then sold at auction and the ship returned home laden with the products of slave labor, including sugar, tobacco, and cotton.

In August 1750, six years before Equiano's abduction, 25-year-old John Newton left Liverpool in the north of England in command of the 140-ton slave-ship the *Duke of Argyll*. After going to sea at the age of 11, Newton had led a dissolute life in his early days, before converting to evangelical Christianity in 1748. He began the log of the *Duke of Argyll* by stating that the ship was going on its voyage to the Caribbean "by God's permission." In addition to the second mate, boatswain, cooper, gunner,

JOHN NEWTON
Newton was at various points in his life a seaman, a slaver, and a clergyman. His experiences eventually led him to campaign against the slave trade.

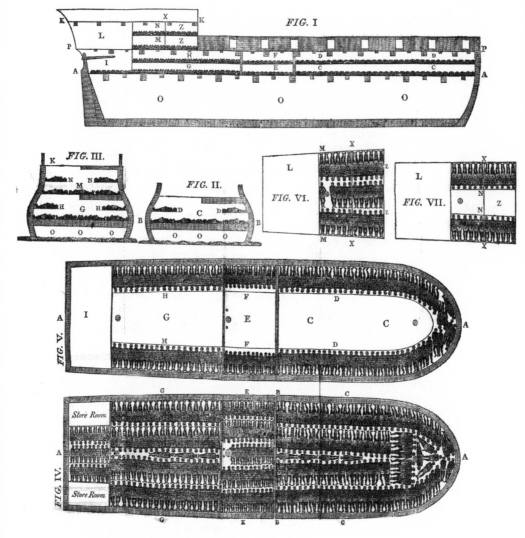

THE SLAVE SHIP *BROOKES*
This ship's plan, dated 1879, shows the
crowded conditions in which slaves were
forced to travel, in order to maximize profits.

steward, cook, tailor, and fiddler there were 11 able seamen aboard.
With the ordinary seamen and apprentices, this made up a total crew
of 30—barely enough to control the expected cargo of 200 slaves
while also sailing the ship. As the ship sailed southward, the carpenter
built partitions below decks that would separate the men, women,
and boy slaves, while the gunner installed guns that completely
dominated the main deck to deter any possible attemps at revolt.

Since this deck was where the slaves would be brought up for exercise, nettings were set up around it to prevent them from jumping overboard. The ship arrived off Sierra Leone in West Africa on October 23: "The passage from England has not been the shortest, but remarkably pleasant, and free from disaster," Newton wrote.

Europeans rarely captured slaves themselves but bought those who were already enslaved. On October 25, Newton went ashore and was shown seven slaves. After rejecting the older women, he picked two men and a woman. Newton soon found that Captain Ellis of the slave ship *Halifax* had cornered most of the business on that part of the coast. Furthermore, French ships had been blockaded during a recent war, so colonies such as Martinique and Haiti were eager for slaves and French captains were prepared to pay high prices. The *Duke of Argyll* spent the next few months moving up and down 150 miles of West African coast looking for slaves for sale, anchoring offshore and landing longboats through the surf. The boats were also used for lengthy trips up rivers to find more slaves. Getting a full cargo was a slow process. When, on February 22, 1751, the longboat returned with just two men, two women, and a boy, Newton described this as a "long month's purchase."

Newton declared that no one was to be trusted among the slave-trading agents ashore: "Whites, blacks and mulattoes are all double and designing alike." On board the *Duke of Argyll*, Newton's crew left a good deal to be desired. He gave two of them "a good caning" and one sailor was put in irons. Later he tried to desert, but some Africans recaptured him, for which Newton rewarded them with a gallon of brandy.

Newton did not record the names of any of his slaves, only the numbers they were given on purchase, and he showed no particular grief when some died of disease after being brought on board. He recorded the death on January 9 of No. 11, "a fine woman slave," who suffered "a lethargick disorder, which they seldom recover from." When woman No. 79 died, Newton speculated that it might be the diet of rice the slaves were given twice a day and planned to try them with beans and peas. A few days later, he recorded that girl No. 92 was sent on shore to die, in order to "free the ship of a nuisance." In all, a dozen slaves died before the ship left Africa. Sailors also succumbed to tropical diseases and Newton especially felt the loss of his trusted first mate on January 20.

PORTUGUESE SLAVE SHIP
Slave ship the *Diligente* crosses the Atlantic in this
1838 painting. Despite the the Anglo-Portuguese
treaty of 1810, which limited slave trading in
Portuguese colonies, the illegal transportation
of slaves continued until the 1860s.

Newton did not fear revolt by the female and boy slaves, but as soon as he brought 12 adult males on board he chained the men up. He may have used the cruel system in which men were shackled together in pairs, facing in opposite directions. Newton observed: "… they cannot move, either hand or foot, but with great caution, and with perfect consent. They must sit, walk and lie, many months…" As for the women, they were allowed some freedom of movement, but were exposed to potential sexual abuse by the crew. Newton cracked down on this practice on his ship, but wrote that: "In some ships, perhaps in the most, the license allowed, in this particular, was almost unlimited." Equiano described women and girls as "often exposed to the wanton rudeness of white Savages."

On May 22, after seven months on the West African coast, the *Duke of Argyll* finally set sail for Antigua in the West Indies. It was not uncommon for slaves to attempt a revolt soon after setting to sea, and this is what happened aboard Newton's vessel. One of the slave boys had developed a large ulcer and was freed from his chains and allowed up on deck. Once there, he managed to pass a large spike through the gratings to the slaves below, who used it to release about 20 captives from their irons. The men were almost ready for a breakout when they were discovered by the crew and the revolt was foiled. "They still look very sullen and have doubtless mischief in their heads if they could find opportunity to vent it," Newton wrote in his log.

As was usual on slave ships, the captives on the *Duke of Argyll* were allowed on deck in small groups to exercise, but on June 12, it became so cold that they had to be taken down again. Over the next few days, confined to the hold, slaves began to die of hardship and disease. Nine lives were lost in the course of the voyage. European slavers confined their human cargo to appallingly overcrowded and filthy quarters on the Middle Passage, the slaving route between Africa and South America. Equiano observed this on one voyage.

SLAVES FREED BY THE ROYAL NAVY'S
WEST AFRICA SQUADRON 1808–60:

150,000

SHACKLES
Slaves were often chained
together in transit to
prevent a revolt.

[The ship] was so crowded that each had scarcely room to turn himself. This produced copious perspirations, so that the air soon became unfit for respiration, from a variety of loathsome smells, and brought on a sickness among the slaves. This wretched situation was... aggravated by the galling of the chains, now become unsupportable, and the filth of the necessary tubs, into which the children often fell, and were almost suffocated. The shrieks of the women, and the groans of the dying, rendered... a scene of horror almost inconceivable.

The ship arrived at Antigua on July 3, 1751, with more surviving slaves than was usual on the Middle Passage. The captives' relief at reaching land was short-lived, however. Life on the West Indian plantations was harsh; hard-hearted owners had calculated that it was cheaper to import new slaves than to treat the existing ones well, and the average life expectancy was about nine years. Newton wrote that the *Duke of Argyll* was "very full and lumbered" with her cargo, presumably sugar, on her return journey. On October 7, the ship anchored off Liverpool after a round trip of more than a year.

It is estimated that around 11 million people were transported in the Atlantic slave trade. Both the slaver Newton and the slave Equiano were later prominent activists in the movement to abolish the slave trade. Newton became a clergyman and fervent opponent of slavery, linking up with William Wilberforce and his fellow Christian abolitionists. He wrote hymns, including "Amazing Grace," two lines of which were particularly apt, given his change of heart: "I once was lost but now I'm found; Was blind, but now I see." Equiano learned to read and write after being bought by a Royal Navy officer and purchasing his own freedom. From 1786, he too became active in the abolitionist movement, his 1789 autobiography helping to support the cause. Opposition grew in the United States, Portugal, and across Europe, and slavery itself was abolished in the British colonies in 1834. Despite the efforts of the Royal Navy's dedicated anti-slave-trading unit, the West Africa Squadron, to suppress it, however, a transatlantic trade in African slaves continued for much of the 19th century.

Cook in the Pacific

O N AUGUST 25, 1768, HMS *Endeavour* set out from Plymouth on England's south coast for a voyage of scientific exploration to the Pacific Ocean. In command was 39-year-old Royal Navy Lieutenant James Cook. The son of a farm laborer, Cook had learned his seamanship in a collier (a cargo ship that carried coal) among the intricate waters of England's east coast. He had joined the Royal Navy in time to serve in the Seven Years' War (1756–63) against France and other nations, and, after the war, distinguished himself by conducting a masterly survey of the Newfoundland coast. This drew him to the attention of the British Admiralty, who chose Cook as a suitable officer to lead an important scientific voyage.

Cook had 85 seamen and marines under his command on the *Endeavour*. Also on board was a party of scientists headed by naturalist Joseph Banks—only 25 years old but already a fellow of the Royal Society and a leading light in the scientific world. Banks and his companions were eager to document new species of plants and animals, and their presence on the voyage proved invaluable. However, the official purpose of the voyage was to observe the transit of Venus across the face of the sun, which would occur in June 1769. If this could be measured accurately, it would be of great value in calculating the distance of the earth from the sun. Cook's wider mission was to carry out a detailed exploration of the Pacific, in search of a vast southern continent, the Terra Australis Nondum Cognita ("southern land not yet known"), whose existence was predicted by theorists such as Scottish

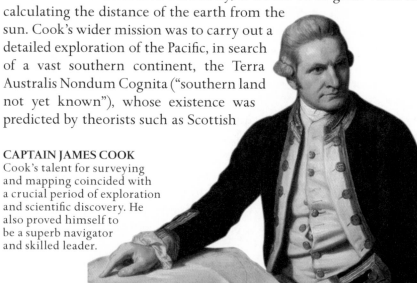

CAPTAIN JAMES COOK
Cook's talent for surveying and mapping coincided with a crucial period of exploration and scientific discovery. He also proved himself to be a superb navigator and skilled leader.

COOK'S VOYAGES

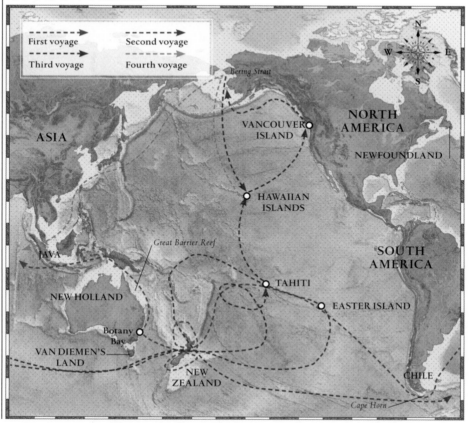

geographer Alexander Dalrymple. If this fabled continent—thought to be far larger than Australia—did exist, then it could be claimed for Britain's expanding empire.

The British and French had begun to show an interest in the Pacific Ocean—beyond plundering Spain's possessions there—in the late 17th century. Initially, this took the form of privateers combining their search for gold with exploration and scientific enquiry, as when the English pirate and naturalist William Dampier led a British Admiralty expedition to New Holland (Australia) in 1699–1701. Interest stepped up after 1763, when France ceded almost all its territories in North America to Britain at the end of the Seven Years' War. The French began to look for new outlets for expansion in the Pacific, while the British tried to forestall them. A race began to explore and occupy the remaining uncharted areas of this vast region. British Captain Samuel Wallis became the first European to land on Tahiti in 1767. The following year, Louis-Antoine de Bougainville led the first official French expedition to the Pacific. He visited Tahiti and his descriptions of the island as a tranquil paradise led to the myth of the "noble savage" untouched by civilization. Bougainville also mapped many island groups for the first time, and documented the customs and lives of their inhabitants.

Tahiti was to be the first objective for Cook's expedition and the site from which the transit of Venus would be observed. The *Endeavour* was a converted collier, sturdy and able to carry plenty of provisions but, according to Banks, "more calculated for stowage, than for sailing." Conditions for the long sea journey were cramped. Cook had to give up his cabin to the scientists and draftsmen and the junior officers were unable to stand upright in their cabins on the lower deck. On the outward voyage, Cook tested the latest preventive measures against scurvy. Caused by a deficiency of Vitamin C, the disease had always

MAORI WAR CANOE
Cook encountered hostility from Maori tribes off the coast of New Zealand, and the crew of the *Endeavour* had to fight off attacks by Maori warriors in war canoes.

been a major cause of death on longer sea voyages. Cook fed his men a diet that included "portable" condensed vegetable soup and sauerkraut. He reported that they were consequently "in general very healthy." The *Endeavour* reached Cape Horn at the southern tip of South America in January 1769. Going ashore on Tierra del Fuego to collect plant specimens, Banks lost two servants, who died of exposure in the bitter cold. Cook then shaped course for Tahiti, where the party arrived on April 13 after an eight-month voyage.

A tent was set up with the astronomical instruments, but the measurement of the transit of Venus was not a complete success— the problems of distortion that marred the observation would not be fully understood until the 20th century. The Tahitians proved a major distraction for the British visitors. Midshipman James Magra remarked that: "The women... have agreeable features, are well proportioned, sprightly, and lascivious." Banks and Cook mused on the islanders' seamanship and navigational skills, learning with surprise how widely they sailed (see pp.14–19).

In August, Cook left Tahiti to scour the seas for the lost southern continent. Two months later, the *Endeavour* made landfall in New Zealand. Cook's party was the second group of Europeans known to have reached New Zealand, the first having been Dutch sailors led by Abel Tasman in 1642. Cook observed that the warlike Maoris were very different than the Tahitians, writing in his journal, "it is impossible to see, without astonishment, the degree of madness to which they will elevate themselves even in their harangues, that are preparatory to a feigned battle." Setting out to chart the New Zealand coast, Cook sailed around both islands and carried out a remarkably accurate survey, confirming that neither island was joined to a large southern continent.

On April 1, 1770, Cook left New Zealand to look for land to the west. He knew of the existence of "New Holland"—modern-day Australia—which had been sporadically visited by Europeans since the early 17th century. The Dutch had landed on the inhospitable north and west coasts of Australia, and East Indiaman the *Batavia* had been wrecked there in 1629 (see pp.126–33). Abel Tasman had seen what he called Van Diemen's Land (later renamed Tasmania) in 1642, but failed to establish whether it was an island. William Dampier had landed in northwest Australia in 1699, but abandoned an attempt to approach eastern Australia in the following year. Cook was the first European sailor to explore this fertile east coast.

After his crew sighted Australia on April 19, Cook found a way past the treacherous Great Barrier Reef. He then turned north to head along the coast, seeing people on a beach with "very dark skin or black colour," and on April 28 found a bay in which to anchor and replenish. A few natives came to look at the strangers, but it was difficult to establish communication and a few shots were fired to warn them off. The bay was originally dubbed Stingray Harbour, but when Banks found a large quantity of interesting plants there it was renamed Botany Bay. After a week collecting specimens, Banks' collection grew so large that he had to start pressing plants inside books to save space. Cook himself observed the soil and thought it "capable of producing any kind of grain."

The expedition continued along the Australian coast—naming mountains and headlands after British aristocrats, admirals, and politicians—for another six weeks. Then disaster struck. Cook was

BANKSIA SERRATA
This genus of flowering plant, discovered by Banks and recorded in his collected engravings, *Banks' Florilegium*, is named after the scientist himself.

usually far too careful to sail in the dark along a strange coast, but the night of June 11–12, 1770 was lit by a full moon and there was no obvious place to anchor, so he proceeded slowly in light winds. Just as a crewman was casting the lead into the water to measure its depth, the ship suddenly struck coral and stuck fast. Cook tried to find a way out. The crew laid an anchor and hauled on the chain, and everything possible was thrown overboard to lighten the ship, including drinking water, guns, stores, and stone ballast. But despite dropping around 50 tons, when high tide came the ship still did not move. Meanwhile, water was leaking through the damaged hull into the hold. More anchors were laid out, attached to blocks and tackles. At the next high tide, some crewmen pulled with everything they had, while others furiously worked the pumps to get the water out of the hold. At 10:20 pm on June 12, more than 24 hours after grounding, the *Endeavour* began to float off the coral.

One of the crew measured the depth of the water in her hold and discovered it was a dangerous, but not catastrophic, 3 ft 9 ins (114 cm). The pumps were just keeping them afloat. Sails were set to move the ship slowly forward and find a suitable beach on which to ground it. Cook decided to "fother" her to stop the leak; he had heard about the process, but despite his experience, had never seen it done. Midshipman Jonathan Monkhouse stepped forward; he had once served on a merchant ship that had used the technique successfully. He found an old sail and covered it with bits of oakum and wool. Ropes were attached to each corner, so the sail could be manipulated, and then it was drawn underwater. If it could be got over the hole, the materials would be sucked in and plugged it. Then, according to Banks, "in about half an hour to our great surprise the ship was pumped dry, and upon letting the pumps stand she was found to make very little water." On June 17 she was run ashore to begin repair.

Having successfully got the *Endeavour* ashore after the accident, the travelers had to face the stark fact that they were some 10,000 miles (6,000 km) from home and more than 2,500 miles (4,000 km) from the nearest Europeans at the Dutch colony of Batavia (Jakarta) on Java. There was a real possibility they could spend the rest of their lives where they had landed, unless they could repair the *Endeavour*. The ship was stripped of everything moveable and a camp was set up on shore. Wood was found inland and the carpenter and his mates toiled to repair the timbers and planking. They could only work on the hull for a few hours each day, when the tide was low.

At last, after more than six weeks, the ship was ready to sail. They made their way to Batavia for more extensive repairs. Thanks to Cook's insistence on a good diet for his crew, there had been no deaths from scurvy, but the men picked up malaria and dysentery while in the insalubrious Dutch colony. When the *Endeavour* sailed again, 40 men were seriously ill. Twenty-four of them died before the ship reached Cape Town. The expedition arrived home in April 1771.

Cook's journey had been a great success. It had surveyed New Zealand and mapped the east coast of Australia, making the first recorded landfall there and claiming the area for Britain. Banks had collected

THE *ENDEAVOUR* ASHORE
After beaching the damaged *Endeavour* on a
riverbank in northern Australia for repairs,
Cook named the river after his ship.

NEW SPECIES DISCOVERED BY
JOSEPH BANKS:

1,300

a vast number of natural history specimens, many of them previously unknown to science. In June 1772, Cook received a second set of orders from the Admiralty: to continue the search for the elusive southern continent. Banks demanded ultimate authority over this expedition, but the Admiralty refused—the days of "gentlemen" commanding experienced seamen were over. Cook set sail with two ships, but without Banks. On the three-year voyage, he circumnavigated the Antarctic, but could not break through the ice to find the polar continent that lay beyond it. Promoted to captain, he embarked on a third voyage in 1776. His mission was to find the Northwest Passage, believed to link the Pacific and Atlantic oceans across the top of America. En route, he and his crew became the first Europeans to land on the Hawaiian Islands. After exploring and mapping the northwest coast of America, they reached the Bering Strait, where, frustratingly, a wall of ice revealed there was no navigable passage. They returned to Hawaii in early 1779. There, on February 14, Cook was killed by locals during a quarrel about the alleged theft of a boat.

Meanwhile, in 1778, Joseph Banks advised a parliamentary committee that the area around Botany Bay (now New South Wales) would be suitable as a settlement for British convicts. In 1787, the "First Fleet" set out for Australia, carrying 504 male and 192 women prisoners. The settlement in Botany Bay was soon abandoned—Cook's favorable assessment of the soil proved to be wrong and there was a lack of fresh water—and the British moved to nearby Sydney Cove, laying the foundations for a future great city.

Finding Latitude

In order to navigate with any degree of
certainty, seafarers must be able to determine
their latitude—their distance north or south
of the equator—which involves measuring
the angle of elevation of the noon sun (or
of certain stars at night) above the horizon.
The traditional intrument for making
such a measurement is the sextant.

Index mirror

Filters for
index mirror

Split-screen
horizon
mirror

Astrolabe

The first instrument designed to calculate
latitude with precision was the astrolabe.
Invented by the Ancient Greeks for use
in astronomy, it was later refined and
developed in the Arab world. It was made
of several components that could be
moved to give the user a representation
of the sky at a desired date and time. With
it, sailors could determine
their latitude if they knew
the time (and vice versa)
and had an easy way
of finding stars
that were useful
for navigation.

ASTROLABE,
LAHORE, 1642

Mirror
shade in
red glass

Handle

The inlaid silver
scale shows arc
minutes (one
sixtieth of a degree)

The arc is one
sixth of a circle,
giving the sextant
its name

The scale shows the degrees
north and south of the equator,
with zero degrees at the right

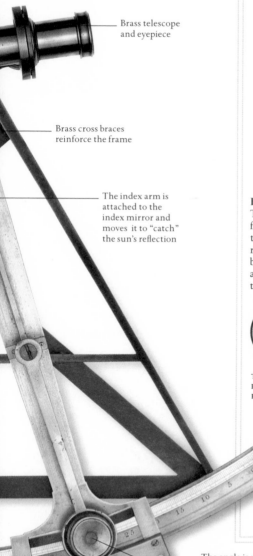

SEXTANT
LONDON, 1791

Invented in the mid-18th century, the sextant consists of a telescope mounted behind a semi-reflective window, used to measure the altitude of heavenly bodies to determine a ship's position (see box, right).

— Brass telescope and eyepiece

— Brass cross braces reinforce the frame

— The index arm is attached to the index mirror and moves it to "catch" the sun's reflection

— The angle is read through a magnifying glass on the index arm

Using a sextant

During the day, a sextant is used to measure the angle of the sun at noon above the horizon. At night, it is used to measure the angle of the North Star above the horizon in the Northern Hemisphere and the angle of the Southern Cross constellation in the Southern Hemisphere.

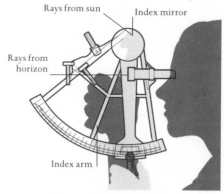

Rays from sun   Index mirror

Rays from horizon

Index arm

LINING UP WITH THE HORIZON
The observer looks through the telescope and focuses on the horizon. He or she then releases the index arm to find the star's or the sun's reflection in the index mirror. This is possible because the left half of the horizon mirror is a normal mirror and the right half of it is transparent.

THE HORIZON IS REFLECTED BY MIRRORS

THE MIRROR IS MOVED TO ALIGN THE STAR

THE STAR IS ALIGNED WITH THE HORIZON

ALIGNING THE STAR
Once the star or the sun is reflected in the index mirror, the observer moves the index arm until the reflection of the star aligns with the horizon. The angle of elevation can then be read on the scale at the bottom of the sextant.

John Paul Jones and American Independence

IN THE LATE 18TH CENTURY, Edinburgh, the capital of Scotland, was at the height of its prestige and prosperity. But in September 1779, news arrived that a squadron of American ships was about to attack the defenseless city by sailing up the Firth of Forth, the estuary near which it stands. Across the Firth, in the county of Fife, a Presbyterian minister prayed for deliverance from the imminent threat: "Now, dear Lord, don't you think it a shame for you to send this vile pirate to rob our folk... The way the wind blows, he'll be here very soon, and who knows what he might do?" Ironically, the "vile pirate" bringing the Revolutionary War to the British Isles was himself a Scot, by then using the name John Paul Jones.

Born in the village of Kirkbean, near Kirkudbright, on the southwest coast of Scotland in 1747, he had originally been named John Paul. At the age of 12, he was apprenticed on a merchant ship from Whitehaven, not far across the English border on the south shore of the Solway Firth. He worked mostly on vessels trading with the West Indies, including slave ships (see pp.146–53), and by 1768 he had risen to command of a small ship. Then he ran into trouble. In 1770, he was briefly imprisoned for flogging a sailor who subsequently died and in 1773, he killed the leader of a mutiny on board his ship in the West Indies. Fearing prosecution if he returned to Britain, he took refuge in the colony of Virginia and adopted the name "Jones" to conceal his identity. He was thus in America when the revolt of Britain's American colonies against British rule began in 1775.

Confrontation between Britain and the colonies developed chiefly because of the imposition of taxes by the distant British Parliament, in which the colonists had no representation. This led to widespread protests in America and inspired the slogan: "No taxation without representation!" There were numerous incidents between Americans and the British authorities, often taking place at sea. In June 1768, the sloop *Liberty*, belonging to wealthy Bostonian merchant John Hancock, was seized for violating many of the strict British-imposed customs

THE BOSTON TEA PARTY
In an iconic act of American resistance to British rule,
protestors dumped three East India Company ships'
cargo of tea into Boston Harbor.

laws. In Boston in December 1773, a group of colonists disguised as
Native Americans protested about the tax on tea by boarding three
East India tea ships, splitting open tea chests and hurling the contents
into the sea. The incident later became known as the Boston Tea
Party, and it triggered a sharp escalation in America's struggle against
British rule. By summer 1775, the American colonies were in open
revolt and they declared their independence on July 4, 1776.

To counter this, the British government was forced to support an
army fighting some 3,000 miles (4,800 km) from home and needed
hundreds of thousands of tons of shipping in order to do it. The
Americans wanted to disrupt this transatlantic supply route, but
initially had no navy or warships. In October 1775, the Continental
Congress, set up to act as a governing body for the rebel colonies,
ordered the creation of a Continental Navy, which would later become
the United States Navy. "Gentlemen seamen" were recruited by a poster
signed by John Hancock, by then president of the Congress. The seamen
were offered a chance to "distinguish themselves in the glorious cause
of their country, and make their fortune." Most of those who came
forward were probably more interested in the second of these aims.
The motives of John Paul Jones are unclear, but he found a position as
a lieutenant in the new navy. After demonstrating his competence in
operations aboard the frigate USS *Alfred* and the sloop USS *Providence*,

in June 1777 he was given command of a sloop-of-war, the USS *Ranger*, with 14 small 6-pounder guns and 140 men. In November, he set sail across the Atlantic with orders to take the war to the enemy.

The *Ranger* first made port in the River Loire in France, a country that was then neutral, but sympathetic to the American cause. At first, Jones met with frustration. He had hoped to be given command of a much better ship, *L'Indien*, which was under construction in the Netherlands, but the Dutch government was not prepared to breach neutrality by selling it to the Americans. For the time being he had to put up with the *Ranger*. Jones's position was strengthened considerably in early 1778, when France entered the war and signed an alliance with the American colonies. He received the first international recognition of the new "Stars and Stripes" American flag when his 13-gun salute was returned by a French warship on February 14.

Jones's first attack on Britain was launched in 1778. The *Ranger* set sail from France on April 10 and headed north through the Irish Sea. Jones decided to raid his old port of Whitehaven, where several hundred vulnerable merchant ships were at anchor. He did not intend to take prizes, as a privateer would have done, but to destroy the ships

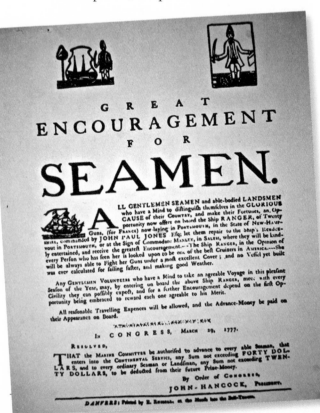

RECRUITING POSTER
John Paul Jones issued
this poster to gather
crew for the *Ranger* in
1777, prior to crossing
the Atlantic and
raiding Britain.

"I wish to have no connection with any ship that does not sail fast; for I intend to go in harm's way"

JOHN PAUL JONES

in a blow against a weak point in Britain's defenses. His crew were not pleased with the prospect of burning ships rather than capturing them—the ship's surgeon, Ezra Green, maintained that "nothing could be got by burning poor people's property." Under cover of darkness on April 22–23, two boats carrying 40 men were sent ashore at the port, but half of them repaired to an inn, while one went around banging on doors to warn people of the impending danger. Back aboard the *Ranger*, the surgeon waited "in expectation of seeing the smoke of the town and shipping ascend as the smoke of a furnace," but nothing had happened by daybreak. The landing party went back on board having burned only a single collier.

Later that day, Jones crossed the familiar waters of the Solway Firth and landed with 12 men in southern Scotland. He planned to take a hostage, local minor noble the Earl of Selkirk, in exchange for the better treatment of American seamen held in British prisons. Selkirk, however, was not at home. Some of Jones's men pointed out that "in America no delicacy was shown by the English, who took away all sorts of moveable property, setting fire... to towns and to the houses... without distinction." They demanded the right to plunder the house and, against his better judgment, Jones gave in. Anxious to establish his reputation as a gentleman, he later wrote to Lady Selkirk in explanation and refunded the value of the items. Although the attacks on Whitehaven and the Selkirk estate had minimal practical effect, their psychological impact was considerable. The British regional military commander Sir James Oughton later reported that Jones had "thrown the whole western coast into consternation."

Before the Whitehaven raid, the Americans had seen the Royal Navy sloop HMS *Drake* anchored across the North Channel in Carrickfergus, Ireland. Jones resolved to attack her before returning

THE *BONHOMME RICHARD*
Under John Paul Jones's command, the *Bonhomme Richard* entered a pitched sea battle with the English ship HMS *Serapis* in 1779.

to France. Again, his crew were unwilling—a naval ship would put up a good fight and yield little prize money. But their captain was determined. On the afternoon of April 24, the *Drake* came out to fight in a light breeze and a gun action continued for more than an hour. The British captain and first lieutenant were killed and 20 of the crew were put out of action. Lowering the ship's flag was the usual signal of surrender, but since the *Drake*'s ensign had been shot away, the surviving British officer indicated surrender by waving his hat. The *Ranger*, which had also suffered losses, made her way back to Brest in France with the prize.

In 1779, the French gave Jones a new ship to command. The USS *Bonhomme Richard* was an eccentric vessel—a French merchant ship built for the East Indies trade in 1765, with two decks of guns on a length of 145 ft (44 m). She did not sail as well as a single-decker frigate and, with only six old 18-pounder guns, she would not be able to take on a larger ship of the line armed with 32-pounders. Jones set sail in August with a crew of 207 officers and seamen, only 79 of whom were American—many were French volunteers and most of the petty officers were British. The ship also carried 137 French marines. Jones initially had seven ships under his command. His aim was to sail around the north of Scotland into the North Sea. His fleet became separated in storms off Ireland and he had only three of the original ships when, on August 13, he sighted the Pentland Hills behind Edinburgh.

Jones made detailed plans for an attack on the city's port of Leith, which he believed was very weakly defended—the guns of Edinburgh Castle were 2.5 miles (4 km) away, with barely the range to reach the sea, and there was no militia for local defense. Each of Jones' ships was to provide men for the landing party, and when the city was captured, a letter would be sent to the Lord Provost of Edinburgh offering terms.

It would claim that the captors could burn Leith town to ashes, "did not the plea of humanity stay the hand of just retaliation." And they would demand an indemnity of £100,000. Jones's three ships tacked up the Firth of Forth, capturing a small Scottish merchant ship, but a boy managed to escape from it in a boat and his report alerted the army in Edinburgh. Jones lowered boats and his marines got ready to land. The only Royal Navy ship afloat in the Firth was the HMS *Three Sisters* of 20 guns, which took up a position off the harbor mouth to prevent a landing. Then a squall struck Jones' ships and the boats had to be hoisted in. Contrary winds drove the landing boats the wrong way down the Firth, and the landing had to be abandoned, but the mere presence of an enemy in the Firth had caused panic ashore.

Jones headed south down the east coast of England. On September 23, off Flamborough Head in Yorkshire, he came upon a convoy of 41 ships carrying lumber from the Baltic Sea, escorted by two Royal Navy warships. Battle was joined between the *Bonhomme Richard* and the leading British ship, the 44-gun HMS *Serapis*. She too was a small two-decker, but she had a full battery of twenty 18-pounder guns. The discrepancy in firepower was increased when two of the *Bonhomme Richard*'s 18-pounders blew up early in the action, leaving her with only four. The two ships jockeyed for position at close range, with Jones hoping to board. After the *Bonhomme Richard*'s bow became entangled at the *Serapis*'s stern, the British ship's captain, Richard Pearson, asked if the Americans had surrendered. Jones replied stonily, "I have not yet begun to fight."

The ships pivoted as the wind shifted, and deadly fire was shot from both sides. The British deployed their heavy cannons, tearing holes in *Bonhomme Richard*'s hull at point-blank range. At the same time, musket-armed French marines and Americans in the *Bonhomme Richard*'s tops aimed downward to clear the enemy decks. An American seaman climbed out along the yardarm, which was overhanging the *Serapis*, and dropped hand grenades into her hold, igniting a gunpowder charge and causing many

JOHN PAUL JONES
Born in Scotland, Jones had a turbulent career prior to his emigration to America. He went on to be one of its leading naval commanders in the Revolutionary War.

THE BATTLE OF FLAMBOROUGH HEAD
Fought on September 23, 1779 off the coast of
northern Britain, the Battle of Flamborough
Head became one of the most celebrated naval
battles between Britain and America, where
John Paul Jones was hailed as a hero.

RICHARD PEARSON'S PISTOLS
This pair of cannon-barrel flintlock pistols belonged to Captain Richard Pearson of British ship the *Serapis*.

casualties. But the *Bonhomme Richard* was holed below the waterline and in such a bad condition that British prisoners captured from a merchant ship had to be freed from the hold to help with pumping her. One prisoner escaped to the *Serapis* and informed Captain Pearson that his opponent was close to defeat. Equally sure of a British victory, the *Bonhomme Richard*'s chief gunner, Henry Gardner, tried to haul down the American flag to surrender, but he was felled by Jones, who remained defiant. Then a shot from the *Bonhomme Richard* almost severed the *Serapis*'s mainmast. Captain Pearson lost his nerve and it was he who surrendered. Forty-nine men had been killed and 67 wounded in Jones's ship, compared with 54 dead and 75 wounded in the *Serapis*. As the *Bonhomme Richard* was sinking, Jones had to transfer his men to the captured British ship, which he then sailed to the neutral port of Texel in the Netherlands.

The battle of Flamborough Head made Jones a legend, but it was to be his last engagement with the American navy. His exploits had dented British morale and raised American spirits, but caused little material damage. Ultimately, it would be the armies across the Atlantic and the great battle fleets of Britain and France that would determine the result of the war. On March 16, 1781, the British and French fleets met at the entrance to Chesapeake Bay in Virginia. Neither side lost a ship but the battle was a strategic victory for France and its American allies. It ensured that the British Army under General Charles Cornwallis, besieged in Yorktown by American General George Washington, would not be relieved by sea. Cornwallis's surrender sealed the fate of British power in North America. Despite defeating the French at the Saintes in the West Indies in April 1782, the following year, Britain recognized the independence of the 13 colonies that would form the United States of America. After the war, Jones returned to Europe and briefly served as an admiral in the fleet of Empress Catherine II of Russia, performing creditably in fighting between the Russians and Ottoman Turks in the Black Sea. He died in France in 1792.

GIVE HIM THE SCHLEY DEGREE.

CHAIRMAN OF PAUL JONES INQUIRY BOARD.—Captain Jones, did you or did you not say,
"Damn the *Alliance!* Let her take care of herself!"

CALLED TO ACCOUNT
This satirical cartoon from 1905 depicts John Paul
Jones before a court of inquiry, called to defend his
conduct. The poster behind the senior naval officers
shows "the loop of the *Bonhomme Richard*."

The Battle
of Trafalgar

AUGUSTE GICQUEL DES TOUCHES stood on the forecastle of
the French 74-gun *Intrèpide* as she sailed into action off Spain's
south coast, between Cadiz and the Strait of Gibraltar, on October 21,
1805. His ship was part of a combined Franco-Spanish fleet under
Admiral Pierre de Villeneuve that was fighting Britain's Mediterranean
Fleet under Admiral Horatio Nelson at a crucial moment in the
Napoleonic Wars. Serving as an ensign—a junior officer—Gicquel
was about to take part in the culminating engagement of an entire
era of naval warfare: the Battle of Trafalgar.

In the six wars fought between Britain and France from 1689 to 1802,
the two oceanic powers developed fleets in which the key classes of
warship were ships of the line and frigates. Ships of the line, as their
name suggests, were designed to fight as part of a fleet in a single line, a
tactic that made best use of their gun power in firing broadsides. The
74-gun ship of the line—with two full decks of heavy guns—was the
ideal compromise between gun power and mobility. Three-deckers,
with 98 to 120 guns, were clumsier and slower, but their extra height
meant that in close action they could pour fire on the decks of smaller
ships. Supporting the ships of the line, the small, fast frigates, each with
a single deck of guns, carried out a range of tasks including reconnaissance,
escorting convoys of merchant ships, and
raiding enemy shipping.

Gicquel had seen service both on
frigates and ships of the line. Born in
Britanny in 1784 to aristocratic parents,
he belonged to the social class that had
traditionally provided officers for
France's navy, but the French Revolution

ADMIRAL HORATIO NELSON
A gifted leader and unconventional
tactician, Nelson lost an arm
and the sight of one eye
in combat.

THE LEAD-UP
TO THE "GLORIOUS
FIRST OF JUNE"
This battle in the
Atlantic was the first
large-scale naval
engagement between
Britain and France
during the French
Revolutionary Wars.

of 1789 brought radical upheaval. Many aristocrats were arrested, executed, or fled into exile. With the old aristocratic officers gone, the revolutionary navy found replacements by promoting petty officers or transferring captains from merchant ships, but the former lacked education and the latter lacked daring. From February 1793, revolutionary France was at war with Britain. In this time of turmoil, at the age of nine the aristocratic Gicquel joined the navy as a ship's boy on the frigate *Gentille*. In the summer of 1794, within a few weeks of beginning his naval career, Gicquel found himself in an Anglo-French battle in the North Atlantic. On a day known as "13 Prairial" in France, following the Revolutionary calendar, and the "Glorious First of June" in Britain, this was the first great naval engagement of the French Revolutionary Wars. Gicquel's frigate passed on signals from the flagship but did not take part in the main fighting. The French fleet lost six ships of the line, but succeeded in protecting a vital convoy delivering grain to France.

In 1799, as the Revolutionary Wars raged on, Gicquel was promoted to midshipman on the 74-gun *Desaix*. On July 6, 1801, the *Desaix*, commanded by Captain Christy de la Pallière, was part of a squadron of three ships of the line that encountered six British ships of the line off Algeciras, near Gibraltar. In the ensuing battle, while the *Desaix* exchanged fire with HMS *Hannibal* at 200 yd (180 m), HMS *Caesar* came aft and raked her along the gun decks of the French ship. Half the crew of the *Desaix* were killed or wounded and Gicquel's tiny cabin was shot to pieces. Despite this, by the end of the action the *Caesar* and two other British ships were disabled. Six days later, the French squadron was joined by a Spanish squadron that included two huge 112-gun ships, but during a British counterattack, both these ships were set alight. "The flames rose to the sky, illuminating the squadron

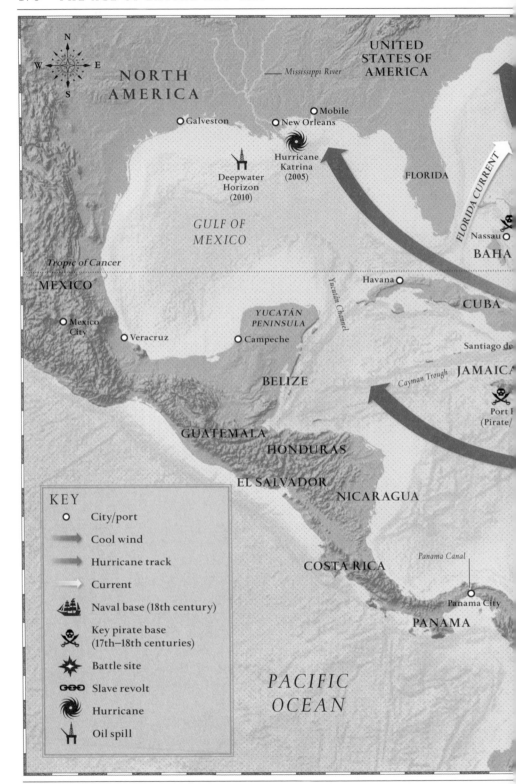

NORTH
AMERICA

Mississippi River

UNITED
STATES OF
AMERICA

Galveston

Mobile

New Orleans

Hurricane
Katrina
(2005)

FLORIDA

FLORIDA CURRENT

Deepwater
Horizon
(2010)

Nassau

BAHA

GULF OF
MEXICO

Tropic of Cancer

Havana

CUBA

MEXICO

Mexico
City

Veracruz

YUCATÁN
PENINSULA

Campeche

Yucatán Channel

Santiago de

Cayman Trough

JAMAICA

BELIZE

Port F
(Pirate/

GUATEMALA

HONDURAS

EL SALVADOR

NICARAGUA

Panama Canal

COSTA RICA

Panama City

PANAMA

PACIFIC
OCEAN

KEY

○   City/port

→   Cool wind

→   Hurricane track

→   Current

Naval base (18th century)

Key pirate base
(17th–18th centuries)

Battle site

Slave revolt

Hurricane

Oil spill

The Caribbean Sea and the Gulf of Mexico

The Caribbean, one of the world's largest seas, is a semi-enclosed extension of the North Atlantic. It is separated from the ocean by a cresent-shaped string of islands known as the West Indies. Both the Caribbean and the Gulf of Mexico, an ocean basin connected to the Caribbean via the Yucatán Channel, are dominated by trade winds from the northeast, and are subject to annual hurricanes. Two deep ocean trenches on the seabed of the Caribbean also put the region at risk from earthquakes and tsunamis.

STREAM

r STREAM

Puerto Rico Trench

AITI
380
ve revolt
91–1804)
O Port-au-Prince

DOMINICAN
REPUBLIC
O Santo Domingo

PUERTO RICO

ANTIGUA &
BARBUDA

Antigua
(British)

*NORTH
ATLANTIC
OCEAN*

Battle of the
Saintes (1782)

Martinique
(French)

CARIBBEAN SEA

ST LUCIA

Barbados
(British)

BARBADOS

tagena
anish)

TRINIDAD
& TOBAGO

O Port-of-Spain

Trade winds

VENEZUELA

Orinoco River

MBIA

PIRATES OF THE CARIBBEAN

The ships that plied their trade between the Caribbean and Europe in the 17th and 18th centuries provided lucrative opportunities for pirates (see pp.136–45), and during this period the region became notorious for their villainous activities. Some towns, however, such as Port Royal in Jamaica, prospered greatly by allowing the pirates to trade their plundered goods unhindered.

and the entire Straits with a horrible clarity," Gicquel wrote later. He could hear screams of terror before the Spanish ships exploded with the loss of around 2,000 men.

In March 1802, the Treaty of Amiens brought the recurrent warfare between France and the other powers of Europe to an end. Within a year, however, the peace collapsed and war resumed between Britain and France. Napoleon Bonaparte, a general who had risen to power during the revolution, continued to consolidate his power, crowning himself emperor in 1804. He mobilized an army on the northern French coast in preparation for an invasion of Britain. In 1805, needing to achieve naval control of the English Channel before he could ferry his troops across to England, Napoleon planned to lure the British fleet away from European waters by threatening their colonial possessions in the West Indies.

By this time, Gicquel was an ensign aboard the *Intrèpide* in France's Mediterranean base at Toulon, which was blockaded by the British under Nelson. In March 1805, the *Intrèpide*, along with 11 other French ships under Admiral Villeneuve, managed to slip past the blockade and head for the West Indies. Nelson set off in pursuit, but initially sailed in the wrong direction. Joined by six Spanish ships of the line— Spain had allied with France in 1804—Villeneuve reached the French West Indian colony of Martinique a month ahead of the pursuing Nelson. Then, having drawn the British admiral to the West Indies, the Franco-Spanish fleet sailed for Europe. Nelson sent a frigate home with the news and it spotted Villeneuve's fleet in mid-Atlantic. A British squadron was hastily assembled and confronted Villeneuve off Cape Finisterre, Brittany, on July 22. In an indecisive encounter, the British captured two Spanish ships. The battle was strategically important, however, because it made Villeneuve head to port in Spain instead of sailing to the Channel. In August, Napoleon abandoned his planned invasion of England and withdrew his army from Boulogne.

By September 1805, Admiral Villeneuve was in Cadiz with an enormous fleet of 33 French and Spanish ships of the line, having picked up more ships on the way. Chosen to lead the British fleet blockading them, Nelson arrived off Cadiz later that month. The French and Spanish had no confidence in their ability to fight Nelson's fleet. They knew that their gunnery was inferior—as Gicquel wrote, in exchanges of cannon fire "our losses were always incomparably higher than those of the English." Having already won battles at the Nile in 1798 and

Copenhagen in 1801, Nelson was confident and fully aware of his enemy's weaknesses. His crews were well trained after years at sea, whereas the Franco-Spanish fleets had spent a lot of time blockaded in port. Many of the British sailors had been pressed into the navy against their will, but morale was excellent, for Nelson was a charismatic leader.

Villeneuve was goaded by Napoleon into taking action. On October 18, believing that if he stayed in port he would be fired, he prepared to sail out of Cadiz toward the Mediterranean. With movement slow in light winds, battle was eventually joined three days later off Cape Trafalgar, on the Spanish coast. The French and Spanish formed a line of battle to meet Nelson but the crews were badly trained—in some places the ships were two or three abreast, in others there were large gaps in the line. Nelson only had 27 ships of the line against Villeneuve's 33, but he organized them in two columns to attack headlong. His aim was to concentrate his force on a single area and break through the enemy's line, achieving local superiority of numbers. Attacking in column, exposed to broadsides during a long approach, would be risky if the enemy's gunnery was adequate, but Nelson knew that it was not.

On October 21, a British column led by Admiral Cuthbert Collingwood penetrated toward the rear of the Franco-Spanish line, with each ship enduring heavy fire until it was through, then turning

THE LINES OF BATTLE
This plan of Trafalgar shows the formation of the ships.
Nelson used a bold move known as "breaking the line"
to smash through the French and Spanish defenses.

to attack individual French or Spanish ships. Nelson led the other column in the HMS *Victory*, penetrating near the center and engaging Villeneuve's flagship, the *Bucentaure*. Captain Jean-Jacques Lucas of the *Redoutable* came up to aid Villeneuve. Lucas had reacted to the deficiency in gunnery by training his men in musketry, with one dramatic effect: Nelson was hit on the shoulder by a musket ball fired from the rigging of the *Redoutable*. It passed though his lungs and lodged in the base of his spine. He was carried below decks, mortally wounded, but the fight went on.

Gicquel's ship, the *Intrèpide*, was near the head of the Franco-Spanish line in a squadron under Admiral Pierre Dumanoir. Instead of turning back to join the fighting in the center and rear of the line, Dumanoir kept on his course—a decision that later led to accusations of cowardice. The captain of the *Intrèpide*, the rough, daring, and barely articulate Louis Infernet, "had another view of his duty," however. On his own initiative, he turned his ship toward the fray. Stationed on the forecastle, Gicquel could see the 74-gun *Redoutable* being overwhelmed by the *Victory*, "but still resisting with such valour that she almost took Nelson's ship by boarding." He observed: "Everywhere the English had the advantage of numbers... Having the wind they were able to go anywhere where they were most needed..." Meanwhile, below decks on the *Victory*, Nelson was dying, gasping for breath as his lungs filled with blood. Yet still he asked about the progress of the battle, as the more effective British gunnery wore down the Franco-Spanish fleet.

Amid the smoke and confusion, Gicquel saw an opportunity he knew would appeal to his captain. A British ship, the HMS *Orion*, was about to cross their bows and fire into them. Gicquel thought they could turn the tables by ramming and boarding the *Orion*, and sent a midshipman to suggest it to the captain. Dreaming of taking a British

NELSON'S SIGNALS
This chart is a record of the signals used by Nelson at the Battle of Trafalgar in 1805.

"There was fire from above, fire from below… orders and hearing were out of the question: everything was done by signs"

A BRITISH MARINE OFFICER AT THE BATTLE OF TRAFALGAR

prize, Gicquel got his boarding party ready for action, but nothing happened. Deciding to tell the captain himself, he headed off, but en route found the midshipman lying face down on the deck—he had taken fright when another British ship, HMS *Britannia*, had come alongside and begun firing. Gicquel gave the man a kick but then spotted Infernet brandishing his sword threateningly. "Do you want to cut my head off, Captain?" Gicquel asked. "Certainly not you, my friend," Infernet replied, "but that's what I mean to do to the first man who speaks to me of surrender." But the opportunity to fight back had gone, the *Orion* had already fired a murderous broadside and passed ahead, and the *Britannia* was creating havoc alongside.

Gicquel was lucky to survive the encounter. He described the scene on board the *Intrèpide*: "… our guns were disabled, and the batteries heaped up with the dead and dying." With most of the Franco-Spanish fleet having surrendered, the *Intrèpide* had to give in too. Gicquel wrote, "It was impossible to keep up a resistance… Our flag was hauled down… the only one still flying."

The British had captured 19 French and Spanish ships and destroyed one. But there was another ordeal to come. In the aftermath of the battle, a storm blew in, wreaking havoc among the already damaged ships. The *Intrèpide* was dismasted and threatened to sink. The wounded were passed out to safety through the gunports until only Gicquel and two other seamen were left on board. Gicquel finally abandoned her as she foundered and was picked up by his old adversary the *Orion*. Only four of the 19 prizes survived the storm.

Trafalgar was a great victory for the British, destroying Napoleon's maritime strategy and sealing the supremacy of British sea power. The downfall of Napoleon in 1815 was the beginning of a century of relative peace in Europe, and Gicquel went on to serve the restored monarchy.

Finding Longitude

By the 18th century, sailors had long known how to establish their latitude by measuring the angle of the sun above the horizon at noon (see pp.162–63). Determining longitude (the distance east or west), however, was still problematic, for it required the use of a timepiece that was reliable at sea over time—and such a clock was only invented in 1736. It was called the Sea Clock (or H1), and its inventor was John Harrison.

A spring drives the oscillating motion of the weights

John Harrison

Yorkshire-born carpenter John Harrison responded to the British Board of Longitude's offer of £20,000 to whoever could solve the problem of longitude by presenting his H1 Sea Clock in 1736. It was the first of four such clocks that he would design, and it lost only a few seconds on its test run to Lisbon. His final design (H4) was the size of a pocket watch, and gave a measurement that was accurate to within one nautical mile.

JOHN HARRISON
(1693–1776)

Dial showing the time in seconds

Dial showing the time in minutes

Dial showing the days passed

SEA CLOCK (H1)
BRITISH, 1736
H1 was built between 1730 and 1735 and weighed 75 lb (34 kg). Unlike conventional timepieces, it was controlled and balanced by springs, so that, unlike a pendulum clock, it was independent of the direction of gravity.

Stablizers

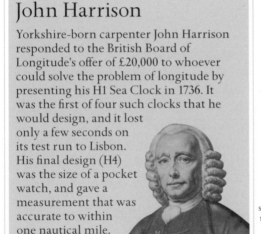

Two pairs of oscillating weights (the top pair visible here) drive the clock mechanism. The horizontal motion of the weights is not affected by the pitching and rolling of the ship.

A second set of spring-controlled weights sits at the lower end of these staves. When the top spring expands, the bottom springs retracts, and vice versa.

Solid brass framework

Crowns and cherubs decorate the dial plate

Dial showing the time in hours

Calculating longitude

The key to establishing longitude lies in calculating local noon (when the sun is at its highest), and checking the time with a chronometer set to Greenwich Mean Time (GMT). If, for example, the chronometer shows that it is 2 pm, then the ship (below) must be 30° west of Greenwich, since, given the curvature of the earth, 15° of longitude is traveled for every hour's difference in the time of local noon. If the time is 10 am, then the ship must be 30° east of Greenwich.

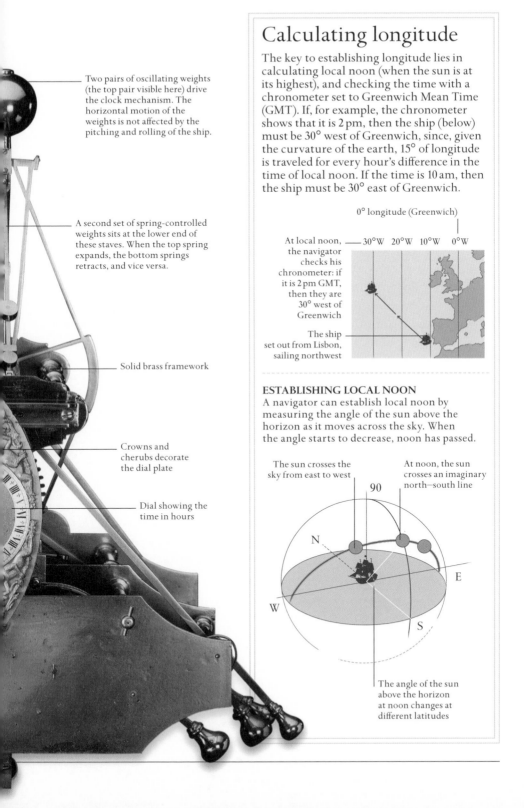

0° longitude (Greenwich)

At local noon, the navigator checks his chronometer: if it is 2 pm GMT, then they are 30° west of Greenwich

30°W 20°W 10°W 0°W

The ship set out from Lisbon, sailing northwest

ESTABLISHING LOCAL NOON
A navigator can establish local noon by measuring the angle of the sun above the horizon as it moves across the sky. When the angle starts to decrease, noon has passed.

The sun crosses the sky from east to west

At noon, the sun crosses an imaginary north–south line

90

N

E

W

S

The angle of the sun above the horizon at noon changes at different latitudes

Death in the Arctic

THE WHALING SHIP *Resolution* of Whitby, England, had a field day on the edge of the Arctic ice on June, 15, 1811. The whalers had already butchered one whale when a suckling whale, still dependent on its mother for milk, surfaced close to one of the ship's boats. Such a young whale would not yield much blubber, but the crew knew its mother would take extraordinary measures to protect it, so they pierced it with a harpoon. Sure enough, the grief-stricken cow circled the ship, unable to abandon her child. Captain William Scoresby describes her, "running furiously and frequently stopping short and returning seemingly in great agony for the loss of her young…" The whalers in the first boat kept the calf alive while five other boats hunted the mother, which fearlessly approached them. Twice the harpooners tried to stick their weapons into her and failed. On the third attempt they speared her, and soon she was bristling with harpoons. The mother took an hour to die, and the calf was killed too. The mother was "a pretty fine fish," Scoresby wrote, but the calf yielded only three or four inches of blubber, and a bone from its skull to make an ear trumpet.

Twenty-one-year-old Captain Scoresby watched all this from the crow's nest of the *Resolution*. He was a man so religious that he felt guilty for indulging in "worldly and vain'" conversation on the Sabbath, but he did not object when his men were still "flensing" the whales, or stripping their flesh, on Sunday June 16. He was also a budding scientist who spent his winters at Edinburgh University. Neither science nor religion made him see whaling as cruel. However, when his men repeated this trick with a cow and her calf two years later and the whales escaped, he did not know "whether to rejoice or regret"— perhaps suggesting some pang of remorse at his part in the slaughter.

Men have been killing whales for their own use for more than a thousand years. By the 12th century, Basque sailors were hunting the Biscayan right whale. They ventured far afield in its pursuit, reaching Newfoundland by the 16th century. Dutch whalers began hunting in the Greenland Sea in the 17th century, where they were soon followed by Basques, Danes, Germans, and British. From the 18th century, North American whalers in particular pursued sperm whales on long voyages in the South Atlantic and Pacific. Whale oil was highly valued, especially for use as lamp fuel. By the 19th century, it was vital to Britain's rapidly growing textile industry, which used it to condition wool for spinning. The Greenland or bowhead whale was particularly prized. Living in freezing cold water on the edge of the Arctic ice, it developed a layer of blubber up to 19 in (50 cm) thick. This was the whale's main attraction to the hunters, but its mouth also contained about 300 baleen plates—strong, flexible material to filter its food that was used to make corsets.

In 1813, 66 British ships set out for the Davis Strait, west of Greenland, and a further 73 for the Greenland Sea, including seven from Captain Scoresby's home port of Whitby. Scoresby himself took command of a new ship, the *Esk* of 350 tons, built to cope with the Arctic ice. The captain's cabin had been outfitted, Scoresby wrote, "in the best style," by the finest carpenters in Whitby. The ship was equipped with six boats to chase the whales, each with a harpooner, a boat steerer, and a line-manager, who controlled the rope attached to the harpoon as it was fed out. In addition to a surgeon, carpenter, armorer, and cook, the ship needed 16 skilled seamen. Whalers were protected from the Royal Navy's press gangs during the whaling season, but experienced hands were nonetheless hard to come by during the Napoleonic Wars. The *Esk* sailed to Shetland to recruit extra men there, but even then the crew was weak. Six of them were raw lads 12 to 16 years old.

Scoresby's new ship proved not as robust as she looked. As she sailed north to the hunting grounds, her hull began to leak and the pumps were barely able to manage. However, on April 17, they reached

DRAWING BY WILLIAM SCORESBY, 1820
A whale tosses a harpooner's boat into the air. Even without such dramatic accidents, mortality rates among whaling crews were high.

IN THE ICE
Tenders from English whaling ships in pursuit of their prey off Greenland navigate an ice floe in the 1750s.

a latitude of nearly 79 degrees north on the edge of the Arctic ice and began to prepare the whaling boats for action, equipping each with two harpoons, six ropes 120 fathoms long, and six or seven oars. Two days later, the *Esk* started to drift stern first toward the ice in a flat calm. The crew lowered three boats into the water to tow her, but were unable to change her course. Scoresby dropped a sea anchor of his own design to slow her down, which also proved ineffectual. The crew reckoned they were two hours away from disaster when a breeze got up and blew them away from the ice.

Soon after midnight on April 22, they sighted a whale. They launched the boats and at 3 am made the first harpoon strike. Harpooners tried to avoid the massive, thick skull of the bowhead whale, but a hit anywhere else would "admit of the full length of the instrument, without danger of obstruction," as Scoresby wrote. The harpoon had barbs at the end, making it hard for the whale to free itself once pierced. As the whale dived, the crew in the boat wound the rope round a bollard to slow it. Friction made the rope smoking hot and the men had to wet it to stop it from catching fire. The crew joined ropes together to hold the whale as it dived to a depth of nearly 800 fathoms—so deep that Scoresby believed it might suffer damage from the water pressure. Eight ropes were attached to the whale, which ran deep under the water until it was exhausted. When it broke the surface, it was too tired to escape. By this stage in the hunt, Scoresby wrote, "The sea, to a great extent around, is dyed with blood, and the ice, boats, and men, are sometimes drenched with the same." The crew was jubilant.

Scoresby was lying in his cabin on April 24, when he heard movement on deck and the cry of "man overboard!" John Dodd, a line-manager described as "encumbered with a Flushing extra jacket, & two pairs of mitts on his hands," had fallen into the sea from the mizzen topsail yard. By the time the captain got on deck, Dodd was already some way astern and had sunk out of sight into the icy water. In the freezing cold Arctic, he would have succumbed to hypothermia within minutes.

The whaling continued. On May 3, Scoresby's crew came across another mother, with a newborn calf. When harpooned she did not dive for as long as the bowheads usually did—her protective instincts kept her close to her child. The men killed her and left her baby to die alone. Later in the month they caught two more whales. After each kill, the crew had to carry out the malodorous, hard labor of flensing. They brought the carcass alongside the ship and held it in place with ropes while the harpooners climbed onto it, wearing spurs to increase their grip. Under the direction of the "spectioneer," or chief harpooner, they cut the flesh into oblong strips of up to half a ton each, which were hauled on deck by tackles. Then they turned the whale over, and did the same on the other side. Greenland whalers such as Scoresby's crew tended to cut the flesh into smaller pieces and stuff it into casks, in contrast to South Seas whalers who boiled the flesh down into oil on board ship.

There were no more sightings until June 7, when the lookout in the crow's nest made "the joyous cry of 'a Fall, a Fall.'" This time the whale was in a tricky position among the ice floes. It dived deep with a harpoon in its back, then surfaced near the edge of the ice. The harpooners took several hours to strike it again, when it was "speedily dispatched."

On June 10, the *Esk* became trapped in the ice. A long ice floe was blown across the moored ship's position, blocking it from exit to clear water and forcing smaller floes against its hull. Scoresby feared the ship would be crushed:

... by a careful watch, under the care of Divine Providence, we may evade the most alarming pressures, but should the Ice close us immoveable we can then make no effort towards the preservation of the ship & can only have confidence in Him who is alone able & willing to save to the uttermost those who put their trust in Him...

WHALING HARPOON
Once the harpoon was lodged in the whale's thick hide, the harpooner would keep hold of the rope and run the creature to exhaustion.

Fortunately, after three days a gap appeared and a wind got up, allowing the ship to sail into a clear area of water about a quarter of a mile square. The crew then cleared a small exit into open sea by moving pieces of ice weighing up to 100 tons. Forty men went onto the ice to haul the *Esk* through the gap they had made, which closed again as soon as the ship had reached open water.

Over the next two weeks, they killed eight more whales. "Surely the Lord is on our side," Scoresby wrote. There was a difficult chase on July 9, when a whale was spotted blowing in a hole in the ice. The crew dragged a harpoon and line 350 yd (320 m) over the ice and struck the whale just as it was about to dive. It ran out 10 lines and was seen blowing at several different holes until it reached the edge of the ice. A second harpoon struck home. The victim dived again and broke the surface through a foot of ice. A brave sailor, seeing that one of the harpoons was about to come loose, jumped on

THE USES OF A WHALE
This lithographic plate from around 1850
illustrates the whale's "… Employment
During Life and Uses After Death."

the whale's back, cut out the harpoon and stuck it in again. The whale was killed.

By July 22, Scoresby realized they were "now out of reach of further Success this voyage,"

WHALES KILLED 1930–1931:

37,00

though the casks in the hold were not full. The crew prepared for the homeward journey, hoisting three sets of jawbones in the rigging, cutting the blubber off two whales' tails, and clearing the deck to stow the boats. They also readied the ship's guns, for the outbreak of the War of 1812 between Britain and the United States brought the risk of attack by marauding American frigates. The *Esk*, however, sailed homeward without incident. Three weeks later, the ship anchored off Whitby. Scoresby was rowed ashore and reported to a crowd of sailors' relatives that he had "nothing but good news to communicate"—despite Dodd's drowning. He found his mother, sisters, and wife "in full health & our Dear Child likewise Blessed." The price of oil was at a record high of £50 per ton and the voyage made nearly £10,000—equivalent to over $790,000 (£500,000) today. Scoresby continued in the trade until 1823, when he entered the church and his annual income dropped from about £800 to £40.

Scoresby published *An Account of the Arctic Regions with a History and Description of the Northern Whale-fishery* in 1820, a scientific work that has stood the test of time, but also in the long term contributed to the near extinction of the bowhead whale. The slaughter increased early in the 20th century with harpoon guns, steam whalers, and factory ships—37,000 whales were killed in 1930–31 alone. By that time, whale oil was becoming less economically important, with coal, gas, electricity, and mineral oil fulfilling most of its functions. However, it was well into the second half of the 20th century before the world fell in love with whales and whale conservation became an issue. Commercial whaling has been banned since 1986, although some countries—notably Japan, Norway, and Iceland—continue to lobby for the ban to be lifted.

Steam and Emigration
1815–1914

During the 19th century, steamships with metal hulls replaced wooden sailing ships, transforming ocean trade and travel. This revolution proceeded in stages. The first steam vessels, propelled by paddle wheels, were only suitable for travel on rivers, lakes, and coastal waters, but from the mid-19th century, ocean-going steamships driven by propellers became more common. Although fast tea clippers gave a final flourish to the age of sail, by the 1870s, sailing ships were scarcely used on ocean routes. Steamships contributed to a rapid expansion in world trade—which increased tenfold between 1850 and 1913—and soaring emigration from Europe, primarily to the United States. Although the transatlantic slave trade was abolished, hundreds of thousands of voluntary travelers crossed the ocean, encouraged by the relative speed and safety offered by steam transportation. By the early 20th century, passenger lines such as Cunard and White Star were operating luxury transatlantic services with ships powered by steam turbines and linked to land by the newly invented wireless telegraphy.

The advent of steam, iron, and steel transformed naval warfare. Steam-powered gunboats became the symbol of European imperialism. The first clumsy battle between rival steamships was fought off Virginia, during the American Civil War in 1862. Within 30 years of this epoch-making event, every country aspiring to be a major power wanted its own expensive fleet of steel-hulled steam battleships, armed with turret-mounted guns firing explosive shells. In the years leading up to World War I, Britain and Germany engaged in a battleship-building contest, a naval arms race that exacerbated international tension. Meanwhile, naval operations extended below the waves with the introduction of submarines, and mines and torpedoes threatened the traditional dominance of the prestigious large warships.

Fire on the Oceans

O N AUGUST 17, 1807, American inventor and engineer Robert Fulton decided that his experimental new boat, the *Clermont*, was ready for her first real trip, 150 miles (240 km) up New York's Hudson River—even though "there were not perhaps thirty persons in the city who believed that the boat would ever move one mile an hour, or be of the least utility..." The *Clermont* had been outfitted with a small steam engine and primitive side paddles, and looked like no other vessel at the time, since all other ships were powered by sail. The sight of her chugging past astonished people watching from the shoreline, and several crewmen out on the river beat a hasty retreat from this mechanical monster marching on the tide, lighting its path with fire. As Fulton's biographer wrote:

> The first steam-boats... used dry pine wood for fuel, which sends forth a column of ignited vapour many feet above the flue, and whenever the fire is stirred, a galaxy of sparks fly off, and in the night have a very brilliant and beautiful appearance. This uncommon light first attracted the attention of the crews of other vessels... when it came so near that the noise of the machinery and paddles were heard, the crews... in some instances shrunk beneath their decks in the terrific sight, and left their vessels to go on shore.

Despite the alarm it caused, the *Clermont's* maiden voyage was a great success, and later versions of the steamboat opened up the Hudson River to easy navigation, which was crucial to the development of New York as one of the world's greatest seaports. However, Fulton was not the only one to have the idea of harnessing steam power to propel passenger vessels.

Across the Atlantic in Helensburgh, on the shore of Scotland's Firth of Clyde, an enterprising civil engineer and hotel owner, Henry Bell, built a 25-ton, six-horsepower steamboat called the *Comet* in 1812 to transport his customers from the booming city of Glasgow. The *Comet* was a commercial success and was soon followed by other steamboats: in Russia, the *Elizabeth* was converted to steam in 1815 and successfully operated a service between St. Petersburg and Kronstadt, while Sweden built her first steamer, the *Stockholmshäxan*, in 1816. In the same year, the *Prinzessin Charlotte* was the first steamship to be built in Prussia, and the *Ferdinando Primo* of Naples became the first steamer to operate in the Mediterranean in 1818.

Back in the United States, Captain Moses Rogers, one of the first men to specialize in commanding steamboats, purchased a ship that was under construction and outfitted her with steam engines and paddle wheels as well as sails. The newly converted ship, named SS *Savannah*, was owned by a consortium determined to launch the first steam-propelled ship (see pp.196–97). However, the *Savannah* attracted very few passengers and the consortium decided that she should be sold in Europe—and so, in 1819, she set sail on an historic, 29-day journey to Liverpool in northern England. On the voyage she relied more on sail power than her steam engines, which were used only for around 100 hours out of a total 582, but she was spotted under steam by several ships who thought she might be on fire. When she arrived in Liverpool, thousands of people thronged to see this astonishing new ship, and the British press gloomily reported: "The Americans have beat us on our own element... adieu to the greatness of Old England." Passengers were not, however, ready for long-distance steam travel, and the consortium was unable to sell the *Savannah*. From then on, the main thrust in the development of the ocean steamboat came from Britain rather than the US.

By 1825, there were 53 steamboats operating on Scotland's River Clyde alone—with many more on the rivers, estuaries, and coasts of Europe—but there were still no passenger vessels crossing the Atlantic. In Britain, the Great Western Railway from London to Bristol was scarcely under construction when the young consulting engineer Isambard Kingdom Brunel suggested, half-jokingly, in 1835, that the line could be extended westward by a steamship service to New York. The railway's directors seized upon his idea, and a 236 ft- (-72 m) long paddle steamer was ordered in Bristol and christened the *Great Western*. Others

ENGINE-ROOM TELEGRAPH
Crew on the bridge transmitted orders to the engine room to speed up, slow down, or stop using two telegraphs connected by a wire-and-chain mechanism.

were sceptical: Irish scientific writer Professor Dionysius Lardner—who clashed with Brunel on more than one occasion—claimed that "they might as well talk of making the voyage from New York to the moon." The ship was launched in 1837 and taken to the Thames in London for trials, but disaster struck when she prepared to sail back to Bristol, as chief engineer George Pearne recorded:

> A fire broke out in the region of the chimney, from the oil in the felt in the steam chests having ignited, which threatened destruction of the ship… I crawled down, after a strong inhalation of fresh air, and succeeded in putting on a feed plunger and opening all the boiler feed cocks… We shortly got the engines and hand pumps to work, and all hands baling, pumping, etc, succeeded in extinguishing the fire.

The *Great Western* survived the fire, but it was not the last time Pearne would have to tend to problems aboard. Meanwhile, a rival had entered the race to cross the Atlantic by steam power. A consortium chartered the *Sirius*, built for the service between London and Cork in Ireland, hoping to beat Brunel at his own game. The *Sirius* was only 208 ft (63 m) long—much smaller and slower than the *Great Western*, but she left Cork on March 28, 1837, before Brunel's ship was ready to set sail for New York.

More than 40 *Great Western* passengers canceled their bookings upon hearing of the fire, and Mr. Foster of Philadelphia, PA, was one of only seven people who boarded the ship in the afternoon of April 7, 1837. He noted that everything was "pell-mell" aboard the ship: "… spars, boards, boxes, barrels, sails, cordage, seemingly without number, stirred well together, coals for the ground work, baggage to infinity; captain scolding, mates bawling, men growling and passengers in the midst of it all, in the way of every thing and every body." At

ISAMBARD KINGDOM BRUNEL
Here wearing his characteristic top hat, Brunel was one of the pioneers of transatlantic travel. He designed both the *Great Western* and the *Great Britain* steamships.

THE *GREAT WESTERN*
Wooden paddle-wheeler the *Great Western*
was the first steamship purpose-built for
crossing the Atlantic. She was 236 ft (72 m) long,
but could still be dwarfed by Atlantic waves.

8 am the next day, the passengers heard the roar of the furnaces as they were started, but it took an hour to raise steam and two more to raise the long chain of the anchor. They finally set off at noon, and Mr. Foster wrote: "Whatever misgivings might previously have assailed us in the contemplation of our voyage, I believe that at this moment there was not a faltering heart amongst us."

The mood changed three days later, however, when the ship was steaming into a headwind. "Seasickness stalks in stifling horror amongst us," Foster wrote, "and the dreadful cry of 'Steward,' the last ejaculation of despair, comes from a dozen nooks..." The following day, on April 11, the passengers were pleasantly surprised by the appearance of a bouquet of flowers on the table in their cabins. "It would be difficult for the uninitiated to conceive how ardently every circumstance on shipboard is taken hold of, however trifling it may be in itself," Mr. Foster noted admiringly. His pleasure was, however, short-lived. The next day he wrote that "the repose of last night might be compared to tossing in a blanket, and a dance of pot-hooks and frying pans was nothing to the glorious clatter among the movables that accompanied it."

Below deck, in the ship's engine room, things were not going well. Stokers normally worked in three watches because of the grueling nature of the job, but more men were needed to keep the engines steaming constantly. On April 12, chief engineer Pearne divided the stokers into two watches of eight men. They were not happy, but

Early Steamships

First proposed by French physicist Denis Papin in 1690, the idea of steam-powered ships did not become a practical reality until the development of Scottish inventor James Watt's steam engine in 1763–75. Pioneered by Robert Fulton (see p.192), steam-powered shipping revolutionized seafaring: by 1807, a US river steamboat service was in operation, and by 1838, transatlantic crossings were possible using steam power alone.

Steamship paddle

Paddle wheels were driven in a rotary motion by a system of piston rods, levers, crankshafts, and flywheels, powered by a simple steam engine.

The boiler produces steam, which is sucked into the cylinder via a valve

The steam pushes the piston forward, driving the crankshaft to turn the wheel

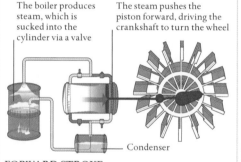

Condenser

FORWARD STROKE
Steam is sucked into the cylinder, and it pushes the piston forward, driving exhaust steam from the cylinder into the condenser.

Steam is sucked into the cylinder via the farthest valve

The steam drives the piston back, pulling the crankshaft to keep the wheel turning

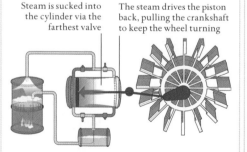

BACKWARD STROKE
Steam enters the other end of the cylinder, driving the piston back. The condenser turns the exhaust steam into water to feed the boiler.

Mizzenma

Coppered hull prevents rottting

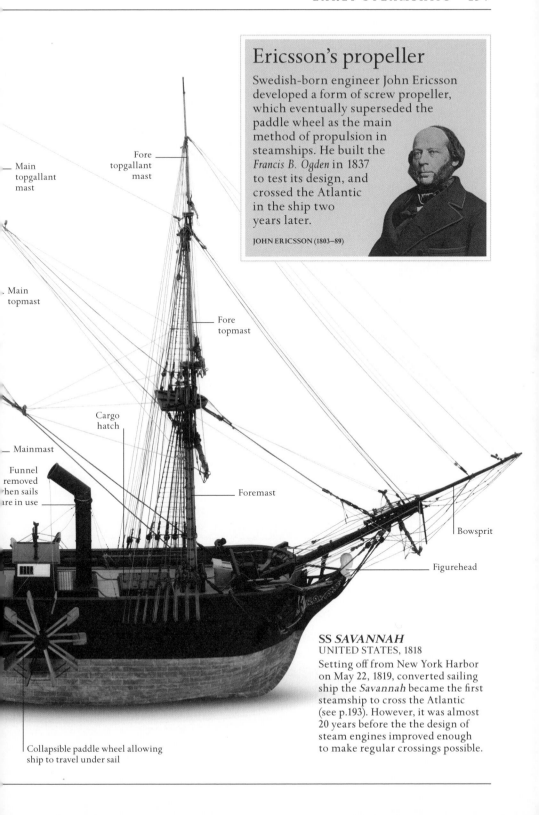

Ericsson's propeller

Swedish-born engineer John Ericsson developed a form of screw propeller, which eventually superseded the paddle wheel as the main method of propulsion in steamships. He built the *Francis B. Ogden* in 1837 to test its design, and crossed the Atlantic in the ship two years later.

JOHN ERICSSON (1803–89)

Main topgallant mast

Fore topgallant mast

Main topmast

Fore topmast

Cargo hatch

Mainmast

Funnel removed when sails are in use

Foremast

Bowsprit

Figurehead

Collapsible paddle wheel allowing ship to travel under sail

SS *SAVANNAH*
UNITED STATES, 1818

Setting off from New York Harbor on May 22, 1819, converted sailing ship the *Savannah* became the first steamship to cross the Atlantic (see p.193). However, it was almost 20 years before the the design of steam engines improved enough to make regular crossings possible.

the captain told them "to abide by such regulations for their working as should be made." Pearne had learned his trade at engine builders Maudsley and Company in London, and probably had little experience at sea. He was soon suffering from "mental depression" and from "anxiety to have the engines and all"—although in general he thought they were "a piece of magnificent perfection." On April 17, the ship stopped to tighten the screws of the paddle wheels. A lead line was cast over the side and established that the ship was in 25 fathoms of water on the Grand Banks off the coast of Newfoundland, Canada. The voyage was nearly at an end. By this time, all the coal in the center of the ship had been used up and the crew was ordered to take more to the engine room. That night there was "much dissatisfaction prevailing among the stokers, declaring themselves all but incapable of work from fatigue," and Pearne was "troubled to keep them at work."

Mr. Foster was now beginning to enjoy the novelty of the voyage: "The past night and day have afforded us in some measure an opportunity of testing the power of steam against the adverse influences of weather, a gale in our teeth... our ship behaved nobly. She plunged and rolled... yet her motions were easy, and her progress without intermission." The following day, schools of porpoises approached the ship, but when they swam close to the paddle wheels they were startled by the splashing and fled. The weather continued to be extremely variable: on April 21, there was a snowstorm that covered the ship in 2 in (5 cm) of snow, and the passengers relieved the tedium of the voyage with a snowball fight.

45
ATLANTIC ROUND TRIPS BY THE *GREAT WESTERN*

2
ATLANTIC ROUND TRIPS BY THE *SIRIUS*

Below deck, Pearne was worried about the shortage of fuel, despite using sails to assist the passage, and he worked the fore and aft boilers alternately to conserve coal. On April 22, they approached New York and the crew hauled the anchor chains up on deck. The following morning, a schooner came alongside and the pilot climbed on board. At noon, "the cry of land ran throughout the ship; and in an instant there was a rush to the poop, the rigging, the forecastle, the highest points of the vessel."

NEW YORK HARBOR
As the age of steamships developed, New York Harbor
teemed with vessels plying their trade. The banks of
Lower Manhattan were almost entirely taken up
with wharves to accommodate them.

By 3 pm, the ship had passed through the narrows at the entrance to
New York Harbor and been saluted by a fort; but bitter
disappointment awaited. "As we neared the city," wrote Mr. Foster,
"the first object to which our attention was now given was the *Sirius*,
lying at anchor in the North River, gay with flowing streamers, and
literally crammed with spectators, her decks, her paddle-boxes, her
rigging, masthead high."

The *Sirius* had arrived the day before, thus claiming the honor of
making the first steam-powered transatlantic passage. But there
was worse to follow; chief engineer George Pearne, the unsung hero
of the voyage, was severely scalded while supervising the blowing
off of the boilers. A doctor was called, but Pearne died soon
afterward, perhaps worn out by the stress and the "heated
atmosphere" of the engine room. Although she came second in the
race, the *Great Western* could claim a successful voyage. She had made

a faster passage—14 days rather than 18½—and despite Pearne's fears, she still had 155 tons of coal left in her bunkers, and was in good condition. She had also been specially designed for the voyage, unlike the *Sirius*, which had been adapted for the task, and she went on to complete 20 times as many transatlantic round trips as her rival. Colonel Webb, who had booked the *Great Western* for the return passage, claimed that the *Sirius* was "very generally looked upon as a kind of interloper, chartered for the purpose of snatching honours from those to whom they justly belonged." It was the *Great Western* that pointed the way to the future of steamships.

Brunel and his partners were already considering what that future might be. In 1843, the *Great Britain* made its appearance. It was a much bigger ship—the largest ever afloat—and was made of iron and outfitted with the newly developed screw propeller, rather than paddles. For fear of sinking, however, passengers were mistrustful of the use of iron in ocean-going ships, and the *Great Britain* carried very few passengers to New York until her fifth trip in 1846, when she had 180. During that voyage she ran aground on the Irish coast, due to "the most egregious blundering," and to the great distress of the passengers, one of whom later recalled the chaos on board: "Men and women rushed out, the latter from their berths, and some threw themselves into the arms of strangers. We could with difficulty stand.

PADDLE ENGINE ROOM
As steamships grew in size, so their engine rooms took on huge proportions. This 1859 illustration shows two human figures on the left for scale.

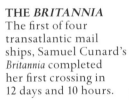

THE *BRITANNIA*
The first of four transatlantic mail ships, Samuel Cunard's *Britannia* completed her first crossing in 12 days and 10 hours.

Oh I cannot tell you the anguish of that night." The passengers were all saved, but the ship was sold and repaired before undertaking a new role—carrying emigrants to Australia.

Nova Scotia-born shipping magnate Samuel Cunard adopted a different approach once the *Great Western* had proved that transatlantic steamships were viable. He moved to Britain, and, instead of investing in one large ship, he used four medium-sized vessels to run a transatlantic mail service between Britain and North America. The first of these ships, the *Britannia*, marked the beginning of a regular transatlantic passenger and cargo service, but, despite luxuries such as a grand dining room, and a fare that included wine and spirits as well as food, the journey on this early ocean liner was far from comfortable—as Charles Dickens found when he sailed to the US in 1842: "... a heavy sea strikes her with the noise of a hundred great guns... she stops, and staggers, and shivers, as though stunned... every plank has its groan, every nail its shriek, and every drop of water in the great ocean its howling voice." Nevertheless Cunard, although technologically conservative, was a far better businessman than Brunel, and his steamships began the gradual transformation of passenger travel on the world's oceans.

Going to America

B Y THE 19TH CENTURY, emigration by sea was not a new concept, but nothing on the scale of the mass emigration from Europe to the United States had ever been seen before. The 1850s was the peak decade for emigration from Britain and Ireland, with nearly 1.7 million people leaving, a million of them for the US and around half that for Canada; the rest were bound mainly for Australia. Other Europeans soon followed, with 2.5 million Germans and over half a million Italians arriving in the US between 1871 and 1905; from 1892, many immigrants were processed through the famous immigration station on Ellis Island in New York.

These huge numbers of ordinary people endured the long and grueling passage for many different reasons—be it from curiosity, ambition, or simply from desperate poverty. A great many went to start new lives. Some could barely afford the passage out, and traveled in the most brutal conditions, particularly during the terrible Irish famine between 1845 and 1852. Following an outbreak of potato blight, Ireland was ravaged by famine and disease: a million people are believed to have died and the same number to have emigrated. Some were paid to emigrate by landlords, while others scraped enough money together to pay for their own fares. In some cases, the travelers aboard these ships found themselves facing an ordeal worse than the one they were fleeing.

Irish migrant Robert Whyte was fortunate to have enough money to pay for a cabin passage to America. Most of the other migrants were in the grim conditions of "steerage" (the cheapest accommodation, so called because it was originally located near the ship's rudder)—but even Whyte's passage was far from luxurious, and he had to share many of the other passenger's hardships. On May 30, 1847, he left his "last footprint" on his native land, as he wrote, and a boat took him out to the brig (a sailing vessel with two square-rigged masts) that was to carry him across the wide Atlantic. He was taken down to the cabin where he would live with the officers: "It was about ten feet square and so low that the only part of it in which the captain could stand upright was under the skylight... The ceiling was garnished with numerous

IRISH-AMERICAN EMIGRATION

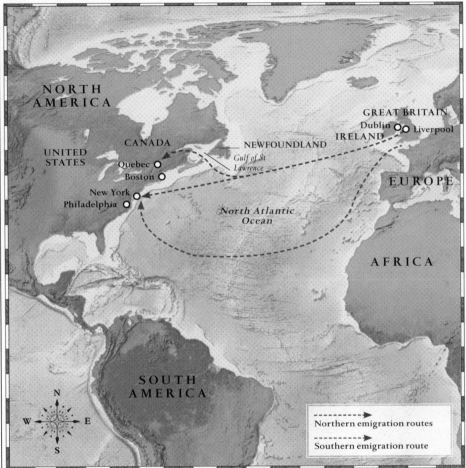

charts… An unhappy canary, perched within a rusty cage, formed a pendant from the centre of the skylight." On meeting the captain—a grizzled and unsocial man—Whyte felt "forced to admire the manly dignity of the rude tar." He also met the captain's wife—universally known as "the mistress"—who had a "goodnatured" face and silver glasses, and a kindness that partly made up for her husband's gruffness. The sailors raised the anchor, the topsails were loosed, and the brig began to glide out of Dublin Bay, entering the North Channel in a southerly wind. That evening, off the Mountains of Mourne, south of Belfast, Whyte leaned against some sacks on deck and was surprised to hear the sound of

IMMIGRANTS EN ROUTE TO ELLIS ISLAND
Immigrants to the United States crowd
the decks of the SS *Patricia*, originally of the
Hamburg-America Line, in 1906. The following
year, over a million immigrants arrived at the
inspection center on Ellis Island, with a one-day
record of 11,747 immigrants on April 17.

a groan. He records: "I jumped up, quite at a loss to account for the strange sound... lo! there was a man crouched up in a corner..." The man was not welcome, and according to Whyte, "the mate at once concluded that he was a 'stowaway,' so giving him a shake to make him stand upright, he ordered him to mount the ladder, bestowing a kick upon the poor wretch to accelerate his tardy ascent. The ragged man confessed that he had been hiding for three days and was brought before the furious captain to decide his fate: "...the captain hastily terminated the deliberation by swearing that he should be thrown overboard. The wretched creature was quite discomfited by the captain's wrath and earnestly begged for forgiveness." Eventually the captain relented, and agreed that the stowaway would be set down upon the first piece of land they passed. The unfortunate stowaway, presumably choosing the lesser of two evils, was satisfied with this verdict. As the crew searched for more stowaways, the passengers were mustered on deck, where Whyte was shocked by their condition: "a more motley crowd I never beheld; of all ages, from the infant to the feeble grandsire and withered crone... One old man was so infirm that he seemed to me to be in the last stage of consumption."

Food was a matter of considerable concern for the 110 passengers and crew. At first they were served out a week's rations "of meal or of bread" all at once, but the half-starved migrants "wasted them most improvidently" and the captain decided to issue food to them daily. They had to cook for themselves on deck in the most basic of conditions:

> The passengers' fireplaces, upon either side of the foredeck furnished endless scenes, sometimes of noisy merriment, at others of quarrels... From morning till evening they were surrounded by groups of men, women and children; some making stirabout in all kinds of vessels, and others baking cakes upon extemporary griddles. These cakes were generally about two inches thick, and when baked were encased in a burnt crust coated with smoke, being actually raw in the centre.

The crew, on the other hand, were comparatively well fed: "They had each 1–2 lbs of beef or pork daily, besides coffee and as much biscuit as they pleased, but it being a temperance vessel, they had no grog, in lieu of which they got lime-juice."

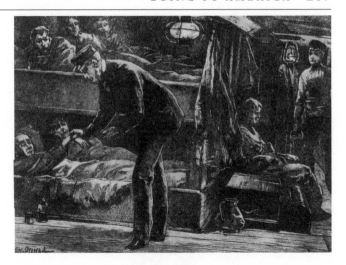

TYPHUS VICTIMS
Many ships provided the bare minimum of food, water, and living space, resulting in the swift spread of disease. The typhus epidemic of 1847 was caused by mass emigration aboard crowded, unsanitary "coffin ships."

One of the passengers was appointed "head committee," and his duties "consisted in seeing that the hold was kept clean, in preventing smoking below, settling differences, etc." However, he soon reported that two women were ill, having succumbed to typhus, the deadly fever spread by lice. Since there were no doctors on board, the captain's wife was recruited to use her amateur nursing skills on the sick women; she prescribed flour porridge with a few drops of laudanum. Whyte was dismayed about the "contagious fever... how could it possibly be stayed without medicines, medical skill or even pure water to slake the patients' burning thirst? The prospect before us was indeed an awful one and there was no hope for us but in the mercy of God." His confidence was further eroded when a shark began to follow the ship, apparently hoping for bodies to be dropped over the side. It did not have long to wait. "At breakfast, I inquired of the mate after the young woman who was so ill yesterday, when he told me that she was dead and when I remarked that I feared her burial could cause great consternation, I learned that the sad ordeal was over, her remains having been consigned to the deep within an hour after she expired."

Before long, a total of 20 cases of typhus had been reported, now also among the crew, and more came to light each day: "A little child who was playing with its companions, suddenly fell down and for some time was sunk in a death-like torpor from which, when she awoke, she commenced to scream violently and writhed in convulsive agony. A poor woman, who was warming a drink at the fire for her husband, also dropped down quite senseless and was borne to her berth."

Whyte described the grisly symptoms of the illness:

> ... the first symptom was generally a reeling in the head, followed by
> swelling pain, as if the head were going to burst. Next came excruciating
> pains in the bones and then swelling of the limbs commencing with the
> feet, in some cases ascending the body and again descending before it
> reached the head, stopping at the throat. The period of each stage varied in
> different patients, some of whom were covered with yellow, watery pimples
> and others with red and purple spots that turned into putrid sores.

ENTRY VISA
Passengers such as this Swedish girl,
pictured on the right with her
mother, were given a visa upon
entry into the US, granting them
unhindered passage for one year.

Due to this plague, a ban on all emigrant ships landing on US shores was already in place by the time the ship reached the US, and the brig was forced to travel to Canada. By the time she sighted Cape North, however, fifty people were sick—nearly half of those on board. Nevertheless, Whyte records that the passengers "expressed great delight at seeing land and were under the impression that they were near their destination, little knowing the extent of the gulf they had to pass and the great river to ascend." A baby was born on board on July 15, and even the tough captain was won over: "... a smile upon the face of the little innocent softened his heart and he soon caressed it with all the endearments he was in the habit of lavishing upon the canary." However, despite having sighted land, the ordeal was not over. The ship was often becalmed or had to tack in contrary winds, and on July 17 there was a terrible storm:

> ... a violent gale arose, lashing the water into tremendous waves
> which tossed us mercilessly about... The roaring wind was drowned
> by the tremendous noise of successive peals of thunder, while the
> forked lightning played about in zigzag lines and the rain descended
> in torrents... They were so buffeted about that the sick could not
> be tended and after calm was restored a woman was found dead
> in her berth...

On July 18, a local river pilot came on board and the weary passengers first met one of the people of their new home, "a heavy, stupid fellow, a Canadian, speaking a horrible patois and broken English." Finally, on July 27, after a voyage of more than nine weeks, the ship anchored at the busy quarantine station off Grosse Île in Quebec. There were many other ships at anchor, however, and the formalities of quarantine delayed their disembarkation even further, while the sick and dying remained untreated. Whyte wrote, "The poor passengers, expecting that they would be all reviewed, were dressed in their best clothes and were clean, though haggard and weak. They were greatly disappointed..."

On July 29, the ship was visited by two Canadian priests, who administered last rites to two of the dying, and baptized the newborn baby. Despite the suffering of the passengers, the priests were impressed by how clean the ship was compared to others they had seen: "In the holds of some... they were up to their ancles in filth. The wretched emigrants crowded together like cattle, and corpses remaining long unburied." It was now possible to replenish their scarce water supplies from the river, though it was polluted with the "vilest matter" of the refuse of other ships. On July 30, the captain was assured that the emigrants would be taken off the next day and they began to demolish their wooden bunks—but still no steamer appeared, so the passengers had to huddle together overnight. At last, on August 1, the surviving migrants were able to leave the ship. One man left describing the captain as "a divil... but a gintleman."

By the 1870s, the journey was usually made under steam, and while it was still uncomfortable, it had at least become relatively safe, even for the steerage passengers. In 1879, the novelist Robert Louis Stevenson traveled in such a ship, which he described with some exaggeration as "a wall of bulwark, a street of white deck-houses, an aspiring forest of spars, larger than a church, and soon to be as populous as many an incorporated town." Between 1820 and 1905, the US received more than 23 million people from Britain and all across Europe in such ships, in what proved to be the greatest migration in history.

NUMBER OF IMMIGRANTS IN THE US BY 1840:

599,000

NUMBER OF IMMIGRANTS IN THE US BY 1850:

1,713,000

China, Japan, and the Perry Expedition

IN THE EARLY 19TH CENTURY, Japan and China were inward-looking countries, cut off from the rest of the world and largely self-sufficient. Between 1839 and 1860, however, several dramatic confrontations with technologically superior Western naval powers forced them to open up to international trade and diplomatic relations. In China, merchants with the British East India Company—which had enjoyed a monopoly on all English trade to the Far East by royal grant since 1600—had begun to exploit the Chinese demand for Indian opium. As this highly profitable trade flourished, leading to opium addiction of epidemic proportions—which the British were happy to fuel to increase trade—the Chinese authorities attempted to stamp it out by banning its import, then confiscating and destroying the opium that traders continued to smuggle into the country. The British objected, and its military response was severe: it attacked or blocked Chinese ports in what became known as the first Opium War.

The Chinese authorities had initially been undaunted by the prospect of facing Britain's naval firepower. According to Yüch'ien, acting governor-general of Liang Kiang and governor of Kiangsu, although British ships were "best in sailing amidst the wind and waves," they were also "unwieldy, taking water to a great depth," which would make them vulnerable in shallow waters, and he thought that they relied too much on heavy guns. However, their belief in the superiority of their own vessels proved unfounded when, in January 1841, a British force of gunboats and steamers landed at Cheng Pi on the Canton River and succeeded in taking its fort, killing 600 men and taking 100 prisoners, with the loss of only 30 wounded. "The sides of the Barbarians' ships were often a foot thick and the cannon were mostly located inside them," one Chinese governor reported disconsolately. They also had "cloth masts and iron anchors, manufactured in such a fashion as to make their working very efficient." China's traditional wooden-hulled junks were no match for Britain's ultramodern fleet, which included steam-powered gunboats. The Chinese were defeated on both land and sea, and were forced to accept the opium imports and to cede the port of Hong Kong to the

British. Their defeat in this conflict was repeated in the second Opium War of 1856–60, and served as a warning to their even more reclusive neighbor, Japan, of the threat posed by European naval technology.

In Japan, successive emperors and their governments had imposed isolation on the country for 200 years, banning Christianity and expeling all foreign traders other than the Dutch, who were allowed to land goods at Nagasaki. Like China, Japan had a long seafaring tradition—using junks similar to those of the Chinese—but it too lagged behind the West in terms of technology, and it had no navy with which to defend itself. It did, however, have a law decreeing that any unauthorized foreign ship that came within range would come under fire. In the 1830s, the United States began to show an interest in Japan, thinking it could provide a base for their whaling ships, or at least offer refuge for their shipwrecked mariners. More importantly, it would also provide a counterpoint to British interests in China and Singapore, especially since the China tea trade was attracting US ships. And so the US decided to launch a diplomatic, naval, and surveying expedition to Japan, primarily to demand a treaty permitting trade and the opening of Japanese ports to US merchant ships.

Commodore Matthew C. Perry, one of the most experienced officers in the US Navy, was assigned to command the expedition. At first, Perry, who was nearing 60 and a distinguished, industrious serviceman with fine diplomatic skills, was not eager to take up the challenge of negotiating with the Japanese, but he soon threw himself into the task. He thought a great deal about his mission and did extensive research into Japan and its hierarchical culture, using the resources of the New York Public Library to their full extent. He discovered that most of the relevant books about this "closed country" had been written by the Dutch, who had gained access through their trade connections. So little was known about Japan and its geography that the US government purchased some sketchy maps of the Japanese coast from the Dutch for Perry for the extortionate sum of $30,000. However, even while he was en route to the Far East, Perry still harbored doubts about "the chances of immediate success in bringing this strange government to any practicable negotiation."

The four ships of Perry's fleet were outfitted in East Coast ports of the US and set sail in 1852. The transition between the old and new technologies of sail and steam was still far from complete at the time,

OPIUM AND CONFLICT
A Chinese junk explodes under fire from a steam-powered British ship during the first Opium War. China tried to stop the British East India Company from importing opium due to the effects of addiction on the population.

so the squadron consisted of the steam-powered paddle-wheelers USS *Susquehanna* and USS *Mississippi* and the sailing ships USS *Saratoga* and USS *Plymouth*. The idea was to create such an overwhelming display of force that the Japanese would think it better to negotiate with Perry than to resist his demands. The flotilla's route took them via the Cape of Good Hope, with several stops on the way, including Madeira, Mauritius, Singapore, Hong Kong, Shanghai, and the Lew Chew Islands (Okinawa) in Japan. In every port of call, Perry and his officers recorded their observations of the people, customs, and commerce they encountered, since Perry requested that "each officer of the respective ships will employ such portions of his time as can be spared from his regular duties and proper hours of relaxation, in contributing to the general mass of information which it is desirable to collect." They reached the Lew Chew Islands on May 26, 1853, where Perry issued special orders about discipline aboard ship and maintaining friendly relations with the inhabitants. He received the local dignitaries, who were given a tour of the fleet—and who showed "imperturbable gravity" until they were shown the steam engine, when "their assumed indifference was fairly overcome…" They were the first Japanese to encounter steam engines, the source of the power that allowed Americans and Europeans to dominate the world.

Perry's fleet—now dubbed the "black ships" by the Japanese because of the smoke they belched out—assembled in Tokyo Bay in July 1853. A crewman reported: "… signals were made from the Commodore, and instantly the decks were cleared for action, the guns placed in position and shotted, the ammunition arranged, the small arms made ready… in short, all the preparations made, usual before meeting an enemy." The squadron proceeded up the river with the sailing ships in tow, and the Japanese were "much puzzled, doubtless by the rapid progress of the steamers against the wind." At five in the afternoon, the four ships anchored off the city of Uraga. A gun was fired from

MATTHEW C. PERRY
A veteran of the Mexican–American War and the War of 1812, Commodore Perry played a key role in the opening up of Japan in the mid-19th century.

OPIUM USERS IN CHINA IN THE 1830s
Chinese estimate:
4,000,000

British estimate:
12,000,000

the shore and boats came out, and Japanese officials tried to board the *Saratoga*: "They attempted to climb up by the chains, but the crew was ordered to prevent them, and the sight of pikes, cutlasses, and pistols, checked them, and when they found that our officers and men were very much in earnest, they desisted from their attempts to board."

On July 14, the ships prepared for landing. "All on board the ships were ready from the earliest hour, making the necessary preparations. Steam was got up and the anchors were weighed, that the ships might be moved to a position where their guns would command the place of reception." Officers and men were selected to accompany the Commodore ashore, all who could be spared from normal ship's duties. A signal was hoisted from the flagship for 15 boats from the different ships to assemble. They were led ashore by two Japanese boats and the Americans noted the skill of the Japanese scullers, for "our sturdy oarsmen were put to their mettle to keep up with their guides." After dropping anchor, the flagship fired a salute, which echoed among the hills, and the Commodore stepped into his barge to be rowed to the land. On landing, two huge sailors stood on either side of the Commodore as his personal bodyguard. As Perry himself later described it:

The marines led the way, and the sailors following, the Commodore was duly escorted up the beach. The United States flag and the broad pennant were borne by two athletic seamen, who had been selected... on account of their stalwart proportions. Two boys, dressed for the occasion, preceded the Commodore, bearing in an envelope of scarlet cloth the boxes which contained his credentials and the President's letter.

The China Seas

The Sea of Japan, and the East and South China Sea—known collectively as the China Seas—are mostly shallow. In addition to being the world's second busiest shipping lane, the South China Sea accounts for more than eight percent of the world's fish catch. The Sea of Japan is almost entirely enclosed from the Pacific, and its low salinity and high levels of dissolved oxygen contribute to the huge quantity and diversity of its fauna. In recent years, gas and oil deposits have been discovered in the East China Sea.

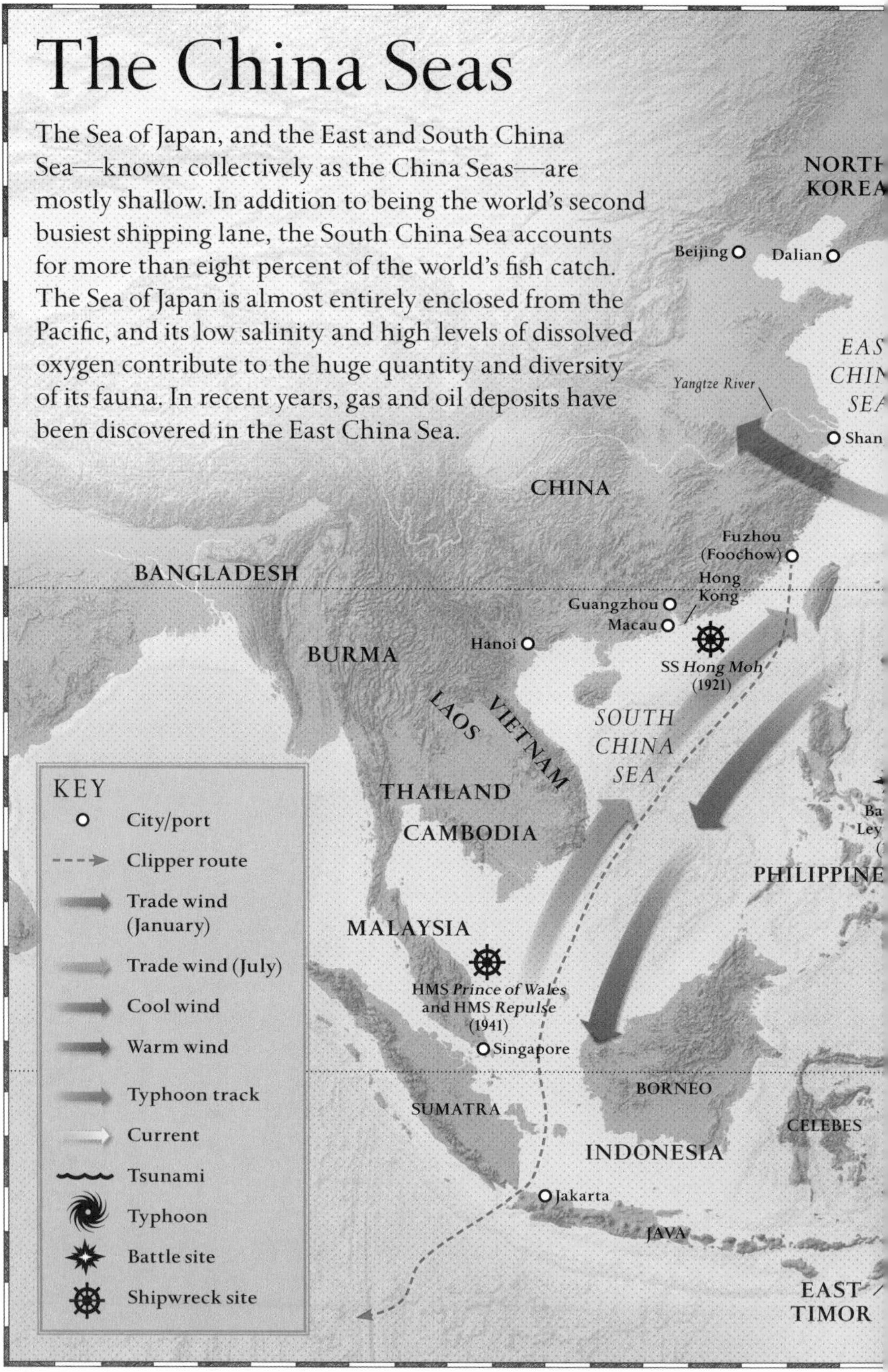

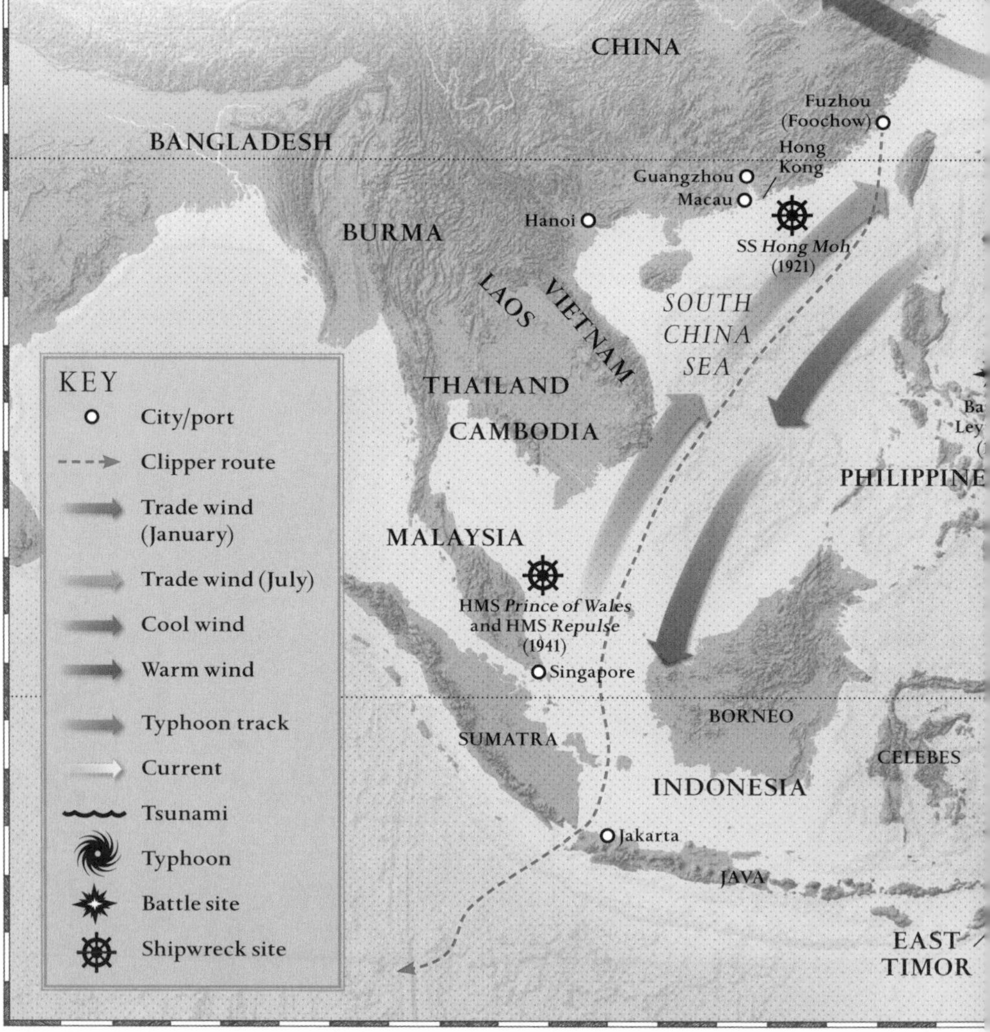
Beijing
Dalian
Yangtze River
CHINA
Fuzhou (Foochow)
BANGLADESH
Hong Kong
Guangzhou
Macau
Hanoi
BURMA
SS *Hong Moh* (1921)
LAOS
VIETNAM
SOUTH CHINA SEA
THAILAND
CAMBODIA
MALAYSIA
HMS *Prince of Wales* and HMS *Repulse* (1941)
Singapore
BORNEO
SUMATRA
CELEBES
INDONESIA
Jakarta
JAVA
EAST TIMOR
KEY
City/port
Clipper route
Trade wind (January)
Trade wind (July)
Cool wind
Warm wind
Typhoon track
Current
Tsunami
Typhoon
Battle site
Shipwreck site

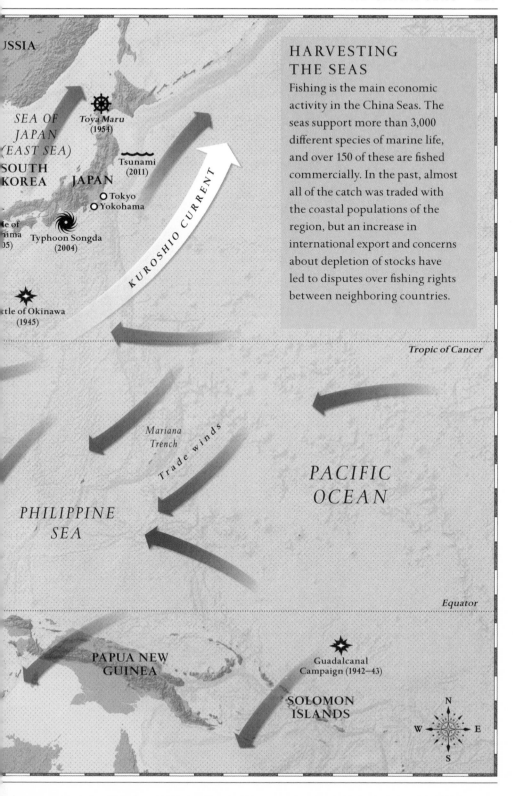

RUSSIA

SEA OF
JAPAN
(EAST SEA)

Toya Maru
(1954)

Tsunami
(2011)

SOUTH
KOREA   JAPAN

O Tokyo
O Yokohama

le of
hima
05)   Typhoon Songda
(2004)

KUROSHIO CURRENT

ttle of Okinawa
(1945)

HARVESTING THE SEAS

Fishing is the main economic activity in the China Seas. The seas support more than 3,000 different species of marine life, and over 150 of these are fished commercially. In the past, almost all of the catch was traded with the coastal populations of the region, but an increase in international export and concerns about depletion of stocks have led to disputes over fishing rights between neighboring countries.

Tropic of Cancer

Mariana
Trench

Trade winds

PACIFIC
OCEAN

PHILIPPINE
SEA

Equator

PAPUA NEW
GUINEA

Guadalcanal
Campaign (1942–43)

SOLOMON
ISLANDS

N
W   E
S

COMMODORE PERRY'S JAPANESE SQUADRON
This contemporary woodcut shows Commodore
Perry's gunships on their way to Japan in 1853. The
picture exaggerates the scale of the expedition: in
reality, only four ships set out, crewed by around
1,600 men, and carrying 144 guns.

It was the Prince of Izu who met with Perry and accepted the letter
from President Fillimore. After much ceremony, in which gifts were
exchanged, it was agreed that Perry should return in the following
spring to hear the emperor's response. And so, with several months
to spare, Perry surveyed the Japanese coast and sailed to China, where
trade with the West was flourishing. It was while he was in China,
however, that Perry learned that the Russians were also interested in
negotiating with the Japanese, so he requested more ships to sail
from America to join him. When the reinforcements arrived, the
larger force of seven ships—four sailing ships, three steamers—and
1,600 men made its way to Japan.

Some of the crews of the new ships, however, were inordinately
wild. William B. Allen, a cabin boy aboard the 18-gun sloop-of-war USS
Vandalia, describes in vivid detail the problems aboard his ship. As soon
as the *Vandalia* set sail from Philadelphia, one seaman cut his wrists to
avoid going to sea, and when the men were allowed ashore in Singapore,
Allen wrote, "the most ludicrous scenes occurred daily, some coming
aboard with faces battered and bruised and swollen in consequence of

fighting amongst themselves and old grudges…" At Macao in August there was a fight between two of the crew, one of whom later died. A seaman and a cabin boy were sentenced to a month in irons for "mutinous conduct and language," and at Whampoa in China a drunken seaman fell overboard and was never seen again. Another man fell overboard at sea in November, but was saved "more frightened than hurt." Stephen Murray was not so lucky. At the end of December, he fell from the mizzen rigging, "striking the brass railing around the poop, bending it like pewter, and breaking his thigh in the descent to the Quarter deck." John Burns died in another accident on the same day.

In spite of such problems, Perry dropped anchor in Yokohama Bay, 26 miles (42 km) from Edo, the Japanese capital, on February 13, 1854. He went ashore from the steam frigate USS *Powhatan* with much pomp and ceremony, and he and his men—even the military band – were armed to the teeth with the latest weaponry. Japanese officials awaited them on the beach:

> The Commodore now embarked from the *Powhatan* in his barge, under a salute from the *Macedonian* of seventeen guns. The Commodore, on landing, was received by the group of officers, who, falling in a line, followed him. The bands now struck up a lively tune, and the marines… presented arms as the Commodore, followed in procession by his immediate staff, his guard of fine-looking sailors and a number of his subordinate officers, proceeded up the shore. A group of richly costumed Japanese guards, or retainers, with banners, flags and streamers, were gathered on each side of the entrance to the treaty house. As the Commodore and his party passed up between these, they were met by a large number of Japanese officials who came out, and uncovering, conducted them into the interior of the building. As they entered, by a preconcerted arrangement, howitzers which had been mounted on the bows of the larger ships' boats… commenced firing in admirable order a salute of twenty-one guns in honour of the emperor, which were succeeded by a salute of seventeen for… the high commissioner, and the hoisting of the Japanese striped flag from the masthead of the steamer *Powhatan* in the bay.

The emperor had given his answer: he would agree to some, but not all of the American demands. Perry then tried to convince the Japanese how both China and the US had benefited from trade. It took considerable negotiation and further displays of military might to

FIRST LANDING
Commodore Perry arrives in Japan on July 8, 1853. The following year the two countries signed the Treaty of Kanagawa, ending centuries of Japanese isolation.

make the Japanese agree to everything on the table, but they finally relented and signed the Treaty of Kanagawa on March 31, 1854. Perry had succeeded in his basic aims: the Japanese agreed to open the ports of Shimoda and Hakodate to American ships and to assist US mariners if they were shipwrecked, rather than imprisoning them. It was only a start, but the negotiations showed the Japanese how much they stood to gain by entering into trade with the modern world. Indeed, Japan's encounter with America galvanized the country into a program of modernization that soon had it competing with and even triumphing over western powers. For it would not be forgotten that the Treaty of Kanagawa had been signed under duress—a fact that made it a matter of honor for the Japanese to defeat the West at its own game, and ultimately to avenge its humiliation.

After a civil war, the Japanese founded a modern navy in 1872. They bought ships from Britain, absorbed all the methods of the European navies, and merged them with Samurai tradition. The

new navy was first tested in 1894, when a dozen Japanese ships met a similar force of Chinese vessels off the Yalu River in the north of Korea; within five hours, five Chinese ships had been sunk, leaving the remainder at the mercy of the Japanese, all of whose ships had survived. A similar drama played out on May 27, 1905, when the Russian fleet faced the Japanese navy off the island of Tsushima (see p.281). In one of the most decisive battles in the age of steam, the Russians were all but annihilated. The Battle of Tsushima, as it became known, was the first real conflict between modern, armor-plated warships with big, rifled guns, and as such it was carefully studied by all the great navies of the world. It showed that battles could be fought at far greater ranges than had previously been possible, and that Europeans could be defeated by a modernized Asian power. The Perry expedition had unleashed forces far beyond America's control—a fact that was finally visited on the West when Japanese forces destroyed the US naval base in Pearl Harbor in 1941 (see p.318).

The Birth of Oceanography

T HE STAGECOACH LEAVING Lancaster, Ohio, in the United States, was overcrowded on the evening of October 17, 1839, but the driver broke the rules and allowed three passengers to sit on the roof. As a naval officer and Southern gentleman, 33-year-old Lieutenant Matthew F. Maury felt obliged to give up his seat to a lady, and perched on top of the coach. It was a dark night, and some way into the journey the stagecoach overturned, flinging Maury onto the ground. Immediately he felt an intense pain in his right leg, and he knew that his seagoing career was over. It was a devastating moment for a seaman in the prime of his life, but it was thanks to Maury becoming desk-bound that he embarked on work that changed our view of the oceans. At the time, the common view was that the oceans were little more than voids that had to be crossed to get from one place to another— even the naturalist Charles Darwin had called them "a tedious waste, a desert of water" on his voyage around the world in the early 1830s. Maury, however, saw them as dynamic systems that should be studied in their own right, and his efforts gave birth to a new branch of scholarship—the science of oceanography.

Maury's studies began when, after a long convalescence, he was appointed Superintendent of the Depot of Charts and Instruments in Washington, DC. He started by gathering information from various captains, promising that "if each one would agree to cooperate in a general plan of observations at sea, and would send regularly, at the end of every cruise, an abstract log of their voyage to the National Observatory at Washington, he should, for so doing, be furnished free of cost, with a copy of the charts and sailing directions that might be founded upon those observations." He approached Commodore William Crane, the chief of the Bureau of Ordnance and Hydrography, who "at once appreciated the importance of the undertaking, and entered... most heartily into the spirit of it." Maury prepared a circular letter to American captains, "requesting them to furnish this office with all kinds of information touching navigation, that might come in their way." There was no response at first, so Maury "then went to the

MINIATURE SEXTANT
Developed by Edward Troughton around 1800, the
pocket sextant was widely used by scientists at sea. This
example belonged to the naturalist Charles Darwin.

old log books of the Navy, and obtained
authority to construct from the materials
afforded by them, a set of 'Wind and Current
Charts.'" However, not many log books were
available, and Maury faced an uphill task:

> I then brought the subject to the notice of the men of science
> of the country, with the view of procuring their countenance to the
> work; and, in papers read on the currents of the sea before the National
> Institute, and the Association of American Geologists and Naturalists,
> now the American Association, I explained the meagre state of our
> information with regard to the currents of the sea, urged the value of
> what was locked up in the old sea chests of mariners, and pressed the
> importance to science, commerce, and navigation, of the information
> which navigators might give concerning the phenomena of the ocean.

Data soon began to flow in, although the coverage was uneven:

> In some districts I have obtained as many as 1800 observations for a single
> month; whereas, in another month in a neighboring district, I have not
> been enabled to obtain a single observation; such is liable to be the case as
> long as some parts of the ocean, as there must be, are frequented more than
> other parts, or as long as crops come to market at different periods of the
> year, and commerce has its seasons of annually recurring activity...

Where large numbers of log books were available, he selected them at
random, wondering:

> Are the observations sufficiently numerous to afford the data for a fair
> average? The answer in this case depends upon the opinion of him who
> undertakes to reply; but to be sure of erring on the right side, if err I
> must, I have aimed to get at least, on the average, 100 observations for
> every month in every district. This is my aim; but practically I have
> found it difficult to accomplish it...

Through his research he soon identified a major error in the route from the East Coast of the United States south to Rio de Janeiro in Brazil. Mariners had long believed it was necessary to make a wide detour to the east to avoid dangers off the Brazilian coast, thus running into the doldrums and often losing weeks off the voyage. Maury was able to show that there were favorable currents close inshore off Cape St. Roque and told his readers: "Stand boldly on, and if need be, tack and work by under the land." In 1848, Captain Jackson of Baltimore proved that the route was viable and returned 35 days earlier than expected.

In 1847, Maury published the first of his Wind and Current Charts—sheet 1 of the North Atlantic. His survey of that ocean was complete by 1849, and was followed by sheets on the South Atlantic, the Indian Ocean, and the Pacific over the next seven years. A typical chart featured arrows to indicate the direction of the wind in a particular month, with the width of the arrow showing how much the wind might vary. Other charts were divided into 5-inch (13-cm) squares, with circles indicating how much the wind blew from each direction that month. There were also charts showing the temperature of the ocean, which was essential to finding the Gulf Stream. Maury explained how useful the charts could be: "Perhaps it might be the first voyage of a young navigator... If so, there would be the wind and current chart. It would spread out before him the track of a thousand vessels that had preceded him... Such a chart... would show him... the experience also of each master as to the winds and currents by the way, the temperature of the ocean, and the variation of the needle."

It was claimed that by using the charts and directions, the voyage from New York to California would take 135 days instead of 183. The outward journey from England to Australia could be reduced from 124 days to just 97, and the return passage from 124 days to 67. In 1853, in a new spirit of cooperation, the major maritime nations held a conference, and agreed to record further data using Maury's methods.

MATTHEW F. MAURY
Nicknamed the "Pathfinder of the Seas," Matthew Fontaine Maury was the world's first oceanographer.

"There is no calling of men that has done more for philosophy than the mariner"

MATTHEW F. MAURY

Until the 1840s, there had been no real interest in measuring the depth of the world's oceans. Seamen obviously needed to know if they were about to go aground in shallow water, and when approaching Europe they often cast the lead (measured the depth of the water using a lead line) to determine when they were in "soundings" (shallow water) or on the continental shelf. Otherwise, they did not need to know exactly how much water lay beneath them. This changed with the invention of the telegraph. On land, the development of electricity had led to telegraph lines being set up on both sides of the Atlantic in 1837. At first, these were used mainly by railroad networks which communicated using the code developed by Samuel B. Morse. The first underwater cable was laid across the English Channel in 1851, but in the US, Cyrus Field was promoting the installation of a much longer cable—right across the Atlantic Ocean. This attracted the attention of Maury, who wrote about the area between Newfoundland and Ireland in 1854:

> ... the bottom of the sea... is a plateau, which seems to have been placed there especially for the purpose of holding the wires of a submarine telegraph, and of keeping them out of harm's way. It is neither too deep nor too shallow; yet it is so deep that the wires but once landed, will remain for ever beyond the reach of vessels' anchors, icebergs, and drifts of any kind.

The first Atlantic cable was laid in 1858 but it soon failed, due to faulty insulation. In 1866, Brunel's *Great Eastern* was adapted to carry a single length of cable that could extend across the ocean. The second attempt to lay the cable was successful, and from July that year, it was possible to communicate across the Atlantic in seconds rather than weeks.

The success of his Wind and Current Charts inspired Maury to plan a much larger project. There were already many pilot books that gave sailing directions for various ports and seas, and sometimes expanded into the history, culture, geography, and biology of the areas concerned.

CABLE REPAIRS AT SEA
Men aboard the *Great Eastern* attempt to repair a damaged transatlantic cable in 1866. From 1865 to 1872, the ship laid four transatlantic telegraph cables (including the first, unsuccessful one), and one between Aden and Bombay.

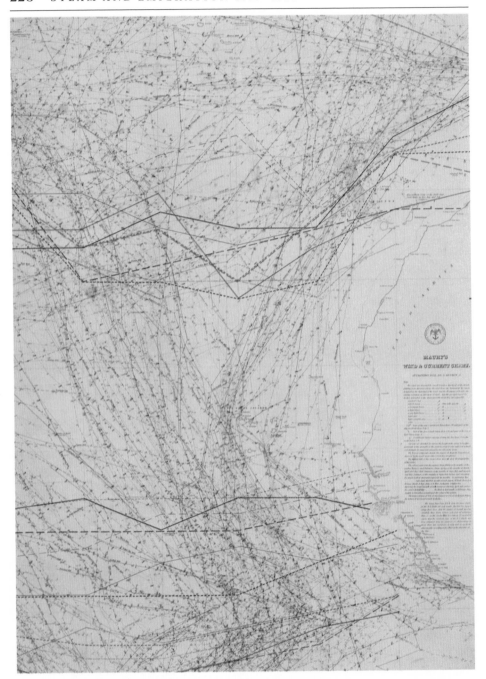

M. F. MAURY'S WIND AND CURRENT CHART
This astonishingly complex collection of data
revolutionized both scientific knowledge of the
oceans, and the ability of ships' captains to
navigate them.

HMS *CHALLENGER*
Frontispiece from the journal of HMS *Challenger*, the ship sent on the first ever dedicated voyage of marine research and discovery.

Maury, however, was the first to tackle the subject of the oceans as a whole, and in *The Physical Geography of the Sea* he went further than anyone else in trying to generalize and theorize about them. He had some success in the first of these endeavors, but considerably less in the second. His book was first published in 1855, and was soon translated into many languages, but it did contain some serious errors. Maury refused to believe that the surface currents of the oceans were caused by winds. He was obsessed by the Gulf Stream and listed theories about its cause, but did not, unfortunately, advocate for the correct one—that it was the outflow of warm water from the Gulf of Mexico.

On the other side of the Atlantic, European scientists were taking an intense interest in the fruits of Maury's labors. Engineers were planning to lay cables across more of the world's oceans, and the long-standing belief that nothing could live in more than 300 fathoms of water was being challenged. An around-the-world voyage was promoted by Edinburgh University and the Royal Society of London to put Britain at the forefront of ocean exploration. The expedition was lent the steam frigate HMS *Challenger* by the Admiralty, with all but two of her 18 guns taken out, and outfitted with laboratories and the latest scientific instruments. Captain George Nares, a well-known writer on seamanship, was put in charge of the vessel, while Professor C. Wyville Thomson headed the scientific department of six. The voyage began in rough weather in December 1872, and over the next four years the ship toured the Atlantic and the Pacific, and visited the Southern Ocean, though not the Indian Ocean.

The voyage led to the publication of 50 volumes of reports, which proved that there was life at the bottom of the oceans, revealed the shapes of the deep basins beyond the Atlantic, and made contributions to many sciences, including hydrography, meteorology, and geology as well as botany and zoology. It was the true beginning of the science of oceanography—a term that was invented to describe the work of the scientists involved.

Saving Lives at Sea

IN THE MID-19TH CENTURY, being a sailor was still a dangerous business. Seafaring had the highest mortality rate of any profession, with one in five mariners dying at sea; merchant ships were often recklessly overloaded, or were in such poor condition that they were barely seaworthy. It was claimed that corrupt ship owners could over-insure their vessels, which would then be worth more sunk than afloat—in some cases, it was felt, with little concern for the lives of their crews. What was needed was a set of internationally binding safety regulations that gave rights to mariners and limited the amount of cargo a ship could carry—and no one fought harder to establish this than British politician and social reformer Samuel Plimsoll.

Plimsoll was severely critical of the 1871 Merchant Shipping Act, which made it a criminal offence for seamen to refuse to board a ship, even if it was known that the vessel was unseaworthy, and he proposed a new Merchant Shipping Bill to redress the situation. However, on July 22, 1875, the British Prime Minister, Benjamin Disraeli, addressed the House of Commons to say that the bill would have to be dropped, due to a crowded program of reform. After containing himself for several hours, Plimsoll then beseeched the House, "I earnestly entreat the right hon. Gentleman at the head of Her Majesty's Government not to consign some thousands of living human beings to undeserved and miserable death." He railed against "shipowners of murderous tendencies outside the House, and who are immediately and amply represented inside the House..." and reminded the House that "every winter, hundreds and hundreds of brave men are sent to death, their wives are made widows and their children are made orphans, in order that a few speculative scoundrels, in whose hearts there is neither the love of God nor the fear of God, may make unhallowed gains." When the members called on him to name names, he mentioned Edward Bates, the Member for Plymouth, and claimed; "I am determined to unmask the villains who send to death and destruction—" at which his words were lost in a storm of voices, including repeated cries of "Order!" The speaker intervened to ask if he had used the word "villains" to refer to members of the House, and Plimsoll replied, "I did, Sir, and I do not mean to withdraw it." This was considered "altogether un-Parliamentary," but Plimsoll refused to apologize

SAMUEL PLIMSOLL
British politician Samuel Plimsoll fought tirelessly to improve the lives of seamen, and saw to the passing of legislation that reduced the use of unseaworthy vessels.

and was politely asked to leave the chamber. On the following day, *The Times* commented, "… when we remember the years Mr. Plimsoll has laboured at the subject, and the frenzy of grief he must have felt when he saw another year passing fruitlessly away, we are ready to pardon his passionate outbreak the moment he expresses his regret at his want of self-command."

Plimsoll's detractors pointed out that numerous developments had taken place over the previous 60 years to make seafaring safer—and it was true that new lighthouses had been built (including the Bell Rock off the east coast of Scotland in 1810, and Skerryvore to the west in 1844) and that they had been revolutionized when they had begun to incorporate a new and far more powerful lens developed by French physicist Augustin-Jean Fresnel in 1822. Likewise, Henry Greathead and others had designed lifeboats with built-in cork buoyancy, and the National Institution for

> "… every winter, hundreds and hundreds of brave men are sent to death, their wives are made widows and their children are made orphans"
>
> **SAMUEL PLIMSOLL**

the Preservation of Life from Shipwreck (the forerunner of the Royal National Lifeboat Institution) had been set up in Britain in 1824. The United States Life Saving Service had been formed in 1848, and France had founded the Société Centrale de Sauvetage des Naufragés in 1865. Examinations were also being introduced for entry onto merchant ships. On being examined for Mate in 1883, novelist Joseph Conrad wrote, "... the scheme of the test he was applying to me was... the sort of passage I would not wish to my bitterest enemy. That imaginary ship seemed to labour under a most comprehensive curse."

Despite these developments, however, safety at sea had never been given the proper legal attention, and it seemed that only a major disaster involving a high-profile ship would give the subject the hearing it deserved. Public interest in the issue had flared in 1838 when Grace Darling, the daughter of a British lighthouse keeper, used a rowing boat to rescue passengers from the stricken *Forfarshire* off northeast England. But in 1859, there was a shipwreck that shocked the public more than any other, and encouraged reformers such as Plimsoll to fight even harder for their cause.

The *Royal Charter* was an unusual ship, with an iron hull, the lines of a clipper, and a 200-horsepower steam engine for use in calms. She was built for Gibbs, Bright and Company by William Patterson, who had also built the *Great Britain* (see p.200). Though slightly smaller, the *Royal Charter* was intended to follow up the success of the *Great Britain* on the Australia run. The frantic days of the gold rush were over by the time she entered service in 1855, but she soon found a lucrative market transporting prospectors returning with their fortunes. She left Melbourne in August 1859, carrying 511 passengers and crew. She made a fast passage, and 58 days later, on October 24, she anchored at Queenstown in Ireland to discharge a small number of passengers by pilot boat. Midshipman Frederick Foster took the chance to post a hurried letter to his parents: "You may expect me and one or two friends at your house Tuesday or Wednesday night, so be prepared. How is Alice? Remember me kindly to her and all."

The ship proceeded up the Irish Sea toward Liverpool. However, unknown to its passengers and crew, around 600 miles (960 km) away, off Cape Finisterre in France, local sailors had started to notice especially strong winds. These soon brewed into a powerful storm, which passed north-northeast and deepened, with winds reaching

speeds of 50–100 mph (80–160 kph) as the storm hit the English
Channel. Captain Thomas Taylor of the *Royal Charter*, meanwhile, had
no way of knowing this, and was making the fastest speed he could to
the end of the voyage—straight into the gathering storm. On the
afternoon of the 25th, passengers and crew crowded the decks to view
the *Great Eastern*, by far the largest ship of the day, at anchor off
Holyhead on the island of Anglesea. A *Times* correspondent on board
the *Royal Charter* described the moment the storm arrived:

> The wind gradually freshened during the afternoon, though not very
> much, till over the mountain came a thin black haze, which rose into
> the air with ominous rapidity and overspread the sky. The sea and wind
> kept rising as the glass fell, and before eight it blew a heavy gale from the
> eastward, with fierce squalls and storms of rain. As night wore on, the
> wind increased and it came in fearful gusts, tearing away among spars
> and rigging with a hoarse sustained roar that was awful to listen to...

Anxious to complete the voyage, and perhaps a little complacent about
the strength of his iron hull, Captain Taylor pressed on past the Skerries
off the northwest corner of Anglesea in Wales, by which time some of
the passengers were already becoming nervous. At about 9 pm, the ship

THE WRECK OF THE *ROYAL CHARTER*
The *Royal Charter* was one of numerous ships wrecked by the
savage storm of 1859, which was later named in honor of it.
Hundreds of passengers and crew lost their lives.

was encountering very strong winds; Taylor turned her inshore off the north coast, but the wind direction shifted to the east-northeast and she was battered by the gales. She dropped anchor, but even a hundred fathoms of chain on the rocky seabed combined with the power of the engine could not stop the ship from being driven slowly backward toward the coast. Then, at 1:30 am, the port chain cable snapped near the hawse hole where it exited the ship. The starboard anchor was not enough to hold the ship steady, and each gust of wind drove her relentlessly toward the shore. The crew cut away the masts and rigging to try and prevent further drift, but to no avail. With a terrible grinding of metal, the ship crashed onto the rocks at Moelfre in Anglesea around 7 am.

The terrified passengers assembled on deck. Some of the prospectors were weighed down with as much of their gold as they could stuff into their pockets, and many of the women "dressed in great haste and agitation" so that "their clothes had become mixed together." They began to fear the worst, and chaos broke loose: "Nothing but confusion on deck, fore and aft passengers, saloon, cabin, and steerage all mixed together, fathers and mothers clasping their children in their arms, wives clinging to their husbands, shrieking and crying, 'Save me, save me' 'Don't leave me.'" Captain Taylor tried to calm them over the noise of the wind: "Now, ladies, you need not be afraid. We are on a sandy beach, and embedded in the sand. We are not ten paces from the shore, and the tide will leave us dry, and in ten minutes we will all be safe." But having spent two months away at sea, he had miscalculated the tide: it was actually rising, and was beginning to swamp the listing ship. Lifeboats were useless in these circumstances: "the sea was so rough that no boat could have lasted five minutes in it." The *Royal Charter*'s crew sought more drastic measures. Seaman Joseph Rogers was later described as "a short dark set man very black hair and beard but the very type of an English sailor"—though he was actually Maltese, and his real name was Joie Rodriguez. Unlike most British sailors, he

JOSEPH ROGERS
The Maltese hero of the *Royal Charter* disaster was praised for his bravery in national newspapers. His actions helped save 31 lives.

was a good swimmer. He tied one end of a rope around his waist and lowered himself into the raging waters. As he modestly recounted later, "The sea between the ship and the rocks was very heavy. I partly swam and partly was washed ashore. I was three times washed back to the ship." He was badly injured by the battering of the waves, but successfully reached shore and was dragged in by local villagers, who then set up a hawser between the shore and the ship. They slung a boatswain's chair—a harness used to haul sailors up and down the mast—under the rope, and one by one began to pull the soaking passengers slowly ashore. Others tried to swim for the shore, and some of the prospectors were dragged under the water by the weight of gold in their pockets. Eventually the ship could take no more punishment from the wind and waves and "broke like the snapping of a tobacco stump." The seas surged over the ruins of the ship and washed away all the passengers and crew who were still on board.

Just 18 out of the hundreds of passengers survived, plus five out of the 11 riggers, and 18 men from the 100-strong crew. No officers survived, nor any women or children. Charles Dickens visited the scene two months later and met the local vicar, the Reverend Stephen Hughes. He had buried 145 bodies, "when not identified, in graves containing four each... Several bodies had been exhumed from the graves of four, as relatives had come from a distance and seen his register; and, when recognised, these have been reburied in private graves." Local craftsmen had worked night and day, even on Sunday, to produce enough coffins, and residents had feared that there was not enough room in the cemetery to bury them.

Very few storms have names. Perhaps the most famous is the Trafalgar storm, which sank many of Nelson's prizes after the battle. The *Royal Charter* storm, as it became known, joined that select group: more than 200 other ships were lost or damaged in that storm, and some 800 lives lost, more than half of them in the *Royal Charter* alone. In the age of railroads, telegraph, and newspapers, news of the disaster traveled quickly and became a subject of national mourning. At the time, the forerunner of the British Meteorological Office was a four-man team headed by Robert FitzRoy, who had the title of Meteorological Statist to the Board of Trade. As a result of the disaster, FitzRoy set up barometers in fishing ports and arranged for storm signals to be erected on

FRESNEL LENS
Known as the stepped Fresnel lens, this optical system for lighthouses projects a sweeping parallel beam of light to warn shipping of hazards—each lighthouse has a different light pattern.

headlands. Using data sent by telegraph around the coast, he prepared "synoptic charts" of the weather, and set up the world's first gale warning system.

Such was the state of the world's shipping when Samuel Plimsoll tried to pass legislation to secure the safety of ships. His bill was rejected by Disraeli in 1875, but the following year Disraeli saw how badly he had misjudged the situation. It is true that Plimsoll was overemotional, and that his book, *Our Seamen*, was inaccurate and misleading in places—and that he singularly failed to prove his theory of a conspiracy of insurers and owners outfitting "coffin ships" for their mutual profit—but he had became a popular hero—"the seaman's friend," as he was known—and it was thanks to his arguments that a new Merchant Shipping Act was passed in 1876. This new act compelled British ship owners to paint a series of lines on their ships, collectively called the Plimsoll Line, indicating the maximum depths at which they could float in various conditions. In 1906, this law was extended to include all foreign ships visiting British ports, and in 1930 the International Load Line Convention was ratified by 54 nations, finally creating international agreement on the application of load line regulations. The rights of seamen were also recognized in the act of 1876, and another amendment in 1877 established rules regarding their engagement by shipowners and their shipboard accommodation.

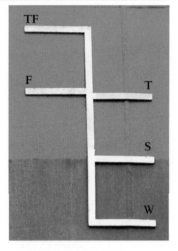

THE PLIMSOLL LINE
Samuel Plimsoll's groundbreaking safety regulation to prevent overloading in ships is still in use today. From top to bottom, the markers are for tropical freshwater, freshwater, tropical seawater, summer seawater, and winter seawater respectively.

But safety at sea is never absolute, and there were many gaps in the regulations. One of the most striking of these, it turned out, was the outdated rule that related the capacity of a ship's lifeboats to tonnage rather than the number of passengers. That would play a major part in the heavy loss of life when the *Titanic* sank in 1912, an event that came to overshadow the *Royal Charter* as the most famous maritime disaster in history.

RMS *TITANIC*
In the most famous sea disaster of all time, the *Titanic* sinks slowly after hitting an iceberg. She was drastically underequipped with lifeboats as per the regulations of the time, resulting in the loss of 1,502 lives.

The *Alabama* and America at Sea

THE UNNAMED "SHIP NO.290" had often aroused suspicion as her elegant hull was being built in the Laird Brothers' Yard, just across the River Mersey from Liverpool in England. Supposedly a civilian ship, she had fine lines, a sailing rig, a powerful 600-horsepower steam engine, and a screw propeller that could be raised for sailing and lowered for steaming, but there was absolutely no sign of any passenger or cargo accommodation. Had anyone chosen to speculate, there was an obvious customer for such a sleek, fast vessel—the southern "slave states" of America, known as the Confederacy, that were in rebellion at the time against the United States of America, having seceded from the Union in 1861. The British authorities could not allow a warship to be built openly for a rebel government, but she had no obvious signs of any armament, so there was no clear argument for halting her construction.

On July 29, 1862, the ship left the Mersey, supposedly for a trial run, carrying a party of men and women who expected to return with her to the river that night. But businessman and Confederate secret agent James D. Bulloch, who had orchestrated the construction of the mysterious ship, had other plans. In a discreet maneuver, a tug came alongside and quietly took the passengers away, and the ship—which was soon named the CSS *Alabama*—set sail for the Azores. There she met the Confederate ship, the CSS *Bahama*, which was carrying the *Alabama*'s officers, guns, and military stores, and a team of engineers.

Over the next few days, the crew set furiously to work transforming the ship. Lieutenant Arthur Sinclair noted: "The carpenter and mates assisted by the engineers were measuring and putting down the 'circles' for the two pivot-guns. The boatswain and mates fitting train and side-tackles to the broadside guns. Gunner stowing the magazine, shot and shell lockers. Sailmaker looking after his spare sails, and seeing them safely stored in the sailroom." At last, on August 24, the ship took its final form—a heavily armed Confederate warship, complete with a formidable 110-pounder rifled cannon as its main armament. Captain Raphael Semmes took his place at the stern with his officers grouped around him, wearing the gray uniforms of the Confederacy with "a redundancy of gold lace."

The fierce, resolute, impressively learned Semmes was a 53-year-old Marylander who had served in the United States Navy before taking up international law—an unusual accomplishment for a sea captain, but one he found useful in deciding which ships he was entitled to capture and destroy. Like his fellow Confederate, the oceanographer M. F. Maury (see pp.222–29), he studied the geography and trade routes of the oceans in great detail, which made it easier for him both to track down enemy ships and to stay out of danger. He was bitterly opposed to the "Northern vandals" who were invading his home state, and was determined to use his new vessel to scourge Union shipping. He read his commission from President Davis, hoisted the Confederate flag, and tried to persuade the British crew of the *Alabama* to enlist in the service of the Confederacy. His rousing speech was sweetened by an offer of double the Royal Naval rate of pay (in gold), as well as the usual ration of grog. Eighty-five of the sailors agreed, and the *Alabama* entered service as a Confederate warship. Semmes was ready to attack "Northern commerce on the high seas with a vigor and relentlessness that seemed absolutely malignant…"

CAPTAIN RAPHAEL SEMMES ON BOARD THE CSS *ALABAMA*
Semmes ran a strictly disciplined ship, and his officers (including First Lieutenant John Kell, behind him) were of high quality.

"The sailor is as improvident, and incapable of self-government as a child"

CAPTAIN RAPHAEL SEMMES

CIVIL WAR RECRUITMENT POSTER
The Virginia Coast Guard needed sailors to man their ships during the Civil War. Their role included transporting supplies and troops to Union garrisons.

The *Alabama* was one of a dozen Confederate ships designed to counter the northern states' dominance of the seas by raiding their commerce. Before the war, the US had the second largest merchant fleet in the world after Britain, at six million tons. The southerners hoped that by inflicting huge losses on the northern Yankee fleet, the profit-conscious Yankees could be deterred from attempting to reconquer the rebel states. The *Alabama* was quick to enter the fray. Semmes remained in the Azores after commissioning, and soon claimed his first victim— the US whaling ship *Ocmulgee* of Massachusetts, whose captain had mistaken the *Alabama* for a Union gunboat. By the time Semmes had taken the *Ocmulgee* and captured its crew, it was too dark to burn the ship without attracting attention; he waited until morning, then set the helpless whaler ablaze and went on his way. He ordered that the prisoners of his early captures be chained, much to the indignation of their captains, but he later relented and became renowned for his chivalrous treatment of prisoners. After a few more successful captures, he headed west across the ocean toward New York, gaining a fearsome reputation en route.

The *Alabama*'s officers laughed at the exaggerated reports of their plundering that appeared in northern newspapers, although it was true that the ships they captured (the "prizes") were their chief source of supplies. Boarders even took requests for items of loot: "One would want a pocket-knife, another a pipe, some light reading-matter..." Semmes's officers were of very high quality, but his crew was a mixed bunch of various nationalities, including "a large sprinkling of Yankee tars"—he supplemented his original crew with recruits from the ships he defeated. A rowdy bunch, at one stage they had a "quasi-mutiny" due to excessive drinking, and they often deserted when allowed ashore. Semmes was a fierce disciplinarian and wrote,

"Nothing demoralises a crew so much as frequent visits to port. The sailor is as improvident, and incapable of self-government as a child." Some of the enemy crews were enlisted in the *Alabama*, including a slave boy who became a wardroom servant. According to Semmes, there was "that sympathy of master and servant, which our ruder people of the North find it so impossible to comprehend."

In October, the *Alabama* faced a cyclone, which Semmes recorded in great detail, and early in 1863 she came up against Union steamer the USS *Hatteras* off the coast of Texas. The Union commander, Captain H.C. Blake, wrote an account of the battle:

> ... I had gained a distance of but thirty yards from her. At this stage, musket and pistol shots were exchanged. The firing continued with great vigor on both sides. At length a shell entered amidships in the hold, setting fire to it, and, at the same instant... a shell passed through the sick bay, exploding in an adjoining compartment, also producing fire. Another entered the cylinder, filling the engine-room and deck with steam, and depriving me of my power to manoeuvre the vessel...

The *Hatteras* had become "a hopeless wreck upon the waters" and soon sank. By the middle of 1864, after nearly two years of voyaging and plundering in the Atlantic, the Indian Ocean, around the Cape of

PIVOT GUN
The *Alabama* and many other warships of the era used heavy guns mounted on pivots, to allow the guns to aim in different directions.

ATTACKING THE *ALABAMA*
Union sloop-of-war the *Kearsarge*'s superior
gunnery swiftly brought the *Alabama*'s dominance
of shipping routes to an end when they clashed off
Cherbourg in France.

Good Hope, and off the coast of Brazil, the *Alabama* was beginning to
show signs of strain. Semmes commented: "Her boilers were burned
out, and her machinery was sadly in want of repairs... We therefore
set our course for Europe, and on the 11th of June 1864, entered the
port of Cherbourg, and applied for permission to go into dock."

Captain John A. Winslow, in command of the Union screw sloop the
USS *Kearsarge*, was off Holland in pursuit of the *Alabama* when a
message arrived informing him of her location. He set sail
immediately, and the *Kearsarge* arrived off Cherbourg within a day.
Semmes' Confederate flag could be seen flying over the breakwater,
and after some diplomatic maneuvering, the *Alabama* came out to
fight. As battle commenced, the two ships circled each other, trying
to rake one another with cannon fire, all the while drifting westward
with the tide. The surgeon of the *Kearsarge* described the action:

> The firing of the *Alabama* was rapid and wild, getting better near the
> close; that of the *Kearsarge* was deliberate, accurate, and almost from the
> beginning productive of dismay, destruction, and death. The *Kearsarge*
> gunners had been cautioned against firing without direct aim, and had
> been advised to point the heavy guns below rather than above the water-
> line, and to clear the deck of the enemy with the lighter ones.

Under the thunderous onslaught of the *Kearsarge's* cannon fire, the *Alabama* began to sink. She had fired almost twice as much shot as her enemy, but the Union ship's more accurate gunnery won the day. As his ship went down, the injured Semmes threw his sword into the sea, preventing it from becoming a trophy for the Union captain. Most of the *Alabama's* crew were rescued by the *Kearsarge*, but some, including Semmes, were picked up by a passing British yacht, the *Deerhound*, and taken to safety in England.

Over the course of her career, the *Alabama* had captured an astonishing 66 Union ships, and terrified many more, but her efforts were not enough to win the war, and the Confederate armies surrendered in April 1865. She did, however, do permanent damage to the US merchant marine, which never regained the momentum of the years before 1861. The *Alabama* was also the subject of a long legal dispute between the US and the British government, which had allowed her to be built. The issue was eventually settled by Britain paying the US government $15.5 million. Semmes himself, after much legal and political wrangling, was released at the end of the war. Despite his controversial military career, he went on to work in America as a university professor, a newspaper editor, and a county judge.

The US Navy declined in power and prestige for some years after the Civil War, one congressman describing it in 1883 as "An alphabet of floating washtubs." It revived in the 1890s, partly under the influence of Captain A.T. Mahan, an American admirer of British sea power, who gained worldwide fame with his book, *The Influence of Sea Power on History, 1660–1783*. He showed how naval strength had been essential to Britain's rise from being a divided island on the fringes of Europe to being a global power, and advocated similar policies for the US. By 1898, the nation had a reasonably strong fleet of a dozen modern battleships. This expanded substantially, and in 1907 President Theodore Roosevelt sent a fleet of 16 battleships on a high-profile voyage to circumnavigate the world. This Great White Fleet, as it was called, demonstrated above all else that American sea power was now a global force.

CREW OF THE USS *KEARSARGE*
Union captain John A. Winslow's crew was
just as rowdy—and as mutinous—as its
counterparts on the *Alabama*. Nevertheless, 17
of them were awarded the Medal of Honor for
bravery in the battle between the two ships.

The Great Tea Race

IN SEPTEMBER 1866, the clipper ship the *Ariel* reached the English Channel with a cargo of tea a mere 99 days after leaving Foochow in China—an astonishing voyage of around 15,000 miles (24,000 km). According to her proud captain, John Keay, the ship was "a perfect beauty to every nautical man who ever saw her," with "symmetrical grace and proportion of hull, spars, rigging and finish." She was built for speed rather than beauty, however, and Keay was anxious to get his valuable cargo of tea unloaded onto the dock.

The *Ariel* was sweeping toward the finish of one of the most fiercely contested sailing races of all time, and her rivals were close behind. The clippers—incredibly fast merchant sailing ships with long, narrow hulls, elegant lines, and striking square-rigged sails—were competing to be the first to carry that year's crop of tea from China to London; the winner would secure the best prices for his cargo, as well as a prize and a huge amount of prestige. The tea races, as they were known, grew out of the demand for fresh tea from China, and every year for about 30 years the epic race across the oceans between the swift, graceful clipper ships captured the attention of the British public. In London, gamblers placed large bets on the outcome, national newspapers waited eagerly to report the results, and enthusiastic crowds gathered at the docks to cheer the winning ship.

The 1866 tea race was exceptionally close because the design of tea clippers had been virtually perfected during the preceding 25 years. The origins of the clipper went back to 1817, when ship owners started a "fast packet service" of sailing ships—the Black Ball Line—to carry mail quickly between Liverpool and New York. In the United States, fast merchant sailing ships built on the East Coast in the 1840s were given the name "Baltimore clippers" because of the way in which they "clipped" time off the miles. Coincidentally, early clippers were built in Scotland at around the same time. The clippers had narrow, streamlined hulls, and their sails were square-rigged, designed to sail with the trade winds behind them, rather than tacking into the wind. The *Ariel* could fly up to a total of 30 sails—over 26,000 sq ft (2,400 sq m) of billowing canvas—in good

SHIPS OF THE BLACK BALL LINE
Precursors to the clipper ships, these fast sailing ships
delivered mail across the Atlantic on a route known as
the Black Ball Line in the first half of the 19th century.

weather conditions. The clippers' decks were low since they did
not carry guns, and passenger comfort was usually of secondary
concern to sheer speed.

Tea, which had been a luxury in 18th-century Britain, was now drunk
by people of all social classes; the value of tea imports increased
sevenfold between 1817 and 1851 and most of it came from China,
which had opened her doors to foreign commerce. The powerful
British East India Company previously had a monopoly on the tea
trade, with its slow, heavy ships, the East Indiamen (see pp.134–35).
They carried tea along the trade routes slowly, since there was no
competition—the round trip took about a year. In 1834, however, the
company lost its trading monopolies, including tea. American shipowners soon realized that faster ships improved trade—tea fetched
the best prices when it was fresh. In 1845, the early American clipper
the *Rainbow* made the passage from Canton to New York in an
unprecedented 88 days, a fraction of the time it would have taken an
East Indiaman. This stimulated British competition, and ships from
both nations were soon competing to pick up cargoes of tea from the
Chinese ports of Foochow, Canton, Whampoa, Shanghai, and Hong

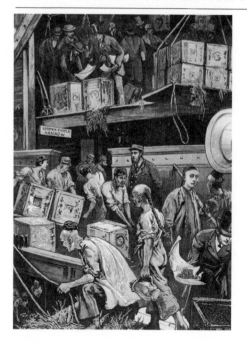

STEVEDORES AT WORK
Chinese stevedores load British ship the *Louden Castle* with 40,000 packages of tea in 1877. Skilled packing was essential to preserve the cargo on the long journey.

Kong. The Americans dropped out of the trade in the 1860s, but the race from China stimulated a second wave of clipper building in Britain, and soon rival British ships were racing to deliver their precious cargoes ahead of the competition.

The *Ariel* was already renowned as one of the fastest ships of her day when the tea race of May 1866 began, so she was given priority on loading at Foochow, ahead of the nine other ships competing. Dozens of sampans arrived on the river carrying different varieties of tea, which Chinese stevedores expertly loaded onto the clippers, ramming the tea chests in as far as possible. This was skilled work, since the cargo had to be packed tightly so that it did not move around in rough seas; it was also important to keep the tea dry, because water—or even the stench of the bilges—could ruin it. The *Ariel* took on 123,900 lb (56,200 kg) of tea, slightly more than her main rival, the *Taeping*. Of the other ships vying with the *Ariel*, the *Fiery Cross* had won several tea races in the early 1860s and was famed for her speed, while the lighter, newer clipper the *Serica* had beaten her in the race of 1864.

On May 28, the *Ariel* began the long tow down the River Min while the other ships were still loading their cargo, but she lost her lead when was forced to anchor after her tug lost control, and the other ships caught up with her. The following day, the clippers were unable to sail due to bad weather, but Captain Keay made good use of the time and had his crew adjust the trim of the ship—its balance in the water—by moving stores and equipment around. It was something of an obsession of his and essential for good sailing. Early on the morning of the 30th, the *Ariel* set her sails and steered around Turnabout Island; the *Fiery Cross* had already set off ahead of her, and the true race was now on.

THE GREAT TEA RACE

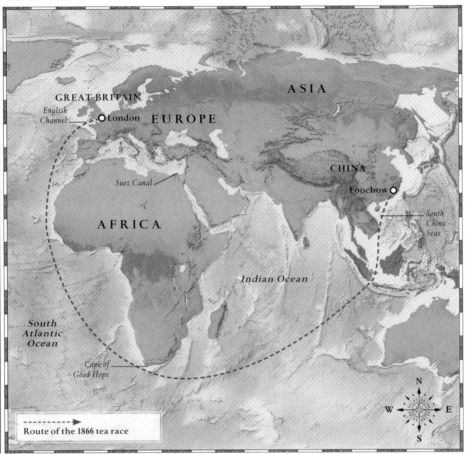

Route of the 1866 tea race

Keay was still worried about the ship's trim—he wanted her to be about six inches deeper at the stern than in the bows, and he even made the crew move heavy cables into his own cabin to increase the weight aft. The ships were heading for the South China Seas. These were dangerous waters—on the *Ariel*'s first voyage there the previous year, Captain Keay had been woken by "screaming and loud cries" from a nearby sampan; a dozen pirates had boarded it, and crews from neighboring ships had to help fight them off. By June 5, the *Ariel* was "tacking as necessary" in light and unfavorable winds in the South China Seas, and keeping close inshore at night, hoping to pick up the land breeze around midnight. She was in the lead, but by the 9th, the *Taeping* was only 3 miles (5km) behind her and gaining ground. The *Ariel*'s crew toiled long and hard against the constantly changing winds: "In all staysails; clewed up royals and down flying jib. 2 a.m. moderate; set all sail again." On the 16th, the *Ariel* crossed the equator and four days later, despite "Faint baffling airs," she passed Anjer in the channel between Sumatra and Java, sometimes used as a layover point on the tea races, and charted a course out into the open seas of the Indian Ocean.

The most important human factor in a clipper race was the attitude of the captain. The *Ariel*'s Captain Keay was considered a daring navigator. He needed a strong constitution, especially during the early part of the voyage, for he wrote: "My habit during these weeks was never to undress except for my morning bath, and that often took the place of sleep. The naps I had were of the briefest, and mostly on deck." Like all good clipper ship captains, Keay knew how to take a calculated risk: "He was a seaman of iron nerves… not a sailor on board but admired him." Obsessed by weight distribution, he had a large chest filled with heavy metal, which the crew then dragged

around the deck until Keay was satisfied that the ship's trim was perfect. Of the other captains, Donald MacKinnon of the *Taeping* was reputed to be one of the finest sailors of his day, while Captain George Innes of the *Serica* was known as a hard man with an explosive temper.

Clipper crews were comparatively small, to reduce labor costs in competition with the steamers, but they were highly skilled and contemptuous of all other sailors, particularly those who worked on the steamships. One of the Polish novelist Joseph Conrad's characters was inclined to "chuck the sea forever and go in a steamer," and a clipper sailor described the steamship crews as "Those miserable thieves." During quiet moments on the voyage, the *Ariel's* crew trimmed the sails as required and carried out routine maintenance. In June 1866, Keay recorded: "Watch lacing the foot of the upper topsails to the jackstays of lower topsail yards. Scraped and oiled the bower anchors and chains outside the house to lessen rust; opened the quarter-hatch to ventilate the hold better while weather is fine."

PASSING THE LIZARD
The *Ariel* and *Taeping* pass the Lizard on the southwestern tip of England in 1866. Even after sailing across vast expanses of open seas, there was still very little distance between them.

Soon after passing Anjer and joining the Indian Ocean, the *Ariel* picked up the powerful trade winds: she covered an astonishing 330 miles (530 km) in a single day on June 26, and at least another 200 miles (320 km) every day for the next week. Winds were variable until July 14, when, approaching the Cape of Good Hope, they were swept up in strong currents, making the ship "almost unmanageable"; at one stage she swung around against the action of the rudder and began to go backward. Off the Cape, they easily overtook the British ship *Tantallon Castle* out of Bombay, but even so, their progress was slow. Winds were now light, the current was still against them, and they made only 82 miles (132 km) per day—the glory days of 300 mile-(480 km) -per-day passages were a long way behind them. Heading northwest after rounding the Cape, Keay noticed the ship was out of trim again, because the crew had used up a large amount of the drinking water, lightening the stern; he had the men bring two tons of coal aft to balance this out. Soon the wind freshened and they achieved a passage of around 220 miles (350 km) per day. By the 30th, food was short: both the ship's pigs had been slaughtered, and when a passing schooner asked if they could spare any provisions, the answer was a resounding "No." They crossed the equator on August 4, unaware that both the *Taeping* and the *Fiery Cross* had now drawn level with them.

By September 1, they were finally approaching home waters. Early in the morning of the 5th they sighted the Bishop's Rock lighthouse off the Cornish coast, and throughout the day the seamarks flashed past as they made their way east along the southern English coastline—the Lizard, Portland, and, by evening, the Isle of Wight.

"The modern clipper, without auxiliary power, has accomplished a greater distance in a day than any steamer has ever known to reach"

MATTHEW F. MAURY

CLIPPER CARDS
As the number of clipper ships competing on the same routes grew, shipowners promoted their vessels with colorful cards, handed out at docks and warehouses.

Farther along the coast, off Dungeness near the eastern end of the English Channel, the *Ariel*'s great rival the *Taeping* was still visible behind. The *Ariel* hailed a pilot cutter, whose crew told them they were the first China ship that season. Captain Keay replied, "Yes, but what is that to the westward? We have not room to boast yet." As he wrote later, "Instinct told me it was the *Taeping*." After racing nearly halfway around the world driven only by the wind, there was scarcely a mile between the two ships as they arrived off Deal, near the entrance to the Thames.

The *Ariel* and *Taeping* both hired tugs off Deal to tow them up the Thames to London—one of the paradoxes of the great sailing ships was that they were entirely dependent on steam-powered tugs at the beginning and end of each voyage. This, perhaps the greatest sailing race of the era thus ended on a note of farce, as the *Taeping*'s tug was faster and she eventually docked 20 minutes before the *Ariel*. The *Serica* arrived just a few hours later, and the *Fiery Cross* around 36 hours after that—an extraordinarily close finish after traveling such a huge distance.

In the spirit of true sportsmanship, the captains of the *Ariel* and *Taeping* agreed to share the premium of 10 shillings per ton for the first ship in, and to split the reward of £100 for the captain. The tea race—the closest of all—had captivated the public and the results were duly published in national newspapers the *Telegraph* and the *Daily Mail*.

The race of 1866 inspired the building of more clippers. However, the Suez Canal opened in 1869, cutting straight from the Indian Ocean through the Red Sea to the Mediterranean and therefore providing a short cut for cargo ships traveling between Europe and the Far East. It was not a practical route for sailing ships, since they relied on wind direction, but steamships could now make the journey far more quickly, bypassing the long and hazardous route round the Cape of Good Hope. Tea was also carried to Europe overland on the "tea road" through Russia. The age of the great sailing ships was almost at an end.

Clipper Ships

Designed to carry cargo at speed, clippers covered distances of 250 nautical miles per day, around one third more than other sailing ships of the time. They achieved this through vast areas of sail and narrow hulls, and in 1854, a clipper logged the speed record for a sailing vessel—22 knots.

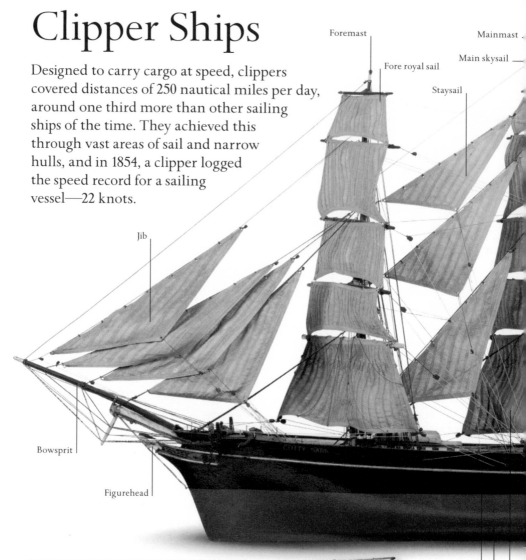

Foremast

Mainmast

Fore royal sail

Main skysail

Staysail

Jib

Bowsprit

Figurehead

Hull made of wood on an iron frame,

Hold

Main course-sail

Gold rush clippers

When gold was found in California in 1848, scores of prospectors arrived via San Francisco to seek their fortune. Without railroads, the best route from New York was by sea around Cape Horn, and clipper captains found work carrying hopeful prospectors to and from the goldfields.

CARD ADVERTISING A
CLIPPER'S PASSENGER SERVICE

THE *CUTTY SARK*
DUMBARTON, 1869

The *Cutty Sark* was one of the last great tea clippers. She was powered by 32,000 sq ft (2,790 sq m) of sail, compared to the 12,900 sq ft (1,200 sq m) of the clippers' predecessors, the East Indiamen (see pp.134–35).

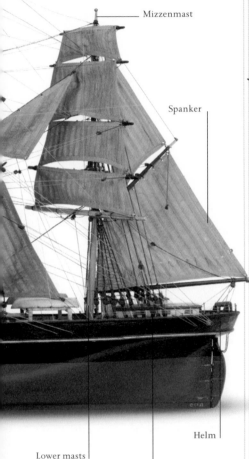

— Mizzenmast

Spanker

Helm

Lower masts made of iron

Officers' accommodation in the raised poop deck

Sailmaker's, carpenter's, and bosun's quarter

Sailing rigs

Most clippers were square-rigged barques (see below), but as they grew in popularity they were outfitted with a variety of different sail configurations.

THREE-MASTED BARQUE, c.1864
Barques carried square sails, as well as a sail known as a spanker on the mizzenmast at the rear. Four-masted barques were also built.

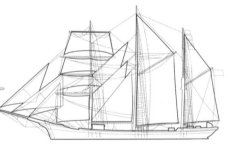

THREE-MASTED BARQUENTINE, c.1871
Barquentines combined square sails on the foremast with easier-to-handle fore and aft sails on their main and mizzenmasts.

FOUR-MASTED SCHOONER, c.1890s
With fore and aft sails on all masts, schooners could sail very close to the wind. American schooners would have up to four or five masts.

John Holland and the First Submarines

IN 1881, A SMALL CROWD had gathered in New York Harbor. They watched curiously as a short, bespectacled Irishman clambered into a peculiar, cigar-shaped metal craft floating in the water. He slammed shut the hatch above him, and, as the crowd watched, the vessel sank slowly from view until it was completely submerged in the harbor waters. Inside the boat, its inventor, a bookish schoolteacher called John Holland, was piloting his experimental submarine with a colleague:

> … almost immediately the boat began to settle, giving us the suggestion of slowly descending in an elevator… A second or two later everything grew dark and we were entirely submerged, and nothing could be seen through the ports except a dark green blur. Our next sensation was a slight jar, when the vessel struck the bottom.

The boat came to a standstill in around two fathoms of water. Holland opened a valve to blow the water out of the tanks, and to his great relief the boat began to rise back toward the surface.

> The green blur of the ports in the conning tower grew lighter… suddenly the light of full day burst through, almost dazzling me… a cheer burst from a crowd of observers on the dock, among whom opinion was equally divided as to whether we would ever emerge from our dive or not.

JOHN HOLLAND
The Irish inventor stands in the conning tower of his submarine, *Holland VI,* in April 1898, in Perth Amboy, New Jersey.

Holland's submarine, called the *Fenian Ram*, had passed its test. It was the first submersible design to maintain positive buoyancy, rather than simply to take on ballast until it sank. Although it never saw service, it would launch a revolution in sea warfare with consequences far wider than the inventor could ever have intended.

Before Holland's breakthrough, the vast majority of sailors had only been interested in what was under the sea if their ship was likely to hit it. Pearl divers had operated in India and the Persian Gulf since ancient times, and the diving bell had been in use since 1535, when Francesco di Marchi went deep in Lake Nemi near Rome, and experienced the agonies of air compression: "When I was going under water... it seemed a steel dagger had been put into me, which transfixed me from ear to ear, and I felt a very great pain." Diving bells went on to be used by civil engineers such as Isambard Kingdom Brunel in the 19th century when tunneling under rivers and building crossings such as the Brooklyn Bridge in New York. After the 16th century, however, the idea of a self-propelled submarine, or "submersible boat," remained a fantasy until the Revolutionary War, when the precursor to the *Fenian Ram* was constructed. Designed in 1775 by American patriot David Bushnell, the *Turtle*, as it was known, was little more than a one-man capsule designed to drill holes in the hulls of the British warships anchored in New York Harbor. Although its various ventures failed (including a famous attack on the British warship HMS *Eagle* on September 6, 1776) its presence was never detected by the enemy, demonstrating that the chief virtue of the submersible was stealth.

Thirty years later, American engineer Robert Fulton persuaded the French to build another submersible, called the *Nautilus*, but the idea proved too radical even for the French revolutionaries. As a consequence, Fulton promptly changed sides and offered his invention to the British, who were equally cautious about the idea. Admiral of the Fleet Lord St. Vincent railed that it was foolish "to encourage a mode of warfare which those that command the sea did not want, and which, if successful, would deprive them of it." During the Civil War, the southern Confederate States of America were eager to use a submarine to challenge Union sea power, and in 1863, Confederate marine engineer Horace L. Hunley built his submarine in Mobile, Alabama. Called the *H.L. Hunley*, it was man powered, like its predecessors, with eight men operating crank

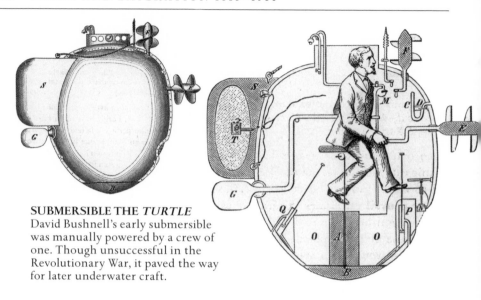

SUBMERSIBLE THE *TURTLE*
David Bushnell's early submersible
was manually powered by a crew of
one. Though unsuccessful in the
Revolutionary War, it paved the way
for later underwater craft.

handles that drove a propeller mounted inside an old boiler at the
stern. Sadly, her operations say more about the determination of
Confederate sailors than the quality of her design; she sank twice and
most of her crews were drowned. However, on her final mission in
February 1864, in Charlestown Harbor, she successfully sank the USS
Housatonic by ramming her with a spar torpedo. Unfortunately, after
becoming the first submarine to sink another vessel, the *Hunley* herself
was lost at sea while returning to her naval station.

Such was the situation when John Holland, an Irish schoolteacher and
inventor living in the United States, first unveiled the *Fenian Ram* to the
public. He had long believed that submarines were the key to
overthrowing British sea power and furthering the Irish nationalist
cause. The very name *Fenian Ram* neatly expressed both his support for
the Irish cause and his intentions toward the British fleet. Having
proved the *Ram*'s ability to descend—and more crucially to ascend—in
the trial in New York Harbor, he went on to test it under power with his
engineer George M. Richards. It was outfitted with a gasoline engine,
which was more compact than a steam engine, but demanded more air.

> Richards and I entered the boat… After a little kicking and muttering he
> succeeded in getting it started. We then let in the clutch and the boat
> started forward. When we reached the far side of the basin I turned her
> around and threw out the clutch, causing the boat to slow down and stop.

He closed the hatch and began to travel along underwater:

> We then proceeded along awash; that is, with only the little tower showing above the surface… I next threw forward the lever on the right side of my seat (controlling the diving rudders aft). Immediately the nose of the boat went down and before I realised it our gauge showed a depth of 10 feet. I now drew the lever back to centre, and the boat straightened out on an even keel… After running about one hundred yards submerged I steered the boat up… I then opened the valve and expelled my ballast, causing the boat to rise and assume her normal position.

Holland's pioneering control system was later used in practically every submarine built. He also tested a gun that could be fired underwater, which offered some promise. However, with no periscope and little help from the compass, the boat was very difficult to navigate. An even greater setback came when he fell into dispute with the financial backers of the *Fenian Ram*, which culminated in them seizing the boat from him. Undeterred by this, or by the rival inventors of most of the other maritime nations, Holland continued with his designs, having successfully secured various other backers. His fifth model, called the *Plunger*, was armed with two torpedoes, and at 85 ft (26 m) long was his largest model to date. It was built with US government support, but its construction was hampered by interference from the government, as well as overheating problems in the fire room, and it never left dock.

Holland's sixth submarine model, the *Holland VI*, was launched in New Jersey in 1897; at 53 ft (16 m) long, it was considerably smaller than the *Plunger*. It was not the first submarine to use an electric motor, which needed no air and was ideal for operating underwater,

DEATHS IN SUBMARINES PRE-1914

USA: 2	FRANCE: 57
GERMANY: 3	RUSSIA: 70
JAPAN: 14	BRITAIN: 79

but it had an innovative 45-horsepower gasoline engine that operated on the surface and charged the batteries of the electric motor. This submarine was equipped with the "Holland Pneumatic Dynamite Gun," which used a combination of air and gunpowder to fire a shot up to 1,000 yd (900 m) into the air, or around 30 yd (27 m) underwater, and had a tube for launching a torpedo, with storage space for two more torpedoes. It also boasted, according to Holland, "a spirit compass, a pressure gauge, which indicates the exact depth at which the boat is travelling; bell pulls for starting and stopping; two speaking tubes; whistle pull; indicators showing the position of both rudders; together with two controllers for the steering engine." The crew consisted of a commander and his assistant, an electrician, an engineer, a gunner, and a machinist who acted as assistant gunner. Holland claimed that the vessel had a range of 1,300 nautical miles and a speed of six to ten knots, and that with electric light and a water closet the crew could, "comfortably live on board for 40 hours." With this model, Holland finally proved that a workable submarine was possible.

USS *HOLLAND* IN DRY DOCK
The United States Navy's first submarine was
named after its creator. John Holland's designs
made submarine warfare a reality in the early 1900s.

In 1900, Holland sold his patents to the Electric Boat Company, which became the US Navy's builder of submarines for the next century or so. The company licensed the design to other world powers: in a twist of irony, the British Royal Navy was licensed to build his submarines, and the first British model bore the name of an Irish nationalist—*Holland No 1*. Nevertheless, Admiral Fisher of the Royal Navy was jubilant: "Even the bare thought makes invasion impossible! Fancy, 100,000 helpless, huddled up troops afloat in frightened transports with these invisible demons known to be near." The modern submarine also proved popular with other world powers, and customers included the Imperial Japanese and Russian navies, and the Dutch navy. But far from being able to "comfortably live on board" as Holland had predicted, life in a submarine was hard in 1910, as Captain Sydney Hall recalled of an early British boat:

> Clothes cannot be dried, fires are not permissible, in cold weather it is difficult to keep reasonably warm, the amount of fresh water precludes any attempt at personal cleanliness and the roar of the Engines is all over the boat… To many the smell inside a submarine after she has been a short time at sea, which is absolutely peculiar to itself, is most revolting, All food tastes of it, clothes reek of it, it is quite impossible to wear any clothes again after they have been used in it.

If this were not bad enough, several of the early boats sank, and it was even rumored that Holland had tampered with the designs to harm his old enemy, the British—but there is no hard evidence of this. Indeed, when the German navy began to build submarines in 1906, Holland may even have tried to warn the British of the danger. Nevertheless, the submarine proved itself to be vital for naval dominance, and went on to play a pivotal role in warfare and politics across the world for the next century or so—from all-out combat in the World Wars, to the nuclear patrols of the Cold War and beyond.

Early Submarines

Early submersible vessels were built from around the 18th century onward, but it was only around the turn of the 20th century, with the use of the electric motor and diesel engine, that the submarine became a viable means of transportation. Over the decades that followed, the invention of the submarine created an entirely new form of naval warfare, and had a profound influence on naval strategy worldwide.

Early submarines in fiction

Published in 1870, Jules Verne's classic science-fiction novel *20,000 Leagues Under the Sea* tells the tale of Captain Nemo and his submarine *Nautilus*. Though entirely fictional, it helped fuel popular interest in the idea of underwater travel and the military potential of subsurface vessels. The book's title refers to the distance traveled—not the depth of the dive.

JULES VERNE'S POPULAR NOVEL, 1870

Propeller

Propeller shaft

Auxiliary motor

Main motor (gasoline engine)

Aft ballast tanks

Flood valve

HOLLAND VI/USS *HOLLAND* (SS-1)
NEW YORK, 1897
Named after her inventor, John Holland (see pp.258–63), USS *Holland* (SS-1) was the US Navy's first commissioned submarine. Launched on May 17, 1897, her design and features formed the basis of early 20th-century submarines.

How a submarine dives

To submerge the submarine, the vents at the top and bottom of the outer hull are opened, allowing water into the ballast tanks—water tanks between the inner and outer hulls—until it loses buoyancy. Its engines then power it forward and its hydroplanes are set to force it downward, until the ballast tanks are completely full and it has achieved neutral buoyancy—the same density as the surrounding water, in which state it will neither rise nor sink. The upper vents are then closed.

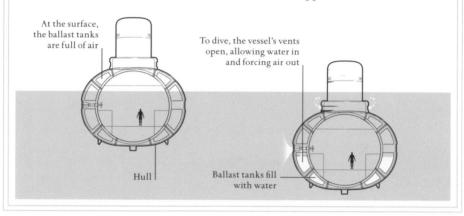

At the surface, the ballast tanks are full of air

To dive, the vessel's vents open, allowing water in and forcing air out

Hull

Ballast tanks fill with water

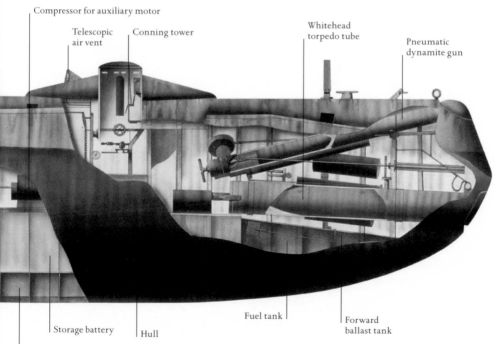

Compressor for auxiliary motor

Telescopic air vent

Conning tower

Whitehead torpedo tube

Pneumatic dynamite gun

Storage battery

Hull

Fuel tank

Forward ballast tank

Main ballast tank

To the Other Side of the World

REACHING AUSTRALIA AND NEW ZEALAND—the British colonies in the Antipodes—required a much longer journey than the voyage across the Atlantic, and although steamships were becoming common in the 1880s, many emigrants still traveled by sail. Early in 1884 on the River Clyde in Scotland, 361 such emigrants joined sailing ship the *Otago* for a voyage to Queensland. The *Otago* had been built on the Clyde in 1869, the same year as the famous clipper the *Cutty Sark*, but unlike most of the clippers she was never a speedy ship—even her sister ship, the *James Nicol Fleming*, made far faster passages.

There were only three cabin passengers aboard the *Otago*, living aft of the officers' quarters; the rest of the passengers were in "steerage" (the cheapest accommodation). The largest group were the 180 men, women, and children traveling as families or married couples. The Hunter family consisted of two adults and three children, or three and a half "statute adults," since each child counted as half an adult. They had to share cramped living conditions of "two beds, one immediately above the other, 6 feet long by 3 feet 6 inches wide." The upper berths were preferred, because they had air and light from the portholes. The family also had a

PORT CHALMERS, NEW ZEALAND
This small port was one of the main entry points
for European emigrants to the country in the
19th century. It is still in use as a port today.

small sitting space and table, and a tiny bench that also served as a locker for mess utensils. "What a 'wee hoose' for our family, and what strange surroundings!" commented Mr. Hunter.

Also aboard were 158 single men, who were prone to rowdiness and known as a volatile group. They lived forward in a space 82 ft (25 m) long, where there was "no attempt at privacy at all." On the other hand, the 20 single women on board were strictly guarded, for they were regarded as highly vulnerable in the confines of a ship. They were accommodated in part of the public area used for officers and cabin passengers, with a separate cabin for the matron who supervised them.

On the morning of February 2, the *Otago* weighed anchor and a tug took her down the Firth of Clyde. Most of the passengers had never been to sea before. Hunter observed: "Nearly everybody has been troubled with sea-sickness today. I had my breakfast, then went on deck, and immediately became sick. Some of the passengers were quite helpless." On the 6th, they lost sight of Ireland. Apart from a few glimpses of isolated islands, this was to be their last sight of land until they reached Australia some months later. Fourteen-year-old Katie Cashin said goodbye to her homeland, probably for the last time. She wrote a poem to mark the occasion:

> Adieu, adieu, fair Erin's Isle
> My own, my native land;
> Oh! sad my heart, when I beheld,
> Thy slowly sinking strand.

The passengers soon got to know the officers and crew. The captain, Hugh Falconer, tended to remain aloof, as befitted his station. The surgeon, Dr. Thomas F. Macdonald, was a fully qualified physician, but his responsibilities were broader than that. Under the ship's regulations, he had sole responsibility for the welfare, morality, and discipline of the passengers, as well as their health—he was "invested... with supreme authority on board in everything not connected with the sailing of the ship." The ship's cook, James Selkirk, was a professional entertainer, and a great favorite at concerts as a singer and comedian. However, he was far less popular in the galley: "We never knew what it was to have our food properly cooked, unless during the time the cook was laid aside from duty," the passengers grumbled. Even worse, he bullied the passengers from steerage who were sent to help him. Charles Clarke, a lay preacher from Birmingham, complained that he made him feel "no longer a man, but a serf, placed for the time being under the 'King' of the galley."

The ship had not gone far when the crew and passengers were reminded of matters of life and death. In the evening of the 8th, Thomas Williamson wrote:

> The wind rose to a gale, and the sea ran mountains high. Everyone retired very early to bed, but not to sleep. We could hear the boxes in the hold rolling from one side to the other, and in our imagination threatening to knock a hole in the side of the ship. Amidst all the noise and roaring of the wind and sea, the mate's voice was heard crying out 'All hands on deck.' We had lost one of the sails. I thought the night would never come to an end.

The weather was still rough two days later, and it was claimed that "even the sailors could scarcely keep their feet on deck." Nevertheless, the steerage passengers were expected to earn their passage by working in the galley and by carrying coal; if they refused, they were denied dinner. On February 23, as they headed out into the ocean to the west of Portugal, one of the passengers, Keith Cameron, produced the first edition of a ship's newspaper, *The Gull*, "with a genuine desire of affording the emigrants… some little change in their monotonous life…" Two copies were written out by hand and circulated, and there was a reading of it on Saturday afternoons.

"We never knew what it was to have our food properly cooked, unless during the time the cook was laid aside from duty"

ANONYMOUS PASSENGER

"CONSTABLE HAGERTY'S MIDNIGHT BATH"
Day-to-day life aboard the *Otago* was the subject of gentle satire in the ship's unofficial handwritten newspaper, *The Gull.*

The other passengers gathered together to produce concerts and musical entertainments. The first was held on March 6, when the ship found fair weather off the coast of Africa and was making good progress toward the doldrums. The traumas of the storm were behind them for the moment, and the passengers had recovered from their seasickness. The "*Otago* Minstrels" included several members of the crew, such as the boatswain, and many passengers. Concerts were held almost weekly for the rest of the voyage; among the favorites were Selkirk, and young Katie Cashin, who "gave several recitations on board in truly dramatic fashion."

Some passengers and crew preferred more domestic pleasures, such as baking and sewing. Able Seaman John Schael was a model maker of some skill, and produced a replica of the clipper ship the *Maulsden*, one of the fastest ships on the Australia run. Others had less wholesome pastimes. One passenger, Charles Gardner, smoked cigarettes incessantly, even during concerts, and some of the men kept lighting their pipes below decks, creating a fire hazard. According to *The Gull*, "The married and single men, with the assistance of a few sailors, have hit on a new and edifying source of amusement for the evenings—viz, stealing each other's hats and caps; and, by way of a change, treading on the toes of little girls who may unfortunately get in the way." By late March, a group of single men were gambling regularly at the card game "Napoleon" and pitch-and-toss in their quarters in the early hours of the morning, joined by some of the married men; two brothers lost £5 between them, and so did the cook's assistant. There was a strong temperance (antialcohol) faction on board, including the passenger Samuel Hunter, who longed for ginger beer after bouts of seasickness, but there were also many who preferred something stronger. In theory there was no alcohol on board except for medicinal purposes, but

Keith Cameron noted, "whisky, rum and gin were sold regularly all through the voyage, *not as medical comforts*; and Captain Falconer pocketed a tidy little sum from the sale of liquor. He drew more than £20 for whisky, £19 for gin, and £12 for rum…" The abstemious Hunter also noticed some of the men "lounging about the cabin-door in the dark as the loafers do at home beside a public house door."

Trouble flared up on April 10, while the ship was south of the Cape of Good Hope. Some of the men claimed to be too sick to carry coal, so their food and water were stopped. Complaints were then lodged against the surgeon; "in some cases he had to be asked two or three times before being induced to see a sick person" and "the single girls on the poop demanded *all* his attention and *got it too*." Samuel Hunter complained about poor food, the conduct of the doctor and the cook, the lack of a library, and many other issues. *The Gull* sided with the dissenters, but was suppressed by Captain Falconer.

At 4 pm on May 11, Able Seaman William Brown called from the masthead that he could see land ahead. The healthier passengers scrambled as far up the rigging as they could, and about 40 miles (65 km)

CAPE OF GOOD HOPE
Emigrants on their way to Australia passed the cape
on the southern tip of Africa, though they rarely
saw it since most ships passed farther south to reach
favorable winds.

away they could see Cape Otway, near Melbourne. Two hours later, the light on King's Island, at the entrance to the Bass Straits between Australia and Tasmania, was visible from the deck. One woman stood precariously on a hatch until she could see it, then let out an unforgettable shriek of joy. The ship was traveling fast in a southwesterly wind and made 240 miles (390 km) that day, so the light was some way astern by the time the emigrants went to bed that night. They woke the next morning to find themselves within the Straits, enjoying their first view of trees and houses for more than three months. They passed a coastal steamer and exchanged messages. It was the first vessel they had seen since the *Belfast* nearly two months earlier. "Glad indeed grew the hearts of the emigrants," reported an unpublished edition of *The Gull*. Close to the end of their voyage, however, tragedy struck. Four-year-old Daniel Robertson was a great favorite on board, "with his winning ways and wistfully sweet voice." He had been complaining of "a sair heid." On the evening of the 12th, his mother's birthday, he died of "congestion of the brain." The carpenter made a small coffin, and the passengers and crew gathered for the burial at sea:

> At 6:30 the faces so recently smiling in gladness... grew strangely sad and overcast when they witnessed the preparations being made for consigning to the deep the remains of Daniel Robertson... we saw the tiny shrouded form going down to endless rest in the heart of the beautiful sea, the faces of the women, gathered in a mournful group, were wet with tears, and the little girls present were sobbing bitterly.

On the morning of the 19th, the crew dropped anchor off Cape Moreton lighthouse near Brisbane. The single men, sensing an end to their ordeal, made an effigy that they accused of "the most outrageous, villainous, and diabolical" of crimes, including responsibility for the shortage of food. They staged a mock execution from the yardarm and threw the "corpse" overboard. The pilot came on board to take the ship into port, and was greeted with loud cheers. On the 24th, a tug finally arrived and the ship tied up in Brisbane. The whole voyage had taken a grueling 120 days. The *Otago*'s sister ship, the *James Nicol Fleming*, had made a slightly longer voyage to Dunedin in New Zealand in 69 days; a steamship would have taken less than 60 days.

The Birth of the Luxury Liner

THE SECOND HALF of the 19th century marked the beginning of a golden age of ocean travel. The invention of the marine steam engine, which reduced journey times over long distances, led to an increased interest in foreign travel for pleasure. This, along with the millions of Europe's poor and dispossessed traveling to new homelands, was the foundation on which numerous shipping fortunes were made.

In 1885, 28-year-old Albert Ballin became head of passenger operations for Germany's Hamburg-American shipping line, and two years later he joined the board as director. Born in Hamburg to a Jewish family that had emigrated from Denmark, Ballin was described by the magazine *Die Weltbühne* as "an idealist as an observer, a realist in action," and was said to possess "a curious mixture of iron will and opportunistic worldly wisdom, combining a lively synthesising imagination with a coolly calculating appraisal of the facts." He was also touchy and overly sensitive, and hugely ambitious, and he soon developed a loyalty to the shipping company that was unsurpassed by any other director, shareholder, or employee. At that time, the Hamburg-American Line (known as Hapag in Germany) had 22 ocean-going steamers, with a total of 60,500 tons. The company, which had been founded in 1847, had adopted the motto of the Hanseatic League (a medieval organization of guilds)—"My field is the World." Ballin was determined to make that notion a reality, and his vision had a profound effect on world shipping.

When Ballin looked at the shipping business, he saw seas dominated by British commerce. It was a fact of which he had been aware

ALBERT BALLIN
An ambitious businessman and innovator, Ballin pioneered a new kind of passenger shipping.

since the beginning of his career, when, working for his father's company, he had arranged countless passages on British ships for emigrants traveling to the United States. The US had largely abandoned ocean commerce since the depredations of the *Alabama* and other Confederate warships that ravaged its merchant shipping during the Civil War (see pp.240–47). By 1890, only nine percent of American seaborne trade was carried under the US flag. Elsewhere, France was still licking its wounds after defeat in the Franco-Prussian War, and Germany (united in 1871) was a new nation still undergoing industrialization.

Britain, by contrast, had the largest and most efficient fleet in the world. It had exploited the skills of canny businessmen such as Arthur Anderson of P&O and Samuel Cunard (see p.201), and had led the way technologically—building not only the first iron and the first steel ships, but patenting the compound and triple expansion engines (which greatly increased fuel efficiency) and constructing specialized craft such as refrigerated ships and oil carriers. By the 1890s, British shipbuilders were producing some 80 percent of the world's new tonnage, and Anglo-Irish engineer Charles Parsons was on the verge of developing the steam turbine, to increase the speed of ocean liners.

The term "ocean liner" has its roots in merchant shipping. By the late 19th century, this was divided into two types of vessel: the tramp steamer and the liner. Tramp steamers were part of a global economy, hired to carry a single cargo—usually coal or grain—or to supplement the liner routes on busy times, rather than to operate regular routes. Despite the name, they were not necessarily run down or in bad condition. The term "liner," on the other hand, simply meant a ship operating a regular route, or "line." These vessels did not have the glamorous association they enjoy today, but they carried passengers as well as cargo, and their decks were often crammed with migrants en route to new lives in the US or Australia.

The stormy winter months made the transatlantic crossing a grim experience for passengers, and Ballin was aware that his liners on that route were underused. He considered deploying them on recreational voyages in southern waters, and in 1891, conducted a Mediterranean cruise in the company's largest vessel, the *August Victoria*, which had previously remained in dock during the winter. In a departure from the basic conditions of the majority of passenger ships, the commercial emphasis was placed firmly on leisure and escapism.

For two months her passengers will constitute a self-contained community, released from normal ties, freed from the cares and burdens of office and business… everyone will be free to do as they please, to socialize or to set themselves apart… The most ample care has been taken to look after physical wellbeing, but music and sport will also make the hours fly by…

The idea was not new, but Ballin's version of the luxury cruise proved popular with passengers. Ever the perfectionist, he combined his global vision with an eye for detail, and made numerous voyages on his own ships and those of other companies, taking notes on the minutiae of the luxury passenger experience:

List of Moselle purveyors wants revision—notices on board to be restricted as much as possible, those which are necessary to be tastefully framed—sailing lists and general regulations to be included in the passengers' lists—state room on board the *Kaiser Friedrich*: key, latch, drawer; no room for portmanteaux and trunks; towels too small—*Deutschland*: soiled linen cupboard too small—stewards *Oceanic* white jackets—celery glasses—butter dishes too small—large bed pillows—consommé cups—playing cards—toast to be served in a serviette (hot).

In 1901, Ballin made an around-the-world voyage, partly to look at prospects for a passenger service to the newly acquired German colony of Tsingtao in China, and jotted down detailed observations on the ports he visited. At Port Said in Egypt he went to bed as coal was being delivered but could not sleep:

The steamer had scarcely taken up her moorings when several hundreds of dusky natives, wildly screaming and gesticulating, and making a noise that almost rent the skies, invaded her in order to fill her bunkers… Just imagine a horde of natives wildly screaming at the top of their voices, and add to this the noise produced by the coal incessantly shot into the bunkers…

"Superbly beautiful" was how he described the entrance to exotic Singapore: "The steamer slowly wended her way through the channels between numerous small islands clad with the most luxurious vegetation, so that it took us two hours to reach the actual harbour," he enthused—while the Chinese city of Shanghai was dubbed "the New York of the Far East." On the business side, he

CONTENTS OF AN ATLANTIC LINER
A steamer taking emigrants to America at the beginning of the twentieth century would need to carry huge amounts of food.

established a branch of Hamburg-American in Hong Kong, set up an office in Shanghai, acquired two shipping lines, and opened negotiations with the Japanese.

The North Atlantic was by far the most prestigious liner service, and it was there that the Germans hoped to make an impression. In 1897, German shipping company North German Lloyd challenged British dominance by building the *Kaiser Wilhelm der Grosse*. At more than 14,000 tons, she was the largest liner ever built at the time, and became the first German ship to win the unofficial but highly coveted Blue Riband for the fastest transatlantic passage. In 1898, the line carried almost a quarter of the passengers to New York, including more first- and second-class passengers than the British Cunard line. Hamburg-American responded in 1900 with the 16,500-ton *Deutschland*. She too won the Blue Riband (in 1902), making the passage from Eddystone Lighthouse off the southwest coast of England to Sandy Hook, New York, in 5 days, 15 hours, and 45 minutes. The voyage was not without mishap, however—she was dogged with vibration and mechanical problems, lost her rudder in the mid-Atlantic, and had to be steered with her engines—and Ballin, who disliked costly and wasteful competition, never attempted to win the Blue Riband again. Instead, Hamburg-American adopted the slogan "Luxury instead of speed" for its Atlantic services, reasoning that passengers would be in no hurry to end five or six days of comfortable living.

Indeed, ships with tastefully designed interiors were becoming the standard. One of the earliest examples of these was the *America*, a steamer in which, according to US author Richard H. Dana in 1856, the ladies' cabin was "a very pleasant room, made to look as much as possible like a room in a house on shore. The walls are papered, and there is a marble

**DINNERTIME ON AN
INDIA-BOUND P&O LINER**
Passengers at dinner in the P&O liner *Himalaya*
on the way to India in 1891 experience both
the luxury of their surroundings, and the
discomfort of the rough sea.

SS *IMPERATOR*
Advertised as the "World's Largest Ship" in 1913,
the *Imperator* of the Hamburg-American Line was
one of the most luxurious liners of its day.

"The splendour of these ships… may be taken… as a gesture of confidence and hope"

WILLIAM BERTRAND,
FRENCH MINISTER OF THE MARINE

fire place, with grate and mantle piece. All has quite a domestic, cosey look." In 1913, Hamburg-American commissioned the ambitious *Imperator*, and British writer Adam Kirkaldy was impressed with the opulence on display: "She has no fewer than eleven decks… There is a winter garden on board, a Ritz restaurant, a theatre, a Roman swimming bath, a ball-room, a gymnasium… Luxury is being carried almost too far."

The luxury liners plying the Atlantic were only part of Hamburg-American's worldwide services, however. Like many shipping lines, Hamburg-American made most of its profits by carrying freight. By 1914, it was the biggest shipping company in the world, operating 442 ships (nearly half of them ocean going) of more than 1.4 million tons on 74 different services to more than 350 ports. The German shipping industry had grown alongside it, to eight times its 1885 tonnage.

That very year, however, because the prospect of war in Europe loomed large, Germany's success was threatened. Ballin was horrified at the idea of European conflict. He reported to his Kaiser that he had been "successful in establishing complete concord among Germans, British, French, Italians, Austrians, and a whole series of small nations on questions affecting their highly important shipping interests, and in replacing unbridled and economically disastrous competition by friendly agreements." He thought he could do the same for diplomatic relations, and attempted to negotiate a peaceful resolution as mediator with Britain, through the German-born British businessman Sir Ernest Cassel. War, however, did indeed break out in 1914, and amid the carnage that engulfed Europe, the majority of Hamburg-American's ships were blockaded. Ballin committed suicide in 1918, two days before the end of the war, but Hamburg-American survived. The fleet went on to endure World War II, and finally merged with North German Lloyd in 1970, becoming the Hapag-Lloyd line that operates today.

The Great Arms Race

The design of warships fluctuated greatly during the second half of the 19th century, as one change followed another in rapid succession. Iron and steel hulls were outfitted with ever-stronger armor, and guns (which were now rifled and breech-loading) could fire explosive shot rather than solid balls over greater distances. Steam was becoming universal and the major warships no longer carried sails even as backup. In 1890, however, the situation stabilized when a new type of battleship evolved. This had a high hull to meet the waves, a ram bow, and usually four main guns in two turrets. The British Royal Navy was still the most powerful in the world at the time, and had ships carrying a variety of 12-inch, 6-inch, 12-pounder, and 3-pounder guns, but her supremacy was being challenged by the burgeoning navies of Russia, the United States, and Italy. In 1897, a new threat emerged when Admiral Alfred Friedrich von Tirpitz became State Secretary Imperial Naval Office. He knew that he had no hope of building a fleet as big as the Royal Navy, so he adopted the "risk theory": if the German navy was large enough—though still smaller than the vast British fleet—Britain would risk losing so many ships in a war against Germany that she would be unable to fight a second enemy. It was a dangerous plan, since Britain could attack before the German navy had built up strength, but he forged ahead with his plans nonetheless and had a fleet of 20 battleships by 1904.

The same year, Admiral Sir John "Jackie" Fisher, a Royal Navy veteran who understood

ADMIRAL ALFRED FRIEDRICH VON TIRPITZ
A skilled naval reformer who began his career in torpedo boats, von Tirpitz built the German navy into the second largest in the world.

the need for modernization, became Britain's First Sea Lord. Ebullient and opinionated in a service that valued silence and conformity, he was initially charged with reducing spiraling naval costs. This he did, by withdrawing ships from imperial duties and scrapping scores of old gunboats that would be ineffective against a modern foe. Just such an force emerged in 1905, when Russia fought a war with the rising power of Japan. The two fleets met at the Battle of Tsushima (see p.221), and the Japanese, although inferior in numbers, captured or destroyed eight out of the nine Russian battleships, as well as three armored ships and eight cruisers. The most striking feature of the battle was the unprecendented range at which it was fought. The two fleets opened fire at 7,000 yd (6,400 m)—much farther than conventional naval battles of the time—and the Japanese scored decisive hits within 20 minutes. Back in London, Fisher realized that long-range gunnery was the key to success. A ship's guns needed to be as large as possible and should all be of the same caliber so that misses could be easily corrected. To turn these ideas into reality, he channeled his resources into constructing the first all-big-gun battleship—HMS *Dreadnought*. She was built in Portsmouth Dockyard in just over a year, from 1905 to 1906, rather than the normal two-and-a-half years.

Instead of the traditional armament of mixed-caliber guns, the *Dreadnought* had ten 12-inch guns, with a secondary armament of light 12-pounders for fighting off torpedo boats. She also had the latest turbine engines, making her the fastest battleship in the world. In a single stroke, the *Dreadnought* transformed naval warfare; she also rendered Britain's existing fleet of 50 battleships obsolete. Fisher was widely criticized for this. His rival, Admiral Sir Charles Beresford, described it as "putting all one's naval eggs in one or two vast, costly, majestic but vulnerable baskets"—to which Reginald Bacon, the *Dreadnought*'s first captain, replied, "Knowing as we did that the *Dreadnought* was the best type to build, should we knowingly have built the second-best ship type?"

Von Tirpitz had been wrong-footed. His plans had been inflexible and the size of his ships had been limited by the width of the Kiel Canal, a strategic waterway connecting the training area of the Baltic to the operational area of the North Sea, which was too narrow to allow a ship the size of a dreadnought through. There was only one solution—to increase the width of the canal and to start building German dreadnoughts. The canal was duly widened between 1907

Dreadnoughts

The overwhelming success of Japan's battlehip fleet against Russia in 1904–05 (see below) instigated a new age of naval technology. Britain's Royal Navy constructed HMS *Dreadnought* in response, combining the first all-heavy-gun armament with the superior speed of steam turbine engines. Outgunning every other warship afloat, it gave rise to a new class of battleship.

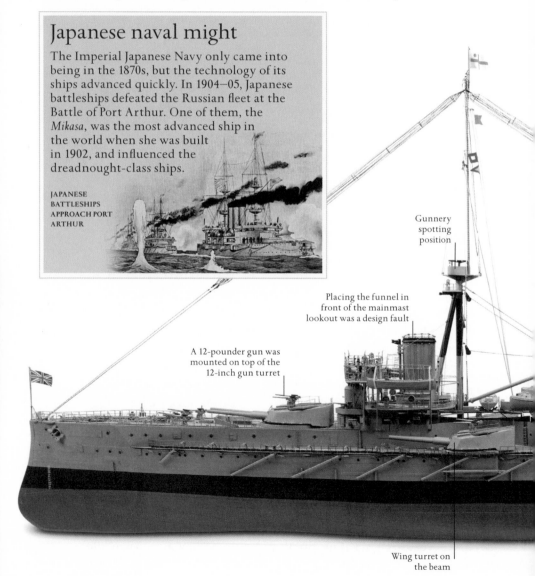

Japanese naval might

The Imperial Japanese Navy only came into being in the 1870s, but the technology of its ships advanced quickly. In 1904–05, Japanese battleships defeated the Russian fleet at the Battle of Port Arthur. One of them, the *Mikasa*, was the most advanced ship in the world when she was built in 1902, and influenced the dreadnought-class ships.

JAPANESE
BATTLESHIPS
APPROACH PORT
ARTHUR

Gunnery spotting position

Placing the funnel in front of the mainmast lookout was a design fault

A 12-pounder gun was mounted on top of the 12-inch gun turret

Wing turret on the beam

Gun turrets

One of the characteristic features of dreadnoughts was the use of heavy, far-ranging armament in order to avoid traditional close-range combat. To achieve maximum impact, early designs experimented with the position of gun turrets, although these also varied from nation to nation.

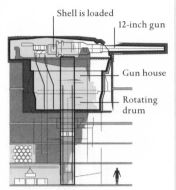

Shell is loaded

12-inch gun

Gun house

Rotating drum

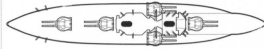

BRITISH DREADNOUGHT, 1906

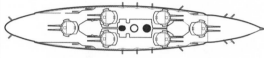

GERMAN DREADNOUGHT, 1908

GUN TURRET POSITIONS
The first British dreadnought models featured three turrets in a central line and two on the wings, while German ships tried four wing turrets combined with one fore and one aft, all carrying two guns each.

GUN TURRET DESIGN
Protected by armored barbettes and supported by a bed of rollers enabling the guns to rotate, dreadnought gun turrets required a crew of around 30 men to operate them. The shells and propellant charges were so heavy they had to be hoisted for loading.

HMS *DREADNOUGHT*
GREAT BRITAIN, 1906

At 527 ft (106 m), with ten 12-inch guns and a speed of 21 knots, the *Dreadnought* was the very first all-big-gun warship, and the first of a new class of ship. She saw only limited action in World War I, since she was being refitted during the major naval engagement of the war, the Battle of Jutland, in 1916 (see pp.288–99).

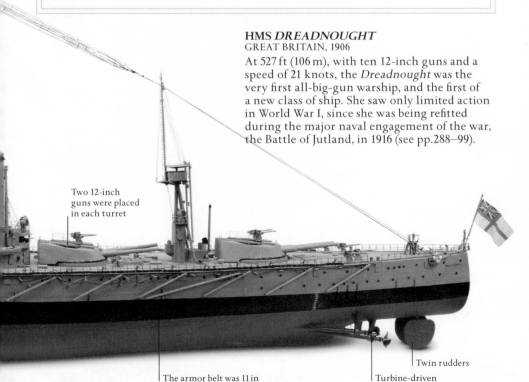

Two 12-inch guns were placed in each turret

The armor belt was 11 in (279 mm) thick at the waterline

Turbine-driven three-bladed propellers

Twin rudders

THE BATTLE OF TSUSHIMA
Tsushima did not just demonstrate the efficacy of Japan's industrialized navy; it also proved the devastating power of modern gunnery.

and 1914, and the first German dreadnought, SMS *Nassau*, was launched in 1910. On the face of it, the *Nassau* was inferior to British dreadnoughts, with only 11-inch guns and old-fashioned reciprocating engines, but she had all the benefits of German engineering. Von Tirpitz duly increased the rate of shipbuilding; three more battleships entered service that year, followed by three in 1911, two in 1912, and four in 1913.

Ironically, dreadnoughts were not even Fisher's favorite type of ship. In 1905, less concerned about the prospect of war with Germany, he had commissioned a large, fast cruiser to deal with possible French commerce raiders. This was armed with the same guns as a dreadnought, but traveled considerably faster. As war with Germany became more likely, these new "battle cruisers" were seen as a fast division of the main battle fleet, but their lighter armor made them vulnerable. Fisher referred to them as "eggshells armed with sledgehammers." In the meantime, the latest post-dreadnought battleships appeared. These "super-dreadnoughts" were armed with 13½-inch guns that fired shells nearly 40 percent more destructive than those of a dreadnought.

The new British and German ships excited a great deal of interest among the public. In Britain, membership of the Navy League (a charity that supported the Royal Navy) soared from 14,000 to 100,000 members, and the German equivalent, the *Flottenverein*, founded in 1898, had nearly a million members by 1906. The arms race reached a peak in 1909, when the Navy League's demands for more dreadnoughts—"We want eight and we won't wait!"—were answered, and British naval costs soared even higher. It was not decided, however, where the ships should be based. The Royal Navy still operated mainly from its southern bases at Plymouth, Portsmouth, and Chatham, all designed for war against France. In 1903, land was purchased for a new base at Rosyth in Scotland, but Fisher was against it, fearing that the Forth Bridge might be demolished and the fleet subsequently trapped. He looked at sites farther north, but they were left untouched. Germany, meanwhile, developed the port of Wilhemshaven on its tiny North Sea coast as the main base for its ships. According to the *Encyclopedia Britannica*, "The three entrances to the old and new habours are sheltered by long and massive moles; and the whole complex of docks, building slips, machine shops... forms the government dockyard, which is enclosed by a lofty wall with fourteen iron gates."

Fisher retired in 1910, having achieved much but having made many enemies both inside and outside the service. Just a few months later, Germany put on a dramatic show of strength. On July 1, 1911, Kaiser Wilhelm claimed a protectorate over Morocco, ostensibly to protect its German residents, and sent the gunboat SMS *Panther* to the Atlantic seaport of Agadir. The action caused outrage in France, which wanted Morocco for itself, and in Britain, which feared Germany gaining a good habor on the Atlantic. It precipitated a shake up of the British armed forces and led to Winston Churchill becoming First Lord of the Admiralty at the age of 37. In Fisher's day, First Lords of the Admiralty had been nonentities, whose main role had been to explain naval policies to Parliament. Churchill was very different, taking full command and firing admirals who didn't agree with him. He threw himself into the job and carried out reforms where Fisher had failed, creating a naval staff to plan campaigns, setting up a department of naval aviation, improving conditions for the seamen of the lower

SMS *PANTHER*
Sent to the Moroccan port of Agadir to secure it in
the name of German interests, this small German
gunboat triggered an international crisis.

deck, replacing coal with oil to power the fleet, and building new and even more fearsome battleships, including the Queen Elizabeth class. Equipped with 15-inch guns, these were the most powerful battleships of their day.

By 1914, Britain had a brand-new fleet of 22 dreadnought battleships and ten battle cruisers, whereas Germany had a mere 16 dreadnoughts and six cruisers. Von Tirpitz's fleet had failed to act as an effective deterrent, and Britain was now eager to pursue a more aggressive policy toward Germany. The chance for the two countries to lock horns came in June 1914, when the Austrian Archduke Franz Ferdinand was assassinated in Sarajevo, igniting a powder keg of alliances that led to Germany being at war with France, and Britain joining to defend Belgium. It was hoped that the war would be over by Christmas, but stalemates on land and at sea protracted it until 1918.

WINSTON CHURCHILL, 1912
During his time as First Lord of the Admiralty, Churchill strengthened the Royal Navy to counter the growing threat from Germany.

There never was a single, decisive battle between the Royal Navy and the German High Seas Fleet—though the Battle of Jutland came close in 1916 (see pp.290–99). Britain's warships eventually proved to be vulnerable to attack from a new and far more deadly type of vessel, one that would eventually supplant the battleship as the symbol of naval supremacy—the submarine (see p.315).

The Wars on the Oceans

1914–1945

At the start of World War I in 1914, jingoistic patriots in Britain and Germany looked forward to a contest between the great steel battleships of the rival navies. But the naval war failed to fulfil expectations. Except for a single, frustratingly indecisive encounter at Jutland in 1916, the British and German main battle fleets never met. Instead, German submarines posed the greatest threat to Britain. Sinking thousands of merchant ships, including the passenger liner RMS *Lusitania*, they narrowly failed to cut Britain's essential maritime supply routes.

After World War I, a defeated Germany was disarmed and other major powers negotiated limits on the size of their navies. By the 1920s, the era of mass emigration from Europe was at an end but luxury ocean travel flourished, reaching a peak of opulence in the French liner SS *Normandie* and the British RMS *Queen Mary*, which both entered service in the mid-1930s. Naval aviation came of age too, with the first purpose-built aircraft carriers entering service, but many naval commanders remained obsessed with big battleships.

After World War II broke out in 1939, the vulnerability of even the largest warships to air attack came as a shock. In the Pacific, Japan and the United States, at war from December 1941, fought an intensive naval conflict in which carriers played the leading role. A desperate struggle was waged to keep Atlantic sea lanes open as they came under attack from German U-boats. Merchant seamen suffered heavily in the front line of this conflict. The superior naval power of Britain and the United States was a crucial factor in achieving ultimate military victory. It allowed amphibious landings to be made on Japanese-held Pacific islands and on the coasts of German-occupied Europe, culminating in the massive armada assembled for the D-Day landings in Normandy in June 1944.

The Battle of Jutland

IN THE PEACEFUL summer of June 1914, a squadron of British dreadnought battleships and cruisers made a courtesy visit to the German port of Kiel during its annual regatta. The atmosphere was cordial on the surface, but Commander Georg von Hase, gunnery officer on the German battle cruiser SMS *Derfflinger*, observed the British crews with a cold, prejudiced eye: "The tall Teutonic type was far rarer than among our men," he later commented. "Indeed, I observed that a large number looked strongly Jewish, a thing which astonished me, as I knew that the Jews had a fundamental aversion to seafaring." Sublieutenant Stephen King-Hall of Britain's Royal Navy concluded, "If we ever cross swords, it will be with gallant opponents."

At all levels of the German navy, the British were regarded as the main potential enemy. Richard Stumpf was a seaman on the battleship SMS *Helgoland*, one of the ships built as part of Germany's naval arms race with Britain in the years leading up to the war (see pp.280–87). According to Stumpf, when news came through at the beginning of August 1914 that Germany was at war with Russia, the men were disappointed because they really wanted to fight the British. "We built our navy against the false and treacherous English!" When it became clear that Britain was going to declare war on Germany, Stumpf wrote in his diary, "All of us breathed a sigh of relief."

From the start of the war, Britain and Germany decided to conserve their huge and vastly expensive battle fleets. Not prepared to risk engagement except on favorable terms, the battleships of the German High Seas Fleet mostly stayed in port, reducing Stumpf and his comrades to the role of spectators. When a German naval force defeated a weaker British one off South America at the Battle of Coronel in November 1914, Stumpf hailed a "wonderful victory." He was also greatly excited by "the heroic deeds of our incomparable cruiser the *Emden*," which raided British shipping in the Indian Ocean. Even when the Germans were defeated by a much larger British naval squadron at the Falkland Islands in December the same year, he commented, "If the situation had been reversed... the battle would have lasted a mere five minutes."

Stumpf was most enthused by the performance of German U-boats. When the submarine *U-9* shocked the British by sinking three cruisers in September 1914, Stumpf cheered on her return to

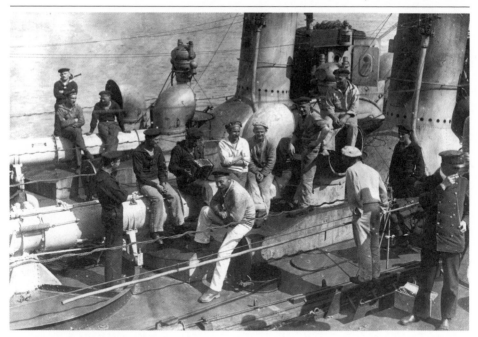

LIFE ON BOARD A GERMAN SHIP
The crewmen of a German torpedo boat enjoy
a rare moment of leisure in 1916. The lightly armored
vessels were designed to carry out torpedo attacks
on much larger enemy warships.

port. The following May, Stumpf and his fellow sailors gave the same enthusiastic welcome to the submarine *U-20* after it had sunk the passenger liner *Lusitania* with heavy civilian losses. Stumpf proclaimed, "Our German submarines have overthrown all the theories of naval warfare."

Stumpf, however, craved real action. On leave he met soldiers who mocked his uniform: "I was ashamed to be a sailor because they maintained that we did nothing but lie in port and that we did not dare to face the English fleet. I did not tell them that this was virtually true..." The High Seas Fleet had settled into a monotonous and stifling routine in port.

> ... at six we eat dinner and then we write letters, play cards or play music until 7:30... It is usually 8:30 before the noise quiets down and all the hammocks are slung... Groups of three or four men sit in a corner smoking their pipes which taste all the better now that smoking is forbidden... Often they continue spinning their yarns until eleven o'clock or until someone falls asleep.

All seamen shared a hatred of loading the ship with coal—heavy and filthy labor, which usually had to be done immediately after a patrol. The crew of the *Helgoland* once had to do it in front of civilians off the resort of Swinemünde:

> We began loading at 8:30... Our dusty work was watched with intense interest by ladies and gentlemen dressed in fragrant white clothes who rowed out to the ship. We were pleased when in a short time these people turned as dark as we were from the coal dust... Then the searchlights were turned on to illuminate our work and we continued... Finally, by one o'clock the last of the eight hundred tons had disappeared into the insatiable bunkers... The men were utterly exhausted. A layer of coal dust inches thick covered the entire deck.

Discontent among the crews was exacerbated by class conflict. There were some good officers in the German navy, but many were remote and aristocratic, something that at least one prewar captain approved of: "Experience teaches us that, as a rule, in Germany military qualities and the faculty of leadership, engendered by tradition and education, may be found with greater probability in the sons of certain classes than those of others..." On the *Helgoland*, one officer believed that, "the less educated a nation is, the easier it is to govern!" The food got worse over the years, which exacerbated the inequality:

SMS *HELGOLAND*
Despite being struck by a 15-inch British shell, the *Helgoland* sustained minimal damage during the Battle of Jutland.

ESTIMATED DEATHS AND INJURIES IN WORLD WAR I:

35,000,000

"While we have to content ourselves to live on half rations of bread," Stumpf wrote, "on the officers' mess they hold feasts and drinking bouts at which six or seven courses are served."

Late in May 1916, the High Seas Fleet left port to sail into the North Sea, hoping to surprise a detached portion of the British fleet and destroy it. After such a long period of inactivity, ordinary German sailors such as Stumpf, on board the *Helgoland*, doubted they would see real action. Von Hase, on SMS *Derfflinger*, described the scene in romantic terms: "The sun rose magnificently, covered the sea with its golden rays and soon showed us the picture of the whole High Seas Fleet proceeding to meet the enemy." The core of the fleet consisted of 16 dreadnought and six pre-dreadnought battleships, which formed a single line in action, as battleships had done for centuries. Ahead of them steamed five battle cruisers, with almost as much armament, but with greater speed and less armor. They provided a heavily armed reconnaissance force, and took part in the general gun action as required. In support were nine light cruisers, also in a reconnaissance role, and 60 torpedo boats, whose role was to deter submarines, fight off enemy torpedo boats, and launch torpedo attacks of their own.

Von Hase was desperate for the operation to be the real thing: "My career seemed so incomplete, so much of a failure if I did not have at least one opportunity of feeling in battle on the high seas what fighting was really like." He was not disappointed. On the afternoon of May 31, the German warships unexpectedly encountered the entire British Grand Fleet, sent out to intercept them.

On the face of it, the British force was materially superior—it had more ships of every type, armed with bigger guns. But the Royal Navy had several fatal flaws. Its ships, especially the Battlecruiser Fleet under the dashing Admiral Sir David Beatty, had had much less

THE BATTLE OF JUTLAND
The smaller German fleet inflicted greater losses than their more numerous opponent. Nevertheless, Britain retained strategic control of the North Sea.

exercise in gunnery, and British shells tended to explode on impact rather than penetrating German armor. The British battle cruisers, meanwhile, were too lightly armored to give effective protection against accurate German shell fire. The British fleet also suffered from poor signaling procedure that left subordinate commanders without adequate orders, a situation that they failed to remedy by using their initiative.

The battle that followed was named Skagerrak by the Germans, but was known to the British as Jutland. The initial encounter of the battle took place between the rival battle cruisers, with von Hase soon in the thick of the action. From the fore control position on the *Derfflinger*, he directed the fire of eight 12-inch guns over ranges of up to 12 miles (20 km). He was heavily reliant on technology, including the Zeiss range finder and the range clock. These computed factors such as range and bearing, wind resistance, and the movement of both ships—his own and the target. Skilled petty officer gunlayers kept their weapons constantly trained as the ship pitched and rolled. At 6 pm, under German shell fire, the British battle cruiser HMS *Indefatigable* blew up. This dramatic event was unseen by Commander von Hase, who was completely occupied in directing the shooting against another ship. The *Derfflinger* engaged the battle cruiser HMS *Queen Mary* until 6:26 pm, when von Hase observed:

First of all a vivid red flame shot up from her forepart. Then came an explosion forward which was followed by a much heavier explosion amidships, black debris of the ship flew into the air, and immediately afterwards the whole ship blew up with a terrific explosion... nothing but a thick, black cloud of smoke remained where the ship had been.

Both groups of battle cruisers headed north, Beatty leading the Germans toward the main body of the British Grand Fleet. The fleet's commander, Admiral John Jellicoe, skillfully deployed his battleships to sail in line across the Germans' path. This classic maneuver, known as "crossing the T," allowed all of his gunfire to be concentrated on their leading ships, as von Hase soon became aware: "At 8:15 pm, we came under heavy fire. It flashed out on all sides. We could only make out the ships' hulls indistinctly, but... enemy ships were all around us... It was now perfectly clear to us that we were faced with the whole English Fleet."

As the *Helgoland* came into action in the center of the German fleet, Stumpf, who had been observing the action as a lookout, reluctantly went down to his battle station in the ammunition chamber of a gun turret. In the stifling heat he heard the bridge announce, "Enemy has commenced firing. First volley 1,000 meters short." Then, "A violent wind blew through the chamber, the gun tower shook, 'Bang, bang!' our first broadside was off." But the

Modern Warships

The laying down of HMS *Dreadnought* (see pp.282–83) in 1906 marked the beginning of a new era of naval warfare—one in which the world's great powers built ever more powerful battleships, and the nuclear submarines that dominate the seas today.

HMS *CONQUEROR* (1911)
One of four Orion-class British super-dreadnoughts, the *Conqueror* fought at the Battle of Jutland in 1916 (see pp.290–99). Unlike the *Dreadnought*, her 13.5-inch guns were mounted along the centerline.

SMS *DERFFLINGER* (1913)
German battle cruiser the *Derfflinger* bombarded several English coastal towns during World War I, and took part in the battles of Dogger Bank and Jutland (see pp.290–99).

USS *BAINBRIDGE* (1920)
The *Bainbridge* was one of 156 Clemson-class destroyers produced for the US Navy from 1919. In World War II she made three convoy escort voyages to Newfoundland and Iceland.

BISMARCK (1936)
Pride of the German navy, the *Bismarck* saw battle just once, in 1941, during which she destroyed the British battle cruiser HMS *Hood*, before being sunk herself (see pp.308–17).

VITTORIO VENETO (1940)
The *Vittorio Veneto* was one of only three fast battleships built for the Italian navy between the world wars. In 1941, she participated in the Battle of Cape Matapan off the southwest coast of Greece.

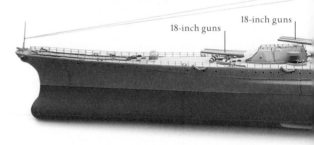

18-inch guns   18-inch guns

18-inch guns

YAMATO (1941)
The *Yamato* and her sister ship the *Musashi* were the biggest and most powerfully armed battleships ever built. The *Yamato* was the flagship of the Japanese fleet throughout 1942.

LE REDOUBTABLE (1971)
France's first ballistic missile submarine was equipped with the M20 missile, which was capable of delivering a one-megaton warhead at a range of over 1,864 miles (3,000 km).

JSS GEORGE WASHINGTON (1992)
With space to accommodate 80 aircraft, this American nuclear-powered supercarrier is 1,092 ft (333 m) long, 244 ft (78 m) wide. .

HMS LANCASTER (1992)
This British type-23 frigate carries Harpoon antiship missiles, Sea Wolf anti-aircraft missiles, Stingray antisubmarine torpedoes, and a Westland Merlin helicopter.

HMCS VANCOUVER (1993)
Belonging to the Canadian navy, the Vancouver is a Halifax-class multi-role frigate. She carries antisubmarine torpedoes, surface-to-air missiles, and a Sea King helicopter.

HMS ASTUTE (2010)
Armed with conventional torpedoes, Spearfish guided torpedoes, and Tomahawk cruise missiles, the British Astute is a nuclear-powered attack submarine.

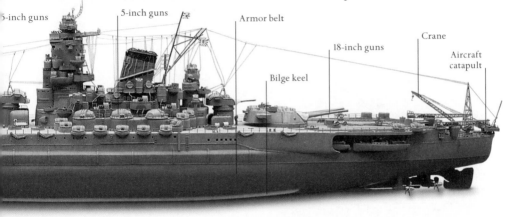

5-inch guns
5-inch guns
Armor belt
18-inch guns
Crane
Aircraft catapult
Bilge keel

German fleet's commander, Admiral Reinhard Scheer, ordered his ships to turn away in succession to avoid the devastating British fire. When he turned again to try to head back to his base, once more Scheer saw the Grand Fleet drawn up in line ahead of him. In desperation he ordered a "death ride" of the battle cruisers—a risky defensive maneuver—to protect the rest of the fleet, while his torpedo boats launched an attack. To his surprise the British ships turned away, for Jellicoe was not prepared to risk his battleships being sunk by German torpedoes.

Although Jellicoe's action gave the High Seas Fleet a chance of escape, as night fell it still risked being cut off from its base by the pursuing British warships. After midnight, seaman Stumpf was released from the magazine to resume his duties as bridge lookout. There were minor actions all night as British destroyers sought the German fleet in the darkness. As Stumpf described it, "There they are! The beam of the stern searchlight swooped on a gray shape and held fast. Mighty flames shot away from all our guns... Another broadside and a hit! I distinctly saw the pieces flying..." The following morning, the German ships completed the return to their home port. They had lost one battle cruiser, one old battleship, nine other ships, and 2,500 men. The British had lost three battle cruisers, 11 other ships, and 6,000 men.

The Germans believed they had won a great victory over the Royal Navy and Stumpf thought it was a "heaven-sent day." The British had a sense of disappointment that rankled for decades, but they had won a strategic victory. As their jubilation faded, the Germans accepted that they had been forced to retreat from the North Sea. Giving up any hope of catching a detached portion of the British fleet, the High Seas Fleet hardly left port again. The Germans instead put their energy into a new submarine campaign against merchant shipping, which caused the United States to declare war on Germany in April 1917, after

ADMIRAL REINHARD SCHEER
Known as a fierce disciplinarian and an accomplished tactician, Scheer commanded the German fleet at Jutland.

BRITISH SOUVENIR
This silk scarf commemorates
Britain's "victory" at Jutland.
In fact, the battle was far from
conclusive, and both sides
claimed to have won.

seven US merchant vessels were sunk. The High Seas Fleet lost its sense of purpose, as the best men were drafted away to the U-boats.

By October 1918, with Germany facing defeat in the war on the Western Front and its allies surrendering, the Admiralty in Berlin ordered the fleet to sea on a final, suicidal mission. But the war-weary sailors had no desire to sacrifice their lives in a futile gesture. Mutiny broke out in several ships, witnessed by Stumpf on the battleship SMS *Thüringen*: "the... crew simply locked up the petty officers and refused to weigh anchor. The men told the captain that they would only fight against the English if their fleet appeared in German waters." The authority of the officers collapsed, and following the naval mutiny there was a general revolt across Germany. With the country in the grip of revolution and their allies defeated, Kaiser Wilhelm II fled and a new German government was forced to accept stringent armistice terms. These included the internment of much of the High Seas Fleet in the British base at Scapa Flow in Scotland. In June 1919, the fleet salvaged some honor by scuttling itself in protest as the Treaty of Versailles imposed humiliating peace terms on Germany. Writing years later in 1926, von Hase claimed:

> Our German youth will grow up in an enslaved Germany in which foreign Powers are compelling us to work for them... Brave Germans, old and young alike, must, and will, see that our nation does not lose its inherent characteristics in feeble, servile and un-German conceptions of life and the world.

It was an attitude that bore terrible fruit over the next few years, as the Nazi party played on such feelings to assist its rise to power.

High Society at Sea

"**WELL DOROTHY AND I** are really on the ship sailing to Europe as anyone could tell by looking at the ocean… I always love a ship and I really love the *Majestic* because you would not know it was a ship because it is just like being at the Ritz…" Thus Lorelei Lee, the American heroine of Anita Loos' hit 1925 novel, *Gentlemen Prefer Blondes*, began her transatlantic adventure. She was joined by hundreds of thousands of Americans in the 1920s, crossing the ocean in very different conditions from those their predecessors had endured.

The age of mass migration was over. In 1921, the United States Congress passed the Quota Acts, which severely restricted immigration. Instead of poor emigrants from Europe, the typical ocean travelers were now wealthy Americans traveling the other way. In 1920, around 60,000 Americans crossed the Atlantic to visit Europe; by 1926 this figure had risen to 365,000. The shipping lines had to change their image for a new upmarket clientele. British-owned Cunard, for example, had formerly relied heavily on emigrants in steerage, but by 1927 had reinvented itself as a luxury line.

Anglo-American scriptwriter and author Basil Woon, a frequent transatlantic voyager, divided the "regular" American passengers into four types: there were, "Professional Men, meaning writers and others bent on 'investigating conditions' in Europe"; there were, "Professional Women, meaning actresses, alimony hunters, and ocean vampires"; there were society people, ranging from the very

GLAMOUR AT SEA
Luxury liners sometimes attracted movie stars, in this case Raoul Walsh, Mary Pickford, and Douglas Fairbanks aboard the *Olympic*.

rich such as the Rockefellers and Vanderbilts to "a Swedish masseur turned gigolo"; and there were buyers for large stores, often "highly-paid and extremely energetic women," who sought out "baby linen, millinery, dresses, laces, flowers, lingerie, handbags, lampshades, and so forth." Woon ranked students and tourists as "exceptional" travelers, in contrast to the "regulars."

A passenger could choose to go on a small ship that was slower, cheaper, and often more congenial. According to Woon, however:

> If... you are in the Social Swim, or if you want your name in the papers, or if you are a person to whom time means money, or your idea of the sea is something best hung up in a nice frame in the parlor, or if you... insist on fresh caviar with your luncheon and plovers' eggs with your dinner, or if you are just rich enough to want the world to know it, you will take a big, fast ship.

Liners retained a strong national flavor. In the Prohibition era, from 1920 to 1933, American ships had the disadvantage of being officially "dry." The United States Line stoutly denied rumors of bootleg liquor on board. The ships of the Compagnie Général Transatlantique had a strong appeal for Woon: "... the French Line ships are a foretaste of France. You disembark from one of them with precisely the sensation you have on leaving Paris." Italian ships mostly sailed directly to the Mediterranean. The star was the 32,000-ton *Roma* of 1926, one of the few newly built large ships in service, with a marvelous interior based on Renaissance art. The Holland-America Line ships were "among the finest and most efficiently-managed on the Atlantic." For many travelers, however, the Cunard Line's classic RMS *Mauretania*, launched in 1906, remained the doyenne of Atlantic travel. When the *Mauretania* was damaged by a fire in 1921, Cunard took the opportunity to re-outfit her interior and convert her to oil fuel instead of coal, which increased her speed and reduced the crew. She was refurbished again at the end of 1926 to meet French competition, with new carpeting, smaller tables in the dining rooms, and the veranda café replaced with a greenhouse.

The German lines (see pp.272–79), meanwhile, had been virtually eliminated from the market following Germany's defeat in World War I. Many German ships that had been confiscated as reparations under the peace terms imposed in 1919 reappeared under fresh names and flags.

CUNARD LINE POSTER
After its reinvention as a luxury line, Cunard rose
swiftly in the field. Posters such as this, from around
1930, were intended to convey prestige and opulence.

The newly formed United States Line had the *Leviathan* (ex-*Vaterland*) and
the British White Star line operated the 56,000-ton *Majestic* (ex-*Bismarck*—
not the ship of the same name that took part in World War II) which
claimed to be the largest ship on the transatlantic route.

The war had done much to level class differences ashore, and this
was partly reflected on board a liner. First class was still prestigious—a
passage to Europe would cost a minimum of US$285.50 in the *Mauretania*
in the summer, compared with US$152.50 in second class—but second-
class passengers were nearly as comfortable. Ships still had steerage,
though it no longer had the horrors of the prewar years, and third class
was now divided into "tourist" and "steerage" classes. The former was
filled with students while as Woon observed, steerage now had: "Clean
cabins for two, three, and four! Lounges, smoking-rooms, deck space!
Bathrooms!" But the very concept of "steerage" excited the philanthropic
instincts of some of the richer passengers. "On every ship there is the
Eager Gentleman or no-less Eager Lady who goes around with his or her
nose in the air looking for a Charitable Object. Every day she will visit
the steerage, and if one day she actually does discover that the wife of a
returning Slavic immigrant has given birth to a baby, why joy, oh joy!"

Woon advised a first- or second-class passenger that "a dinner-
jacket is as necessary to an ocean traveler as a tailcoat to a waiter.
Without it you may not, except on the first and last nights out, come
down to dinner. Without it you will have to sneak out of the smoking-
room at eight p.m." For the daytime, "Weird though it may be, the
Plus-Four... is now considered absolutely the only garment fit to
wear for promenading during daylight hours on deck." It was
important to choose the time of joining the ship and to dress

"If your ship sails late at night it is permissible—in fact, 'the thing' to go aboard in dinner clothes"

BASIL WOON

appropriately. "If your ship sails late at night it is permissible—in fact, 'the thing' to go aboard in dinner clothes. If it sails very early in the morning some lines will allow you to go on board the night before, so that you are happily asleep at the moment of departure." In 1927, the New York skyline was not the spectacle it later became, and seasoned travelers might well sleep as they sailed out of the city.

The novice passenger, on the other hand, was beginning "the Great Adventure of his life" as the ship pulled away from the pier in New York, wrote Woon: "No matter how hardened to novelty his heart may be, he will thrill to every minute of the first twenty-four hours. The hoisting of the gangway, the perceptibly widening ditch of water between ship and dock, the shrill good-byes, the snorting tugs, the realisation that actually you are *Off!* There is no sensation in the world like it." The passengers were now cut off from the world for at least five days, except for the radio, which could be very expensive to use.

The ship would reach the Gulf Stream on the second day out, where the weather was warmer and a coat was no longer needed on deck. Rough weather was felt less on a big ship, but Woon offered advice on seasickness and recommended passengers to wedge themselves into bed in rough weather. He suggested a tour of the ship if the weather permitted: "You will see the kennels, the slaughterhouse, the steerage, the garage, the stables, the second-class, the stokehold... and if you are lucky you may even be shown the navigating bridge." It would be "one of the most interesting experiences of your life."

Social life was an integral part of the voyage and was dominated by "the Sets"—sporting, bridge, poker, drinking, dancing, and exercise ("these last are great nuisances"). There were also "the seasick set, and the gossipy set." But the "Exclusive Persons" were separate from these— "an ambassador, a foreign diplomat, a great author, a moving picture actress, a cardinal of the Church of Rome, or even an Olympic champion. Each rapidly gathers a little circle of worshipers, forming frequently groups madly jealous of one another." Celebrities were common on the great ships and Basil Woon had no hesitation in dropping their names, though very few of them are recognizable today, even among the stars of the silent screen. They mostly had their favorite ships. "David W. Griffith is frequently aboard the *Olympic*... Mae Marsh, Albert Warner, Thomas Meighan, John Zanft, Sessue Hayawakawa, and Charlotte Greenwood like the *Leviathan*, a ship often chosen by

Douglas Fairbanks and Mary Pickford. Charles Chaplin travels little, but has been seen aboard the *Majestic*..." Celebrities and dignitaries were often more approachable than they would be on shore:

> ... members of the Atlantic Who's Who are agreeable persons; free from the little mannerisms of conceit which too often distinguish them ashore. There is something ego-dwarfing in the contemplation of a horizon with nothing upon it but water. There is also a baffling quality of indifference to fame about the very procedure of the ship itself... the Hollywood beauty who most of her life has merely to raise a shapely eyebrow to have the tiniest wish gratified, discovers that not even she, no not even she, can make the ship stop that circular movement which plays such havoc with the proper digestion of one's lobster mayonnaise.

Romance was also part of the voyage for Woon. "A girl you wouldn't turn around to look at twice on Fifth Avenue becomes, by the second day out, a 'pretty little thing'; by the fourth day she is a 'peach'; by the sixth she is the 'sweetest thing you ever saw'... You are madly, passionately, ravingly, crazy about her..." But that did not survive the voyage: "... you get your eye filled with visions of feminine loveliness on Piccadilly or the Boulevards... A week later you have difficulty in recalling her name."

As the ship neared Europe, passengers gambled on when Eddystone Lighthouse off the English coast would be sighted. Most of the liners called at Southampton and Cherbourg, people disembarking according to preference for London or Paris.

The Wall Street Crash of 1929, ushering in the Great Depression, hit the transatlantic trade. Meanwhile the prewar ships were wearing out. Cunard planned a new and greater liner to replace the *Mauretania*, which was launched in 1936 as the *Queen Mary*. It was a great event, for the liners were now symbols of national prestige, and around the same time France launched an equally impressive liner, the *Normandie*. These luxurious ships brought the golden age of the transatlantic liners to a new peak. However, the era of the grand ships, and their bold defiance of the tough economic times, did not last long. The outbreak of World War II in 1939 plunged the world's oceans into conflict once more, and the ships were either confined to port or put to use as troop ships. Many did not survive the war.

THE *MAURETANIA* DISEMBARKS
A tender takes American passengers and
their luggage ashore from Cunard liner
the *Mauretania* in Plymouth, England, after
a transatlantic crossing in 1925.

The Battle
of the Atlantic

IN THE SUMMER OF 1940, Lieutenant-Commander Joseph Wellings of the United States Navy, on leave in Boston prior to assuming command of a destroyer in Honolulu, was unexpectedly ordered instead to take up an appointment as Assistant Naval Attaché in London. At this point in World War II, France had surrendered and joined Poland, Norway, the Netherlands, and Belgium under Nazi occupation. Air battles were taking place daily over southern England, and a German invasion of Britain was expected at any moment. The US had stayed neutral at the beginning of the war and there was no immediate prospect of American involvement, but Vice Admiral Herbert Leary told Wellings forcefully: "Damnit, we are not going to fight the British. Tell them everything you know and get as much information out of them as you can." Wellings' appointment gave him an outstanding opportunity to observe British naval procedures and tactics in the conflict that would become known as the Battle of the Atlantic.

Dependent on imported food and fuel for survival, Britain had an absolute need to protect its merchant shipping from German attack. It was fortunate for the British that, when the war began in September 1939, the German navy was only in the early stages of a planned major expansion. Although German surface raiders played a part in attacks on merchant ships, submarines constituted the main threat. Admiral Karl Dönitz, commander of the German U-boat fleet, was clear that, "the focal point of warfare against England, and the one and only possibility of bringing England to her knees, lies in attacking her sea communications in the Atlantic." U-boat building was accelerated, so that from 26 U-boats capable of Atlantic operations at the beginning of the war, there were 64 in service by the fall of 1940. The defeat of France allowed the Germans to establish submarine bases on the French Atlantic coast from which to raid transatlantic sea lanes.

Resuming defensive tactics developed to counter German submarines in World War I, the British organized their merchant ships—except the very fastest ones—into convoys. Ordered to Britain, Wellings was first sent to Halifax, Nova Scotia, where he prepared to

THE BATTLE OF THE ATLANTIC 1939—45

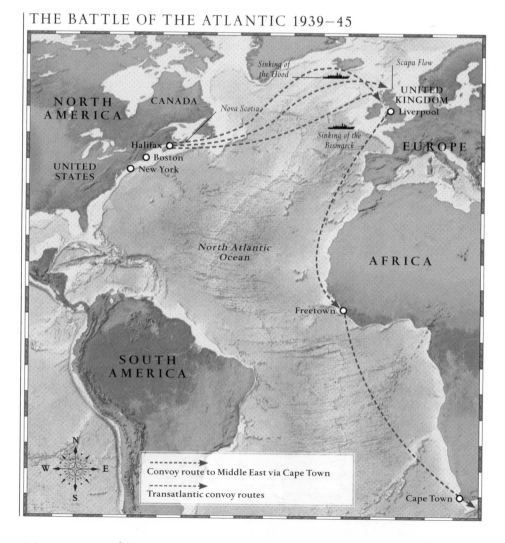

join a convoy of 42 merchant ships about to cross the Atlantic under
naval escort. He attended a conference in Halifax with the captains of
the naval escort vessels and merchant ships, as well as the convoy's
commodore, a retired naval officer whose job was to keep the merchant
ships in order. Each captain was given a pack of instructions as he left
the room. An hour and a half later, their ships raised anchor and began
to sail out of the harbor. The escort was headed by the converted
merchant ship HMS *Montclare*, armed with 5.5-inch guns, while
Wellings traveled in the commodore's ship, HMS *Hilary*, a former
passenger liner, leading the center column of the formation. At one

point, the convoy became disorganized in fog despite constant sounding of horns, but otherwise the voyage was thankfully without serious incident. The *Hilary*'s crew listened to the radio, hearing the news that US President Franklin Roosevelt had given 50 old destroyers to the Royal Navy in exchange for the use of bases. The convoy encountered no U-boats. After 12 days sailing at a speed of 9 knots, often zigzagging along the way, they were met by local escorts off the west of Scotland. The ships then split up to head for their separate destinations, the *Hilary* and 14 other vessels making for Liverpool.

Wellings was soon given a more in-depth view of the antisubmarine war. After experiencing German bombing in London, where the sustained air raids of the Blitz were just beginning, he was sent north to join the destroyer HMS *Eskimo* at Scapa Flow in the Orkneys. She was one of the famous Tribal class, among the most glamorous ships in the Royal Navy. As Wellings observed, destroyers were "always on the go," their duties including protecting convoys from U-boats. When Wellings took part in an antisubmarine exercise, the ship was dogged by mechanical trouble. It was clear that the Royal Navy was suffering from too fast an expansion, since two-thirds of the destroyer's officers and crew were new. But Wellings was impressed with the ship's captain, Commander St. John Aldrich Micklethwait, who had already won the Distinguished Service Order twice. Wellings noted:

At sea the captain was on the bridge during all maneuvers, including large changes in course. At other times he remained in his emergency cabin, reading light literature and sleeping. He… could not remain on the bridge all day and all night and be mentally and physically alert when an emergency arose.

SAILOR ON BOARD HMS *ESKIMO*
A sailor on board the Tribal-class destroyer *Eskimo* demonstrates a signaling lamp. Joseph Wellings joined the *Eskimo* at Scapa Flow in 1940 for antisubmarine exercises.

By 1941, the U-boat war was beginning to accelerate. A hundred British merchant ships were lost to enemy action in February, building up to 154 in April as the Germans adopted "wolf pack" tactics, with groups of U-boats collaborating to attack a single convoy. British convoy escorts were equipped with asdic, a sonar underwater detection device that was quite effective at finding submerged U-boats. But the submarines could not be detected on the surface at night. Wellings reported on U-boat tactics and British countermeasures:

> At night submarines approach from bow or quarter on surface with conning tower awash usually fire at ranges of one to two thousand yards and retire on surface in same direction from which they approached... Local escorts fire starshells on side of convoy in which ship torpedoed or submarine sighted. If side unknown all sides illuminated. Object is to sight submarine, force it to dive and then conduct intensive asdic search and attack.

It was in March 1941 that British Prime Minister Winston Churchill first coined the expression "the Battle of the Atlantic," and he later echoed German Admiral Dönitz's view on the importance of submarine warfare (see p.308) when he wrote, "The only thing that ever really frightened me during the war was the U-boat peril."

German surface raiders were also a threat to merchant convoys. Warding them off was the job of the Royal Navy's larger warships. Wellings spent time on board the great battle cruiser HMS *Hood*, the pride of the Royal Navy, in winter 1940–41. The *Hood* was based at Scapa Flow in Scotland, lying in wait in case one of the German raiders came out for a sortie into the North Sea or Atlantic. Wellings was impressed with the size of the ship and the friendliness of the officers, though he considered their seamanship poor—it took four hours to moor up to a buoy in strong winds. Despite rationing ashore, Wellings found the food on board was surprisingly good. After Christmas dinner he told his wife: "The only thing lacking was cranberry sauce." But life at Scapa Flow was extremely boring. When the ship sailed to Rosyth near Edinburgh, there was a holiday atmosphere in the wardroom at the thought of visiting the city.

In February 1941, Wellings was sent to the cruiser HMS *Birmingham*, which was escorting a convoy of 29 large ships taking troops and munitions to Egypt and the Middle East via Cape Town. Because of

HMS *RODNEY*
The British ship used her devastating 16-inch guns
against the battleship *Bismarck*. Prior to World War II,
the *Rodney* and her sister ship, HMS *Nelson*, were
considered the most powerful battleships afloat.

concern about attacks by surface raiders, for a time they were joined
by the battle cruiser HMS *Renown* and the aircraft carrier HMS *Ark
Royal*, which he wrote, "presented a beautiful silhouette on the
western horizon." The threat did not materialize and Wellings was
back in Britain by the end of April.

Wellings was then delighted to hear that he was to join the battleship
HMS *Rodney*, which was going to his home town of Boston to be re-
outfitted. The *Rodney* left the Clyde on May 23, but hopes of a
Wellings family reunion were soon dashed. The powerful German
battleship *Bismarck*, accompanied by the cruiser *Prince Eugen*, had left
port and sailed into the North Sea on course for the Atlantic, posing
a serious threat to Allied shipping. At 8 am on the 24th, the *Rodney*
received a terse but shocking radio signal from the battleship HMS
Prince of Wales, which had engaged the *Bismarck* with the *Hood* in the
Denmark Strait south of Greenland: "*Bismarck* fire extremely
accurate—straddling *Hood* on second or third salvo. Fire
immediately broke out in *Hood* near after port 4-inch AA twin

mount, spreading rapidly to mainmast. At 0600 an explosion occurred between the after funnel and the mainmast in *Hood* and she sank within 3 to 4 minutes." Only three men from *Hood*'s 1,418 crew survived. Wellings did not record his emotions on the loss of many friends, but the Royal Navy's shock was obvious enough. Sub-lieutenant Ludovic Kennedy of the destroyer HMS *Tartar* wrote, "The *Hood* gone—the most famous, most loved of British warships, the one above all that epitomized the Navy and the country? It seemed almost impossible to believe... If this is what the *Bismarck* could do in six minutes flat, what might she not achieve against the convoys from America?"

Now it was even more important to stop the *Bismarck*. The *Rodney* was one of many ships ordered in pursuit. The German battleship was lost for a time in the Atlantic, but then sighted by aircraft. Fairey Swordfish biplanes (affectionately known as "Stringbags") launched from the carriers HMS *Victorious* and *Ark Royal* attacked the *Bismarck* with torpedoes. Wellings kept copies of the reports of some of the pilots from the *Victorious*:

> The *Bismarck* was taking avoiding action by turning hard to starboard and it appeared that she was not willing to be attacked from the starboard side. The attack appeared to be rather straggly and drawn out. *Bismarck* fired a few rounds at us and we retired to shadow from 10 miles astern having seen at least five Swordfish attack and retire homewards. *Bismarck* seemed to be in trouble for some time after the attack, her course was erratic and white smoke was issuing from the funnel.

The huge German warship, despite her fearsome reputation, began to yield under the assault. Soon her steering gear was damaged by one of the torpedo attacks, and she was cornered by the *Rodney* and another battleship, HMS *King George V*, as well as several cruisers and a destroyer flotilla. Seeing her opponent's weakness, the *Rodney* opened fire with her 16-inch guns, the largest in the fleet—Wellings's first action with

ALLIED SHIPS SUNK BY GERMAN U-BOATS IN WORLD WAR II:

2,775

SURVIVING THE *BISMARCK*
An injured German seaman, rescued after the
sinking of the *Bismarck*, is taken ashore at the
British coast. The *Bismarck*'s captain, Ernst
Lindemann—who had commanded it for its
entire service history—went down with the ship.

the Royal Navy. The recoil of the full broadside had a startling impact, as recorded by another American passenger on the *Rodney*, Chief Petty Officer Miller: "Cast iron water mains were ruptured and in many instances broke, flooding compartments... All electric lights were disintegrated and bulbs and sockets snapped off the heads..." This was as nothing, of course, to the devastation inflicted by the *Rodney*'s shells on the *Bismarck*. After heavy shelling, the famous German battleship sank. Only 115 out of more than 2,000 of her crew were saved. Her demise marked the end of German warship raids in the Atlantic, and was widely celebrated in the British press.

The battle-weary Wellings eventually returned home to the US in mid-June 1941. On entering Boston Harbor, he records: "I really became homesick. I knew every buoy in the channel, and almost every rock on the bottom from my younger days sailing..." To his delight, his wife was there to meet him, "looking radiant and beautiful on the pier." Later that year, the US entered the war, fighting alongside Britain against Germany and Japan.

The Battle of the Atlantic continued unabated, and was the longest single campaign of the war. After the sinking of the *Bismarck*, it consisted almost entirely of U-boat attacks and the attempts to defend merchant ships from them. As Allied countermeasures improved, the U-boat crews suffered the heaviest losses of any branch of the services during the war—about two in every three men who served on U-boats lost their lives. The death toll was also appalling among Allied civilian merchant seamen—26,000 British merchant sailors were killed, besides those of other Allied nations. It was only in the spring of 1943 that the U-boat threat was defeated as the Allies equipped many more ships with radar detection, increased the number of escorts, and provided much more extensive air cover over the Atlantic. These successes directly affected the outcome of the war: they enabled Britain's merchant convoys to continue importing vital supplies, and they paved the way for the buildup of American and Canadian forces that carried out the crucial Normandy landings in 1944 (see pp.326–33).

ROYAL NAVY MANEUVERS
British battle cruisers including HMS *Hood*, pictured last in line, undertake maneuvers in the English Channel in 1939. The *Hood* later exploded after being hit by German shells off Scapa Flow in 1941, and sank within minutes.

The Battle of Midway

THE MAINTENANCE CREWS of the Japanese aircraft carriers *Akagi*, *Kaga*, *Hiryu*, and *Soryu* did not have much sleep on the night of June 3–4, 1942. They were preparing for an attack on Midway Atoll, two tiny American-held islands in a strategic position in the central Pacific. As the ships sailed through bad weather, their crews toiled in the dark, overcrowded hangars below deck to get 108 planes into order. The aircraft were brought up by elevator and the crews ranged them on the aft part of the flight deck. Maintenance Lieutenant Hirosho Suzuki described the work on the *Akagi*: "We mechanics really had tight working conditions on a flight deck that was filled with aircraft, and if just one plane moved abruptly, we could be killed." During the 15 minutes it took to warm up the engine of each aircraft, Hirosho kept in mind the day on which a man had been killed by a spinning propeller.

The four carriers were unmistakably Japanese with their long low hulls, flat decks, and tiny superstructures. The *Akagi*, converted from a battle cruiser while under construction in the 1920s, had a long flight deck on her 771 ft (235 m) hull and a speed of 31 knots. The *Kaga* was of the same 1920s vintage. Originally planned as a battleship, she was shorter and slower at 28 knots. The *Soryu* and *Hiryu* were smaller, purpose-built carriers better designed for attack than defense, with very light armor but a good speed of 34 knots. At 4:30 am on June 4, the four ships turned into the wind to allow the aircraft to take off. On a flag signal from the *buntaicho* (division officer), each pilot in turn revved up his engine and headed forward at full power. The first aircraft had the shortest take-off run. There was always tension as it left the deck and dipped briefly from sight before rising well above the carrier. The rest of the aircraft were launched in sequence, until the whole formation was ready to head toward Midway.

Morale among the Japanese naval aircrews was high. Their surprise attack on the American base at Pearl Harbor, Hawaii, which initiated the Pacific War in December 1941, had been planned with meticulous care, and executed with great daring. Japanese naval aircraft had sunk or damaged much of the American Pacific Fleet, destroyed hundreds of aircraft, and killed 3,681 personnel. United States aircraft carriers had been out on exercise at the time and remained intact to dispute Japanese sea power, but nonetheless Japan had scored some almost unbelievable victories since then, conquering the Philippines and inflicting a humiliating defeat on British imperialism by taking Singapore. The pilots on the Midway mission were confident combat veterans, most of whom had taken part in the attack on Pearl Harbor. "What's important in the world of naval aviators are your flying abilities," one Japanese pilot said, "not your rank or number of lines on your good conduct badge." Unlike their American or British counterparts, the majority of Japanese naval aircrew were not commissioned officers. Many were not even petty officers, but basic seamen.

The airmen flew three different types of aircraft. The two-seater Aichi Type 99 dive-bomber (known to the Americans as "Val") delivered an accurate bombing attack in a steep plunge from high altitude. The three-seater Nakajima Type 97 torpedo-bomber (known as "Kate") usually attacked ships in a low-altitude torpedo run, but could also carry conventional bombs. Fighter escort was provided by the famous Mitsubishi Type Zero. The fighter pilots in these regarded themselves as an elite and they loved their aircraft. "The Type Zero was a superb fighter," one pilot recorded. "I felt as if I was soaring and the aircraft was part of me." The Japanese pilots had not yet discovered its greatest fault—to save weight, it had practically no defensive armor.

The sweeping formation of Japanese aircraft headed toward Midway. It comprised of 36 of each type, the "Kates" armed with bombs rather than torpedoes for attack on land targets. Around (30 miles) 50 km from

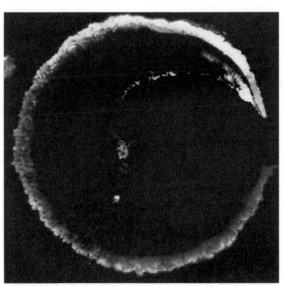

EVASIVE ACTION
Photographed from an American B-17 bomber, a Japanese aircraft carrier maneuvers in a full circle to avoid attack during the Battle of Midway.

UNDER FIRE
A Japanese torpedo-bomber barely avoids
heavy American anti-aircraft fire as it flies
in low over the water toward its target.

their destination, the first wave of the battle began, and the Zero fighter
pilots' combat skills were tested as they were attacked by a force of 25 US
Marine fighters based on the islands. Most of the American fighters were
obsolete Brewster F2A-3 Buffaloes, about which an American officer
wrote, "any commander that orders pilots out for combat on an F2A-3
should consider the pilot lost before leaving the ground." The fighters
engaged, and in the ensuing air battle 15 of the American planes were
shot down. Some of the "Kate" bombers met intense anti-aircraft fire
over the target. Power stations, a hangar, and oil storage tanks were hit
by Japanese bombs, creating a large column of black smoke.

Eleven Japanese aircraft were lost. The remainder flew back to their
carriers to find that the ships were under attack by American B-17
Flying Fortress bombers from Midway. High-level bombing of ships
hardly ever inflicted damage but it forced the carriers to take evasive
action and delayed landing until the attack was over. The pilots then
had to face the challenge of landing on a carrier at sea: each aircraft had
to turn toward the ship 650 ft (200 m) away and approach at an angle of
seven degrees, then gradually reduce the speed with throttle and flaps
while avoiding a stall, which could be fatal. As the ship pitched and
rolled, the pilot glanced at green and red lamps adjusted by the *hikocho*,
or air officer, to show the correct angle of landing.

Admiral Chuichi Nagumo, the commander of the Japanese carrier
force, ordered that the planes be re-armed for a second strike on
Midway. But then Japanese plans began to go awry. The Japanese high

command had believed that the only air opposition would come from the weak forces based on Midway itself, that all the American carriers were out of action or elsewhere. But the US had cracked Japanese naval codes, giving them advance knowledge of the attack on Midway. The US Navy had sent three carriers to the area—the USS *Enterprise*, the USS *Hornet*, and the USS *Yorktown*, which had been repaired with amazing speed after being badly damaged only a month before at the Battle of the Coral Sea. When Chuichi was informed that American warships had been sighted, including a carrier, he ordered aircraft preparing for the second strike on Midway to be armed instead for a strike against ships. Maintenance Petty Officer Kaname Shimoyama commented: "There was utter confusion on *Akagi*; it would have been much easier to leave our aircraft as is. Inside our hangar there was very little room, and it was very hard to do this job... When I looked at all this confusion, even though I was a low-ranking person, I thought, is it really wise to be doing this?"

Meanwhile the American carriers had launched their aircraft— Dauntless dive-bombers, Devastator torpedo-bombers, and Wildcat fighters—to attack the Japanese carriers. But the various groups became separated. The American fighters were nowhere near the torpedo planes and dive-bombers they were supposed to protect. Arriving first at their target, all 15 aircraft of *Hornet*'s torpedo squadron were shot down by Zeroes hurriedly launched from the four Japanese carriers. When *Enterprise*'s torpedo-bombers arrived 15 minutes later, 10 of the 14 were lost, with no hits on the carriers. Watching the American torpedo aircraft deliver their low-altitude attack without fighter escort, Petty Officer Haruo Yoshino, an aircrewman on board the *Kaga*, began to doubt what he had been told about American cowardice.

Despite the confusion of the Americans' air assault, it was here that the battle reached a critical turning point. The US torpedo bombers had failed to hit their targets, but they had drawn the Japanese fighters low down and exhausted their ammunition. When the high-flying American dive-bombers arrived, they found the Japanese carriers unprotected, and launched a devastating attack. Dauntlesses from the *Enterprise* attacked the *Akagi* and *Kaga*, while those of the *Yorktown* dived onto the *Soryu*. All the carriers were in a highly vulnerable condition, with fuel and bombs on deck and in the hangars. Hiroshi was in the operations center of the *Akagi* at the time and witnessed the destruction:

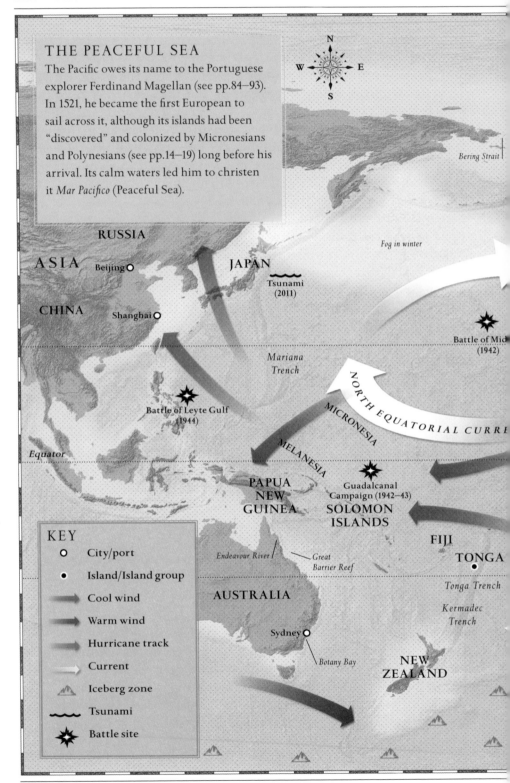

THE PEACEFUL SEA

The Pacific owes its name to the Portuguese explorer Ferdinand Magellan (see pp.84–93). In 1521, he became the first European to sail across it, although its islands had been "discovered" and colonized by Micronesians and Polynesians (see pp.14–19) long before his arrival. Its calm waters led him to christen it *Mar Pacifico* (Peaceful Sea).

Bering Strait

N
W   E
S

Fog in winter

RUSSIA

ASIA   Beijing○   JAPAN
                          〰 Tsunami
CHINA   (2011)
        Shanghai○   Battle of Mid
                                                  (1942)

                          *Mariana
                           Trench*
                                    NORTH EQUATORIAL CURRE

        Battle of Leyte Gulf
            (1944)   MICRONESIA

Equator   MELANESIA
                                          Guadalcanal
                          PAPUA   Campaign (1942–43)
                          NEW
                          GUINEA   SOLOMON
                                        ISLANDS
                                                      FIJI
KEY   TONGA
                                                          •
    ○   City/port
                     Endeavour River — Great   *Tonga Trench*
    •   Island/Island group   Barrier Reef
                                                      *Kermadec
         Cool wind   AUSTRALIA   Trench*

         Warm wind

         Hurricane track   Sydney○
                                                      NEW
         Current   *Botany Bay*   ZEALAND

    ⛰   Iceberg zone

    〰   Tsunami

    ✸   Battle site

The Pacific Ocean

With a surface area of 63.8 million sq miles (165.25 million sq km), the Pacific is the largest ocean on earth, covering more than 30 percent of its surface. It extends from the Arctic in the north to the Antarctic in the south and is bounded by Asia and Australia in the west and the Americas in the east. It is also the deepest of the world's oceans, and it is home to the Mariana Trench, which contains the deepest point on earth. The Pacific is fringed with mountain ranges, many of them volcanic.

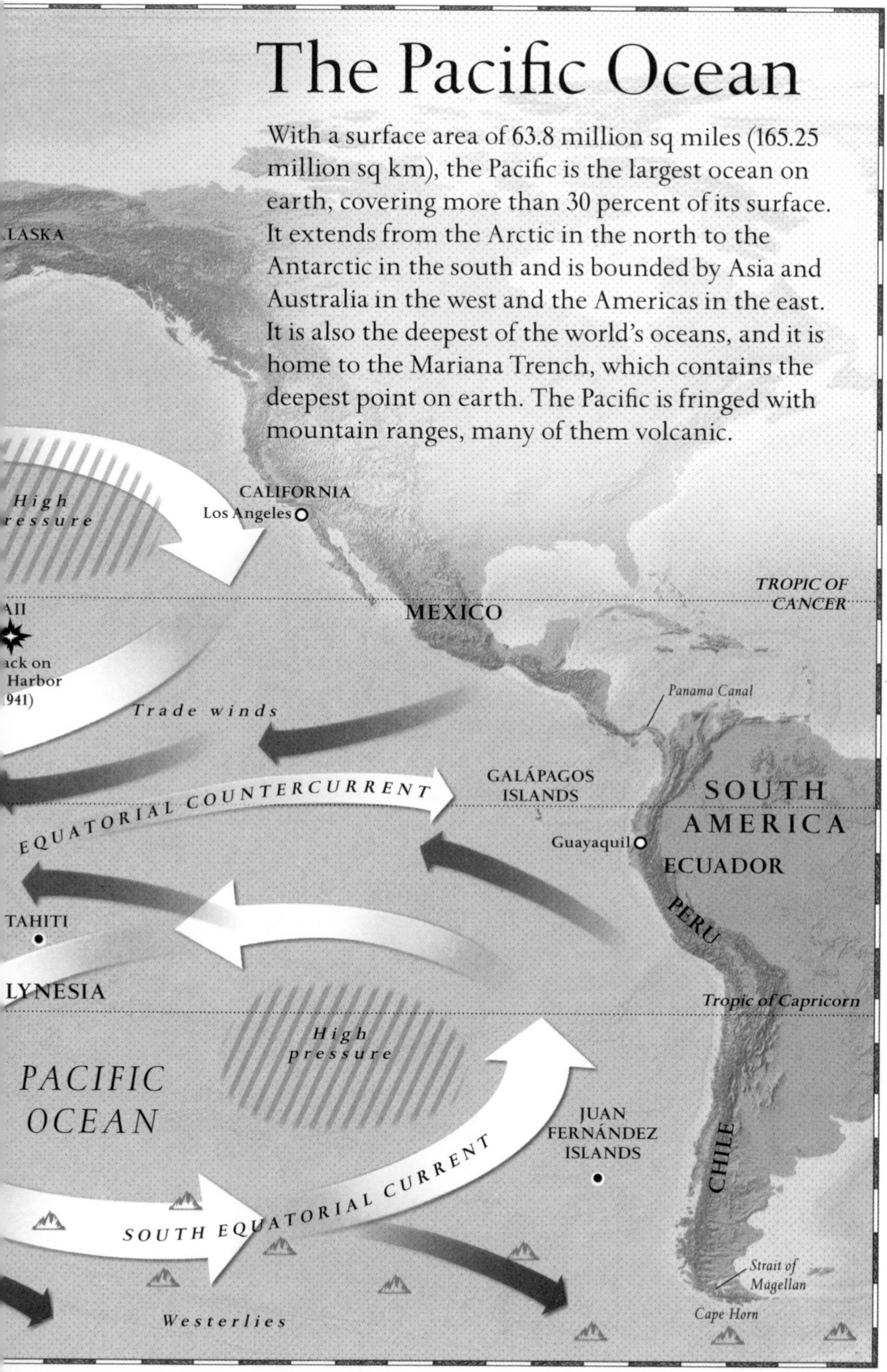

ALASKA

High pressure

CALIFORNIA
Los Angeles O

TROPIC OF CANCER

AII

ack on Harbor 941)

MEXICO

Panama Canal

Trade winds

EQUATORIAL COUNTERCURRENT

GALÁPAGOS ISLANDS

SOUTH AMERICA

Guayaquil O

ECUADOR

PERU

TAHITI

LYNESIA

Tropic of Capricorn

High pressure

PACIFIC OCEAN

JUAN FERNÁNDEZ ISLANDS

CHILE

SOUTH EQUATORIAL CURRENT

Strait of Magellan

Westerlies

Cape Horn

Once again, a warning blared out that we were being attacked. The first bomb was a near miss, but I was knocked down by the force of the blast… I wasn't hurt, except that my face was all black. Then there was a direct hit on our carrier that caused a big explosion. This bomb landed squarely on the Zero fighters sitting on the flight deck. As the aircraft ignited a big fire rose up… I thought that the *Akagi* would split in half due to the big explosions…

Taisuke Maruyama went up to the flight deck of the *Hiryu*, the only carrier that was not under attack. "I couldn't believe my eyes when I saw the terrible sight of our damaged ships… On board the *Kaga* I could see airplanes exploding; soon it became an inferno. Also, in the middle of that, bombs exploded in a chain reaction. *Akagi* was in the same situation when two bombs hit the ship." Three out of four Japanese carriers were fatally damaged. Within the space of a few minutes, the balance of power in the Pacific was shifting dramatically. The Japanese command believed they only had one American carrier against them and that the *Hiryu* was still operational. Returning Zero pilots landed on her decks, including ace pilot Kaname Harada of the *Soryu*. His damaged plane was dumped over the side, and another one was readied for him. Meanwhile strikes took off against the American carrier. The Japanese found the *Yorktown* defended by 28 fighters. Taisake, in his "Kate" torpedo-bomber, was one of those who faced the American Wildcats: "We were attacked again and attempted to escape, but our aircraft was very slow due to the 800-kilogram torpedo… the tail of our aircraft looked like a honeycomb… and the left fuel tank was leaking very badly. Nevertheless, I didn't want to die until I dropped my torpedo." He successfully launched it, and believed it was one of two to hit the *Yorktown*. The American carrier was also hit by three bombs, and was seriously damaged.

"Vengeance will not be complete until Japanese sea power is reduced to impotence"

US ADMIRAL NIMITZ

**DAUNTLESS
DIVE-BOMBERS**
Above the US Navy
aircraft carrier USS
Enterprise, a squadron
of Douglas SBD-3
Dauntless dive-bombers
flies in formation.

Back on the *Hiryu*, Kaname was called on deck as his new plane was
ready. He took off just as another American attack began. He was
only 800 yd (730 m) from the deck when the ship was hit by dive-
bombers from the *Enterprise* and the *Yorktown*. Soon the *Hiryu* too was
ablaze and Kaname faced a carrier pilot's nightmare—he was in the
middle of the ocean with no carrier to land on. Flying around in
circles, he regretted not bringing his pistol to end his life, since he
believed some of his colleagues did. Eventually he saw a destroyer and
ditched his plane into the sea close to her, but she was attacked by
American B-17s and made off. Stranded floating in the Pacific in his
waterlogged aircraft, it was dark before he managed to attract the
attention of another destroyer, which picked him up. Delight turned
to horror when he arrived on the deck to find it covered by horribly
wounded men from the other ships, with missing limbs, severe burns,
and mangled bodies. He urged the ship's doctor to treat them first,
only to be told that he was a priority since he could return to battle,
while the others were useless for fighting.

The Japanese had relied on a quick victory in their war against the
US, but that was now unlikely. In addition to the four carriers, they
had lost many of their most skilled pilots, and the standard of their
aircrew declined rapidly as the war progressed. Despite the loss of the
Yorktown, the Americans had regained their confidence and soon went
on the offensive at Guadalcanal. Their industrial strength was crucial,
with factories and shipyards working at maximum production. The
defeat at Midway was concealed from the Japanese people, but in the
long term it ensured American victory in the Pacific.

The D-Day Landings

IN JUNE 1944, United States General Dwight D. Eisenhower had to make one of the biggest decisions in history. Based at Southwick House, outside Portsmouth in southern England, Eisenhower was Supreme Commander of Allied invasion forces preparing to land in German-occupied Normandy. Hundreds of thousands of men—chiefly American, British, and Canadian—and more than 6,000 ships and boats had been ready for the operation to take place on Monday, June 5, but the landings had been postponed at the last moment because the weather was too bad. If there were any further delays, the tides and the moon—needed for its illumination—would not be in the right combination for another month. The troops and sailors would pass their peak of readiness, the Germans would have more time to prepare the defenses, and there was every chance of a security leak. Hope was fading when Group-Captain James Stagg, a Royal Air Force meteorologist, produced a new weather report: "... there will be an interval of fair conditions which... should last at least until dawn on Tuesday." There is some question of exactly what Eisenhower said, but one version suggests it was, "OK, let her rip." The landings were set for the morning of June 6.

The British were responsible for the lion's share of the naval side of the Normandy landings, with 112,000 Royal Navy sailors engaged alongside 53,000 Americans. Both countries had to learn fast to mount the most complex military operation in history. In the US,

EISENHOWER AND CHURCHILL
The American and British leaders confer with Field Marshall Sir Alan Brooke, Chief of the Imperial General Staff and Churchill's principal military advisor, on the progress of the war in 1944.

the Marine Corps had developed techniques for amphibious landings and put them into practice fighting the Japanese in the Pacific. Landings on European shores posed different challenges from Pacific islands, however, with wind and tide a greater problem than surf. Britain had neglected amphibious operations before World War II, but the defeat of the British Army in Europe in 1940 and the evacuation from the beaches at Dunkirk had caused a drastic rethink. Prime Minister Winston Churchill had ordered the setting up of Combined Operations to develop appropriate material and techniques. In 1943 and early 1944, the British and Americans carried out landings in Sicily and Italy that provided troops and landing craft crews with some experience of actual conditions. But nothing was a full preparation for Normandy, where they would meet strong beach defenses and the force of the German army.

Between them, the US and Britain evolved a bewildering collection of landing craft types, in three main classes. The largest were landing ships, which were not intended to land on the beaches, but carried smaller craft to within range of the shore. These minor landing craft (or landing boats) were designed to carry a platoon of more than 30 men, the smallest unit commanded by an officer. The British Landing Craft Assault (LCA) had armored sides and two engines, giving a maximum speed of around 7 knots. The American equivalent was officially known as the Landing Craft, Vehicle, Personnel (LCVP) but more often called the Higgins Boat after its designer, Andrew Higgins. It was similar in size to the LCA but with a large single engine that gave a speed of about 10 knots. It was light and unarmored so that it could pass over sandbanks. However, most troops preferred the security given by the light armor of the British LCA. The LCVPs and LCAs were launched from landing ships a few miles off the beaches. The third class, major landing craft, were larger vessels designed to make the whole journey from the embarkation port to the beach under their own power. These included the Landing Craft, Tank (LCT), jointly evolved by the US and Britain, which was able to carry up to nine heavy fighting vehicles (see pp.328–29)—it was essential that they landed not long after the infantry, to provide support. Within each of the three classes, craft could also be divided by function—those intended to land infantry, or vehicles, or to carry out other support tasks, which included gunfire support, fighter aircraft direction, navigation, and even providing floating kitchens.

Landing Craft

Landing craft were developed in World War I, as the need to mobilize large numbers of troops and weapons rendered the conventional method of landing via a ship's boats obsolete. It was in World War II, however, that amphibious warfare came of age. Tens of thousands of landing craft were produced to a variety of designs, primarily for the navies of the United States and Britain.

LANDING CRAFT (TANK)
GREAT BRITAIN, 1942–45

The Landing Craft (Tank) was initially developed by the British Royal Navy, and subsequently adapted for use by the US Navy from 1942 onward. An amphibious assault ship for landing tanks onto beachheads, it was employed in the Normandy landings in 1944,

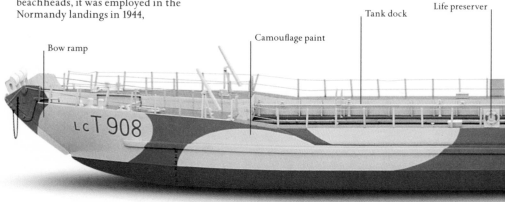

Tank dock

Life preserver

Camouflage paint

Bow ramp

Lc T 908

Landing craft design

A wide range of landing and amphibious craft was produced during World War II. Whether they were used to transport infantry or tanks, or as amphibious assault vehicles, most had design features in common, such as a flat bottom and a flat frontage with a ramp that could be lowered, instead of a bow. These enabled the landing vessels to run up onto the seashore and unload their cargoes quickly and efficiently, but they also made the craft uncomfortable for passengers and difficult to control.

DUKW AMPHIBIOUS TRUCK, 1942

Naval assault and landings

From 1942, Allied naval forces honed their expertise in troop landings. After their success in escorting troops to North Africa in late 1942, British and American warships went on to cover the landings in Southern Italy and Sicily the following year, and played a crucial role in the success of the large-scale invasion of Normandy in June 1944.

A TOTAL OF 1,213 WARSHIPS, 4,126 LANDING CRAFT, AND 1,600 SUPPORT VESSELS TOOK PART IN THE NORMANDY LANDINGS

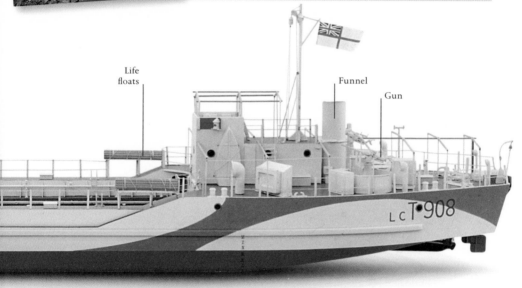

Life floats

Funnel

Gun

LCT·908

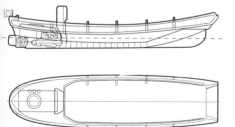

DAIHATSU
A World War II Japanese landing craft, the Daihatsu had a similar, but superior, design to the LCVP (right) which made it more seaworthy.

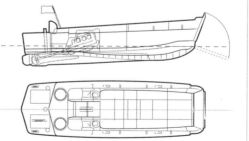

LCVP HIGGINS
The US Navy's World War II Landing Craft, Vehicle, Personnel (LCVP) was based on a boat built for use in swamps.

The troops were to go ashore on five Normandy beaches, code-named Omaha, Utah, Gold, Juno, and Sword. The Americans were to land at Omaha and Utah, the British at Gold and Sword, and Canadians and British at Juno. The Germans were convinced that the Allies would invade by the much shorter route across the Straits of Dover, but they had not left Normandy undefended, building concrete bunkers proofed against shell fire, and various types of beach obstacles between high and low water. The great bulk of the invasion force was based in southern England. When the order to start was given, the ships sailed toward an assembly area code-named Piccadilly Circus, south of the Isle of Wight. From there the different groups headed toward France under cover of darkness, sailing down channels that had been swept for mines. Strong escort forces were positioned on the flanks to keep away German U-boats and torpedo boats. The Allies had almost total air superiority since most of the Luftwaffe had been withdrawn to defend Germany against bombing. During the night, paratroopers and glider-borne troops were flown into drop zones near the landing beaches. Naval and air bombardment attempted to soften up the German defenses in preparation for the landings.

Sublieutenant "Jimmy" Green of the Royal Naval Volunteer Reserve was in charge of the six LCAs carrying American troops to be launched from the *Empire Javelin*, a Landing Ship Infantry (Large). The ship first left Portland Harbour on the south coast of England on the evening of June 4, but turned back when the initial attempt was canceled. She sailed again the next night, making an uneventful but choppy crossing of the English Channel. Green was roused in the early hours of the morning. His LCAs were to be the first wave to come ashore at Omaha Beach. Because the sea was rough, he was told, it had been deemed necessary to launch earlier than initially planned in order to reach the beach at the prescribed time. Green climbed on board LCA 910, where he was joined by Captain Taylor Fellers of the

TROOPS PUT
ASHORE ON D-DAY:
—————————————
132,175

US Army with 31 of his men, "a friendly but shy bunch of fresh-faced country lads" from D Company of the 116th Regiment. Very few of the landing craft crews had known anything about the sea before the war, so Green

D-DAY LANDING IN NORMANDY
American troops go ashore on Omaha Beach on
June 6, 1944—D-Day. They had to wade through
waist-deep water under heavy fire, and more than
2,500 American soldiers died in the landings.

considered himself very lucky to have Leading Seaman Martin, an
expert sailor from Newfoundland, alongside him. The boat was
lowered to the sea and immediately hit in the stern by the next
landing craft, LCA 911, causing a leak that had to be bailed out.

Green's LCAs had a long journey to the shore, because the
Americans insisted on launching 11 miles (18 km) off to be out of
range of enemy gunfire. On the way they overtook an LCT floundering
in the waves. Clearly it would not land its tanks ahead of the infantry.
Out of their sight, another armored force was in greater trouble.
Duplex Drive (DD) amphibious tanks—Shermans equipped with a
flotation screen and a propeller—were supposed to "swim" ashore
and land first, but nearly all of them were lost in the waves. Another
big idea was to use Landing Craft (Rocket) to bombard the beaches.
Green watched in dismay as one fired its missiles: "Not one came

anywhere near the shoreline." More promising was one Landing Craft (Gun) that went close inshore ahead of Green's flotilla and scored a hit on a fortified German guard post, but it soon moved on.

The boats went in line-ahead formation to pass through minefields, but changed to line-abreast for the final approach to the beach. Before going in, Green was distressed to see LCA 911 sinking nearby, but he had no room to pick up survivors and had clear orders to get to the beach. The general plan was to land soon after low water, while the beach obstacles were still exposed. Green arrived at the right time and in the right place—though none of the other flotillas did, since they were nearly all swept farther east by the wind and tide. The landing ramp was lowered and the troops exited into water up to their waists, wading 20–30 yd (18–27 m) to the shore. But then they had to cross 100 yd (90 m) of open beach that, contrary to expectations, had not been cratered by naval gunfire.

As Green headed back to the parent ship, there was catastrophe on the beach behind him. Situated between the cliffs at Pointe du Hoc and Port-en-Bessin and backed with 100 ft (30 m) bluffs, Omaha was always going to be tough. Almost everything went wrong on the day. Few of the troops landed in the right place and much of the heavy equipment did not land at all. Naval and air bombardment had failed to damage the German defenses, and the invaders were not just faced with the German 716th Static Division as they expected, but elements of the battle-hardened 352nd Division. US Sergeant Harry Bare was one of those caught by heavy fire from machine guns, rifles, and shells:

> Our boat dropped its landing ramp somewhere near Les Moulins, and my lieutenant, the first off, took a shot in the throat, and I never saw him again. As ranking non-com, I tried to get my men off the boat, and make it somehow under the cliff. I saw men frozen in the sand, unable to move. My radio man had his head blown off three yards from me. The beach was covered with bodies, men with no legs, no arms—God, it was awful.

A little later in the morning the American novelist Ernest Hemingway, at the time a war correspondent for *Collier's Magazine*, was in an LCVP launched from the transport ship USS *Dorothea L. Dix* as part of the seventh wave of the landings at Omaha. The landing craft was commanded by US Navy Lieutenant Robert "Andy" Anderson. On the way in they were impressed with the fire of the battleship

USS *Texas*, bombarding German positions onshore. "There would be a flash like a blast furnace from the 14-inch guns," Hemingway wrote, "… Then the yellow-brown smoke would cloud out and… the concussion and the report would hit us… like a punch with a heavy, dry glove." One soldier commented, "I guess there won't be a man alive there," but in reality naval gunfire was rarely accurate enough to destroy enemy strongpoints.

Anderson's map of the area was blown overboard. Hemingway believed he had memorized it and tried to help, but there was a desperate search for the right beach. "There is the Colleville church. There's the house on the beach. There's the Ruquet Valley on Easy Red to the right. This is Fox Green, absolutely." But craft were circling in a confusing manner offshore and they did not go in yet. Hemingway could see that the landing was not going well. "'There's something as wrong as hell', I said to Andy. 'See the tanks? They're all along the edge of the beach. They haven't gone in at all. Just then one of the tanks flared up and started to burn with thick black smoke and yellow flame." In some ways it was worse for the secondary waves as the tide rose to cover the beach obstacles and restrict the troops to a narrow strip of sand under the enemy guns. Anderson finally got directions from an officer on the beach with a megaphone. "Do you see that ruined house? Fox Green beach runs for eleven hundred and thirty-five yards to the right of that ruined house." Eventually they headed for a spot where the army officer on board thought his unit was. They landed the men under machine-gun fire and Anderson called out, "Get her out of here!"

By that time the tide of battle was beginning to turn on Omaha Beach. Small parties began to penetrate the gullies, and destroyers moved in close to shore to give gunfire support. By the afternoon it was clear that the assault had been successful. Meanwhile the force for Utah Beach had landed too far to the east, but was coherent and unopposed. The British and Canadian landings at Gold, Juno, and Sword had been successful with comparatively light casualties, though they did not move inland as fast as planned and it took a month to capture the first-day target of Caen. Over 132,000 soldiers had been put ashore on D-day in the largest amphibious operation in history. Eisenhower's decision had proved correct, and the Allied armies were able to advance through Europe to end the war.

The Global
Ocean

1945–PRESENT

In the modern era, much of the glamour and excitement associated with ocean voyages has gone. Although passenger jets largely replaced ocean liners for long-distance travel by the 1970s, ships remained central to warfare and international trade. The tonnage of merchant shipping on the world's oceans increased six-fold between the 1950s and 2000, and huge oil tankers were built that would have dwarfed the *Titanic*. Computer technology meant that giant container ships could be operated by a crew of fewer than 20—however, using this new technology was not without risk, and the 20th century saw the first oil slicks caused by wrecked tankers. In warfare, navies adapted to a high-tech age. Armed with missiles instead of guns, relatively small warships could deploy more effective firepower than the old big-gun battleships, while aircraft carriers grew in size and carried supersonic jets. The largest carriers were driven by nuclear power, which gave them virtually unlimited range, while the first nuclear-powered submarines were introduced in the 1950s and were capable of remaining submerged almost indefinitely; some of them were armed with nuclear missiles, as were surface warships. The United States established an overwhelming naval dominance, unchallenged after the dissolution of the Soviet Union in 1991. The role of the US Navy and its allied forces was primarily to attack land targets with sea-launched missiles and carrier aircraft as part of the projection of global power.

In the age of computers and GPS navigation, ocean travel has mostly become safe and routine—however, smuggling and piracy are still rife in the more lawless corners of the world. The romance of the sea inevitably declined, but an element of glamour stayed on in the form of luxury cruise ships, while the lure of adventure inspired oceanic yachting races and long-distance voyages by lone sailors. The exploration of the ocean depths, meanwhile, opened up a new world as little known as the far reaches of outer space.

The Container Revolution

ON APRIL 26, 1956, a hundred dignitaries were given lunch at Port Newark, in New York harbor, and watched as a crane loaded 58 heavy 33-ft (10-m) containers onto the deck of a converted tanker. It took eight hours for the ship to be loaded, and she set sail the same day for Houston, Texas. Days later, when she arrived at her destination, the dockworkers were "amazed to see a tanker with all these boxes on deck," according to one witness. "We had seen thousands of tankers in Houston, but never one like this. So everybody looked at this monstrosity and they couldn't believe their eyes." The ship's name was the *Ideal X*, and she was the first of a new type of vessel that would revolutionize international trade.

In many parts of the world, the 1950s are often seen as a conservative age, typified by men in gray suits and women back at home after their wartime service, yet the second half of the decade saw some of the greatest social, economic, and political revolutions in history. The West (including North America, Western Europe, Australia, and New Zealand) enjoyed continuous economic growth, minimal poverty, low unemployment, and rising standards of living. West Germany and Japan were integrating into the western world, which formed a single trading bloc. Youth culture took off, the civil rights movement gained momentum, millions of families were buying television sets, washing machines, and cars for the first time, and the age of mass travel began with the introduction of the Boeing 707 jet airliner in 1958. Amid all this, the start of the container revolution passed by almost unnoticed.

The "father of containerization," as he became known, was an American entrepreneur called Malcolm McLean. Like Brunel—the railroad

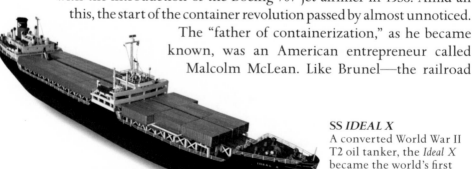

SS *IDEAL X*
A converted World War II T2 oil tanker, the *Ideal X* became the world's first container ship in 1955.

THE PRE-CONTAINER ERA
Dockworkers unload foodstuffs from a merchant ship
in 1931. Loose cargo was unwieldy and time-consuming
to load on and off ships.

"WHY U.S. NEEDS NEW SHIPS"
This *Popular Science* magazine cover from
1946 illustrated the need for reform in the
postwar shipping industry.

engineer who founded transatlantic steam travel (see p.193)—McLean came from a different transportation sector. Born in North Carolina in 1914, he bought his first truck in 1934, and by the early 1950s had developed the second-largest trucking company in the United States, with 1,776 vehicles. From the very beginning, however, he had noted the inefficiency of the port system: "I had to wait most of the day to deliver the bales, sitting there in my truck, watching stevedores load other cargo… I watched them take each crate off the truck and slip it into a sling, which would then lift the crate into the hold of the ship." As an alternative, he considered the possibilities of moving goods by sea along the east coast of the US. A ship could carry hundreds of truckloads with comparatively small fuel costs, and required only a small crew instead of hundreds of drivers. There were also far lower maintenance costs for a ship, and none for the water itself (unlike roads, which needed regular repairs and funding through taxes). He toyed with the notion of driving trailers straight onto ships, but a better idea was to lift the trailers onto the ships without their chassis, which would give them maximum space and allow them to be stacked. He bought an old wartime T2 tanker called Potrero Hills and converted her to carry containers on her upper deck, renaming her the *Ideal X*.

McLean designed boxes that were strong enough to support the weight of several others on top, and had cranes installed at Newark and Houston ports. Every container had sockets at each corner that engaged with the spreader bar hoisted by the crane, so there was no need for a worker to touch the container during loading or unloading, except to secure it on deck. US antitrust laws prevented McLean from owning both trucking and shipping firms, so he was obliged to sell his trucking company when he bought the Pan-Atlantic Steamship Company, which he later renamed Sea-Land in honor of its new role. When the *Ideal X* finished her maiden voyage at Houston, shippers were astonished that the containers had been moved so cheaply and that the goods were dry and undamaged. McLean then outfitted a second ship, the Gateway City, which was designed so that containers could be carried in her hold as well as on deck. Though shorter than the *Ideal X*, she could carry nearly four times as many containers.

Standardized containers had been used in shipping for centuries, from the amphorae of ancient Greece to the medieval casks, or "tuns," that give their name to "tonnage" as the measure of a merchant ship's capacity. But in the 1950s, much cargo was still being shipped as individual items, known as "break-bulk," and major ports employed vast forces of casual labor to move it. The condition of these workers was highlighted in the 1954 movie *On the Waterfront*, which was based on a series of articles printed in the *New York Sun* revealing the corruption and crime that were rife in US dockyards. Father Corridan, the New York waterfront priest who was the model for Karl Malden's character in the movie, claimed that "the heart of the matter is the system of hiring along the waterfront. Men are hired as if they were beasts of burden, part of the slave market of a pagan era." In London, too, the work was hard and often dangerous. As one worker wrote, "If your cargo was brown sugar, and the bags were all encrusted together, you'd have to separate them with a crow bar. You pried the bag up enough to be able to slip a chain under a sack weighing anything up to three hundredweight." When unloading frozen meat, "the worst thing is to go down too far, and make your working space too deep. Because once the cold air started getting out of it, they'd start sliding on you."

The accident rate at the docks was even higher than in the construction and mining businesses—but it did, at least, provide employment for the dockworkers, and when the safer system of containerization appeared, it met with huge resistance from workers on both sides of the Atlantic. Watching the *Gateway City* set off, one official of the International Longshoremen's Association hoped that she would sink "right here." In Britain, the dockers were militant and powerful supporters of workers' rights, and their strikes would shake the government as late as 1972.

Containerization progressed steadily after the voyages of the *Ideal X* and *Gateway City*, and the Matson Line operated services from New York to

TOTAL LENGTH OF CONTAINERS ON A MODERN SHIP IF LAID END TO END:

54 MILES
(87 KM)

Venezuela. Then, in 1966, the Sea-Land ship *Fairland* made the first transatlantic container voyage, calling at Rotterdam in the Netherlands, Bremen in Germany, and Grangemouth in Scotland. Heavy US involvement in the Vietnam War from 1965 consolidated the importance of containers, showing how they improved military supply chains. As a result, in 1968, the first in a series of international conferences established standard sizes for containers—the "20-foot" container, for example, was 8 ft (2.4 m) wide, 8 ft 6 in (2.5 m) high and 20 ft (6 m) long.

Deals between shipping companies and dockworkers were struck in many ports, such as Seattle, where maritime worker Jerry Tyler recorded one particular speech: "We can fight the employers on this container issue and we can cost them millions of dollars. But we're going to lose. You cannot fight progress." The speaker proposed "trading no opposition to containers for better health and welfare, early retirement and nobody loses a job." However, in many cases the power of the workers and the unions—or in some cases of organized crime—was bypassed when new ports were built and obscure ones expanded. Felixstowe, for instance, was little known until its growth in the 1960s and 1970s made it Britain's biggest container port, while nearly all the London docks were closed.

By 1970, containerization had become a truly international system, with each container bearing a standard serial number for identification. American companies receded in importance, and most of today's 9,000 ships operate from the Far East (Sea-Land was taken over by the Danish Maersk Line in 1999). The latest ships can carry the equivalent of 15,000 of the "20 foot" containers. Loading and unloading is a highly technical operation, which takes into account the stability of the ship, ease of access at each port, and the isolation of dangerous goods. Architect Danny Marc Samuels describes the work in the port of Houston, the destination of the first container voyage:

> The density of trucks on the roads carrying containers increases until finally they line up in 26 rows at the entrances to the facility, an average of 1,600 in or out each day. Each truck yields its load to a rubber-tired gantry crane [which] stacks the containers in well-ordered rows... Usually with no more than two moves... they are positioned for loading onto ships, separated for different parts of the hold by destination and weight (heavier containers... lower in the hold). Then in a final move from gantry to truck to giant wharf crane, the containers are loaded on board.

"BREAK BULK"
Loose "break-bulk" cargo is loaded in Amsterdam Port in 1950, shortly before the era of the container. Today the port is the second busiest in the world, and mostly carries "bulk" (unpackaged) cargo.

Writer Maria Staal watched this process from a ship docked at the port of Gioia Tauro, in Italy:

> Several port workers, or stevedores, had come on board… The nerve center during cargo operations was the ship's office on the main deck. From there also the stability of the ship was monitored… To avoid capsizing, water was pumped in and out of the ballast tanks to keep it level. Soon the cranes were off-loading the containers from out deck.

The first great shipping revolution was the development of the three-masted ship in the 15th century (see pp.72–73), while the second was the introduction of steam power in the course of the 19th century (see pp.192–201). The container was only one part of the third great shipping revolution—the 1950s and 60s also saw the introduction of the bulk carrier to replace the old tramp steamer (see p.273). Today, 95 percent of the world's goods still travel by sea, with only a few high-value items transported by air. The cost of sea travel has now become negligible—about one or two percent of the price of the goods transported, while in the 1950s it was up to 25 or even 50 percent. A television set that sells for $700 costs $10 to transport across the oceans, and a liter of gasoline is transported to the US at a cost of half a cent. Such radical economies have led to an enormous increase in international trade, and have contributed to the emergence of China, Japan, and South Korea as economic powerhouses—consequences that were unthinkable when the *Ideal X* set sail, but are a direct result of McLean's revolutionary system for speeding up shipping procedures.

The Cuban
Missile Crisis

AT AROUND MIDNIGHT ON OCTOBER 1, 1962, four Soviet submarines (B-14, B-36, B-59, and B-130) slipped their moorings at half-hour intervals and headed out of the Arctic port of Saida Bay near Murmansk, in the Soviet Union. To the crews inside, the nature of the mission was unclear, but they knew it was a special operation because there was tropical equipment on board and teams of intelligence officers had joined them, taking up space in the already overcrowded submarines. Captain Dubivko of the B-36 was proud that the vessels (which were all of the Model 641 class) were among the best diesel-electric submarines in the world, but they were not nuclear submarines and would have to spend much of their time on the surface since traveling underwater was much slower. Each boat carried the normal complement of 22 torpedoes (10 in the launch tubes and 12 spares), but one in each vessel was armed with a nuclear warhead, a fact that was unknown to American intelligence. As the submarines passed Kola Bay, the captains opened their secret orders, which instructed them to head across the Atlantic to Cuba, the Soviet Union's new ally. They were then to set up a submarine base at Mariel Bay, near Havana, largely to deter American attacks on the island. The orders on the use of nuclear torpedoes were ambiguous; those from the admiral in command said that they should be fired if they were attacked, but the written orders said that they could only be used on explicit instructions from Moscow.

The years from 1957 to 1963 saw unparalleled tension between the world's two superpowers, the United States and the Soviet Union, and their NATO and Warsaw Pact allies. Both sides had hydrogen bombs that were at least a thousand times more powerful than those dropped on Japan in 1945, and both had ballistic missiles that could deliver them over distances of thousands of miles. The Soviets had demonstrated their rocket capability by putting the world's first satellite, Sputnik I, into space in 1957, and the first man into space in 1961, leaving the American space program lagging behind. At the same time, there was an escalating number of international crises. In 1960, the Soviets shot down an American U2 spy plane over Soviet territory, and in 1961, the

THE CUBAN MISSILE CRISIS, 1962

Walnut line
Soviet submarines
Soviet transport ships

UNITED STATES

FLORIDA

Key West

Mariel Bay

Havana

CUBA

Bay of Pigs

Sargasso Sea

Turks Island Passage

HAITI   DOMINICAN REPUBLIC

North Atlantic Ocean

Walnut line

South Pacific Ocean

SOUTH AMERICA

N
W   E
S

Berlin Wall was built. There was also conflict in the developing world, where both sides competed for support in the newly liberated colonies. When guerrilla leader Fidel Castro overthrew the corrupt Batista regime in Cuba in 1959, he had not intended to form an alliance with the Soviets, but he was isolated by the US and felt that he had no alternative. Three national leaders of very different characters thus became locked in combat—the bull-like Soviet premier Nikita Khrushchev, the sophisticated US president John F. Kennedy, and the loquacious Castro, who had a strong following in the developing world and among the left wing in the West—and after an American-

KHRUSHCHEV AND KENNEDY
The two leaders had met in 1961, the year before the Cuban missile crisis, at the tense Vienna Summit.

backed invasion of Cuba was defeated at the Bay of Pigs in 1961, it seemed that Kennedy was already off balance. Then, in October 1962, American intelligence confirmed that the Soviet Union was installing weapons, including nuclear-tipped medium-range ballistic missiles, in Cuba to deter an American attack and to give the Soviets a strategic platform in the Caribbean. The US repsonded by demanding that the Soviets dismantle all missile bases in Cuba and return the weapons to the USSR. Kennedy rejected the idea of countering with a missile attack on Cuba, deciding instead to "quarantine" the island—a term that was deliberately chosen instead of "blockade," since the latter implied an act of war. The navy was instructed to set up the "walnut line" about 500 miles (800 km) north of Cuba, with destroyers stationed at 50-mile (80-km) intervals, and all ships approaching Cuba were to be stopped and searched for missiles. This cordon would be backed up by every available ship in the US navy, including aircraft carriers, and by land-based air patrols.

The Executive Committee of the US National Security Council met at 6 pm on October 23, just before Kennedy announced the quarantine to the world. Kennedy was nervous about the proposed method of signaling to the Soviet submarines—by dropping practice depth charges on them. He had been a naval officer in World War II and he was also worried about the mechanics of boarding a Soviet ship, saying, "They're gonna keep going. And we're gonna try to shoot the rudder off or the boiler. And then we're going to try to board it. And they're going to fire guns, machine guns. And we're going to have a hell of a time trying to get aboard that thing." Kennedy was

SOVIET SUBMARINE NEAR CUBA
This attack submarine was photographed from a US Navy aircraft near Cuban quarantine operations at the height of the Cuban missile crisis.

assured that the Soviet ships had only small crews, and the meeting turned to other matters. The committee met again the following day as the quarantine was taking effect. They knew several Soviet submarines were in the area and feared that these might attack the American ships, but news soon arrived that changed the entire picture. John McCone, head of the CIA, confirmed that a number of Soviet ships had reached the blockade line and had either stopped or turned back. The Secretary of State, Dean Rusk, famously whispered to George McBundy, the National Security Adviser, "We are eyeball to eyeball, and I think the other fellow just blinked."

Things were going Kennedy's way, but out in the Atlantic there was still great danger. The Soviet submarine commanders had crossed the Atlantic on a tight schedule, and now, after two weeks at sea, they received new orders. Instead of heading for Cuba (and possible shore leave) they were to "deploy in a barrier due north of the entrance to the Turks Island Passage and take up combat positions in the Sargasso Sea." No reasons were given, but the intelligence parties on each boat were able to glean from radio broadcasts that Kennedy had announced the quarantine of Cuba, and they believed it to be the start of a US invasion.

As the four submarines set off, the B-130's engines broke down and she had to be towed a the supply ship, leaving just three submarines with mechanical problems as the sole Soviet force standing against the scores of American vessels. They were unaware that the rest of the Soviet ships had turned back. B-4 was not detected by the Americans, but B-59 was bombarded by depth charges and hand grenades from the US destroyers USS *Beale* and USS *Cony*. The

RUSSIAN MISSILES, NOVEMBER 1962
This US intelligence photograph released by the
Pentagon shows eight Soviet ballistic missiles
clearly visible aboard the Russian cargo ship
Anosov, which is transporting them back to
the USSR from Cuba.

bombardment lasted for four hours and, according to Lieutenant Orlov of the B-59's crew, "It felt like you were sitting in a metal barrel, which somebody is constantly blasting with a sledgehammer." The submarine had been underwater so long that her batteries were running low, and only emergency lighting could be used. The temperature rose to 140° F (60° C) in the engine room, so men could only enter for short periods. Air quality declined, and the watch officers fainted one after another. Captain Savitsky was exhausted and knew very little about what was going on above. He ordered the nuclear torpedo to be prepared for use, and according to Orlov, became highly emotional: "Maybe the war has already started up there, while we are doing somersaults here. We're going to blast them now! We will die but we will sink them all—we will not disgrace our navy!"

Orlov's account has been disputed, but if true, this was the most dangerous moment of the whole crisis, and perhaps of world history. Launching the torpedo might have destroyed an American ship with a warhead as powerful as the ones used at Hiroshima or Nagasaki, and the Americans would probably have retaliated with nuclear depth charges— it is difficult to see where it would have ended. Savitsky could not make the decision to attack without consulting his officers, and the executive officer Arkhipov and political commissar Maslennikov were against launching. At 8:52 pm on Saturday October 27, B-59 gave a recognized international signal to the Americans and surfaced to find itself surrounded by five US destroyers. Jazz was being played aboard one of the ships, so Captain Savitsky concluded that they were not at war.

In B-36, Captain Dubivko was pleased at how much the range of his detecting devices had increased in warmer water, but he had problems communicating when he had to submerge to avoid the Americans. He had heard enough from the radio to know they were not yet at war, but

SATIRIZING THE CRISIS
This political cartoon from 1962 depicts Fidel Castro and Nikita Khrushchev backstage at a theater, holding a "promise by US not to invade Cuba" and a nuclear missile respectively. At the time, the US government did not realize how close to nuclear war they came.

"There was a feeling that if there is war, then it will be inevitable death for everybody"

NIKITA KHRUSHCHEV

he did not know that the crisis was almost resolved. On October 31, he was surrounded by the American destroyers USS *Cecil*, USS *Speed*, and USS *Aldebaran*, and did his best to avoid them, discharging decoys and carrying out evasive maneuvers. However, part of his hull had been damaged and the boat could not go below about 230 ft (70 m). Only the forward and aft compartments were habitable and crew had to be sent there in rotation. Drinking water had been rationed to 9 oz (250 g) per day, and the men were losing weight due to dehydration and developing rashes on their skin. After 36 hours of pursuit, Captain Dubivko had to decide what to do. His batteries were almost flat, and "not observing any aggressive actions on the part of the surface ships... I made a decision to come up to the surface to charge the batteries." As soon as he did so, helicopters appeared overhead and he was surrounded by American ships, one of which signaled "Do you need help?"—to which he replied "We do not need help. Asking you not to interfere with my actions." The *Cecil* followed the submarine for two days while its batteries recharged, then the U-boat submerged and gave the Americans the slip.

It was eventually agreed that the Soviets would remove their missiles from Cuba in return for an American guarantee not to invade. The Americans also secretly agreed to remove their missiles from Turkey, and it looked as if Kennedy had won a dramatic victory. He would almost certainly have won reelection had he not been assassinated in 1963, and Khrushchev fell from power in 1964. The crisis showed the gigantic risks involved in brinkmanship between nuclear powers, and the US and the Soviet Union began to move toward arms limitation and better communications, establishing a "hot line" telephone link between the White House and the Kremlin. However, US intelligence had failed to judge the severity of the crisis. The fact that the Soviet submarines had been armed with nuclear warheads—and had come close to launching them—was not known to the US until 2002.

Exploring the Deep

ON A SUNNY SUMMER'S DAY IN 1943, near Bandol on the Mediterranean coast of France, Jacques-Yves Cousteau and his friends Phillipe Tailliez and Frédéric Dumas assembled the apparatus they had recently received by train from Paris. They were anxious to hide it from the occupying German and Italian troops, and also from Cousteau's own brother, who was a Nazi collaborator. They headed for a secluded cove, where Cousteau tested the equipment in the water:

> I kicked the fins languidly and traveled down, gaining speed... When I stopped, I slowly emptied my lungs and held my breath. The diminished volume of my body decreased the lifting force of the water, and I sank dreamily down. I inhaled a great chestful (of air) and retained it. I rose to the surface... I took normal breaths in a slow rhythm, bowed my head, and swam slowly down to thirty feet... the Aqua-Lung automatically fed me increased compressed air to meet the new pressure layer... I reached the bottom in a state of excitement...

His invention was the Aqua-Lung, a device that enabled divers to swim freely underwater for long periods of time, aided only by a tank of compressed air strapped to their back. It revolutionized underwater exploration and was quickly adopted by the US Navy—who renamed it the SCUBA (self-contained underwater breathing apparatus) system—but it was only the first of Cousteau's many achievements in a life devoted to diving, moviemaking, and oceanography.

Born in the Gironde region of France in 1910, Cousteau was a passionate swimmer and loved boats from an early age. He learned how to dive when his family moved to New York in 1920, and on his return to France in 1930, he bought his first movie camera. He joined the French Naval Academy in the same year, but a car accident left him partially paralyzed in his right arm, preventing him from becoming a naval aviator. He took a post on a naval base in Toulon, where naval officer Philippe Tailliez encouraged him to explore the underwater world of the Mediterranean Sea—and it was here that he, Tailliez, and diving expert Frédéric Dumas experimented with conventional diving equipment.

Diving suits were easy to buy in France, but they were expensive, restrictive, and required a great deal of training. As Cousteau wrote: "I thought of the helmet diver arriving on his ponderous boots... and struggling to walk a few steps, obsessed with his umbilici and his head imprisoned in copper." Like many great inventions, Cousteau's alternative was a combination of several tried and tested elements. The face mask had been developed by Maurice Fernez, and the fins (or flippers) had been patented by Louis de Corlieu in 1933. Compressed air was already being used in a system devised by Commander Yves Le Prieur, but the diver had to open a valve every time he needed to take a breath. What Cousteau contributed, with the help of engineer Emile Gagnan, was a "demand valve," which lets the diver receive air automatically with each breath, at the right pressure according to his depth in the water. The liberating effect of using an Aqua-Lung was described by the Australian writer James Aldridge:

TESTING THE EQUIPMENT
Jacques Cousteau, on the right, tests the new "French lung" with the help of diver Terry Young in 1950.

> ... the moment you are under it, the depth and solidity of the water around you give you a feeling of freedom which even flying cannot yet satisfy above, for no man has yet devised wings for the body itself which is what you feel like under water; a man with wings, free, in a free element. To dive and zoom, with no other power but your legs, is finally to free the body of the need of a single line of gravity running from head to toe.

When the war ended, Cousteau's equipment triggered interest all around the world in underwater "treasure hunting." Cousteau himself found and explored the Roman wreck the *Mahdia*, off the

FILMING UNDERWATER
In addition to his pioneering oceanographic and
conservation work, Jacques Cousteau also created
innovations in underwater camera technology.

coast of Tunisia, but his main interest was marine life and he wanted
to film it, so he developed a camera that could be used at depths of up
to 2,000 ft (600 m). He left the navy in 1949, and the following year he
bought a former minesweeper, which he renamed the *Calypso*, and
equipped her as an oceanographic vessel with instruments for diving
and scientific research. She was made of wood, which meant that she
could be repaired easily in out-of-the way ports without metal-
working facilities, and her shallow draft meant that she could navigate
coastal waters as well as the open ocean. Her most prominent feature
was her "false nose"—an underwater viewing point in the bows,
which was reached by a tunnel ahead of the stem. Some of the cabins
were converted into laboratories and over time she was outfitted with
many different types of sensor, including radar and sonar.

Below decks, the *Calypso* had a small storeroom, a hold for
provisions, a freezer, a machine shop, and an engine room
containing two 580-horsepower diesel engines that could give a
speed of 10 knots. The crew's quarters were somewhat spartan, with
two-tier bunks, but the crew of 17 could be increased to 30 with

some crowding. The hold aft was used to store all kinds of underwater equipment—in 1970, for example, it housed underwater scooters specially designed to negotiate the strong, changeable currents around the Galápagos Islands, and a small submarine with a delicate plexiglass nose. Cousteau was particularly careful in making the *Calypso* suitable for diving:

> … [she has] a wet diving well down through the hull, entered through the galley, so that divers could go into the water amidships, the most stable point on the hull. In bad weather they could avoid passing through the waves at the sides. From cold dives they would climb into the warm kitchen.

The *Calypso*'s first major expedition was to the Red Sea in 1951, where Cousteau and his colleagues went diving to explore the coral reefs:

> … [the Red Sea is] a corridor of marvels—the happiest hours of my diving experience have been spent there… the reef of Shab Suleim was an intaglio of structure with porches of coral, winding couloirs and countless narrow cracks aswarm with beings waiting in the wings like walk-on players at the opera.

Cousteau recounted these adventures in his best-selling book *The Silent World* (1953), followed by a documentary of the same name that stunned viewers with the first color footage of the undersea world. It won an Oscar in 1957, and made Cousteau a household name. His experiments with new equipment continued, and he developed a specially adapted pressure-proof camera that he used at a phenomenal depth of 4 miles (7 km). In 1962, off the coast of Sudan, he built the first of several underwater Continental Shelf Stations, in which divers could live for days on end. Conshelf II, as it was known, had a

COUSTEAU'S INFLUENCE
Jacques Cousteau's underwater exploits fired the imagination of the public and were featured in many magazines, such as this 1950 edition of *Popular Science*.

submarine hanger in which a two-man "diving saucer" (also invented by Cousteau, with Jean Mollard) could dock. "Conshelf III" was set up near Cap Ferrat, between Nice and Monaco, in 1965, and six divers spent three weeks there at a depth of 336 ft (100 m).

In February 1967, Cousteau announced that the *Calypso* was setting sail on a four-year voyage of exploration, largely to film *The Undersea World of Jacques Cousteau*, a new series to be shown on American television. It was a journey that would utilize all the diving and underwater filming technology that Cousteau had developed, and the result was the work he is best remembered for. The theme of the series was marine biodiversity, and its ten episodes, broadcast over two-and-a-half years, highlighted the beauty and fragility of the world's underwater ecosystems. One of its most memorable scenes showed Cousteau's encounter with the marine iguanas of the Galápagos Islands in the Pacific Ocean— creatures that Cousteau admired for their diving ability. As his chief diver, Bernard Delemotte, noted, "iguanas are not very good swimmers, but they are remarkable divers. They are able to go down very rapidly; and they move quickly once they are on the bottom." In the narrow channel between Baltra Island and Santa Cruz, Cousteau followed the iguanas down to great depths. He even performed an electrocardiogram on one, proving that its

AN IGUANA DIVES
In his television series, *The Undersea World of Jacques Cousteau*, the French conservationist followed iguanas for the first time as they dived to great depths.

"We forget that the water cycle and the life cycle are one"

JACQUES COUSTEAU

heartbeat slowed down from 45 to eight or nine beats per minute in deep water. He also showed that iguanas emptied their lungs while diving, to reduce buoyancy, and absorbed oxygen from air carried under their skin.

Such underwater adventures made Cousteau an avid conservationist, and inspired him to produce numerous stand-alone movies highlighting the detrimental effects that humans were having on the environment. He was also a tireless campaigner for the cessation of commercial whaling. As he lamented in 1976:

> Surely whales have more to offer us than "seafood" for our cats, or stays for corsets, or ribs for umbrellas. *Calypso*'s men are intensely aware of the whales' true value; we have seen these gray-black cylinders of flesh from underwater; we have been scrutinized by their cloudy blue eyes; our limbs have been spared the crushing impact of a female whale's fin. We have heard the whales sing. And we want—we very desperately want—to hear them sing again.

Cousteau was aware that a profound change had taken place in the world: "For most of history, man has had to fight nature to survive; in this century he is beginning to realize that, in order to survive, he must protect it." His legacy of countless books, over 120 television documentaries, numerous inventions, and the work of the nonprofit organization Cousteau Society, founded in 1973, has done much to alert the world to that change, and has brought to its attention many of the environmental issues that dominate the news today.

Undersea Exploration

Marine manned submersibles, or unmanned submersible ROVs (remotely operated vehicles), are a type of mini-submarine designed for use in deep-sea activities ranging from oceanographic surveys to the exploration of wrecks. Built to withstand the extreme pressures of the deep ocean, some can operate at depths of 4¼ miles (7 km).

Vertical thruster propels the vessel up or down

Hook for lowering the vessel into the water

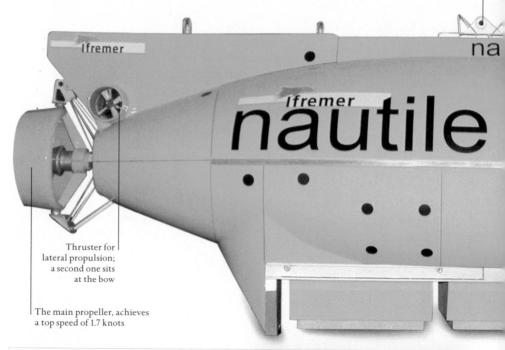

Thruster for lateral propulsion; a second one sits at the bow

The main propeller, achieves a top speed of 1.7 knots

DSV *ALVIN*

Built in 1964 as a improvement on heavier, less maneuverable bathyscapes such as the *Trieste*, the *Alvin* can carry a crew of one pilot and two scientists to depths of 2¾ miles (4.5 km), and has taken part in over 4,000 dives. Equipped with a pair of robotic arms, she can also be outfitted with a range of additional surveying equipment.

THE *ALVIN* USING ITS ROBOTIC ARMS TO GATHER SAMPLES FROM THE OCEAN FLOOR

NAUTILE
FRANCE, 1984

The three-crew submersible *Nautile* can operate to a maximum depth of 3¾ miles (6 km) and stay submerged for eight hours. She has performed over 1,500 dives, and was used to explore the wreck of the RMS *Titanic* in 1987.

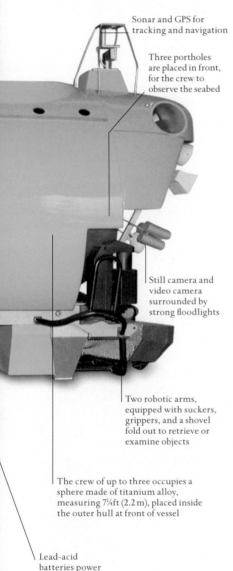

Sonar and GPS for tracking and navigation

Three portholes are placed in front, for the crew to observe the seabed

Still camera and video camera surrounded by strong floodlights

Two robotic arms, equipped with suckers, grippers, and a shovel fold out to retrieve or examine objects

The crew of up to three occupies a sphere made of titanium alloy, measuring 7¼ft (2.2 m), placed inside the outer hull at front of vessel

Lead-acid batteries power the electric motor

Tracking and navigation

Surface vessels use underwater acoustic positioning to track and navigate submersibles. While there are various different systems, all of them use a method of calculating distance according to the speed at which sound travels through water.

USBL AND SSBL NAVIGATION SYSTEMS
In USBL (ultra-short-baseline) or SSBL (super-short-baseline) systems, surface vessels use a hydrophone to track the signal emitted by the beacon on the submersible. This allows the crew on the surface vessel to chart the range and bearing of the submersible in relation to their own position.

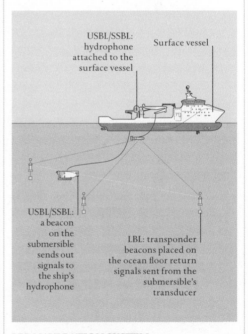

USBL/SSBL: hydrophone attached to the surface vessel

Surface vessel

USBL/SSBL: a beacon on the submersible sends out signals to the ship's hydrophone

LBL: transponder beacons placed on the ocean floor return signals sent from the submersible's transducer

LBL NAVIGATION SYSTEM
The LBL (long-baseline) system offers a more accurate method of underwater acoustic positioning. For this, the submersible carries a transducer that exchanges signals with transponder beacons arranged in set locations on the seafloor. Because the position of these beacons is fixed, the submersible can thus be tracked according to changes in the length and distance of each of the signals.

The Falklands War

AT THE END OF MARCH 1982, 15 British Royal Navy warships arrived in the British overseas territory of Gibraltar, at the entrance to the Mediterranean, after exercises in the Atlantic. The crews enjoyed their "run ashore" on The Rock, as it was known, with its warm climate and exotic scenery. As is common with naval personnel on shore leave, however, they did not follow the news too closely, so it was a while before they realized that there was a crisis growing in the South Atlantic. At around 2 am on April 2, the destroyer HMS *Coventry*'s signals officer, Lieutenant-Commander Ray Adams, picked up a message that Argentina had invaded the Falkland Islands, a remote British colony off the southeastern tip of South America. Although he had only a vague idea where the islands were, Adams woke his captain, David Hart-Dyke, to tell him the news.

Along with Europe's other colonial powers, Britain had lost most of her empire by the early 1980s. India had gained independence in 1947, and the momentum for other territories around the world to follow suit became unstoppable. However, the citizens of one of its remaining colonial possessions had no desire for change. The Falkland Islands, east of Argentina, had been settled by the British in 1833, but Argentina had never recognized Britain's right to the territory, and for many years the Argentine government had claimed sovereignty over the islands, which they called the Malvinas. The British maintained that the islands could not be ceded to Argentina against the wishes of the 2,000 people living there, who were unanimously opposed to Argentine rule. At the time, a brutal military junta, headed by General Leopoldo Galtieri, was governing Argentina, and it desperately needed a success to cover its economic failures and its repression of the population.

LEOPOLDO GALTIERI
As president of Argentina between 1981 and 1982, Galtieri ran the country as a military dictatorship.

Against this backdrop, Britain's government, led by Margaret Thatcher, was cutting its spending. The Royal Navy was to lose much of its global role and concentrate instead on providing a nuclear deterrent with its submarines, and on preparing for antisubmarine warfare against the Soviet Union. In June 1981, it was announced that the aircraft carriers HMS *Hermes* and HMS *Invincible* would be scrapped, the force of frigates and destroyers would be reduced, and the survey ship HMS *Endurance*, based in the South Atlantic, would be withdrawn. In Argentina, this was taken as a sign that the British were no longer able or willing to defend the Falklands. In March 1982, an unofficial Argentine party landed on the island of South Georgia, 600 miles (900 km) east of the Falklands, and also subject to the British government, and raised the Argentine flag.

At 9:30 pm on April 1, 1982, the Argentine destroyer ARA *Santisima Trinidad* anchored off the coast of the Falklands. In a supreme irony, she was of British design, with a hull identical to that of the *Coventry* and her sister ships. Under cover of darkness, men in rubber boats went ashore and crossed the 10 km (6 miles) to the capital, Port Stanley. On the other side of the harbor, a landing ship put amphibious tracked vehicles ashore. The small company of British Royal Marines stationed in the capital was outnumbered, and the Falklands governor, Sir Rex Hunt, ordered them to surrender in the face of overwhelming force. Argentina had taken the Falklands.

The Argentines, however, had gravely underestimated Britain's likely response to their action. Although the vast majority of the British population had never heard of the Falklands, it was felt that no nation could tolerate such a blatant use of force without losing its self-respect. The UN Security Council condemned Argentina's action, and Thatcher emerged as a strong and determined war leader. Just days after the invasion, a British naval task force of 127 ships embarked on the 8,000-mile (12,875-km) voyage to the South Atlantic. It was led by the light aircraft carriers *Hermes* and *Invincible,* with landing ships to carry troops, and every available destroyer and frigate in support. Unfortunately for Argentina, its aggression was ill-timed. The British government had not yet implemented its proposed defense cuts, and the Royal Navy was still able to provide what strategists call a "balanced" force, with a combination of aircraft carriers, landing ships, submarines, and antisubmarine and anti-aircraft escorts. The British Merchant Navy was in long-term decline, but it still had great liners such as the MS *Queen Elizabeth II* and the

TOTAL NUMBER OF DEATHS IN THE FALKLANDS WAR:

913

venerable SS *Canberra*, as well as container ships to transport goods and ferries to carry vehicles. However, Britain's warships were designed for a different kind of war—against Soviet submarines and aircraft in the North Atlantic. The aircraft carriers were small and could only operate helicopters and the unique Harrier jump-jet, which could take off vertically but had a much weaker performance than the latest jets, such as Argentina's French-built supersonic Mirages. The Type 21 frigates of the Amazon class had been built to a private-enterprise design that left them weak and vulnerable. The latest frigate, the Type 22, had the highly effective Sea Wolf short-range anti-aircraft missile instead of a main gun, but there were only two of this type in the fleet, HMS *Brilliant* and HMS *Broadsword*.

The *Coventry* was one of three Type 42 destroyers ordered south with the initial task force. The definition of the type had changed since 1945, and it was now designed to carry long-range anti-aircraft missiles. The Type 42s had been built to reduced size and specification during previous defense cuts, and their Sea Dart missiles were useful for long-range defense of a fleet or a convoy, but they had little to protect themselves at short range. The *Coventry* had a complement of 28 officers and 271 men; 35 of these manned the operations room during each watch in a war zone. Sailors were encouraged to make their wills and to take out life insurance, and there was an air of unreality as they headed out for what might become a real war.

Almost three weeks later, the task force arrived at Ascension Island, the closest British possession to the Falklands, but still some 3,800 miles (6,000 km) away. The ships jettisoned all unnecessary equipment, and in the Type 42 HMS *Sheffield*, "All loose furnishings were to be fully secured, all pictures removed from the bulkheads. The only things we were allowed in our lockers were a number one suit [sailor's uniform], changes of underwear and

ARGENTINE SOLDIERS
Though they held the advantage in tactical position, Argentina's ground forces were let down by their supply chain.

socks, and some warm clothing in case we had to abandon ship."
The *Coventry* was part of a group that was then sent south to take up
position 1,000 miles (1,600 km) north of the Falklands.

The British government had declared a Total Exclusion Zone of
200 miles (370 km) around the Falklands, and anything found in that
area was to be attacked. At the end of April, the makings of an
Argentine pincer movement on the task force was detected, with the
aircraft carrier ARA *Vientecinco de Mayo* to the north and the cruiser
ARA *General Belgrano* to the south. Although the *Belgrano* was outside
the exclusion zone and heading away from the area, on May 2, the
submarine HMS *Conqueror* sank her on orders from London, with 323
crew lost—a decision that remains controversial. Among the British
task force, the reaction was subdued. The *Broadsword*'s chaplain
reported that "... there was no elation in our ship, as we could be in
the same situation ourselves." The only real threat to the British task
force now came from the air, in particular from the deadly Exocet
antiship missiles. On May 4, the communications officer in the
destroyer *Sheffield* looked out to see "a black dot that appeared to be
smoking." It was an Exocet that hit the ship seconds later, killing 20
men. The crew of the *Coventry* saw a pall of black smoke about 30 miles
(48 km) away, and then the news was confirmed. According to her

ARA *GENERAL BELGRANO*
Argentine naval cruiser the *General Belgrano* was
sunk by a British nuclear submarine in 1982,
with the loss of 323 of her crew.

HARRIER JUMP JET
The Harrier is unsual in that it can take off and land vertically—a great advantage in operating from aircraft carriers. It is still in use worldwide.

captain, "Hardly a word was spoken for several hours and people had to struggle to overcome their feelings and fears." On May 3, the *Coventry* had her own action when her helicopter fired Sea Skua missiles at an Argentine patrol craft, killing eight men. Six days later, off Port Stanley, she shot down a Puma aircraft with a Sea Dart missile.

On May 20–21, British troops began landing in San Carlos Water, in the Sound between East and West Falkland. The Argentine Air Force then bombed and sank the frigates HMS *Ardent* and HMS *Antelope*, leaving 23 dead. The *Coventry* was to protect the area from air attack, and she was teamed up with the *Broadsword*, whose Sea Wolfs would complement her Sea Darts. A position was found 10–15 miles (16–24 km) north of the entrance to the Sound. On May 24, the *Coventry* fired a Sea Dart and shot down an Argentine A-4 Skyhawk. Argentine pilot losses were mounting and the British sailors were told that they were now not facing the best of the country's air force. Nevertheless, the British were impressed by the Argentines' almost suicidal bravery. On May 25, Argentina made two targeted air raids on the *Coventry* and the *Broadsword*. The first ended when the *Coventry* shot down an aircraft. The second consisted of four Skyhawks. Captain Carballo and Lieutenant Rinke, flying as "Vulcano flight," dropped a bomb in the sea near the *Broadsword*. It bounced and passed though her afterdecks, damaging the Lynx helicopter.

Meanwhile, Carballo could hear the voices of "Zeus flight"—piloted by lieutenants Velasco and Barrinuevo—over his radio: "My target is in sight, and I am going in." At this point the *Coventry*'s captain ordered her to turn to starboard to give the Sea Darts a better line, but unfortunately he blocked the aim of the *Broadsword*'s Sea Wolfs. A Sea Dart was fired, but its guidance system locked on to the nearby hills, where it exploded. The ship's anti-aircraft guns opened fire and Radio Supervisor MacFarlane "ordered everyone in the radio office to lie down on the deck, hands over the head, in a 'hoping-everything's-going-to-be-all-right position'." Velasco fired his guns at the *Coventry*, then released his three bombs. One detonated in the computer room, killing 16 men, another in the forward engine room. The ship listed rapidly, and there was a three-minute fight for survival. The captain was dazed and communications were down, so there was no specific order to abandon ship, but everyone could see that it was necessary. Men clambered over the side and into life rafts. Fortunately, the weather was calm, it was still daylight, and the *Broadsword* was nearby. One British crewman died during the evacuation and two in the water; 276 survived, and were later picked up by the *Broadsword* and helicopters.

On May 31, British forces made their tortuous way toward Port Stanley, taking Argentine positions along the way, while the landing ships *Sir Tristam* and *Sir Galahad* were bombed. On June 14, after fierce fighting outside the capital, Argentine forces surrendered and the British liberated the town. The short war was the only large-scale naval and air operation since World War II. It claimed the lives of 255 British and 655 Argentine servicemen (and three civilians), and left its mark on both nations. In Britain, the prestige of the Royal Navy was restored and further cuts were halted, while in Argentina, defeat led to the removal of Galtieri and the introduction of democracy. Argentina held its claim to the islands, but the rash invasion of 1982 made any transfer of power unlikely.

Winning the
America's Cup

A GOOD START IS ESSENTIAL in any yacht race, and this was especially true for the 12-man crew of *Australia II* on September 26, 1983. The Australian America's Cup challengers needed to maneuver for position, and to sail over the starting line at the right moment, at a good speed, and as far as possible to windward. There was some confusion in the last few seconds as their boat headed for the line, and when the starting gun rang out over Rhode Island Sound, the big red hull of her US opponent, *Liberty,* was eight seconds ahead. But *Australia II* was toward the windward end of the line. The most dramatic race in yachting history was underway, and so far honors were even.

It was 132 years since the original race, in which the US yacht *America* crossed the Atlantic to victory off Cowes on the Isle of Wight in the presence of Queen Victoria. From then on, British millionaires such as the tea magnate Sir Thomas Lipton and aircraft manufacturer Sir Tom Sopwith lavished fortunes on funding challengers, but for its entire 132-year history the America's Cup trophy had remained in the New York Yacht Club. The *Australia II* was the latest challenger, financed by Anglo-Australian property developer Alan Bond.

By the late 1970s and early 1980s, yachting was no longer an exclusive sport. In the West, many could afford a sailing dinghy, and wealthier professionals could buy decked racing and cruising boats that could take them almost anywhere there was deep enough water. Fiberglass hulls had become less expensive, and electronic aids made navigation much easier and safer. By 1980, it was estimated that one in four Americans was engaged in some kind of boating activity, and one in 20 owned a boat. Dedicated racing yachts, however, were in a league of their own: they were designed and outfitted with no expense spared on the latest technology, and had highly trained crews.

Australia II was designed by the Australian marine architect and yachtsman Ben Lexcen, who had practically no formal education but possessed a wayward genius for yacht design. The boat carried such innovations as all-kevlar running rigging and a carbon-fiber boom, but its most radical feature was its "winged keel." The rules of the America's Cup were strict, and prescribed exactly how deep beneath

AUSTRALIA II
Launched in 1982, the 43-ft
(13-m) racing yacht was one
of the most technologically
advanced contenders in the
1983 America's Cup race.

Ocean Racing

The role of sailing ships in trade and warfare declined toward the end of the 19th century. Around the same time, however, the idea of sailing for sport grew in popularity. The America's Cup yacht race was founded in 1851 and is still going strong today (see below), while more recently, the long distance Volvo Ocean Race (formerly the Whitbread Round the World Race) was launched in 1972. These yachts are designed entirely for speed, which is achieved through sleek, lightweight hulls and by getting as much power as possible from their sail area.

The first America's Cup

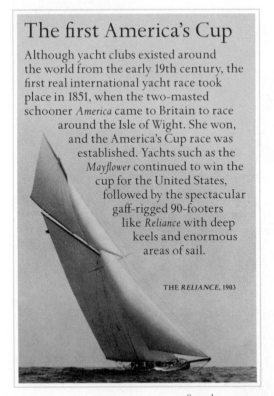

Although yacht clubs existed around the world from the early 19th century, the first real international yacht race took place in 1851, when the two-masted schooner *America* came to Britain to race around the Isle of Wight. She won, and the America's Cup race was established. Yachts such as the *Mayflower* continued to win the cup for the United States, followed by the spectacular gaff-rigged 90-footers like *Reliance* with deep keels and enormous areas of sail.

THE *RELIANCE*, 1903

Mainsail ———

Mast ———

Main boom ———

Rudder ———

Spreader ———

The evolution of racing yachts

The rules of the early America's Cup races stipulated yacht length and sail area only, and the designs of the competing yachts varied from boat to boat, and from one nation and another. The IYRU (International Yacht Racing Union) was established in 1907 with the goal of creating a set of universal categories to enable fair competition between the competing nations. These specifications have changed several times during the Cup's history, leading to a number of variations in yacht design through the decades. Pictured here are some of the key yacht types that have taken part in the race over the last century.

J-CLASS RULE (1930–37)
These beautiful bermuda-rigged yachts had unlimited sail area, but a fixed draft (depth of keel) and length.

12-METER RULE (1958–83)
After World War II, smaller yachts of up to 75 ft (23 m) were used. The race's first safety regulations were also introduced in this era.

IACC-RULE (1992–2007)
Yachts of the 1990s and 2000s featured narrower hulls and distinctive "bulb" keels with a horizontal crosspiece at the bottom.

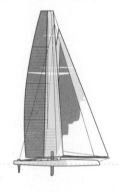

AC72-RULE (2013–)
Catamarans with carbon-fiber wing sails, underwater foils, and 72-ft (22-m) hulls take part in the race today.

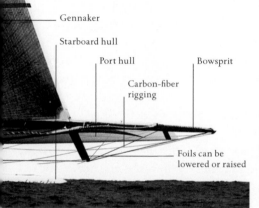

Gennaker

Starboard hull

Port hull

Carbon-fiber rigging

Bowsprit

Foils can be lowered or raised

ALINGHI 5
SWITZERLAND, 2010
The *Alinghi 5* is a 90-ft (27-m) long catamaran. Her 203 ft- (62-m) high mast is supported by 1,750 ft (534 m) of carbon-fiber rigging, and she has a gennaker measuring 11,840 sq ft (1,100 sq m)—one of the three largest ever constructed. Her speed averages 16 knots.

WINGED KEEL
The *Australia II* attracted controversy with her innovative winged keel design. The horizontal fins reduced leeway when the yacht heeled over.

the water the hull of a boat was allowed to go, so Lexcen added "wings" to the lowest part of the fin keel, so that it would actually be deeper when the boat was heeling, helping prevent it from being driven sideways by the wind. The Americans mounted a legal objection to this innovation, but it failed and only served to increase support for the challengers.

Australia II's skipper, John Bertrand, was an intellectual as well as a practical sailor. He had completed a thesis on the aerodynamics of America's Cup sails at Melbourne's Monash University, and in 1972, he was awarded a MSc degree in Ocean Engineering at the prestigious Massachusetts Institute of Technology in the US. He also won a bronze medal in the Finn class dinghy at the 1976 Olympics in Montreal. During the America's Cup final, Bertrand was constantly finding the best course, ready to react swiftly to any change in the wind or maneuver by the opponent, while maintaining overall control of the boat. Beside him stood the boat's tactician, the veteran yachtsman Hughey Treharne, who acted as the skipper's eyes and ears, constantly observing *Liberty* and passing information to Bertrand. "It is to him that I will ultimately listen," the skipper wrote later. The boat's navigator, 27-year-old engineer Grant Simmer, worked with the most up-to-date electronics of the day, using Loran (Long Range Navigation) to find the position of the next marker and the best route to it.

The other nine members of the crew had more physical roles. Shipwright Colin Beashel was charged with trimming the triangular mainsail, the only one aft of the mast, which had a boom to spread its lower edge (its angle and shape had to be set to within a fraction of an inch to get the best performance). Rob Brown helped to trim whichever sail was set forward of the mast. He was not as strong as Beashel, but was valued for his uncanny ability to predict the wind. Skip Lissman was the port trimmer, and his main job was to "tail" the line—that is to pull on the end of it while it was hauled taut on a winch. On the other side of the boat, Scoop Judge was a highly intelligent lawyer who could

WINNING THE AMERICA'S CUP

think fast as well as haul. The actual winch work on the port side was done by John "Chink" Longley, who was 6 ft 4 in (1.9 m) tall and very strong. Longley's opposite number on the starboard side was the even taller Will Ballieu, who had rowed in the 1980 Olympics. The mastman, "Ya" Smidmore, coordinated the numerous lines that ran up the mast for hoisting sails, and he too had a great ability to sense the wind. Peter Costello, the "sewerman," was a major in the Australian army. He mostly worked below deck, handling the seven foresails, or Genoas, and the ten balloonlike spinnakers—all of which were of different sizes and shapes for every variety of wind condition. He passed the right one up when a change was needed, bagged the one sent down, and had each one ready for instant use. As the bow man, Scotty McAllister's main job was to attach the fore edge of the Genoa during a sail change, and detach the one being replaced. According to Bertrand, he was "often in green water up to his eyeballs, horizontally hanging on to a forestay for dear life, as the waves try to sweep him over the side."

As in most yacht races, the America's Cup course was triangular, so the competing boats have to sail at a range of different angles to the wind. The course is around 30 miles (48 km) long, with the first leg mostly into the wind. This was variable in the early stages, on this particular afternoon. *Australia II* tacked to get on the same course as *Liberty*, by turning the boat through the wind and bringing the sails over to the other side of the boat—the only way to progress against the wind. *Liberty* was lighter and faster than during her previous race, and Bertrand was finding it difficult to steer in the swell. *Liberty* pulled ahead as the wind shifted in her favor, and she was four boat-lengths

> "This is real seat-of-the-pants stuff… But the boat feels right, and I'm sure we must push on and keep sailing these angles"
>
> **JOHN BERTRAND,**
> SKIPPER OF *AUSTRALIA II*

THE AMERICA'S CUP TROPHY
Though the race was founded in 1851, the trophy
itself was an off-the-shelf design made in 1848. It is
inscribed with the names of the competing yachts.

ahead as they approached the first marker. *Australia II* turned
to head farther downwind on the second leg, and hoisted
the code-two reaching spinnaker—a colored, parachute-
like sail that would work best with the wind coming over the
side. The wind was shifting to the left, and a great horde of
spectator boats was creating a "wind umbrella" that reduced its
force. When the Australian crew passed the second mark, they
were 45 seconds behind *Liberty*. The wind was behind them
after a turn through nearly 90 degrees, and the green and
gold code-one spinnaker was hoisted to make the best use
of it. Plenty of things can go wrong in setting a spinnaker,
but not on this occasion. *Australia II* began to gain on the
American boat. There was a difference of opinion between the navigator,
Grant, whose instruments suggested that they should steer closer to
the mark, and the instincts of the other members of the crew, who
wanted to make the best of the breeze. In the end, because of the "tricky,
unstable wind," Bertrand decided in favor of the latter.

Australia II had made some gains as she passed the next mark. The
triangular code-two Genoa sail was hoisted, but soon the tactician
Hughey announced that *Liberty* was drawing ahead once more. As the
breeze began to moderate, they changed to the larger code-one
Genoa, a maneuver carried out in a speedy 50 seconds by "clipping,
hauling and pulling." The lighter wind favored the Australians and
they reduced the lead to 15 seconds. Smidmore spotted a gust heading
for the American boat, but there was nothing they could do as *Liberty*
spurted ahead for long enough to restore the gap. As Bertrand
recalled later, they had been "whacked right on the chin."

Australia II rounded the buoy for another downwind run 57 seconds
behind *Liberty*. This was the fifth leg, which had often proved disastrous
in past races, but they had learned some lessons. The code-one spinnaker
was hoisted again and its set was "magical." The boat was now in "that
helmsman's paradise known as 'The Groove,'" with every sail finely
balanced and every crewman doing his job perfectly. She began to gain
on her opponent, and Bertrand noticed signs of doubt on *Liberty*—her
spinnaker was "to my eye a bit wobbly." Both boats made several jibes.

They were close, and Judge called out steering instructions to the skipper. *Australia II* was now slightly ahead, but both boats had to jibe again—if *Liberty* was forced into a collision with her opponent, *Australia II* would be disqualified, so it was vital that she was far enough in front to avoid a clash. The tension was unbearable. Judge called out: "She's going to cross our stern, John. We have half a boat length on them."

The boats passed the final buoy to begin the long upwind leg to the finish line. Bertrand decided on an ambitious sail-change procedure known as the "float drop" to gain a few seconds. The skipper was tense as the Genoa was hoisted. The replaced spinnaker dropped momentarily in the water, and Costello quickly stowed it, "his mighty arms flailing, left-right, left-right, as he [dragged] the big, wet parachute on top of him." They were now 21 seconds ahead and sailing upwind.

Australia II then entered "perhaps the greatest tacking duel in history." The crew tried to match *Liberty's* movements and tacked so often that Bertrand sometimes found himself urged to begin another tack before he had completed the last. It was exhausting: the men on the winches were visibly wilting after hauling the Genoa in so many times. *Liberty* halved the lead to one and a half boat lengths, and both sides got their spinnakers ready as the wind began to shift. Then *Australia II* drew parallel with *Liberty,* but just ahead, and changed course to sail right in front of her, putting her in an almost impossible position. It was nearly over as someone called out the distance to the finishing line: "Four boat lengths...

three boat lengths..." As the gun went off to end the race after four hours and 15 minutes, the crewmen punched the air, leapt up and down, or burst into tears. Back home, the whole nation had stopped to watch the race. The sensational victory was a defining moment for Australian sporting pride, and a triumph of nautical innovation.

CROSS-TACKING
Liberty (below, red) and *Australia II* tack across one another off Rhode Island, during the 1983 America's Cup. It was the closest finish in the race's history.

The *Exxon Valdez* Disaster

CAPTAIN JOSEPH HAZELWOOD had a laissez-faire approach to
running his enormous US oil tanker, the *Exxon Valdez*, so he went
ashore at Valdez, Alaska, late in the morning of March 23 1989,
accompanied by the ship's chief engineer and radio officer. They had
lunch and several drinks in a restaurant, while the ship was loaded
with oil under the supervision of chief mate James Kunkel, second
mate Lloyd LeCain, and third mate Gregory Cousins. A small town
that lies in the shadow of the spectacular Chugach mountains, Valdez
had been rebuilt after a devastating earthquake and tsunami in 1964
because it was the closest ice-free port to the Prudhoe Bay oil fields. It
did not offer extensive shopping facilities, but Hazelwood arranged
for flowers to be sent to his family, the radio officer went to a grocery
store, and the engineer looked for a newspaper. The men met up
again later at a bar, then returned to the restaurant and ordered
pizzas to take back to the ship.

Meanwhile, the loading of the ship was going well, with oil being
pumped at the rate of 100,000 barrels per hour. By 7:30 pm, 1,263,000
barrels were on board. Captain Hazelwood and his companions
shared a taxi back to the port. They went through security at the port
entrance, then took the taxi straight to their ship—walking was
forbidden because of ice in the winter and bears in the summer. When
he was back on the bridge, Hazelwood was surprised to learn that the
departure time had been brought forward by one hour to 9 pm, so
there was only just over half an hour to get ready, but the mates had
done their jobs, the ship was loaded, and everything was in order.

Pilot William Murphy was already on the bridge to guide the ship
out of harbor, along with chief mate Kunkel. An enclosed space about
a third of the 164-ft (50-m) width of the ship, the bridge contained the
radar, sonar for depth-finding, a chart table, and a position for the
helmsman, who did not operate an impressive wheel as in the past,
but a small joystick control. Situated aft and four decks above the
main 987-ft (301-m) hull, the bridge was compact, but there were large
open "wings" on each side for lookouts, and for the captain to
supervise operations while coming alongside a pier—at the time,
seamen still believed that it was essential to feel the wind on one's
face during such maneuvers rather than relying on instruments.

Hazelwood was slightly flustered by the change of plan, but the crew began taking off the mooring lines on schedule at 9 pm. The last line was off 12 minutes later, and the ship began to move away from her berth with the help of two tugboats.

Like most ships of her type at the time, the *Exxon Valdez* had a small crew of 20 men and women in control of 210,000 tons of shipping. She was classified as a "very large crude carrier," which meant that she was over 160,000 tons, but not in the largest category of all, the "ultra large crude carrier" of more than 320,000 tons. "Crude" referred to the type of oil she carried, rather than any lack of finesse in the ship herself. The oil terminal at Valdez had created work for local people and revived the town, but not everyone was happy with its impact on the environment. That very night, campaigner Riki Ott was addressing a meeting of about 30 people, saying that it was only a matter of time before there was a major oil spill.

Meanwhile, pilot Murphy was guiding the *Exxon Valdez* toward the Valdez Narrows, 7 miles (11 km) away, with the tug *Stalwart* alongside in case there was a problem. Captain Hazelwood had been through this passage many times and felt confident enough to leave the bridge, while inexperienced third mate Cousins took over from chief mate Kunkel, who was exhausted after the loading operation. As they approached the Narrows, Murphy reduced the speed to 6 knots to conform with regulations, then the ship eased past Middle Rock, which was generally regarded as the worst hazard in the area.

THE *EXXON VALDEZ*
The 210,000-ton supertanker off Bligh Island
in the narrow channel of Prince William Sound,
Alaska, April 1, 1989.

Murphy increased speed again, but traffic control reported that there were "numerous small pieces of ice" in the channel ahead. Hazelwood returned to the bridge after more than 90 minutes away, because it was time for the pilot to leave. The ship slowed down as a cutter came alongside to pick him up, and Cousins went down to the deck with Murphy to supervise the stowing of the ladder after he disembarked.

In most places, when the pilot leaves, the most difficult part of the departure is over and the crew can afford to relax a little, but in this case, the ship still had to negotiate a long stretch of narrow channel in Prince William Sound. Hazelwood radioed traffic control to report the ship's position. He slurred his speech and forgot for a moment which ship he was on: "Valdez traffic? Ah, Exxon Bata… [Baton Rouge] ah, Valdez." He asked about the ice conditions and was told that there were some "growlers"—small icebergs the size of a house—near the main channel and that he might have to steer to the other side of the shipping lane to avoid them. He was assured that there was no incoming traffic to contend with.

At 11:30 pm, Hazelwood told traffic control that he was altering his course to 200 degrees, which would take him onto the incoming lane. Cousins returned to the bridge a few minutes later and was taken aback to find that the vessel was on automatic pilot, which was not normally used during intricate maneuvers. He was the most junior officer on board, and had very little experience of the area. He had the autopilot switched off and went back to manual steering. He should have been relieved of duty at around 11:50 pm, but LeCain was worn out after loading the cargo and was allowed to sleep on. Maureen Jones took up position on the bridge wing as lookout instead, while second mate Kagan took over the helm. Kagan was another weak link in the chain—he had been promoted from messman, but a recent report stated that he "lacked the necessary skills" to do the job.

Hazelwood set the engines on a computer program that would gradually increase their speed ready for the open sea. He issued vague instructions to Kagan, the gist of which was later disputed. He probably ordered him to pass Busby Island rather than move back into the correct shipping lane. The captain then retired to his cabin, in complete breach of the company regulation stating that two officers should always be on the bridge at such times. Cousins switched off the automatic pilot and resumed manual steering. He took a fix on a lighthouse to establish the ship's position, but delayed turning back

CONTROL ROOM
A high level of electronic automation is required to manage an oil tanker the size of the *Exxon Valdez*. As the disaster revealed, however, the input of the crew remains a critical factor.

into the lane. Shortly before midnight, he ordered Kagan to turn gradually to the right, first with 10 degrees of rudder, then with 20 degrees. Cousins informed Hazelwood of this by telephone, but the captain took no action. "Turning the supertanker around" is a well-known metaphor for difficulty in getting things done, and this was certainly the case on the *Exxon Valdez* that night. The ship slowly turned, but Cousins had left it too late. Just after midnight on March 24, Kunkel was jolted from a deep sleep after working for 24 hours at a stretch as the whole tanker gave six massive shudders.

Hazelwood could no longer ignore the situation and rushed to the bridge. He tried to free the ship using the engines and rudder, but to no avail. It was hard aground on a submerged 28-ft (9-m) deep reef off Bligh Island. Because she had been traveling fast at 12 knots, the ship had struck the jagged rocks of the reef very hard. Kunkel observed that she had already lost "quite a bit of cargo." She was stuck fast by her midsection, with her bow and stern suspended. Several holes had been punched in her bottom and oil was gushing out fast.

This was not the first disaster in the age of the supertanker. In March 1967, the 118,000-ton *Torrey Canyon* hit a reef off southwest England and the world had its first great oil leak, devastating beaches and wildlife in Cornwall and in Brittany, France. The much smaller *Argo Merchant* was stranded off Cape Cod in Massachusetts in 1976, but the wind dispersed most of her oil and a major disaster was avoided. In March 1978, the *Amoco Cadiz* caused the world's worst oil tanker spill to date when she was driven onto the coast of Brittany, France, leaking almost a quarter of a million tons of oil.

The damage to the *Exxon Valdez* was extensive. Eight of her 11 tanks had been penetrated, and although most of the oil was still on board, she eventually leaked an estimated 11 million gallons (38,000 metric tons) of oil. The authorities were completely unprepared for a disaster on this scale and the remote location of Prince William Sound made response efforts difficult—it was accessible only by helicopter, plane, or boat, and attempts to reach the stricken ship were hampered by bad weather. Eighty percent of the oil left in the ship was pumped out into other Exxon tankers, but transferring the thick, heavy oil from temporary storage containers into more permanent ones proved problematic. The authorities floated booms on the surface to limit the spread of the oil and carried out a trial burning between some of them, but the bad weather made this too dangerous to continue.

They then tried to remove the surface oil using skimmers. These were unavailable for the first 24 hours and when they did arrive, they soon became clogged with the thick oil and kelp (seaweed) and it took time to repair them. Dispersants were advocated by Exxon and the other oil companies, but there were not enough waves to mix the dispersant with the water, so these had to be abandoned. Sinking agents had been used by the French after the *Torrey Canyon* disaster, but they were forbidden on environmental grounds.

The oil spill was one of the most devastating environmental disasters ever caused by human error. Around 1,300 miles (2,100 km) of the Alaskan coastline and 11,000 sq miles (28,000 sq km) of ocean were affected by it. It was estimated that a quarter of a million seabirds, 2,800 sea otters, 300 harbor seals, 250 bald eagles, and up to 22 killer whales were killed, and the species numbers are still below their normal levels, since less than ten percent of the oil spill has been recovered. Most of it remains trapped in the sandy soil of the contaminated coastline, and has had a catastrophic effect on animals' breeding cycles.

Captain Hazelwood was convicted of negligent discharge of oil and sentenced to pay a fine of $50,000 and do 1,000 hours of community service. His master's licence was also suspended, but never revoked.

METRIC TONS OF OIL SPILLED BY *EXXON VALDEZ*:

38,000

EFFECT ON WILDLIFE
Scientists attempt to determine whether a gray whale died as a result of oil pollution from the *Exxon Valdez* in 1989. The oil slick has had a lasting effect on Alaskan wildlife and ecosystems.

The Exxon shipping company was charged with failing to supervise the captain or provide sufficient crew for the *Exxon Valdez*. It was fined $150 million, the largest fine ever imposed for an environmental crime, but $125 million was waived in recognition of their cooperation in cleaning up the spill and paying private claims. The official report on the disaster concluded that the oil industry's insistence on self-regulation and the government's weakness with regard to industry pressure had produced a disastrous failure of the system. New legislation on safety measures has since been implemented. The *Exxon Valdez* was eventually refloated and repaired. She served in the Atlantic under several different names until she was finally broken up in India in August 2012.

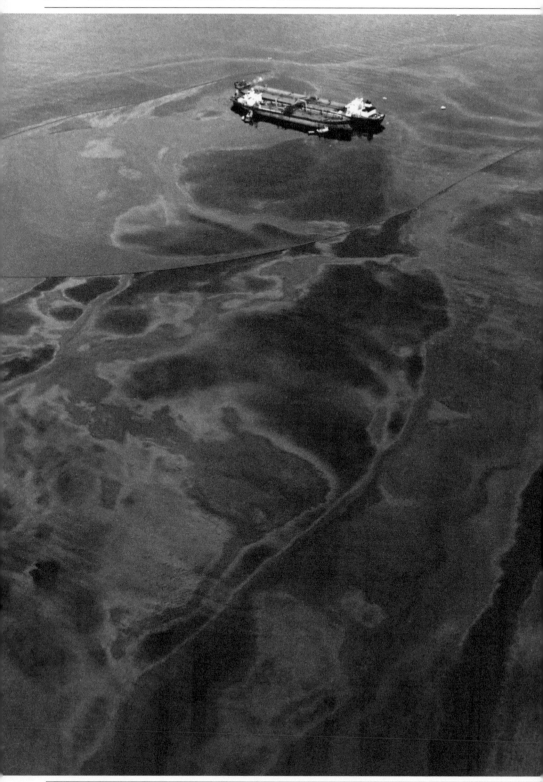

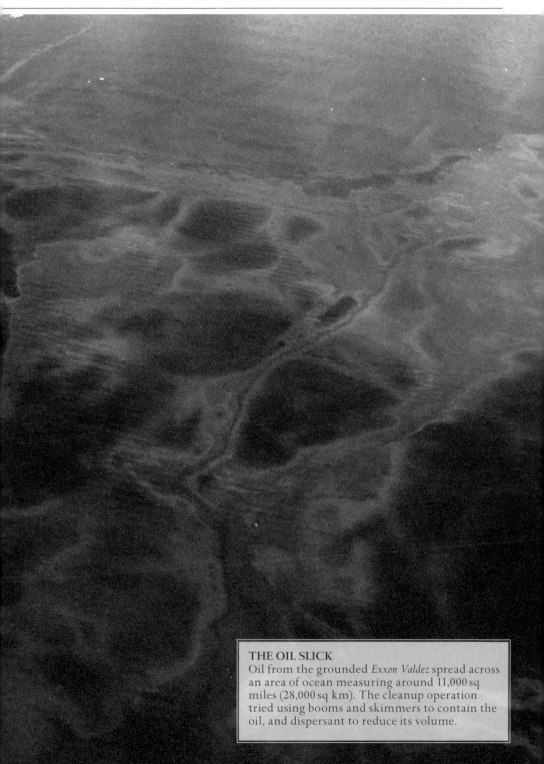

THE OIL SLICK
Oil from the grounded *Exxon Valdez* spread across an area of ocean measuring around 11,000 sq miles (28,000 sq km). The cleanup operation tried using booms and skimmers to contain the oil, and dispersant to reduce its volume.

The Lawless Oceans

TODAY'S OCEANS are home to countless cruise ships and container vessels that symbolize luxury and prosperity. They are also, however, the scene of crimes and horrors that match those of the early emigrant voyages (see pp.202–09) or even the slave trade (see pp.146–53). Refugees flee oppressive regimes in appalling conditions, people are trafficked into slavery, drugs and weapons are smuggled by ship, and terrorists use international waters as a platform for attacks. Of all recent seaborne exoduses, the most infamous took place between 1978 and 1979, when as many as 1.5 million Vietnamese citizens fled poverty and repression in Vietnam in inadequate and overcrowded crafts. It is estimated that between 50,000 and 200,000 Vietnamese "boat people" were lost at sea, although many more made it to settle in the United States, Canada, Australia, and France. In 2000, in a horrific case of people smuggling, 60 illegal Chinese immigrants hid under boxes of

VIETNAMESE "BOAT PEOPLE"
In the late 1970s, many Vietnamese tried to flee
their country. These refugees often traveled in
cramped and unsanitary conditions.

tomatoes in a container truck to make the ferry crossing from Belgium to England. The driver closed the ventilation hatches to avoid detection and all but two of the migrants suffocated.

Drugs and weapons are often smuggled by sea, but one of the greatest problems on the ocean has been the revival of piracy. From the very beginnings of seafaring to its peak in the 17th and 18th centuries (see pp.136–45), piracy had always been been an accepted hazard for international shipping, but in the 1980s, piracy began to flourish once again in the waters around the Strait of Malacca, between Indonesia and the Malay Peninsula. In the first seven months of 1983, there were 47 recorded attacks in the Singapore area alone. Global trade had created a situation in which giant cargo ships loaded with vast quantities of expensive goods were passing deeply impoverished communities, many of them home to fishermen who had been driven out of business by the very same global economy. These ships were typically 1,000 ft (300 m) long and crewed by only 15 or 20 men—too few to prevent pirates from boarding. Pirates could obtain fast boats to pursue ships relatively cheaply, there were plenty of harbors in which to hide, and policing was weak or nonexistent. The pirates wanted to seize the goods on board, not to capture the ships themselves, and their crimes remained fairly low profile. In March 1983, for example, six men boarded the Liberian-registered *Orco Trader* and cut off the captain's nose before they were driven off. Then, in July of the same year, the chief officer of the Swedish *Stena Oceanica* found the radio officer with his hands tied and discovered that the captain's office had been ransacked.

In the 1990s, the regime in Somalia in eastern Africa collapsed and the country was taken over by lawless warlords and religious fundamentalists. Somalia holds just as important a position on the world shipping lanes as Indonesia, because it has a long coastline and numerous harbors at the entrance of the Red Sea and on the route to the Suez Canal. The situation was ripe for piracy and the Somalis brought it to a whole new level, capturing entire ships and demanding outrageously large ransoms from their owners.

One such ship was the German-owned, 13,000-ton chemical carrier *Marida Marguerite*, which left Gujarat, India, in May 2010. She was bound for Belgium, carrying a cargo of castor oil and gasoline additive. Registered in the Marshall Islands, she had an Indian captain by the name of Mahadeo Makane, a Ukrainian chief engineer, Oleg Dereglazov, and a crew of 18 Indians and two Bangladeshis. On May 8, the ship entered "pirate alley," as the dangerous waters between Somalia and Yemen were known, when a blip appeared on her radar. An hour later, Dereglazov spotted a small vessel astern and knew at once from its size, speed, and trajectory that it could only be a pirate ship. The crew of the *Marida Marguerite* had had no weapons training and there was no coordinated security plan, but they ringed the ship with razor wire and stood by to repel boarders with fire hoses. Six men came speeding toward them in a boat, firing Kalashnikov assault rifles, followed by rocket-propelled grenades, which, given the *Marguerite*'s flammable cargo, could have caused a catastrophic explosion. Dereglazov later said, "There would not be ship nor pirates" if they had scored a hit.

The pirates boarded the *Marguerite*. "We did not understand their language. But then fear needs no language," Captain Makane recalled. One of the crew, trainee officer Dipendra Rathmore, tried to radio a nearby Indian Navy ship, but it was too late. "It was utterly terrifying and chaotic," he explained; "We had no choice but to surrender." The pirates ordered the captain to sail toward Somali waters. Two days later, the ship anchored off the Somali coast, where many captured vessels were kept, and was boarded by more pirates. According to Makane, "The first bunch took watches, gold chains, mobiles, laptops... everything that looked nice, boots, jackets, everything... They do not leave even your undergarments."

One of the men who boarded was a suave, multilingual Somali called Mohammad Saaili Shibin. A former schoolteacher and oil company dispatcher, Shibin was now working as a negotiator for the pirates. As US attorney Neil H. MacBride said later at Shibin's trial, "for guys like Shibin, there would be fewer hijackings. The six guys who seize the ship and speak no English, they need a man like Shibin to monetize the ship, the crew and its cargo." Shibin was soon in touch with the ship's German owners by cell phone and put the captain on the line. Makane had to plead: "They are saying if their demands are not met, they will harass us and they will kill us." Shibin then added: "I myself am not a pirate. I work for a local NGO, a human rights NGO in this area. And I volunteered to do this job because I want to save their lives, and I don't want these animals to get rid of your crew, okay?"

Over the next few days, Shibin questioned Makane and the crew about the value of the ship and its cargo, then he called the shipping company again and demanded a ransom of $15 million. The company

THE *MARIDA MARGUERITE*
The German-owned chemical carrier was
intercepted in May 2010 in "pirate alley" between
Yemen and Somalia. Her crew were unarmed.

refused to pay, beginning what would be a seven-month ordeal for the hostages. While Shibin negotiated, the seamen were held in dire conditions: "The pirates took it in turns to keep their guns trained on us—there was never a chance of escape. Nor was there any opportunity to develop a friendship with them. They kept us in a state of terror—we were beaten constantly..." Rathmore recounted. Food was scarce too, as crewman Sudhanshu Pandey recalled: "Though they provided us some food, it was not enough. We were given just enough for subsistence." They were kept in cramped quarters on the bridge while the pirates had the run of the ship. The pirates chewed a narcotic called khat, which made them euphoric and excitable, and Shibin became known as "Dracula" because he only ever appeared at night. He was often on the phone to the shipping company and ocasionally allowed the hostages to call home, as Rathmore described:

> Every few days one of us would be made to call the company and plead for our lives. They would tell us there was nothing they could do—they wanted to force our captors into lowering the ransom. For the first four

months, we were allowed one call a month to our families, so they would also put pressure on the company. Those phone calls were so difficult—we were cut off after just a few words. It was heartbreaking.

In July, another pirate boat came alongside the *Marguerite*, and Makane was ordered to provide it with fresh water. He refused, not wanting to waste valuable fuel on the process, so he and Dereglazov were dragged to opposite sides of the ship and blindfolded, then the pirates fired their guns into the air to convince both of them that the other had been shot, and they were strung up by their arms and left to hang. It was the beginning of 21 days of brutal torture. Makane sought inspiration from *Papillon*, the memoir of a French convict: "Papillon never lost hope. I had to keep the faith," he said. He also found consolation in religion. Rathmore, who at the age of 21 was the youngest member of the crew, avoided the worst of the torture: "Maybe they thought I was too young and unimportant. Some of the older crew members were argumentative, but I made sure never to antagonize the pirates." That did not prevent him from hearing the tortured men screaming for mercy, a memory that haunted him for many months afterward.

After a brief respite, Shibin told the crew of the *Marguerite* that they would be handed over to a terrorist group unless the ransom was paid soon—they had a mere 24 hours to live. The pirates then resumed torturing the officers. Makane and Dereglazov were dangled over the side of the ship as if about to be dropped overboard. Makane then had a plastic bag tied over his head and was threatened at knife-point: "We are going to slaughter you. Now you better tell the truth [about] the fresh water." The fuel was running low and the pirates had become increasingly desperate—they stripped one member of the crew naked and locked him in a freezer.

ESTIMATED COST OF MODERN PIRACY TO
GLOBAL SHIPPING PER YEAR:

$6 billion

The shipping company eventually agreed to pay a ransom of $5.5 million, and on December 28, after 238 horrific days, a small plane appeared and began circling over the ship. The crew of the *Marguerite* was mustered on deck, and shortly afterward a parcel containing the ransom money was dropped from the plane. A German crew then arrived to sail the ship away. Rathmore described how he felt after the long ordeal: "... it felt like being reborn. The first meal, the first shower, the first set of clean clothes all felt extraordinary. Six days later, I was reunited with my family. I looked awful, I was so thin; they just stood and cried... It has not put me off a life on ships, though... I won't let the pirates change my career. They have hurt me enough already." It was over, and the pirates had gotten away, but in 2011, Shibin was caught after being involved in the hijack of an American yacht called the *Quest,* during which four members of the crew were murdered. He had received at least $30,000 as his share of the ransom payment, was found guilty of kidnapping, piracy, and violence, and sentenced to 12 life sentences.

MOHAMMAD SAAILI SHIBIN
US antipiracy forces are increasingly targeting pirates' financiers, and negotiators such as Shibin.

The international community has struggled to suppress piracy. Shipping companies have accepted paying ransom as a normal risk on a voyage, international law is weak, and navies do not always cooperate. The US has been ruthless in pursuit of those who attack its citizens, as has France—it had detained 79 pirates and killed four by mid-2009.

There is nothing glamorous or romantic about modern-day piracy. As Macbride said during Shibin's trial, "this case explodes the myth, if still it exists out there, that pirates are some kind of romantic swashbuckling characters... pirates are brutal, greedy, reckless, desperate criminals who will kidnap, torture and ultimately kill hostages in pursuit of their financial greed."

CELEBRATING THE OCEANS
Despite taking the lives of countless seafarers
throughout history, the oceans still exert a
magnetic appeal. Here, a magnificent array
of traditional yachts race between Brest and
Douarnenez off the French coast, as part of Les
Tonnerres de Brest maritime festival in 2008

Glossary

AFT Toward the stern of a ship.

ASDIC Underwater sound-ranging apparatus for determining the range and position of a submerged submarine. See also *sonar*.

BALLAST Material put in a ship's hold to lower the center of gravity and help keep it upright.

BATTLE CRUISER A class of heavily armed, but lightly armored, ship developed in the years leading up to World War I as a fast battleship.

BATTLESHIP The class of 20th-century warship that carried the greatest number of weapons and was clad with the heaviest armor.

BILGE The lowest part of the interior of the hull, where water collects.

BIREME A galley with two banks of oars on each side.

BOAT Normally a small undecked craft. Submarines and fishing vessels are always referred to as boats.

BOW The front section of a ship.

BREAK BULK Cargo that is carried in single or small units, rather than in large containers.

BRIG A small sailing ship that has two square-rigged masts.

BROADSIDE The simultaneous firing of all the cannons on one side of a warship.

BULKHEAD A vertical partition below decks that separates one part of a ship from another.

CARAVEL A small, maneuverable ship developed in the 15th century with lateen sails on two or three masts.

CARRACK A three- or four-masted sailing ship in use during the 15th and 16th centuries.

CAST THE LEAD To use the lead line to find the depth of the water below a ship.

CATAMARAN A boat with two parallel hulls.

CHRONOMETER An accurate timepiece, originally used for navigation at sea.

CLIPPER A fast sailing ship of the mid-19th century with a very sharp bow, a large sail area, and a short beam in relation to its length.

CLOSE HAULED Sailing as close as possible to the wind without losing speed.

COG/COGGE A clinker-built sailing ship used in northern Europe from the 13th to the 15th centuries. It was powered by a single square sail.

CORSAIR 1. Raider (sometimes regarded as a pirate), particularly one operating off the Barbary Coast of North Africa in the 16th and 17th centuries. 2. A ship operating off the Barbary Coast under government license to raid enemy trade in wartime.

CORVETTE 1. A fast, lightly armed, 20th-century escort vessel often used for antisubmarine operations. 2. A small sailing warship used during the 18th and 19th centuries.

CRUISER A lightly armed, fast warship of the 19th and 20th centuries.

DEAD RECKONING A method of calculating one's position at sea by the ship's speed, the time that has elapsed, and the direction steered.

DESTROYER A small, fast warship armed with guns, torpedoes, depth charges, or guided missiles. The original form of this type of ship was the torpedo-boat destroyer of the late 19th century.

DHOW A lateen-rigged sailing vessel that originated in the Middle East.

DOLDRUMS A belt of light winds or calms along the Equator, where the progress of a sailing ship is likely to be greatly reduced.

DREADNOUGHT Launched in 1906, HMS *Dreadnought* gave her name to a new generation of battleships, faster and more heavily armored than any previous warships.

EAST INDIAMAN One of the largest merchant ships of the 17th and 18th centuries, built to carry goods for trade to and from Asia.

FATHOM An old unit of measurement for depth, equivalent to 6 ft (1.8 m).

FLOTILLA A small fleet, or more commonly, a fleet of small vessels.

FLUYT A Dutch merchant sailing ship with a flat bottom and square hull section, designed to carry cargo and a small crew.

FORE Toward the front of a ship.

FORECASTLE 1. The raised structure at the front of a medieval ship, used as a fighting platform. 2. The front of a ship's upper deck.

FORESAIL The lowest sail on the foremast of a square rigged ship.

FRIGATE 1. A 17th-century sailing ship that was faster than a ship-of-the-line and had just one gun deck. 2. A 20th-century warship with an antisubmarine or general purpose capability.

GALLEASS A large, 16th-century Venetian war galley developed for carrying heavy artillery.

GALLEON The principal European warship of the 16th and 17th centuries. It was longer and narrower than the earlier carrack.

GALLEY 1. An oared fighting ship used mainly in the Mediterranean until the 18th century. 2. The kitchen of a ship.

GENOA The large triangular sail set forward of the mast on a yacht. It overlaps with the mainsail aft of it.

HORSEPOWER A unit for mechanical power. One horsepower is equal to 33,000 lb-ft per minute or 745.7 kw.

IRONCLAD A mid-19th-century warship that was originally built with a wooden hull armored with iron plates.

JIB A triangular sail set forward of the foremast.

JIBE To alter course by turning the stern of a boat through the wind.

JUNK A Chinese or Japanese sailing vessel.

KEEL The long, generally straight assembly of wood or metal that forms the lowest part of the hull of a ship along most of its length.

KNOT A unit of measurement for a vessel's speed through water. One knot equals one nautical mile per hour.

LATEEN SAIL The standard type of sail in the Mediterranean. It is triangular and attached to a long yard set diagonally fore and aft.

LEAGUE Three nautical miles.

LINE A small- to medium-sized rope.

LINE ABREAST A term used to describe ships sailing side by side in a line.

LINE AHEAD A term used to describe ships sailing in a line, one behind another.

LINER Originally, a passenger or cargo-carrying merchant ship with a scheduled route. Later, a cruise ship catering purely for the leisure trade.

LONGSHIP The classic clinker-built Viking vessel, which could be rowed as well as sailed.

LONGSHOREMAN A term used in the US for a worker employed to load and unload ships, often on a casual basis.

MAT-AND-BATTEN SAILS The classic Chinese sailing rig, with sails made of matting and strengthened by battens at different heights.

MIZZENMAST The mast closest to the stern on a ship that has more than one mast.

OCTANT The precursor of the sextant, this was an instrument for measuring the angle of the sun, moon, and stars to the horizon.

OUTRIGGER A secondary hull protruding away from the main hull to provide additional stability. Outriggers were traditionally part of native canoes in the Pacific and Indian oceans.

POOP DECK The aftermost and highest deck on a ship, situated above the quarterdeck.

PORT The left-hand side of a vessel.

PRE-DREADNOUGHT A battleship built or ordered before HMS *Dreadnought* launched in 1906.

PRIVATEER A private vessel equipped to raid enemy shipping in wartime, to raise a profit from the sale of captured vessels.

PROW The bow of a ship, especially if elaborate or highly decorated.

QUINQUIREME A large warship used in ancient Greece and Rome.

RADAR A method of detecting objects by sending out radio waves that reflect back to a receiver upon hitting an object, providing information about its bearing and distance.

REEFING To reduce the area of sail when a strong wind is blowing.

RETOURSCHIP A Dutch East India ship which made the round trip from the Netherlands to the East Indies and back.

RUDDER The main apparatus for steering a vessel, the rudder is a paddle fixed to the stern.

SAMPAN A small Chinese boat with a flat bottom, used as a skiff and sometimes as a floating house.

SCHOONER A vessel with two or more masts carrying fore-and-aft rig and with the main aftermast taller than the foremast.

SCUTTLE To sink one's own ship deliberately, often to avoid it being captured.

SEXTANT A nautical instrument for measuring the angle of the sun or a star to the horizon.

SHIP A vessel with decks, which is large enough and sufficiently well equipped to make voyages.

SHIP OF THE LINE A well-armed sailing warship built to exchange broadsides with the enemy's line and used from the 17th to the 19th century.

SKIPPER The person in charge of a small vessel such as a fishing boat or yacht, or in some cases a seaman under the command of another officer on board.

SHEET A rope used to control the loose corner of a sail.

SLOOP A single-masted sailing vessel with a fore-and-aft rig.

SONAR Previously known as asdic, sonar is an electronic device used to locate underwater objects, mainly in antisubmarine warfare.

SOUNDINGS The depth of water under a ship` as found by casting the lead, or an area where the water is shallow enough to find the depth by these means.

SPINNAKER A large, balloonlike sail set forward of the mast on a yacht and used when the wind is suitable.

SQUARE RIG A sail plan in which the main driving sails are secured to the yards and lay square to the mast in their neutral position.

STARBOARD The right-hand side of a vessel.

STEERAGE A large compartment situated close to the stern and generally just above the propellers. Steerage accommodation usually had only the most basic of amenities.

STEVEDORE A worker who stows the cargo on board a ship, as distinct from a longshoreman or docker, who transports the cargo to the hold.

STERN The rear part of a ship.

TACK To turn a ship's bow through the wind, so that it follows a zigzag course in order to sail into the wind.

TANKER A ship designed to carry liquids in bulk, usually oil.

TRAMP A small cargo ship with no regular route, which delivers and picks up cargo from any destination as required.

TRIM The level at which a ship lies in the water.

TRIMMING Adjusting the angle of the sails to get the best effect from the wind.

TRIREME An ancient Greek or Roman war galley with three tiers of oars on each side.

U-BOAT A German submarine. The term comes from the German word *Unterseeboot*.

WEARING Turning a ship by presenting her stern to the wind.

YARD A horizontal spar that is tapered at the end, used to support and spread a sail.

Bibliography

CHAPTER 1

EXPLORING THE PACIFIC
Joseph Banks, *The Endeavour Journal*, 1768–1771, ed J.C. Beaglehole, Sydney, 1962
Henry Byam Martin, *Polynesian Journal*, Salem, Mass, 1981
Richard Feinberg, *Polynesian Seafaring and Navigation*, Kent, Ohio, 1988
Raymond Firth, *Tikopia Songs*, Cambridge, 1990
Geoffrey Irwin, *The Prehistoric Exploration and Colonisation of the Pacific*, Cambridge, 1992

SEAFARING IN THE MEDITERRANEAN
Lionel Casson, *Ships and Seafaring in Ancient Times*, London, 1994
Homer, *The Odyssey*, translated by E.V. Rieu, London, 2003
Synesius of Cyrene, *Letters*, Livius.org

THE VOYAGES OF THE VIKINGS
A.W. Brøgger and H. Shetelig, *Viking Ships*, Oslo, 1971
Ole Crumlin-Petersen and Olaf Olsen, *Five Viking Ships from Roskilde Fjord*, Copenhagen, 1978
The Saga of Erik the Red, translated J. Sephton, 1880, Icelandic Saga Database
The Saga of Leif Erikson, translated J. Sephton, 1880, Icelandic Saga Database
James Graham-Campbell and Dafydd Kidd, *The Vikings*, London, 1890

ARAB SEAFARING
Ibn Jubayr, *Travels*, translated by R.J.C. Broadhurst, London, 1952
Buzurg ibn Shahriyar, *The Book of the Wonders of India*, translated by G.S.P. Freeman-Grenville, London, 1981
Shelomo Goitein, *A Mediterranean Society*, 6 vols, Berkeley, California, 1967–93
Letters of Jewish Medieval Traders, Princeton, 1974
George Hourani, *Arab Seafaring in the Indian Ocean in Ancient and Early Medieval Times*, Princeton, 1995
G.R. Tibbetts, *Arab Navigation in the Indian Ocean*, London, 1971

THE VOYAGES OF ZHENG HE
Ma Huan, *The Overall Survey of the Ocean's Shores*, translated by J.V.G. Mills, Hakluyt Society, Cambridge, 1970
Gavin Menzies, *1421: The Year China Discovered the World*, London, 2003
Joseph Needham, *Science and Technology in China*, vol 4, Cambridge, 1971
G.R.G. Worcester, *The Junks and Sampans of the Yangtze*, Annapolis 1971

PILGRIMS AND GALLEYS
Felix Fabri, *The Book of the Wanderings of Brother Felix Fabri*, translated A. Stewart, in *Palestine Pilgrims Text Society* vols 7–10, London, 1896–97

John F. Guilmartin Jr, *Galleons and Galleys*, London, 2002
John H. Pryor, *Geography, Technology and War*, Cambridge, 1988

THE BATTLE OF WINCHELSEA
Joe Flatman, *Ships and Shipping in Medieval Manuscripts*, London, 2009
Jean Froissart, *Chronicles*, London, 1978
Gillian Hutchison, *Medieval Ships and Shipping*, Leicester, 1994
Navy Records Society, vol 131, *Select Naval Documents*, Aldershot, 1993

CHAPTER 2

THE NEW WORLD
Samuel Eliot Morrison, *Admiral of the Ocean Sea*, Oxford, 1942
Christopher Columbus, *Journal of the First Voyage*, translated by R.J. Penny, Warminster, 1990

TO INDIA BY SEA
E.G. Ravenstein, ed, *A Journal of the First Voyage of Vasco da Gama*, London, the Hakluyt Society, 1898
Sanjay Subrahmanyam, *The Career and Legend of Vasco da Gama*, Cambridge, 1997

CIRCUMNAVIGATING THE GLOBE
Ian Cameron, *Magellan and the First Circumnavigation of the World*, London, 1974
Antonio Pigafetta, *The First Voyage Round the World*, translated by Lord Stanley of Alderley, Hakluyt Society, London, 1874

THE CONQUEST OF MEXICO
Bernal Diaz de Castillo, *The Discovery and Conquest of Mexico, 1517–1521*, ed Genaro Garcia, translated by A.P. Maudslay, Cambridge, MA, 2003
Florentine Codex; *General History of the Things of New Spain*, ed Arthur J.O. Anderson and Charles E. Dibble, vol 12, Santa Fe, NM, 1982

EXPLORING CANADA
H.P. Biggar, *The Voyages of Jacques Cartier*, Ottawa, 1924
Charles Bourel de la Roncière, *Jacques Cartier et la Découverte de la Nouvelle-France*, Paris, 1931
David B. Quinn, ed, *New American World*, New York, 1979

DRAKE'S PLUNDER
British Library, *Sir Francis Drake*, London, 1977
Sir Julian Corbett, *Drake and the Tudor Navy*, vol 1, London, 1899

CHAPTER 3

COLONIES IN AMERICA
Phillip L. Barbour, *The Three Worlds of Captain John Smith*, London, 1964
Phillip L. Barbour, ed, *The Jamestown Voyages under the First Charter*, 2 vols,

1606–1609, Hakluyt Society, London, 1969
Brian Lavery, *Anatomy of the Ship, Susan Constant*, London, 1988
Samuel Purchas, *His Pilgrims*, vol XVIII, New York, 1965

THE WRECK OF THE BATAVIA
Batavia, *Guide*, Lelystad, 1995
C.R. Boxer, *The Dutch Seaborne Empire, 1600–1800*, London, 1977
Mike Dash, *Batavia's Graveyard*, London, 2003
H. Drake-Brockman, *Voyage to Disaster*, London, 1964

A LIFE OF PIRACY
Plamen Ivanov Arnaudov, *Raveneau de Lussan: Buccaneer Apologist and Mythical Hero, in Elements of Mythmaking in Witness Accounts of Colonial Piracy*, doctorial dissertation, Louisiana State University, 2003
David Cordingly, *Life Among the Pirates*, London, 1995
Raveneau de Lussan, *A Journal of a Voyage Made into the South Sea by the Bucaniers or Freebooters of America*, London, 1698

SLAVE SHIPS IN THE ATLANTIC
Olaudah Equiano, *The Interesting Narrative*, London, 2003
John Newton, *Journal of a Slave Trader*, London, 1962

COOK IN THE PACIFIC
Joseph Banks, *The Endeavour Journal*, 1768–1771, ed J.C. Beaglehole, Sydney, 1962
James Cook, *The Voyage of the Endeavour*, 1768–71, ed J.C. Beaglehole, Hakluyt Society, Cambridge, 1955
Richard Hough, *Captain James Cook*, London, 1994

JOHN PAUL JONES AND AMERICAN INDEPENDENCE
Dr. Ezra Green, *Diary, 1777–78*, Boston, 1875
John Paul Jones, *Memoirs*, London, 1830
Lincoln Lorenz, *John Paul Jones*, Annapolis, 1942
J.H. Sherburne, *The Life and Character of John Paul Jones*, New York, 1851

THE BATTLE OF TRAFALGAR
Auguste Marie Cicquel des Touches, *Souvenirs d'un Marine de la Republique in Revue des Deux Mondes*, 1905
Brian Lavery, *Nelson's Fleet at Trafalgar*, Greenwich, 2004
Peter Warwick, *Voices from the Battle of Trafalgar*, Newton Abbot, 2005

DEATH IN THE ARCTIC
William Scoresby, *An Account of the Arctic Regions*, 2 vols, Edinburgh, 1820
Arctic Whaling Journals, vol 1, Hakluyt Society, London, 2003
Bill Spence, *Harpooned; the Story of Whaling*, London, 1980

CHAPTER 4

FIRE ON THE OCEANS
Ewen Corlett, *The Iron Ship*, Bradford on Avon, 1980
Robert Gardiner, ed, *The Advent of Steam*, London, 1993
James Hosken et al, *The logs of the first voyage, made with the unceasing aid of steam, between England and America, by the Great Western of Bristol*, Bristol, 1838

GOING TO AMERICA
Raymond A. Cohn, *Mass Migration Under Sail*, Cambridge, 2009
Terry Coleman, *Passage to America*, London, 1972
Robert Whyte, *The Ocean Plague; The Diary of a Cabin Passenger*, Boston, 1848

CHINA, JAPAN, AND THE PERRY EXPEDITION
Marius P. Jansen, *The Making of Modern Japan*, Cambridge, Mass, 2002
P.C. Kuo, *A Critical Study of the First Anglo-Chinese War with Documents*, Taipei, 1970
Matthew C. Perry, *Narrative of the Expedition of an American Squadron to the China Seas and Japan*, New York, 1856

THE BIRTH OF OCEANOGRAPHY
M.F. Maury, *Explanations and Sailing Directions to Accompany the Wind and Current Charts*, 1852
The Physical Geography of the Sea, 1855, reprinted Mineola, NY, 1963
Sir Charles Wylie Thompson, *The Voyage of the Challenger*, London, 1877
Francis Leigh Williams, *Matthew Fountaine Maury, Scientist of the Sea*, New Brunswick, 1963

SAVING LIVES AT SEA
Alexander McKee, *The Golden Wreck*, Bebington, Merseyside, 2000
Samuel Plimsoll, *Our Seamen, an Appeal*, London, 1873

THE ALABAMA AND AMERICA AT SEA
S. Dana Greene, *In the "Monitor" Turret*, in *Battles and Leaders of the Civil War*, vol 1, reprinted 1956
John Mackintosh Kell, *The Cruise and Combats of the Alabama* in *Battles and Leaders of the Civil War*, vol 4, reprinted 1956
Raphael Semmes, *My Adventures Afloat*, London, 1869

THE GREAT TEA RACE
Basil Lubbock, *The China Clippers*, Glasgow, 1916
Andrew Shewan, *The Great Days of Sail*, London, 1927, reprinted 1973

TO THE OTHER SIDE OF THE WORLD
Keith Cameron, ed, *The Gull*, Brisbane, 1884
Helen R. Woolcock, *Rights of Passage; Emigration to Australia in the Nineteenth Century*, London, 1986

JOHN HOLLAND AND THE FIRST SUBMARINES
Robert Gardiner, ed, *Steam, Steel and Shellfire*, London, 1992
Simon Lake, *The Submarine in Peace and War*, Philadelphia, 1918
Richard Morris, *John P. Holland, 1841–1914*, Columbia, SC, 1998

THE BIRTH OF THE LUXURY LINER
N.R.P. Bonsor, *North Atlantic Seaway*, London, 1955
Susan Wiborg, *The World is Our Oyster*, Hamburg, 1997

THE GREAT ARMS RACE
Randall Grey, ed, *Conway's All the World's Fighting Ships*, London, 1985
Patrick J. Kelly, *Tirpitz and the Imperial German Navy*, Bloomington, Ind, 2011
Nicholas A. Lambert, *Sir John Fisher's Naval Revolution*, Columbia, SC, 1999
Gary E. Weir, *Building the Kaiser's Navy*, Annapolis, 1992

CHAPTER 5

THE BATTLE OF JUTLAND
N.J.M. Campbell, *Jutland; an Analysis of the Fighting*, London, 1986
Robert Gardiner, ed, *The Eclipse of the Big Gun*, London, 1992
Georg Hase, *Kiel and Jutland*, London, 1921
Richard Stumpf, *The Private War of Seaman Stumpf*, London, 1969

HIGH SOCIETY AT SEA
Engineering Magazine, 1907, *The Cunard Turbine-Driven Quadruple Screw Atlantic Liner Mauretania*, reprinted Wellingborough, 1987
Anita Loos, *Gentlemen Prefer Blondes*, New York, 1925
Basil Woon, *The Frantic Atlantic*, New York, 1927

THE BATTLE OF THE ATLANTIC
Navy Records Society, vol 137, *The Defeat of the Enemy Attack upon Shipping, 1939–1945*, ed Eric Grove, 1997
Joseph H. Wellings, *On His Majesty's Service*, Newport, RI, 1983

THE BATTLE OF MIDWAY
Ikuhiko Hata, Yasuho Izawa, Christopher Shores, *Japanese Naval Air Force Units and their Aces 1932–1945*, London, 2011
E.B. Potter, *The Great Sea War*, London, 1961
Ron Werneth, *Beyond Pearl Harbour*, Atglen, PA, 2008

THE D-DAY LANDINGS
"Jimmy" Green, *The Royal Navy on Omaha Beach*, in BBC History, World War II People's War
Ernest Hemingway, *Voyage to Victory*, in *Collier's Magazine*, 22 July 1944
Samuel Elliot Morrison, *The Invasion of France and Germany, 1944–1945*, Edison, NJ, 2001

Winston G. Ramsay, *D-Day Then and Now*, 2 vols, London, 1995
US Navy, the Navy Department Library, *Ship to Shore Movement, General Instructions*, 1944

CHAPTER 6

THE CONTAINER REVOLUTION
Brian J. Cuddahy, *Box Boats; How Container Ships Changed the World*, Fordham, 2007
Marc Levinson, *The Box — How the Shipping Container Made the World Smaller and the Economy Bigger*, Princeton, 2006
Danny Marc Samuels, *Ideal-X and the Birth of Container Shipping in Houston*, in offcite.org

THE CUBAN MISSILE CRISIS
Peter A. Huchthausen, *October Fury*, Hoboken, 2002
Ernest R. May and Phillip D. Zelikow, *Inside the White House during the Cuban Missile Crisis*, Cambridge, Mass, 1997
National Security Archive, George Washington University; *Recollections of Vladimir Orlov (B-59)*
A.F. Dubivko, *In the Depths of the Sargasso Sea*, from *On the Edge of the Nuclear Precipice*, Moscow, 1998

EXPLORING THE DEEP
Jacques Cousteau and Alexis Sivirine, *Jacques Cousteau's Calypso*, New York, 1983
Jacques Cousteau and Phillipe Doilé, *Galapagos, Titicaca, the Blue Holes*, London, 1973
Jacques Cousteau, James Dugan, *The Living Sea*, London, 1963

THE FALKLANDS WAR
Eric Grove, *Vanguard to Trident*, Michigan, 1987
David Hart-Dyke, *Four Weeks in May*, London, 2007
Ministry of Defence, *Board of Enquiry — Report into the Loss of HMS Coventry*

WINNING THE AMERICA'S CUP
John Bertrand, *Born to Win*, London, 1985
Douglas Phillips-Birt, *The History of Yachting*, London, 1974
John Rousmaniere, *The Americas Cup, 1851–1983*, London, 1983

THE EXXON VALDEZ DISASTER
Alaska Oil Spill Commission, *Spill, the Wreck of the Exxon Valdez*, Appendix N, T/V Exxon, 1989 Valdez Oil Spill Chronology
Richard A. Cahill, *Disasters at Sea: Titanic to Exxon Valdez*, London, 1990

THE LAWLESS OCEANS
John C. Foyne, *Piracy Today*, London, 1980
Dipendra Rathmore, *I Was Kidnapped by Somali Pirates*, The Guardian, 11 June 2011
Roger Villar, *Piracy Today*, ibid

Index

Page numbers for illustrations are in italics.

Acknowledgments

Dorling Kindersley would like to thank the following for their help on this book:

Satu Fox, Gareth Jones, Antara Moitra, Simon Mumford, Nicola Munro, and Ed Wilson for editorial assistance; Joanne Clark, Keith Davis, Phil Gamble, and Chris Gould for design assistance; Margaret McCormack for indexing; Jane Perlmutter for Americanization.

The publisher would also like to thank the following for their kind permission to reproduce their photographs:

(Key: a-above; b-below/bottom; c-center; f-far; l-left; r-right; t-top)

2-3 National Maritime Museum, Greenwich, London: National Heritage Memorial Fund. 5 National Maritime Museum, Greenwich, London: (c). 9 Photo SCALA, Florence: DeAgostini Picture Library (br). 12 National Maritime Museum, Greenwich, London: Ministry of Defence Art Collection (c). 17 Getty Images: Science & Society Picture Library (tl). 18 Getty Images: Dea Picture Library / De Agostini (tl). 19 National Maritime Museum, Greenwich, London: Ministry of Defence Art Collection (t). 21 Corbis: Gianni Dagli Orti (b). 22-23 Dorling Kindersley: Hellenic Maritime Museum (c). 22 Dorling Kindersley: Hellenic Maritime Museum (bl, bc); The Science Museum, London (ca). 23 Dorling Kindersley: Hellenic Maritime Museum (cr); National Maritime Museum, London (clb, crb). Science Museum / Science & Society Picture Library: (tr). 24 The Bridgeman Art Library: Ancient Art and Architecture Collection Ltd. (b). 26 Corbis: Gianni Dagli Orti (bl). 30 Getty Images: Ted Spiegel / National Geographic (bl). 32 Corbis: Yadid Levy / Robert Harding World Imagery (br). 35 The Bridgeman Art Library: De Agostini Picture Library / G. Dagli Orti (tr). 39 Dorling Kindersley: National Maritime Museum, London (br). 40 Corbis: Arne Hodalic. 42 Getty Images: AFP (br). 44-45 National Maritime Museum, Greenwich, London: (c). 44 National Maritime Museum, Greenwich, London: (bc). 45 Corbis: Bettmann (br). Dorling Kindersley: National Maritime Museum, London (cra). National Maritime Museum, Greenwich, London: Pym Collection (crb). 46 Corbis: Chris Hellier (br). 48 Imaginechina: Cheng jiang (br). 50 Photo SCALA, Florence: Photo The Philadelphia Museum of Art / Art Resource (bl). 53 Mary Evans Picture Library: Interfoto / Sammlung Rauch (t). 54 The Bridgeman Art Library: (clb). 57 The Art Archive: Naval Museum Genoa / Collection

Dagli Orti (t). 59 The Bridgeman Art Library: (tl). 61 The Art Archive: Bibliothèque des Arts Décoratifs Paris / Gianni Dagli Orti (tr). 62 Mary Evans Picture Library: IBL Collections (c). 64 Corbis: The Gallery Collection (br). 66 Getty Images: Science & Society Picture Library (tr). 71 Corbis: The Gallery Collection (tr). 72-73 Science Museum / Science & Society Picture Library: (c). 72 akg-images: Michael Teller / National Maritime Museum (cl). Dorling Kindersley: (cla). National Maritime Museum, Greenwich, London: (bl). Science Museum / Science & Society Picture Library: (bc, br). 73 Dorling Kindersley: Hellenic Maritime Museum (bl). Imaginechina: Cheng jiang (bc). National Maritime Museum, Greenwich, London: (tr, cr, br). 74 Corbis: The Gallery Collection (bl). 76 Getty Images: G. Dagli Orti / De Agostini. 80-81 Photo SCALA, Florence: White Images. 83 Science Photo Library: Patrick Landmann (b). 84 Getty Images: G. Dagli Orti / De Agostini (br). 86 The Bridgeman Art Library: Royal Geographical Society, London, UK. 89 Getty Images: Theodore de Bry / The Bridgeman Art Library (t). 91 akg-images: (tr). 92-93 akg-images: British Library. 95 The Art Archive: Biblioteca Nacional Madrid / Gianni Dagli Orti (b). 96 The Art Archive: Museo Ciudad Mexico / Gianni Dagli Orti. 98-99 Getty Images: Apic / Hulton Archive. 100 The Art Archive: Museo Ciudad Mexico / Gianni Dagli Orti (tl). 102 Corbis: Werner Forman (tr). 105 Mary Evans Picture Library: (bl). 106 Alamy Images: Gianni Dagli Orti / The Art Archive (t). 111 National Maritime Museum, Greenwich, London: Caird Collection (tl). 112 The Art Archive: Plymouth Art Gallery / Eileen Tweedy (clb). 114 Getty Images: G. Dagli Orti / De Agostini. 116 National Maritime Museum, Greenwich, London: (c). 119 Alamy Images: North Wind Picture Archives (tl). 121 Corbis: Peter Harholdt (t). 122 Photo SCALA, Florence: British Library board / Robana. 124-125 The Bridgeman Art Library: Photo © Bonhams, London, UK (c). 124 The Art Archive: Private Collection Italy / Collection Dagli Orti (bc). The Bridgeman Art Library: Photo © Bonhams, London, UK (br). John Hamill: (cla). Dorling Kindersley: National Maritime Museum, London: (crb); Caird Collection (cl). 125 Dorling Kindersley: National Maritime Museum, London (tr, cr). National Maritime Museum, Greenwich, London: (cb); Caird Collection (clb). 126 Mary Evans Picture Library: (bl). 127 Getty Images: Andries Beeckman / The Bridgeman Art Library (t). 132-133 The Bridgeman Art Library:

British Library, London, UK (b). **134–135 Museum of London:** (b). **134 National Maritime Museum, Greenwich, London:** Caird Collection (cl). **138 National Maritime Museum, Greenwich, London:** (t). **141 Alamy Images:** AAA Photostock (bl). **142–143 The Bridgeman Art Library:** Peter Newark Pictures. **146 akg-images:** North Wind Picture Archives (bl). **147 National Maritime Museum, Greenwich, London:** (br). **148 Getty Images:** English School / The Bridgeman Art Library (t). **150–151 The Bridgeman Art Library:** Michael Graham-Stewart. **153 © Royal Geographical Society:** (tl). **154 National Maritime Museum, Greenwich, London:** Greenwich Hospital Collection (br). **156–157 Getty Images:** Universal Images Group (b). **159 The Bridgeman Art Library:** (tl). **160 National Maritime Museum, Greenwich, London:** (b). **162–163 National Maritime Museum, Greenwich, London:** Adams Collection (c). **162 National Maritime Museum, Greenwich, London:** Sir William Lawrence collection. **165 Corbis:** PoodlesRock (t). **166 The Bridgeman Art Library:** Peter Newark Historical Pictures (bl). **168 Getty Images:** Interim Archives / Archive Photos (tl). **169 National Maritime Museum, Greenwich, London:** Caird Collection (br). **170–171 The Art Archive:** Chateau de Blerancourt / Gianni Dagli Orti. **172 National Maritime Museum, Greenwich, London:** (tl). **173 Mary Evans Picture Library:** Library of Congress. **174 Getty Images:** Leemage / Universal Images Group (br). **175 National Maritime Museum, Greenwich, London:** (tl). **179 National Maritime Museum, Greenwich, London:** (b). **180 National Maritime Museum, Greenwich, London:** (bl). **182–183 National Maritime Museum, Greenwich, London:** Ministry of Defence Art Collection (c). **182 National Maritime Museum, Greenwich, London:** (cl). **185 National Maritime Museum, Greenwich, London:** (bl). **186 National Maritime Museum, Greenwich, London:** (tl). **187 National Maritime Museum, Greenwich, London:** (br). **188 Getty Images:** Science & Society Picture Library (b). **190 Getty Images:** Science & Society Picture Library (c). **193 Alamy Images:** Interfoto (br). **194 National Maritime Museum, Greenwich, London:** (bl). **195 National Maritime Museum, Greenwich, London:** (t). **196–197 Science Museum / Science & Society Picture Library:** (b). **197 Corbis:** (cra). **199 Getty Images:** Imagno / Hulton Archive (t). **200 The Bridgeman Art Library:** Look and Learn / Peter Jackson Collection (bl). **201 Alamy Images:** Mary Evans Picture Library (tr). **204–205 Getty Images:** Popperfoto. **207 Getty Images:** Hulton Archive (tr). **208 U.S. National Park Service:** (cla). **212–213 The Art Archive:** Eileen Tweedy. **214 The Bridgeman Art Library:** (bl). **218 Corbis:** (t). **220–221 The Art Archive:** Superstock (t). **223 The Bridgeman Art Library:** Royal Geographical Society, London, UK (tr). **224 Corbis:** Mathew B. Brady Studio / Medford Historical Society Collection (bl). **226–227 Getty Images:** Time & Life Pictures. **228 Barry Lawrence Ruderman Antique Maps Inc.** **229 The Bridgeman Art Library:** Royal Geographical Society, London, UK (tl). **231 Mary Evans Picture Library:** (tl). **233 National Maritime Museum, Greenwich, London:** (b). **234 Mary Evans Picture Library:** Illustrated London News Ltd (bl). **236 Science Photo Library.** **237 Alamy Images:** Huw Jones (tr). **238–239 National Maritime Museum, Greenwich, London.** **241 Getty Images:** George Eastman House / Archive Photos (tr). **242 Corbis:** (tl). **243 Corbis:** Lebrecht 3 / Lebrecht Music & Arts (b). **244 Getty Images:** MPI / Archive Photos (tr). **246–247 Corbis.** **249 Getty Images:** Hulton Archive (t). **250 National Maritime Museum, Greenwich, London:** (tl). **252–253 National Maritime Museum, Greenwich, London:** (b). **255 The Bridgeman Art Library:** Peter Newark American Pictures (tl). **256–257 National Maritime Museum, Greenwich, London:** (c). **256 Getty Images:** Transcendental Graphics / Archive Photos (crb). **258 Corbis:** Bettmann (bl). **260 Alamy Images:** Mary Evans Picture Library (t). **262 Corbis:** (b). **264 Getty Images:** British Library / Robana / Hulton Fine Art Collection (cr). **264–265 Getty Images:** Dea Picture Library / De Agostini (b). **266 Corbis:** Hulton-Deutsch Collection (b). **269 National Library of Australia:** Keith Cameron,vn5011407 (tl). **270 The Bridgeman Art Library:** Royal Geographical Society, London, UK (b). **272 Getty Images:** Handout / Getty Images News (bl). **275 Getty Images:** Sean Gallup / Getty Images News (tr). **276–277 Mary Evans Picture Library.** **278 The Bridgeman Art Library:** Cauer Collection, Germany. **280 Corbis:** Bettmann (bl). **282 Corbis:** Bettmann (cl). **282–283 SD Model Makers:** (b). **284 The Bridgeman Art Library:** Peter Newark Military Pictures. **286 The Bridgeman Art Library:** © SZ Photo (b). **287 Getty Images:** Hulton Archive (tr). **288 Mary Evans Picture Library:** Epic / Tallandier (c). **291 Getty Images:** Popperfoto (t). **292 Getty Images:** Hulton Archive (b). **294–295 Alamy Images:** Timewatch Images (t). **296 Dorling Kindersley:** National Maritime Museum, London (cra/HMS Conqueror, clb). © **The Mariners' Museum, Virginia, USA:** (c/USS Bainbridge). **SD Model Makers:** (crb, cla). **296–297 SD Model Makers:** (b). **297 Dorling Kindersley:**

Gary Ombler (cra). **SD Model Makers:** (tl, cr).
298 Alamy Images: Elk-Opid / Photo12 (bl). **299
The Art Archive:** Imperial War Museum / Eileen
Tweedy (tl). **300 Getty Images:** New York Daily
News Archive (bl). **302 Corbis:** Swim Ink 2, LLC.
306-307 Getty Images: Gill / Hulton Archive. **310
Getty Images:** Daily Herald Archive / SSPL (bl). **312
Getty Images:** Hulton Archive (t). **314 Getty
Images:** Popperfoto. **316-317 Getty Images:** Albert
Harlingue / Roger Viollet. **319 Getty Images:**
Library of Congress - edited version / Science
Faction (bl). **320 Getty Images:** George Eastman
House / Archive Photos (t). **325 Corbis:** (tr). **326
Alamy Images:** Coll-DITE / USIS / Photo12 (bl).
328-329 Dorling Kindersley: National Maritime
Museum, London (c). **328 Bovington Tank
Museum:** Roland Groom (br). **329 Mary Evans
Picture Library:** Illustrated London News Ltd (tl).
331 Corbis: Hulton-Deutsch Collection (t). **334
Getty Images:** James Lauritz / Photodisc (c). **336
Fred Koster:** (bl). **337 Getty Images:** Daily Herald
Archive / SSPL. **338 Getty Images:** Popular Science
(tl). **341 Getty Images:** N. V. De Arbeiderspers /
Hulton Archive (tl). **343 Getty Images:** AFP (br).
344-345 Corbis: Bettmann (b). **346-347 Corbis:**
Bettmann. **348 Corbis:** (bl). **351 Getty Images:**
Haynes Archive / Popperfoto (tr). **352 The Kobal
Collection:** Turner Network Television (t). **353
Getty Images:** Popular Science (br). **354 Corbis:**
Tui De Roy / Minden Pictures (b). **356-357 Dorling
Kindersley:** IFREMER, Paris (c). **356 Getty
Images:** Emory Kristof And Alvin Chandler /
National Geographic (br). **358 Getty Images:**
Michael Brennan / Hulton Archive (bl). **360 Getty
Images:** Manchester Daily Express / SSPL (bl). **361
Corbis:** Reuters (b). **362 Alamy Images:** Richard
Cooke (t). **365 Corbis:** Adam Stoltman. **366 Alamy
Images:** Niday Picture Library (clb). **366-367 Getty
Images:** Manuel Queimadelos Alonso (bc). **368 Kos
Picture Source:** (tl). **370 Corbis:** Roger Garwood
& Trish Ainslie (tl). **371 Corbis:** Adam Stoltman
(br). **373 Corbis:** Roy Corral (b). **375 Corbis:** Sergei
Karpukhin / Reuters (tl). **377 Getty Images:**
Natalie Fobes / Science Faction (tl). **378-379 Getty
Images:** Natalie Fobes / Science Faction. **380
Corbis:** Alain Dejean / Sygma (b). **383 Dietmar
Hasenpusch Photo-Productions:** (t). **385 Press
Association Images:** L. Todd Spencer / AP (tr).
386-387 Corbis: Benoit Stichelbaut / Hemis / Terra

Jacket images: *Front and Back:* **Dreamstime.com:**
Joseph Gough (UK PLC); *Front:* **Corbis:** Ocean cb,
crb; **National Maritime Museum, Greenwich,
London;** *Back:* **Alamy Images:** Gianni Dagli Orti /
The Art Archive cla, Enno Kleinert / dieKleinert tc;
The Bridgeman Art Library: tr; **Corbis:** Ocean
cb, Adam Stoltman cra; **Getty Images:** G. Dagli

Orti / De Agostini ca; **The Kobal Collection:**
Turner Network Television tl; *Front Flap:* **Corbis:**
Ocean cb; *Back Flap:* **Corbis:** Ocean cb

All other images © Dorling Kindersley
For further information see: www.dkimages.com

Maps

Maps are provided throughout the book to
illustrate selected features. Please note that they are
for general reference only and are not intended to
be comprehensive.

Measurements

Throughout the book, measurements are given in
the text in both metric and imperial, where the
information is available, with the following
exceptions: nautical measurements are given
without conversions and are explained in the
glossary; tonnage and displacement are expressed
in long tons throughout.